Clifford A. Coombs
Nevis, Minn.
November 29, 1963
Cook Book Club

MENUS FOR ENTERTAINING

Menus for Entertaining

72 PARTIES & 400 RECIPES FOR THE GOOD COOK AND HOSTESS

BY JULIETTE ELKON & ELAINE ROSS

EDITED BY NARCISSE CHAMBERLAIN

Illustrated by John Alcorn

HASTINGS HOUSE PUBLISHERS • NEW YORK 22

Published simultaneously in Canada
by S. J. Reginald Saunders, Publishers, Toronto 2B

Printed in the United States of America

Introduction

Time was when guests for dinner meant just one thing, a formal dinner party—the table spread with damask and laden with crystal and silver, waitresses in starched uniforms, and a rigorously predictable menu centered around squab or fillet of beef. This correct formula had its charms, not the least of which was that it relieved the hostess of any need to think. It became also, in our opinion, something of a bore.

The civilized, three-star-occasion dinner party has not completely vanished, fortunately. But the single standard of entertaining has, we trust never to return in any form. (Let us not, for instance, now carry emancipation to extremes and transform entertaining into one long series of barbecues!) And the standardized menu truly has vanished. Today's hostesses have by and large become their own cooks as well, and varied and imaginative ones at that. Their adventures in the kitchen have produced a whole new notion of good food and how to serve it. Informality has crept in—or should we say swept in—almost everywhere. Entertaining is easier than the command performance it once was and a great deal more fun.

The penalty is, of course, that there are no formulas to rely on any more. You do have to stop and think. Special occasions still have their traditions, but otherwise the only rules left for entertaining are those of good sense and good cooking. To follow these, with an enormously expanded variety of dishes to choose from and all kinds of occasions to fit them to, is not necessarily easy. It is a pleasure to know there are many good ways to plan a party, but the wrong ways to go about it have multiplied alarmingly, too.

The crucial point in applying good sense to good cooking is to apply the good sense to the menu first of all. A collection of marvelous dishes is not automatically a good meal, and any good meal does not automatically succeed for every kind of party. Furthermore, we all do run out of ideas, though this seems absurd with the avalanche of cooking lore available in print nowadays. The avalanche itself is part of the problem, no doubt, but we have been so bold as to add to it on the theory that new ideas and new recipes will always be welcome providing it is made clear what to *do* with them. And what you do with every recipe from scrambled eggs on to a crown roast is to put it in a menu eventually.

So, we have described in general outline every kind of party we could think of that seemed a reasonable possibility for the hostesses of today and plotted a menu, or several, and supplied all the recipes to fit the case. Of course, the situation of every hostess is in some way different from that of the next, and it changes from occasion to occasion besides. So it is up to you to decide which of our menus is the answer to the particular problem of the moment, and, in fact, to decide what variations might suit you better. We don't mean to saddle you with arbitrary instructions but to bolster your supply of ideas and outline a system to make them work.

Most menus adapt to either formal or informal service, for instance, so ours may suit more occasions than we have suggested. We heartily advocate simplification if you think you are getting out of your depths; you could in that case, go through our group of luncheons with an eye to turning them into informal suppers. Or on the other hand, you could tamper successfully with a fairly complex dinner by serving it from a buffet if it is out of bounds for you at a formal table set for sixteen.

In any event, it's foolish to tackle too much and we don't think you will, for we have tried in the paragraphs that precede the recipes in each menu to give you a fair idea of what you are letting yourself in for. We devote a good deal of space here to the sequence of events in the kitchen so that if you are your own cook, and simultaneously intended to be a gracious hostess in the parlor, you can have it clearly in mind what to start and finish when, what to do ahead, and what to save for the last minute. This constitutes a recipe for the menu as a whole, you might say. It isn't a usual thing in cook books and we hope you find it reassuring; recipes alone can't indicate the strategy of a complete meal, and yet the old puzzler of how to make everything come out even can bother even the experts.

Not very many of the menus require any help but yourself in the kitchen. We try to warn you every time you will need help—and for certain grand occasions you will know you want several pairs of extra hands without being told—but do consider the imponderables we don't know about, such as your skill as a cook, how formal or informal an atmosphere will please your guests, whether or not the dishwasher has broken down, and how many children you expect to have underfoot all day. And no matter how much you *can* handle alone, the objective is, after all, for the hostess to come out of this still cheerful as well as still breathing.

Incidentally, those of you who have a jewel in the kitchen to preside over the pots and pans for you will find that we talk most of the time as if she didn't exist. Well, she often doesn't, but we hope our book will meet with her approval if she does in your case. We have made it a point to include meals for casual households, less experienced cooks, and women with a minimum of time on their hands to spend in the kitchen. But there is plenty to challenge the professional pride of a topnotch cook. Furthermore, the menu problem for entertaining doesn't necessarily evaporate just because there are two of you to work on it.

As you will see from the list of menus starting on p. ix, we view entertaining as a very various thing indeed. It rather tickles us that we open this book with a late breakfast for two housewives and have a Christmas Eve open house for one hundred people or so in the same chapter. We fall in happily with quantities of informal entertaining, cooking out of doors, Sunday brunch, and cozy little meals with a few close friends that can hardly be called parties at all. But we also feel strongly about the grand manner in entertaining; it need not be dull, and it does have a place. We have included among other things a garden party, a lavish formal buffet, two wedding breakfasts, a formal tea, and a flock of imposing formal dinners, so you can see we are serious. We don't suggest that all of you have need of a garden party menu, but some of you may, and we really don't know of very many places where you could find out what would be appropriate to the occasion. It seems to us reasonable that we should at least provide the information. If some of these large enterprises strike you as being more sensible for a caterer to attend to than you yourself, this may be true, but how many caterers with an ounce of imagination are there in your vicinity? and do you know how to tell them what you want? We have written mostly on the assumption that the reader is chief cook and bottle washer, and this is a book of food, not one of etiquette, so what we have to say about the large and elegant function is limited to that extent. But we think it ought to be included, for if this kind of party descends upon you unawares, there may be no hostess of the old school around to tell you what goes into it, and we trust you will want something a little livelier than the strictly old school anyway.

We hope this book will not be taken purely as a set collection of menus. With over 400 recipes, it surely constitutes a bona fide cook book, too, and a source to produce ideas for combinations of your own. The categorized index will locate any type of recipe for you, regardless of whether we have tucked it away in a brunch, patio dinner, or midnight supper.* We won't

* Note that, unless otherwise indicated, each recipe serves the number of people proposed in the title of the menu where you find it.

burden you with advice on exactly how to proceed from there, for the art of menu planning is not one that bears too much explaining. One can make a stab at it: Don't combine Vichyssoise, creamed seafood, and a whipped-cream dessert; do consider color, texture, contrast, and the weather; don't get so imaginative that you become eccentric, but do dare to be a little different; give your guests what they like, but surprise them a little, too . . . one bogs down in generalities and contradictions almost at once.

Sound menus themselves speak more clearly than pages of explanation. Our fond hope is that many of ours you will like and rely on just as they stand. But after a while we hope also that the trick of it will become tantalizing and that you, too, will be taken with a passion for menu planning and will ransack our index, and your files and other books also, for dishes to use in menus of your own creation. Either way, whenever you decide to have a party, may it now actually be a pleasure, for a change, to sit down and answer the old question, "What shall we have to eat?"

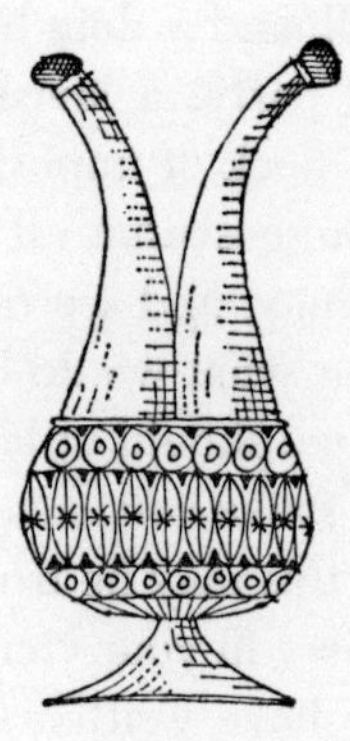

Contents

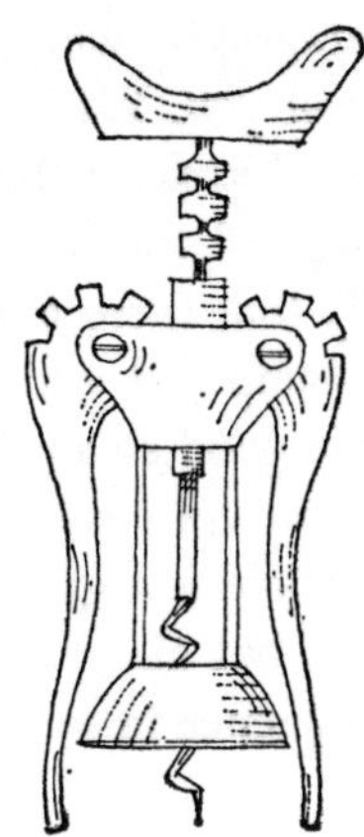

A Note on Wines

Our first concern is that the reader should understand the manner in which the wines that accompany many of our menus have been chosen. Usually, only one wine is called for; we assume you are only planning to give marvelous parties, not run a gourmet society. However, we do suggest as many as three alternative choices in most cases, ranging from inexpensive, to medium-priced, to expensive. The reason for *that* is plain enough.

We have, furthermore, been very specific in naming some of the wines, particularly the finer foreign vintages. This is not because no other bottle will do, but because we occasionally want to make a special point of the particular type of wine we feel would be best with the menu. Every label we suggest will not necessarily be available in every state in the Union. On the contrary, the shipping of wines and liquors is a complex legal affair and the list of what is available can vary considerably from state to state. However, you will usually be able to locate a wine from the same district we mention, or even from the same village in the case of certain foreign vintages. The shipper and importer may differ, for better or for worse, but the wine will have the same basic character.

You will notice, also, that we often suggest American wines. Many of them are truly excellent, they have gained the respect of the experts, and they deserve more attention than they get, even now. Nothing replaces the great vintages of Europe, of course, and many fine imports remain in the middle price range, but we feel that even lesser American wines can be better than inferior imports.

That said, we must apologize to the connoisseurs of wine for the brevity of our discussion of the subject. To tackle it properly would most certainly require a whole companion volume to this one and we have space only for the bare essentials. The understanding and appreciation of wines has grown so enormously in this country of recent years that the paragraphs which follow will seem superfluous as well as incomplete to many of you. Yet we have often been asked to supply precisely this rudimentary information by enthusiasts of wine who have never gotten around to fixing "all the little rules" in their minds. The answer to their question is usually that there are no little rules, at least not ones that cannot judiciously be tampered with. But there is a collection of basic facts which will stand you in good stead if you feel your experience with wine does not quite match your enthusiasm for it. We present them briefly, with the understanding that there is a great deal more to the art of choosing wines than we can say here, but also proposing that you can make no mistake of really dreadful consequence in serving them if you remember the following:

Serve white wines, sweet or dry, and rosés, chilled but not icy; serve red wines *chambré* i.e. a little below room temperature (room temperature in a French *chambre* is cool compared to what we are used to); champagnes are iced.

Uncork red wines an hour before they are poured, to "let them breathe." Red wines usually have some sediment; pour them gently, so the sediment will not reach the glass. Baskets in which bottles can rest quietly on their sides for some time before serving are appropriate for fine red wines; the sediment will hardly be disturbed when the wine is poured. But do *not* use these baskets for serving white wines.

If, when you pull the cork, you find it is rotted or smells of cork and not of wine, return the bottle to your dealer; the wine will have been affected. Use a dependable cork screw, and wipe the mouth of the bottle after you pull the cork. Use a napkin to catch drops from the bottle when pouring if you wish, but do not wrap it around the bottle, thus hiding the label. Very unimportant wines can be decanted into a *carafe* or not, as you choose.

The well-known formality of pouring an inch of wine into the host's glass for tasting before serving guests is for checking the quality of the bottle and getting rid of stray scraps of cork. This should be a completely matter-of-fact procedure, though a little extra ceremony is pardonable if you are pouring a great wine.

The rules for serving what wines with what dishes can only be guides, not rules. Variations of the so-called rules are legion, as you will gather in looking over the choices we have made for our menus. Your palate should be your best guide; you quickly sense, for instance, that certain red wines and red meat are meant for each other. Yet the matter is subtle enough so that there are exceptions. You may not at first feel at ease with your own decisions until you have mulled over the more usual combinations, so these are, roughly: Dry white wine with fish and sea food; red wine with red meat, game and, usually, duck; with other poultry, and veal, pork, and ham, either a white wine or a light, red wine (since you are bound to make a choice here, two rules of thumb are: the kind of wine that may have been used in cooking the dish is the most compatible, or, white wine with the more delicate dishes, red wine with richer fare); red wine with cheese; champagne or sweet white wine with desserts (be careful, though—some desserts will ruin any wine); and rosés, which are particularly good in summer, combine well with almost everything short of sweets providing the menu is fairly simple.

And lastly, never serve a wine that you are not familiar with and know you approve of—not to guests, that is—unless you want to make the occasion into a wine-tasting party. Even then, we feel safer with a tried-and-true bottle or two in reserve.

MORNING, AFTERNOON AND EVENING

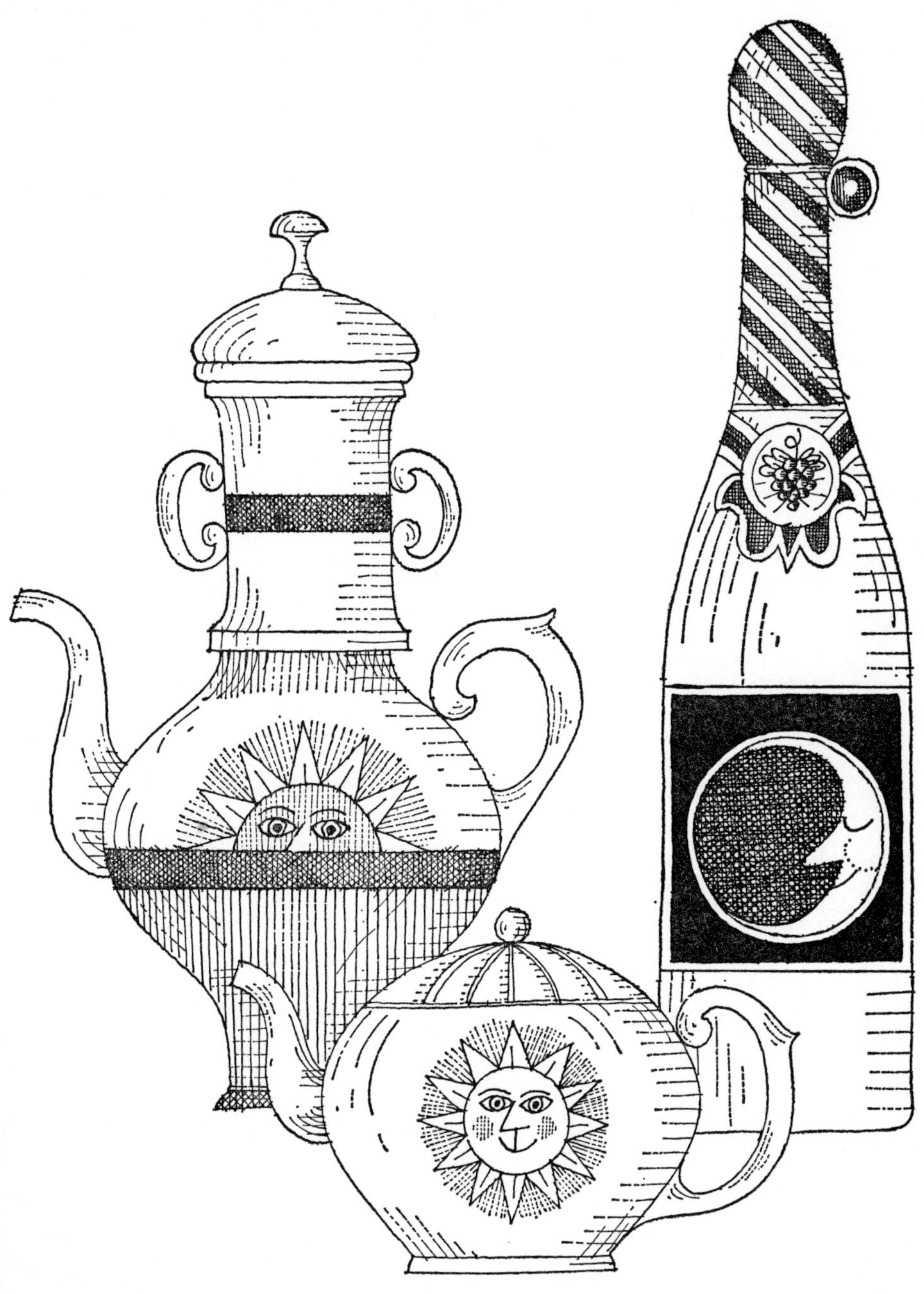

1

Second-Wind Breakfast for Two or Four

UPSIDE-DOWN FRENCH TOAST
COFFEE OR TEA

A second breakfast—providing you had time to have a first breakfast at all—devoted to catching your breath. Who doesn't feel the need of a little renewal after the morning onslaught? A cup of coffee and a special treat shared with a friend on her way home from market or car pool can make new women of both of you.

Upside-Down French Toast is something special, though you are pretty sure to have all the makings on hand without advance warning. It takes only a few minutes to get ready for the oven, and while it bakes you make a fresh pot of coffee and enjoy the first cup along with the chit-chat of the day. Then set toast and coffee on individual trays, carry them to the living room, and sink down into the most comfortable chairs for a deliciously relaxing half hour.

There has been much said about *the* perfect cup of coffee. We can't do better than pass on this information from the Coffee Brewing Institute:

"Start with a thoroughly clean coffee maker; use fresh coffee (buy coffee in quantities which will be used within a week after opening); use freshly-drawn cold water; use full capacity of your coffee-maker; for uniform results, consistent timing is important; coffee should never be boiled; serve coffee as soon as possible after brewing. Best results are obtained by using one standard coffee measure of coffee (or 2 level measuring tablespoons) to each 6 ounces of water."

One point that has always struck us as needing clarification is the use of cold water. According to the experts, cold water from the tap has fewer impurities than hot. Not being chemists, we remain mystified.

Upside-Down French Toast

Preheat oven to 400°. Melt 2 tablespoons butter in a 9-inch-square baking pan. Into the butter stir ¼ cup brown sugar and ¼ cup crushed pineapple, drained of almost all its syrup. Spread this mixture evenly over bottom of pan. In a bowl beat together 1 egg, ¾ cup milk, and ⅛ teaspoon salt. Soak 4 slices bread in milk mixture until soft, then lay over the pineapple and brown sugar in the pan. Bake for 25 minutes, or until lightly browned, and cool 1 minute before inverting on a heated serving platter.

2 tablespoons butter
¼ cup brown sugar
¼ cup crushed pineapple
1 egg
¾ cup milk
⅛ teaspoon salt
4 slices bread

2

Committee Breakfast for Eight at 10 A.M.

BROILED MIXED FRUIT
HILDA'S BRIOCHES (OR
LUCY'S CROISSANTS) WITH SWEET BUTTER
SUNSHINE STRAWBERRY JAM
COFFEE OR TEA

If recipes that yield dozens of *Brioches* or *Croissants* seem out of line for eight people, wait until you've tasted them! And we miss our guess if, at the end of the meeting, Madam Chairman doesn't call for a special vote of thanks to you for having made them. When a morning committee meeting at your house has been under way for an hour, and at ten-thirty or eleven you bring in a tray bearing a pot of steaming coffee, a basket of hot rolls, a crock of sweet butter and another of sun-cooked jam, if the inevitable arguments aren't settled promptly, at least there will be a temporary truce.

The jam has an unbelievably fresh taste as a result of very brief cooking; the rest is up to nature. Just hope that nature is more cooperative than it was the first time we made this. The sun started a hide-and-seek gambit the minute we set the berries outside that delayed the jam for a week. If the sun shows the proper attitude, it should take only two or three days.

Both the *Brioche* and the *Croissant* (see Index) doughs are made the day before. The *Brioche* dough must chill overnight before it is used; the *Croissants* may be shaped, placed on cooky sheets, and refrigerated until the morning. To make either one, you *do* have to get up early to give them time to rise, but if this is against your principles, you can start them two days ahead, do the baking the day before, and heat them in the oven before serving. They are almost as good, but not quite. If you have a freezer, bake them days or weeks ahead, and reheat them, still frozen, in a 375° oven for 12 to 15 minutes; this way they will taste fresh-baked. As to the quantity, we do not truly mean that you won't have a single roll left over, but your family will make short shrift of them unless you freeze the remainder.

The last-minute details of this menu dovetail nicely: Twenty minutes before serving, put the rolls in the oven and start the coffee. When you take the rolls out of the oven, set the fruit under the broiler. While the fruit glazes, you have time to remove the rolls from the tins and pile them in a basket.

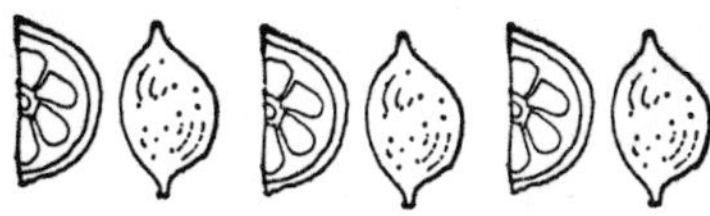

Broiled Mixed Fruit

Peel 2 bananas, halve them lengthwise, and slice crosswise. Peel 2 oranges, remove white pulp, then cut in slices ¼ inch thick; do the same with 1 grapefruit. Add 8 fresh or canned pineapple slices. Lay the fruit in a heavily buttered shallow casserole and sprinkle with ¼ teaspoon cardamon. Warm ¼ cup honey, add ¼ cup orange or pineapple juice, and pour over fruit. Broil until edges show golden and serve hot.

2 bananas
2 oranges
1 grapefruit
8 pineapple slices
¼ teaspoon cardamon
¼ cup honey
¼ cup orange or pineapple juice

Hilda's Brioches

Prepare dough a day ahead. To make 30 small *brioches:* Soften 1 package dry yeast in 3 tablespoons lukewarm water. Scald ½ cup milk and ½ cup water. In a large bowl, cut up ½ pound butter. Pour scalded milk and water over butter. Add ¼ cup sugar, ¼ teaspoon salt, 3 eggs, and 3½ cups unsifted flour. Beat very thoroughly. Beat in dissolved yeast, cover bowl, and refrigerate overnight. In the morning, turn dough out on lightly floured board. Cut off one eighth of dough and reserve. Cut remaining dough into 30 pieces. With lightly floured hands, roll each piece into a ball. Place each one in a well-buttered *brioche* or muffin tin. With wooden spoon handle dipped in flour, make indentation in top of each ball. Cut reserved piece of dough into 30 pieces. Roll into tiny balls and insert one in each indentation. Set in warm place to rise until double in bulk, about 1½ to 2 hours.

Preheat oven to 400°. Brush tops of *brioches* with 1 egg yolk diluted with 1 teaspoon cold water, and bake for 15 minutes.

1 package dry yeast
½ cup milk
½ cup water
½ pound butter
¼ cup sugar
¼ teaspoon salt
3 eggs
3½ cups flour
1 egg yolk

Sunshine Strawberry Jam

Hull 3 quarts firm ripe strawberries. Place them, with 12 cups sugar, in a large pot over medium heat. Stirring constantly, bring to a boil and keep at a rolling boil for 12 minutes. Remove from heat, cool a little, then skim carefully. Pour strawberries in single layer into shallow pans, cover each pan with a pane of glass, and insert a small wedge of paper between pan and glass to allow air to circulate. Stand pans in the sun for 3 days, or until liquid thickens. Stir twice each day. Pour into sterilized jelly glasses and seal with paraffin or vacuum-pack covers.

3 quarts strawberries
12 cups sugar
Paraffin

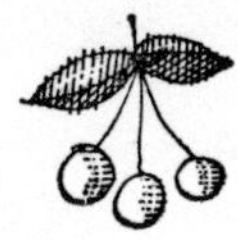

3

Summer Formal Breakfast for Twelve

FRESH STRAWBERRIES CHANTILLY
HAM CORNUCOPIAS À LA RUSSE
RUSSIAN RYE BREAD WITH WHIPPED BUTTER
FLOATING HEARTS
VIENNESE CRESCENTS
DEMITASSE

CHAMPAGNES

Inexpensive: Champagne Punch
Medium-priced: Fortnum & Mason's Cuvée Anglaise, Brut or Mumm's Cordon Rouge
Expensive: Dom Pérignon, Brut

Definitely a hearts-and-flowers menu—we can practically hear the Viennese waltz and the two hearts beating in three-quarter time. You don't necessarily need an engagement or shower or wedding as an excuse for this breakfast, but it's fun to celebrate young love; we hope the occasion comes along.

A "breakfast" that includes Champagne Punch is a little too dazzling to *really* mean breakfast, but that's the romantic old term and no one would dream of changing it. The menu, however, does actually provide luncheon, whether it be served as early as 11:45 A.M. or as late as 1 P.M. In any case, from heart-shaped strawberries to Floating-Heart dessert, everything is keyed to Cupid. Plan your color scheme in his honor, too: a crystal centerpiece with pale pink sweetheart roses in a mist of baby's breath and a lace or lace-trimmed white cloth. Or, if the occasion lacks romantic motivation,

perhaps a pale pink cloth and a container of cranberry glass filled bountifully with clusters of red rambler roses.

You will probably bake the Crescent Cookies some days before, since they keep so well in a tightly covered tin. To get other head starts on this menu, boil and peel the eggs for the Cornucopias *à la Russe* the day before, and make the Liver Pâté (see Index) and the aspic. Cut out the ice-cream hearts and put them on a cooky sheet in the freezer.

You should have two waitresses for efficient formal service. If they come early, they can finish the cooking, but if they come just in time to serve, your morning time table will run this way: Start off with the strawberries so that they have time to chill thoroughly. For an engagement or a wedding party, serve them in champagne glasses instead of glass bowls. Tie a small spray of baby's breath to the stem of each glass with a narrow white satin ribbon. Next, prepare the Cornucopias *à la Russe* on two platters, decorate each, using a heart-shaped truffle cutter for the truffle slices. For a professional touch, reserve a little of the pâté, put it in a pastry bag fitted with a star tube, and top each cornucopia with a rosette. Place them around the mounds of egg salad, seam side down so they keep their shape, and keep the finished platters in the refrigerator. Finally, make the *Sabayon* Sauce.

And now that you have prettied up the food, it's time to pretty up the hostess.

One of the waitresses can slice and butter the bread just before you sit down. Have her arrange the slices on two platters, so that each waitress may pass one after she serves the main course. If the weather is hot, ask your waitresses not to put the desserts on plates until they clear the main course from the table. It's a matter of two or three minutes to fix them, and you do want Floating Hearts, not melting ones.

Fresh Strawberries Chantilly

Hull 2 quarts ripe strawberries and halve them. Whip 3 cups heavy cream with ⅔ cup Vanilla Sugar, below, until it stands in peaks. Fold strawberries into the cream. Spoon into 12 individual glass bowls, and chill in refrigerator for 2 hours before serving.

2 quarts strawberries
3 cups heavy cream
⅔ cup Vanilla Sugar

Vanilla Sugar

Buy 2 vanilla beans at a specialty food shop. Place them in a canister with 1 pound granulated sugar. Cover and allow to remain untouched for a week. From time to time replenish sugar; add 1 vanilla bean every 6 months.

This gives a much finer flavor than vanilla extract and can be used wherever extract is called for. One tablespoon Vanilla Sugar equals ¼ teaspoon extract. Decrease amount of sugar in recipe accordingly.

2 vanilla beans
1 pound granulated sugar

Ham Cornucopias à la Russe

Warm 2 cups jellied beef consommé, and in it dissolve 1 envelope unflavored gelatin. Pour ¼ inch deep into large shallow pan and allow to set in refrigerator (about 3 hours).

Place 20 eggs in a pot with enough cold water to cover generously, and bring to a boil over high heat. Turn off heat and allow eggs to cool in the water for 20 minutes; the yolks will remain perfectly yellow. Peel, chop yolks and whites together, and mix with 1 recipe *Sauce Russe.* Mound in the center of two round platters.

Prepare 1 recipe Mock Goose-Liver Pâté. Spread pâté on 24 thin slices of boiled ham and roll into cornucopias, trimming each one to perfection with kitchen shears. Garnish mound of egg with cornucopias. Slice 2 large truffles, cut into decorative shapes with truffle cutters, and use to decorate. Chop chilled aspic and arrange in a border to finish decorating.

1 envelope gelatin
2 cups jellied beef consommé
20 eggs
Sauce Russe (see Index)
Mock Goose-Liver Pâté (see Index)
24 thin slices boiled ham
2 large truffles

Floating Hearts

From frozen brick vanilla ice cream cut 12 hearts with a heart-shaped cooky cutter large enough to make one portion. Store on baking sheets in freezer. Make *Sabayon* Sauce, using a Garnier cherry-flavored brandy instead of the usual Marsala, and chill. Place ice-cream hearts in individual glass dishes and spoon sauce around the hearts but not over them.

12 squares brick vanilla ice cream
Cherry Sabayon Sauce

Cherry Sabayon Sauce

In top of a 2-quart double boiler, beat together until light and foamy 6 egg yolks and ⅔ cup sugar. Stir in 1 cup Garnier cherry-flavored brandy, and cook over hot water, beating constantly with rotary beater or beater from electric mixer. When sauce has thickened, pour in ½ cup heavy cream, then cool over cracked ice, stirring slowly. Pour around Floating Hearts.

6 egg yolks
⅔ cup sugar
1 cup Garnier cherry-flavored brandy
½ cup heavy cream

Viennese Crescents

Grind 1 cup unblanched almonds. Mix with 4 cups unsifted flour, and work into a soft dough with ¾ pound salt butter and ¼ cup Vanilla Sugar. Work dough with fingers until it is smooth and waxy like clay, then chill for 3 hours.

Preheat oven to 350°. Put small pieces of dough on a lightly floured board, and with the palm of the hand roll into strips as thick as a finger. Break off pieces 2 inches long; bend them into crescents and bake on an ungreased cooky sheet for 10 to 15 minutes. Remove carefully from sheet with a metal spatula and roll in confectioners' sugar. Store between layers of waxed paper in airtight container. Makes about 3 dozen crescents.

1 cup unblanched almonds
4 cups flour
¾ pound salt butter
¼ cup Vanilla Sugar (*see p.* 9)
Confectioners' sugar

Champagne Punch

Slice very thinly, with their rinds, 2 lemons and 2 oranges. Combine with 1 cup peeled seedless grapes and 1 container cubed frozen pineapple. Marinate overnight with 1½ cups extrafine granulated sugar, 1 cup apple brandy, ½ cup Triple Sec, ¼ cup peach brandy, and 1 jar maraschino cherries, with their juice. Freeze a large block of ice in a metal mixing bowl or loaf pan. When ready to serve, place ice in punch bowl, pour mixture over it, and add slowly 6 bottles of chilled dry California champagne. Makes enough for 60 punch cups filled two thirds full.

2 lemons
2 oranges
1 cup seedless grapes
1 container frozen cubed pineapple
1½ cups extra-fiine granulated sugar
1 cup apple brandy
½ cup Triple Sec
¼ cup peach brandy
1 jar maraschino cherries
6 bottles dry California champagne

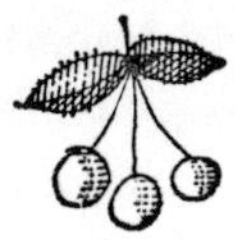

4

Winter Formal Breakfast for Twelve

GLAZED STRAWBERRIES À L'ESPAGNOLE
CAVIAR ROULADE
TOMATOES ST. PETERSBURG
RUSSIAN PUMPERNICKEL WITH WHIPPED BUTTER
RUM CHOCOLATE PUFFS
DEMITASSE

CHAMPAGNES
Inexpensive: Champagne Punch *
Medium-priced: Marcel Frères, Brut
Expensive: Roederer, Brut, Vintage

The fact that we still think of strawberries in winter as the height of luxury undoubtedly dates us—we remember when! Notwithstanding their year-round availability now, there is no fruit more elegant for the first course of a formal winter breakfast. Set a sparkling, crystal stemmed glass heaped high with mammoth glazed berries at each place before your guests come to the table. Echo the color in a paler-hued pink cloth and repeat it in the flower arrangements. If it is late winter, you will find the first spring flowers at the florist. Fill four small, round bread baskets with a variety of flowers in pink, red and white—small tulips or anemones, narcissus, hyacinths, pink and white daisies, and freesia. The system is to pack the baskets with peat moss, cut the flower stems short, and insert them in the moss. Buy plenty of flowers; you will want them solidly massed, since they are the sole table decoration. Naturally, you won't be using candelabra at an 11:45 breakfast.

* see Index

You might use this V.I.O. (Very Important Occasion) menu to entertain V.I.P.'s, in which case the word is probably luncheon rather than breakfast; or for an engagement party, or even a small wedding breakfast. Formal seated service is indicated, with two people waiting at table. Nevertheless, you can do all the cooking yourself.

Make the puffs, their filling and sauce the day before. One of the waitresses can fill them while you are eating. Of course, for a wedding, you will have cake instead. You can make the cake yourself. Frost Louisiana Pecan *Torte* with Seven-Minute Icing (see Index for both) instead of whipped cream. Put it on a large platter and ring the base of the cake with orange blossoms.

Make the *Roulades* early in the morning, fill them, and place them on a buttered cooky sheet; envelop the whole thing loosely in foil, to be reheated later. While they are baking, prepare the strawberries and fill the tomatoes. There is nothing left, then, for you to do in the kitchen. The second waitress should keep an eye on the clock and put both the tomatoes and the prepared *Roulades* in a 300° oven for 25 minutes, just in time to serve after the strawberries.

If someone else is cook, and the *Roulades* are not to be reheated at the last minute, they should be put in the oven a little more than an hour before serving and taken out of the oven when they are done. The heat is then turned down and the tomatoes are put in. The *Roulades* are filled and placed on cooky sheets as above, covered with foil, and set over pots of simmering water to keep hot.

We hope the guest of honor was both very charming and very famous—or that there were two of them, very much in love.

Glazed Strawberries à l'Espagnole

Hull and wash 3 quarts large perfect strawberries. Strain 2 cups raspberry jam and melt it over low heat with ½ cup Madeira. Cool, pour over strawberries, and chill. Serve in individual glass dishes.

3 quarts strawberries
2 cups raspberry jam
½ cup Madeira

Caviar Roulade

Preheat oven to 325°. In a saucepan, over medium heat, melt 4 tablespoons butter and add ½ cup flour, stirring with a whisk or wooden spoon for about 1 minute. Then gradually, still stirring, pour in 2 cups milk and cook for 4 minutes. Remove from heat and add 1 teaspoon sugar and 4 egg yolks. Beat 4 egg whites until stiff but not dry. Grease a 10-by-15-inch jelly-roll tin, and line it with waxed paper, then grease and lightly flour the paper. Spread batter on the paper and bake 40 minutes, or until slightly golden. Turn out on another piece of waxed paper and peel off top paper. Spread with a filling made of 2 ounces grey or black caviar creamed with 2 ounces cream cheese and 2 tablespoons sour cream taken from a ½-pint jar. Roll and place on a heated serving platter. With the hot *Roulade*, serve separately a cold sauce made of 2 more ounces caviar stirred into rest of sour cream.

4 tablespoons butter
½ cup flour
2 cups milk
1 teaspoon sugar
4 egg yolks
4 egg whites
4 ounces grey or black caviar, in all
2 ounces cream cheese
½ pint sour cream

Tomatoes St. Petersburg

Peel, seed, and dice finely 4 large cucumbers. Grate 1 medium onion and add to cucumbers with 1 tablespoon lemon juice and 2 tablespoons butter. Simmer for 5 minutes, adding salt and pepper to taste. Add ¼ cup fine bread crumbs to heated mixture, and cool slightly. Scoop out and drain 12 small tomatoes. Fill with cucumber mixture, and place 1 inch apart in shallow baking pans. Melt 2 tablespoons butter, mix with additional ½ cup bread crumbs, sprinkle over tomatoes, and bake at 300° for 25 minutes. Serve piping hot.

4 large cucumbers
1 medium onion
1 tablespoon lemon juice
4 tablespoons butter
Salt, pepper
¾ cup fine bread crumbs
12 small tomatoes

Rum Chocolate Puffs

Make 12 large cream puffs according to recipe for Basic *Pâte à Chou.* In top of a double boiler, beat 2 eggs and ½ cup sugar. Heat 2 cups milk with 4 ounces semisweet chocolate. When dissolved, add chocolate mixture slowly to egg-sugar mixture, beating continuously. Dissolve 3 tablespoons cornstarch in ¼ cup water and add. Cook filling over hot water until thick, cool, and spoon into pastry tube. Insert tube into bottom of puffs to fill them, and chill until servingtime. Serve with rum-flavored Chocolate Sauce, below.

Basic Pâte à Chou (see Index)
2 eggs
½ cup sugar
2 cups milk
4 ounces semisweet chocolate
3 tablespoons cornstarch
¼ cup water
Rum Chocolate Sauce

Chocolate Sauce

Over low heat melt 12 ounces semisweet chocolate with ¼ cup water. Stir until smooth, and add 1 cup sugar and ½ cup white corn syrup. Boil over high heat until mixture reaches soft-ball stage (234°–238° on a candy thermometer), then add 1 cup light cream. Remove from heat. Warm, then ignite ¼ cup rum, and add to sauce when flames subside. Keep sauce lukewarm in top of double boiler over warm water.

The same sauce can be flavored for other desserts with the liqueur of your choice, such as Cherry Heering or *crème de menthe.* These cordials do not need to be blazed.

12 ounces semisweet chocolate
¼ cup water
1 cup sugar
½ cup white corn syrup
1 cup light cream
¼ cup rum

5

Committee Meeting—Dessert and Coffee at 2 P.M.

Unforbidden Cake
Banana Fan
Richmond Pillow Cake
Roman Coffee

Though dessert and coffee are not officially on the agenda, the ladies of the committee will approve this extra-curricular hospitality, which also provides an interval of small talk and a chance to catch their breath and arrange their thoughts for the meeting to follow. Among the group that meets at your house to discuss a community project or a school "social," there may well be some strangers. What better way to bid them welcome?

Your ladies will like to think that on their account you have really fussed with the table setting as well as with the food. Have everything set out rather formally in the dining room or on a large living-room table. Use one of your handsomest cloths, flowers, and a silver coffee pot if you have one. Have the pot and coffee cups ready with their twists of lemon at one end of the table, the desserts with plates, napkins, and forks at the other. Each lady will help herself as she arrives.

Multiply the coffee recipe as desired. You won't want all three desserts unless there are to be over twenty women at the meeting. Serve either the Banana Fan *or* the Richmond Pillow Cake with the Unforbidden Cake. This last is especially for calorie counters, though that's hard to believe when you taste it.

Make the Unforbidden Cake and the *Pâte-à-Chou* shell the day before; fill the shell an hour before the group arrives. You can cook the cherries and make the fruit purée for the Banana Fan well ahead, but don't peel the bananas or arrange the platter until the last hour.

Unforbidden Cake

Place contents of 1 package of chocolate-chiffon pie filling in a small deep mixing bowl. Bring ¾ cup milk to a boil with ¼ cup strong coffee. Pour into mixing bowl and beat vigorously with rotary beater, or at highest speed of electric mixer, until filling stands in peaks (about 3 to 6 minutes). Then add ¼ cup Vanilla Sugar and beat 1 minute more. Break an angel or chiffon cake into chunks and place these in a 10-inch angel-cake pan with a removable bottom. Sprinkle with a mixture made from ¼ cup flamed dark rum and ½ cup coffee. Stir chunks of cake so they absorb all liquid, then fold in filling and smooth top of mixture. Chill about 2 hours in refrigerator. Insert blade of knife around outside and center tube of pan to detach cake, turn out on a serving platter, and sprinkle lightly with coconut flakes.

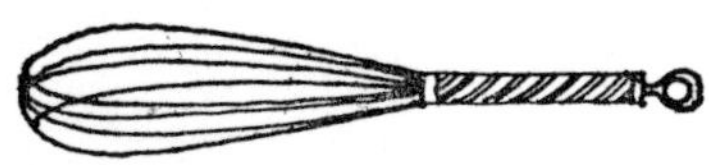

1 package chocolate-chiffon pie filling
¾ cup milk
¼ cup strong coffee
¼ cup Vanilla Sugar (see Index)
Angel or chiffon cake
¼ cup dark rum
½ cup coffee
Coconut flakes

For Lemon Cake: Use lemon-chiffon filling made according to directions on package; sprinkle cake chunks with ¼ cup flamed kirsch mixed with ½ cup water, and proceed as above.

For Strawberry Cake: Use strawberry-chiffon filling made according to directions on package; sprinkle cake chunks with juice from 1 defrosted package frozen strawberries, fold strawberries into filling, and proceed as above.

Banana Fan

Boil 1 cup water and ½ cup sugar together, at a rolling boil, for 4 minutes. Add 2 cups fresh or drained canned Bing cherries, lower the heat, and simmer for 2 minutes. Remove with a perforated spoon, drain, and chill. In an electric blender purée ½ cup each fresh or frozen raspberries, strawberries, and red currants; do this a small portion at a time, using as liquid 1 cup of the syrup in which cherries were cooked. Strain purée and chill.

Shortly before servingtime, peel 8 ripe bananas and halve them lengthwise. Arrange, cut side down, in the shape of a fan on a large shallow silver or glass platter. Arrange cherries in a symmetrical design on upper portion of banana fan. Pour the fruit-purée sauce over cherries, leaving a small semicircle of banana tips uncovered at bottom of fan. Whip ½ pint heavy cream with 1 tablespoon sugar and, with fluted nozzle of a pastry tube, make a thick border of whipped cream along top edge of fan. Serve well chilled.

1 cup water
½ cup sugar
2 cups Bing cherries
½ cup raspberries
½ cup strawberries
½ cup red currants
8 ripe bananas
½ pint heavy cream
1 tablespoon sugar

Richmond Pillow Cake

Preheat oven to 450°. Make ½ recipe Basic *Pâte à Chou,* using 3 large eggs. Spoon out onto a greased baking sheet in a 10-inch ring, leaving a 4-inch hollow center. Bake 12 minutes at 450°, then reduce heat to 350° and continue baking for 40 to 45 minutes, until golden. Cool. Meanwhile, whip 1 pint heavy cream with ¼ cup sugar. Fold in ¾ cup finely crushed peanut brittle. Cut the top from the *chou* ring, and remove any soft dough that may adhere to shell. Fill with whipped-cream mixture.

Make an apricot glaze by sifting 1 cup confectioners' sugar into a bowl and stirring into it, until smooth and ready for spreading, 2 tablespoons strained apricot jam and 2 tablespoons brandy or orange juice. Replace top of filled ring, then brush with glaze.

½ *recipe Basic Pâte à Chou* (*see Index*)
1 *pint heavy cream*
¼ *cup sugar*
¾ *cup finely crushed peanut brittle*
1 *cup confectioners' sugar*
2 *tablespoons strained apricot jam*
2 *tablespoons brandy*
or 2 tablespoons orange juice

Roman Coffee

For 6 demitasses, use a *machinetta* or a drip pot, and ¾ cup Italian dark-roast coffee to 2¼ cups water. Add 1 tablespoon curaçao and a twist of lemon peel to each demitasse.

¾ *cup Italian coffee*
2¼ *cups water*
6 *tablespoons curaçao*
6 *twists lemon peel*

6

Formal Tea Party for Twenty or More

JELLY PINWHEELS *

OPEN-CENTER EGG-AND-TARRAGON SANDWICHES

DILLED RIBBON SANDWICHES

ANCHOVY CHECKERBOARD SANDWICHES

MEDICI CAKES

BUTTERSCOTCH BROWNIES

ALFOLDI SQUARES

BOURBON BALLS

PECAN MINIATURES

PERNOD SPONGE CAKE

TEA AND COFFEE

The United States Tea Council sets forth four cardinal rules for making good tea:

"1. To make the best tea, use your teapot. A teapot is best because it helps keep the water hot during the brewing period.

2. Bring fresh cold tap water to a full rolling boil. Water that has been reheated in a kettle gives tea a flat taste. Only boiling water poured *over* the tea produces the full flavor.

3. Use one teaspoon of tea or one teabag per cup. Don't guess. A teabag is equivalent to a teaspoon of tea—just enough to give you a full-bodied cup of tea.

4. Brew by the clock—3–5 minutes, depending on the strength you like. It takes time for the leaves to unfold and release their flavor. So don't guess—time it by the clock."

To make tea for a large group, the Tea Council suggests preparing a tea concentrate by adding ¼ pound of loose tea to 1½ quarts of boiling water. Cover the pot, let it stand for 5 minutes and strain the essence into a teapot.

* see Index and make 2 recipes

This yields enough concentrate for 40 to 45 cups. To serve, pour about 2 tablespoons of the concentrate into a cup and add hot water.

They also have a word to say about iced tea; use half again as much tea to allow for the melting ice. And, to clear up cloudy iced tea (the result of refrigeration), add a little boiling water.

This menu is intended for twenty people and is meant to be served during the latter part of the afternoon, though you could use some of the cakes by themselves for an early-afternoon dessert-and-coffee. Naturally, you won't use the whole menu for a tea for twenty people; you should probably select about five items: two kinds of sandwiches, two of the small cakes, and, let's say, the Pernod Sponge Cake. Make double batches of each if you have as many as forty people; or, for that number, if you really feel ambitious, make up the complete list as it stands. All of these good things take to freezing—if there should be leftovers—including the sandwiches. We feel a tea table should be generously laden and we expect leftovers rather than not.

Make the sandwiches in the morning and arrange them on platters. Cover each platter with waxed paper and a damp towel, and keep them in a cool place. Bake the Brownies, Medici Cakes, or Pecan Miniatures the day of the tea. It's all right to bake the Pernod Sponge Cake or the Alfoldi Squares the day before, and the Bourbon Balls should be made a few days ahead.

For a formal tea, you need two services—one for tea at one end of the table, the other for coffee at the other end. (It's handy to have a reciprocal lending arrangement with an obliging friend.) Ask from two to four of your close friends to spell each other at pouring, so that you will be entirely free to circulate among your guests. The purpose of the festivities may be anything from lionizing a visiting celebrity to introducing newcomers in the community to their neighbors—in either case your job, once you've taken care of the morning's work in the kitchen, is people, not food.

For teas (and card parties, and desserts at a buffet supper, too), we have used the china dessert-plate-and-cup combinations that have appeared in recent years, and we wonder why they weren't thought of ages ago. What a blessing, particularly at a large tea, where most people eat and drink standing up.

One of your best tablecloths is in order, and have your flower arrangement higher than usual. Don't make it squat, because this time people are standing around looking down on it, not sitting around the table having to peer through it.

Open-Center Egg-and-Tarragon Sandwiches

Make a paste with ¼ pound Tarragon Butter and 8 yolks of hard-cooked eggs. With a 2-inch round cooky cutter, cut 2 rounds from each slice of 2 loaves white bread. Reserve half the rounds as they are. With a second cooky cutter, much smaller than first one, remove center of other rounds, leaving a circle. Spread rounds with tarragon-and-egg paste, then gently press a circle on each one.

¼ pound Tarragon Butter (see Index, Herb Butters)
8 hard-cooked egg yolks
2 loaves white bread

Dilled Ribbon Sandwiches

Prepare ¼ pound Dill Butter. Cut all crusts from 1 unsliced loaf white bread so as to make a perfect oblong loaf. Spread longest side generously with dill butter, then, with serrated knife, cut buttered side into even slice. Repeat procedure until end of loaf. Follow same procedure with 1 whole-wheat loaf. Press white and whole-wheat bread slices together, buttered side *up*, in alternate layers, making loaves 5 slices thick, and turning fifth slice buttered side *down*. Chill for an hour, then slice loaves across layers to make thin sandwiches that will hold together.

¼ pound Dill Butter (see Index, Herb Butters)
1 loaf white bread
1 loaf whole-wheat bread

Anchovy Checkerboard Sandwiches

Using ¼ pound Anchovy Butter, proceed as for ribbon sandwiches above, but cut all slices ½ inch thick and assemble in loaves of only 4 layers. (Make sure all slices are uniform and anchovy butter is spread evenly.) Chill 1 hour.

Cut ribbon loaf into slices ½ inch thick, spreading end of loaf with more Anchovy Butter (another ¼ pound in all) before cutting each slice. Pile 4 of these slices together with ribbon strips running in same direction, but with dark strips above light strips, and light above dark, in a checkerboard design, and with top slice buttered side *down*. Press stack firmly together. Repeat with remaining slices. Chill 2 hours, then cut each stack into thin slices, cutting across strips.

½ pound Anchovy Butter (see Index, Fish Butters)
1 loaf white bread
1 loaf whole-wheat bread

Medici Cakes

Preheat oven to 350°. Mix together 1 pound ground almonds, 2 cups granulated sugar, 5 eggs, ¼ pound chopped citron, juice and grated rind of 1 lemon, 1 tablespoon each sherry and brandy, and 1 teaspoon each powdered cinnamon, allspice, and cloves. Put in a 9-by-11-inch pan, well-greased and dusted with flour. Brush top with 1 egg white, lightly beaten. Decorate with almonds and candied cherries. Bake for 45 minutes. Cool, then cut into 2-inch squares.

1 pound ground almonds
2 cups granulated sugar
5 eggs
¼ pound citron
1 lemon
1 tablespoon sherry
1 tablespoon brandy
1 teaspoon cinnamon
1 teaspoon allspice
1 teaspoon cloves
1 egg white
Almonds
Candied cherries

Butterscotch Brownies

Preheat oven to 350°. Cream ¼ pound sweet butter with 1¼ cups brown sugar. Add 2 eggs, 1 tablespoon light molasses, and 1 teaspoon vanilla. Fold in 1 cup flour and ½ cup chopped pecans. Pour into a well-greased 9-inch-square pan, and bake 30 to 35 minutes. While the cake cools, combine 2 tablespoons confectioners' sugar with ¼ teaspoon instant coffee and ½ teaspoon water to make frosting. Dribble this back and forth in fine zigzag line on cooled cake, and cut in squares.

¼ pound sweet butter
1¼ cups brown sugar
2 eggs
1 tablespoon light molasses
1 teaspoon vanilla
1 cup flour
½ cup chopped pecans
2 tablespoons confectioners' sugar
¼ teaspoon instant coffee
½ teaspoon water

Alfoldi Squares

Preheat oven to 300°. Cream together ½ pound butter, 1 cup plus 2 tablespoons granulated sugar, and 5 egg yolks. Divide batter in half. To one half add juice and grated rind of 1 lime; to the other half add 2 ounces semisweet chocolate, melted. Add 1 cup plus 2 tablespoons flour to each batter. Beat 5 egg whites until stiff but not dry, then fold half of egg whites into each batter. Grease a 10-by-15 inch jelly-roll pan. Cut 2 pieces of waxed paper each a little longer than half the length of pan, then line pan and turn up one end of paper to form a wall across center. Spread batters in pan, one on each side of paper wall, and bake 50 minutes. When done, cool cake in pan for 10 minutes, and 10 minutes more out of pan, then remove paper. Spread light layer with ¼ cup raspberry jam, then cover with chocolate layer; dust heavily with confectioners' sugar, and cut into small squares.

½ pound butter
1 cup plus 2 tablespoons granulated sugar
5 egg yolks
1 lime
2 ounces semisweet chocolate
2¼ cups flour, in all
5 egg whites
¼ cup raspberry jam
Confectioners' sugar

Bourbon Balls

Crush 24 lemon wafers and place crumbs in a bowl with 1 cup finely chopped pecans, 1 cup superfine granulated sugar, 2 tablespoons Dutch cocoa, ½ cup plus 3 tablespoons bourbon, and 2 tablespoons honey, then mix all ingredients. Drop from a teaspoon onto a baking sheet and chill. Then, on waxed paper, roll into marble-size balls. Sift together ½ cup confectioners' sugar and 1 teaspoon cinnamon, roll balls in the mixture, and let stand until sugar is partially absorbed; then roll in sugar mixture again. Store between layers of waxed paper in an airtight container.

24 lemon wafers
1 cup chopped pecans
1 cup superfine granulated sugar
2 tablespoons Dutch cocoa
½ cup plus 3 tablespoons bourbon
2 tablespoons honey
½ cup confectioners' sugar
1 teaspoon cinnamon

Pecan Miniatures

Dissolve 1 package dry yeast in ¼ cup lukewarm water. Into a large bowl, sift 2½ cups flour with 1 teaspoon salt, and make a well in center. Pour in dissolved yeast, ½ cup melted butter, 2 beaten eggs, ½ cup honey, and 1 cup sour cream. Mix all together, then beat well with a spoon and let stand in refrigerator overnight. The next day, soak ⅔ cup dried currants in boiling water until plump, drain, and reserve. Roll out dough ¼ inch thick on a lightly floured board. Dot with bits of butter—a generous tablespoon of it. Sprinkle with ⅔ cup chopped pecans, 1 teaspoon cinnamon, and reserved currants. Dribble 4 tablespoons honey over surface, and roll up like a jelly roll. Cut into ½-inch slices, place in a buttered pan, and let rise in warm place until double in bulk, about 2 hours. Preheat oven to 350°, then bake 15 to 20 minutes, or until light brown. Serve slightly warm.

1 package dry yeast
¼ cup lukewarm water
2½ cups flour
1 teaspoon salt
½ cup melted butter
2 eggs
½ cup honey
1 cup sour cream
Butter
⅔ cup dried currants
⅔ cup chopped pecans
1 teaspoon cinnamon
4 tablespoons honey

Pernod Sponge Cake

Preheat oven to 300°. Beat 4 egg whites until they stand in small peaks but are not dry. Beat 4 egg yolks until pale yellow and fluffy. Gradually add to yolks ¾ cup sifted confectioners' sugar and 2 tablespoons Pernod. Blend in ¾ cup flour, then fold in egg whites. Pour into a well-buttered quart cake mold first sprinkled lightly with about 3 tablespoons granulated sugar. Bake 55 minutes, then unmold onto a rack. When cake is cold, make an icing from ½ package vanilla-icing mix, using 3 tablespoons Pernod instead of some of the liquid recommended on package recipe. Color icing with 2 drops green food coloring. Ice top of cake and drip rest of icing on sides. Cut into 20 thin slices and serve on a platter.

4 eggs, separated
¾ cup sifted confectioners' sugar
2 tablespoons Pernod
¾ cup flour
Butter
3 tablespoons granulated sugar
½ package vanilla-icing mix
3 tablespoons Pernod
2 drops green food coloring

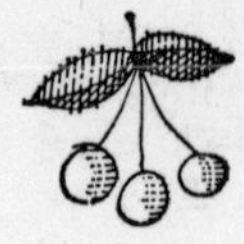

7

Garden Party for Twenty or More

Mint Sandwiches
Queen Mary's Rock Buns
Queen Victoria's Plumb Cake
Chocolate Layer Cake
with Chocolate Butter-Cream Frosting
Louisiana Pecan Torte
Kalte Ente
Punch Frappé
Iced Coffee

When this book was in the talking stage, we spoke of all kinds of parties. Either two great minds were at work, or it was out-and-out thought transference, but at the same moment we came up with the same thought—there *must* be a garden party menu. It was only then we discovered that, years before, each of us had been at the most celebrated one in the world, at Buckingham Palace.

We remember different things about it. Elaine recalls the hundreds of elegant ladies in trailing gowns and picture hats, top-hatted gentlemen in formal attire, the royal bearing of Queen Mary, and the equally regal carriage of her six-year-old granddaughter—as though Elizabeth anticipated her future role. These were fairy-tale sights to an American girl.

To Juliette, familiar with court life in Belgium, the spectacle was not so startling. She remembers the gaiety of brilliant colored uniforms, the block-long tents at one side of the lawn, and especially, under the tents, never-ending tables laden with traditional goodies—rock buns and mint sandwiches, Dundee cake and dark fruitcake, lemonade and orangeade. And, everyone sipped delicious chilled coffee topped with whipped cream from delicate demitasse cups.

The party at Buckingham Palace was *the* model for garden parties all over the world. Entertaining in this way appealed to formal, elegant society in our country, particularly in the South, where weather is kind so much of the year. Southern hostesses, known for the abundance of their tables and with a predilection for sweets, added sinfully rich cakes and *Torten* to the buffet.

The occasions for such a party in this harried twentieth century have become fewer, which we regard as sad indeed and quite unnecessary, too. For if a formal affair is on your spring or summer calendar, it may very well be that neither a formal tea nor a modern cocktail party will quite do. So our garden party may serve as a compromise solution as well as bring back memories of vanished elegance.

You might look over the tea-party menu on p. 17 with an eye to substituting some of those sandwiches or cakes for the ones on this menu, and vice versa—they are interchangeable. As this menu stands, it serves twenty people; for fifty, you will need two Plumb Cakes and three each of the chocolate and pecan cakes. Judge accordingly for any number in between or above.

The baking schedule depends on your freezer space. Bake and freeze the pecan *Torte,* defrost it the morning of the party, and finish it off. (Split the cake into three layers when it just begins to defrost. It is easier to handle and it will defrost faster when it is separated.) If you have room, freeze the chocolate cake, completely frosted and decorated but not wrapped. When it is frozen hard, wrap it loosely in foil or a plastic bag and return it to the freezer. Or you can bake and freeze the chocolate layers ahead if you don't have space for the finished cake.

Without a freezer, you have a heavy baking load the day before the party. That's about as far ahead as you can make the chocolate and pecan cakes

or the rock buns, and still keep them fresh for the party. Wrap them in foil and wait until the next day to frost the cakes. The buns have the friable texture of shortbread; they're a contrast to the very rich cakes and go well with hot or iced coffee.

"Plumb" is an old spelling, not a misspelling. While doing research on this, we cleared up a long-time mystery—why aren't there any plums in plumcake or plum pudding recipes? We learned that, generations ago, "plum" designated not only the fruit we ordinarily think of, but raisins as well.

Kalte Ente is a mysterious name, and we haven't yet determined why such a delicious drink should be called "cold duck." It has charms quite different from the left-over tone of its name. A friend of ours, with a very low tolerance for alcohol, tasted it for the first time in Europe. She was thirsty, the drink was good—need we say more? The next thing she knew, she was back in her hotel room, it was morning, and the sun was shining. Her husband reassures her to this day that not only was she every bit the lady, but perhaps had even a shade more dignity than usual. Lest we alarm you about the potency of this drink, rest easy—after all, how many people will come to your party straight from five hours of sightseeing and with a thirst to match?

Mint Sandwiches

In small bowl of electric mixer, or by hand, cream ½ pound softened sweet butter and add gradually 2 cups sifted confectioners' sugar. Then beat at high speed for 4 minutes, or 20 minutes by hand. Stir in 4 tablespoons chopped fresh spearmint leaves. Use 2 sliced loaves of white bread and 2 of protein bread. Butter white bread heavily with sweet mint butter, cover with protein bread slices, trim crusts, and cut each sandwich into three finger strips. Chill in refrigerator, covered with a damp cloth.

½ pound sweet butter
2 cups confectioners' sugar
4 tablespoons chopped spearmint leaves
2 loaves white bread
2 loaves protein bread

Queen Mary's Rock Buns

Preheat oven to 375°. Into a large bowl sift 4 cups flour with ⅛ teaspoon salt, 1 teaspoon grated nutmeg, 1 teaspoon allspice, 1 tablespoon grated lemon rind, and 2 teaspoons double-action baking powder. Then add 6 egg yolks, 1 cup granulated sugar, and ½ pound softened butter. Work with fingertips until mixture looks like sand-colored bread crumbs. Beat 6 egg whites until stiff but not dry, and incorporate into batter, which should be stiff. Grease and flour 2 baking sheets. With tines of two forks place mixture in small rocky heaps 1 inch apart on baking sheets. Bake 12 to 15 minutes or until dry and golden.

4 cups flour
⅛ teaspoon salt
1 teaspoon nutmeg
1 teaspoon allspice

1 tablespoon grated lemon rind
2 teaspoons double-action baking powder
6 egg yolks
1 cup granulated sugar
½ pound butter
6 egg whites

Queen Victoria's Plumb Cake

Dissolve 3 envelopes dry yeast in ½ cup lukewarm milk. Into a large bowl sift 6 cups flour with 1½ teaspoons ground mace, 2 teaspoons ground cloves, and 2½ teaspoons ground cinnamon. Make a well in the center, and pour in dissolved yeast, 3 egg yolks, 1 cup brandy, and ½ cup warm heavy cream. Then add ½ pound softened butter, 1 cup brown sugar, and 3 tablespoons grated orange rind, and mix together with your hands. Then incorporate 2 cups currants, 1 cup glacéed cherries, and ½ cup blanched slivered almonds, and mix until fruit is well distributed through batter. Butter heavily a large *Kugelhopf* mold or tube pan, spread batter in it, and leave in a warm place for 2 hours.

Preheat oven to 350°. Bake for 1¼ hours, or until cake needle shows clean. Cool cake 5 minutes, then unmold onto a rack. When cold, place on a large sheet of almuinum foil and turn up sides of foil. Warm then ignite ½ cup brandy, and pour flaming over cake. When flames subside, wrap cake securely in the foil, and store at least 5 days before serving.

3 envelopes dry yeast
½ cup lukewarm milk
6 cups flour
1½ teaspoons ground mace
2 teaspoons ground cloves
2½ teaspoons ground cinnamon
3 egg yolks
1 cup brandy
½ cup heavy cream
½ pound butter
1 cup brown sugar
3 tablespoons grated orange rind
2 cups currants
1 cup glacéed cherries
½ cup almonds
½ cup brandy

Chocolate Layer Cake

Preheat oven to 350°. Sift 2¾ cups cake flour with ¼ teaspoon salt and 1½ teaspoons baking soda, and reserve. Over very low heat melt 4½ squares semisweet chocolate in ¾ cup hot water, stir to blend, then remove from heat and reserve. In large bowl of electric mixer, cream ⅜ pound softened butter with 1 cup granulated sugar and ½ cup Vanilla Sugar. Add 3 eggs, then beat at high speed until fluffy, about 5 minutes. Blend in melted chocolate, then add alternately the sifted dry ingredients and 1 cup buttermilk or sour milk. Bake in 3 greased 9-inch layer tins for 20 to 25 minutes. Test after 20 minutes and watch carefully so as not to overbake. This is essential to insure cake's remaining moist.

2¾ cups cake flour
¼ teaspoon salt
1½ teaspoons baking soda
4½ squares semisweet chocolate
¾ cup hot water
⅜ pound butter
1 cup granulated sugar
½ cup Vanilla Sugar (see Index)
3 eggs
1 cup buttermilk or sour milk

Blended Chocolate Butter-Cream Frosting

Put 6 ounces chocolate bits in dry container of electric blender. Cover and blend at high speed 6 seconds. Turn motor off and scrape ground chocolate away from sides with a rubber spatula. Add ¼ cup of coffee, cover, and blend 6 seconds. Then add 4 tablespoons confectioners' sugar, 4 egg yolks, ¼ pound butter, and 2 tablespoons cognac, and blend 15 seconds. If necessary, chill to spreading consistency. Reserve ¼ cup to make border of rosettes with a pastry tube and fluted nozzle. Spread frosting on two bottom layers, and stack layers. Frost cake, decorate, and refrigerate.

6 ounces chocolate bits
¼ cup coffee
4 tablespoons confectioners' sugar
4 egg yolks
¼ pound butter
2 tablespoons cognac

Louisiana Pecan Torte

Preheat oven to 350°. In large bowl of electric mixer beat 10 egg yolks until light and fluffy, and add gradually ½ cup granulated sugar and ½ cup Vanilla Sugar. Add 1¾ cups finely ground pecans, ½ teaspoon salt, and 3 tablespoons dark rum. Blend thoroughly. Beat 10 egg whites until stiff but not dry, and fold them into mixture with 1 tablespoon toasted bread crumbs. Butter a 10-inch springform pan generously and sprinkle with a few bread crumbs. Pour batter into pan, and bake 45 to 50 minutes or until a cake needle shows clean. Cool cake on a rack, then split it in three layers with a very sharp bread knife. Whip 1 cup heavy cream with 1 tablespoon sugar and 2 tablespoons dark rum. Spread layers generously with cream and 1 tablespoon each grated chocolate. Garnish top layer with whipped-cream rosettes pressed through a pastry tube.

10 egg yolks
½ cup granulated sugar
½ cup Vanilla Sugar (*see Index*)
1¾ cups ground pecans
½ teaspoon salt
3 tablespoons dark rum
10 egg whites
Bread crumbs
1 cup heavy cream
1 tablespoon sugar
2 tablespoons dark rum
3 tablespoons grated chocolate

Kalte Ente

Peel 2 lemons in wide, unbroken spiral strips, leaving end of each spiral attached to lemon. Put lemons in large tall glass container, and hang the free ends of peel over container's rim. Pour in 2 bottles Buena Vista Sonoma Valley Sylvaner, or 3 bottles Chilean Riesling, and let wine stand for 15 minutes. Add ice cubes and 2 more bottles wine; then, just before serving, add 2 bottles chilled Almadén brut champagne. Serve in punch cups.

2 lemons
4 bottles Buena Vista Sonoma Valley Sylvaner
or 5 bottles Chilean Riesling
Ice cubes
2 bottles Almadén brut champagne

Punch Frappé

Pour 3 quarts boiling water over 10 sprigs spearmint and 1 cup sugar. Cool, and when cold remove mint, add 12 perfect even-sized mint leaves, and freeze in a metal bowl. Shortly before serving, unmold block of ice and put it in a large punch bowl. Pour in 1½ cups *crème de menthe,* and cover with 3 quarts sweetened cold tea. Serve in punch cups.

3 quarts boiling water
10 sprigs spearmint
1 cup sugar
12 mint leaves
1½ cups crème de menthe
3 quarts cold tea (*see Index*)
Sugar

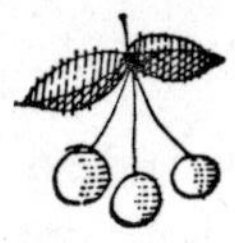

8

Children's Party for Twelve

CHICKEN FRICASSEE IN POTATO NESTS
JELLIED SALADS
ORANGE LAYER CAKE WITH SEVEN-MINUTE ICING
CONFETTI ICE CREAM
HONEY WATER *

We admit it, we are a pair of sentimentalists. We do welcome the chance to awaken that special look on a child's face—the same look of unqualified joy that greets the first sight of Christmas morning or of a candle-lit cake at a birthday party. One glance at a child gazing at a party table you have made *just* for him is all the thanks you want.

Most children prefer familiar foods, so we stick to everyday fare, but in fancy dress. When you have a party for youngsters, by all means prepare everything in advance so you can be on the scene almost every minute in case of crisis. The only last-minute chore with this menu is to heat and arrange the chicken. Have the potato nests ready on cooky sheets, and pop them in the oven while you heat the chicken and add the yolks to the sauce.

The other dishes can, with minor variations, carry out almost any color scheme the occasion may require. Let's see how it works for a Halloween party: Use a solid-orange paper cloth. Get the biggest, brightest pumpkin you can find, let your child help scoop it out, and make a Jack-o'-Lantern for the centerpiece. (Reserve the scooped-out pulp to make Pumpkin Tarts; see Index). Make the first of the jellied salads below, and have one at each place before the children come to the table. Tint the cake icing with a few drops each of red and yellow vegetable coloring, and decorate the cake with licorice shoestrings or candy corn, or stud it with small orange and black gumdrops. If the whole thing looks poisonous to you, you can be sure it's perfect. Sprinkle the ice-cream balls with orange sugar fancies, or stick to the main theme with Sherbet Jack-o'-Lanterns: With an ice-cream scoop, make 12 balls of orange sherbet. Use small licorice gumdrops for eyes,

* see Index

a tiny licorice candy for the nose, and an inch-long piece of licorice shoestring for the mouth. Set in the freezer until needed.

With the above as general guidance, imagination will get you through the entire calendar year. Color is the thing: Red and white, red and green, red, white, and blue, lavender and yellow—the more you think about it, the less edible it sounds, but it's always fun.

Chicken Fricassee

Put a 7-pound fowl in a kettle with enough water to cover, 2 carrots, 1 onion, ½ bay leaf, ⅛ teaspoon dried thyme, and 1 clove. Bring to a boil over high heat, then reduce heat, and poach fowl for 2 hours, or until tender. Set aside 1½ cups broth, and reserve rest for other uses. Cool chicken, discard skin, remove meat from bones, cut in julienne strips, and reserve. Cook 2 packages frozen peas, uncovered, in cup of chicken broth until just tender. Add chicken meat, ½ teaspoon lemon juice, and 1 tablespoon chopped parsley, and remove from heat. Shortly before serving, reheat, then thicken, away from heat, with 2 egg yolks beaten with 1 teaspoon arrowroot or cornstarch. Spoon into individual Potato Nests, below.

1 7-pound fowl
2 carrots
1 onion
½ bay leaf
⅛ teaspoon dried thyme
1 clove

1½ cups broth
2 packages frozen peas
½ teaspoon lemon juice
1 tablespoon chopped parsley
2 egg yolks
1 teaspoon arrowroot or cornstarch

For adults, this recipe will serve six. In this case, augment all ingredients in sauce, above, except green peas, by one-half.

Potato Nests

Preheat oven to 450°. Boil, uncovered, over high heat in salted water, 16 large peeled and quartered potatoes. When tender, pour off water, replace pan on low heat, and shake gently to dry potatoes out. Force through food mill or mash with electric mixer. Add ¼ pound butter in small pieces, 2 egg yolks, ½ cup milk, and salt to taste. Mold into twelve heaps on a greased baking sheet, press the bottom of a teacup into each heap to hollow it in shape of a nest, and use tines of a fork to mark outside of nest. Brush outside of nest with beaten egg. Bake 10 to 12 minutes, or until nests are golden. Remove with a spatula and fill with Chicken Fricassee.

16 potatoes
¼ pound butter
2 egg yolks
½ cup milk
Salt
1 egg

Jellied Salads

Soften 3 envelopes plain gelatin in ½ cup cold water. Open 2 No. 2½ cans Elberta peach halves. Strain juice from can through a fine sieve lined with cheesecloth. Heat juice with enough water to make 5½ cups in all. Add softened gelatin and stir until dissolved. Place ½ peach in shallow glass dish. Use 2 raisins to make eyes and several currants for eyebrows and mouth. Cover with the peach jelly, cool, then chill in refrigerator.

Variations:

In pyrex cups, place cut-up fruit and cover with 6 cups strained orange juice in which 3 envelopes plain gelatin and 1 cup sugar have been dissolved as above. Chill, then unmold on lettuce.

In pyrex cups, place a spiced apple, cover with 6 cups cider in which 3 envelopes plain gelatin have been dissolved as above. Chill, then unmold on lettuce.

3 envelopes plain gelatin
½ cup cold water
2 No. 2½ cans Elberta peach halves
24 raisins
Currants
or
Cut-up fruit
6 cups orange juice
3 envelopes gelatin
1 cup sugar
Lettuce
or
12 spiced apples
6 cups cider
3 envelopes gelatin
Lettuce

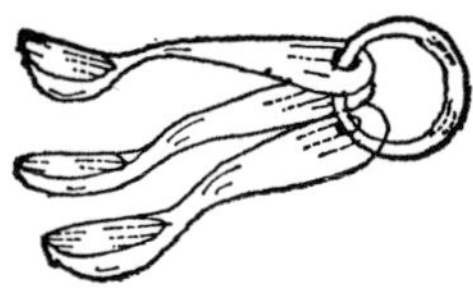

Orange Layer Cake

Preheat oven to 375°. Sift together twice 2⅓ cups cake flour with 2½ teaspoons double-action baking powder, ½ teaspoon salt, and ¼ teaspoon baking soda. Cream ⅔ cup butter, gradually add 1 cup granulated sugar, and beat until fluffy and light. Add 3

egg yolks, one at a time, and 1 teaspoon grated orange rind. Gradually blend in sifted flour alternately with 1 cup orange juice and ¼ cup Vanilla Sugar. Beat 3 egg whites until stiff but not dry and fold carefully into batter with rubber spatula. Butter three 9-inch layer-cake pans. Drop 1 tablespoon flour into each pan, and tap sides of pan gently and rotate to spread a thin veil of flour over butter. Pour out excess flour, then divide batter evenly between three pans, and bake 30 to 35 minutes. Turn layers out to cool on a cake rack. Assemble with ¼ inch of orange marmalade spread between layers. Frost with Seven-Minute Icing, below.

2⅓ cups cake flour
2½ teaspoons double-action baking powder
½ teaspoon salt
¼ teaspoon baking soda
⅔ cup butter
1 cup granulated sugar
3 egg yolks
1 teaspoon grated orange rind
1 cup orange juice
¼ cup Vanilla Sugar (see Index)
3 egg whites
Butter
3 tablespoons flour
2 cups orange marmalade
Seven-Minute Icing

Seven-Minute Icing

In top of quart-size double boiler, over boiling water, combine 1 unbeaten egg white, ¾ cup granulated sugar, ¼ teaspoon cream of tartar, 2 tablespoons water, and ⅛ teaspoon salt. Beat constantly with rotary beater or electric beater for 7 minutes. Remove from heat. For Halloween, flavor with 2 tablespoons frozen concentrated orange juice, and add 2 drops each yellow and red vegetable food coloring. For other occasions, use 1 teaspoon vanilla or almond or lemon extract, and vegetable colors as required. Continue to beat until frosting stands in high peaks. With a spatula, spread at once on cooled cake. For Halloween decorate with black gumdrops and shoestring candy. For other occasions, use appropriate coloring and gumdrops to contrast.

1 egg white
¾ cup granulated sugar
¼ teaspoon cream of tartar
2 tablespoons water
⅛ teaspoon salt
1 teaspoon vanilla
or almond or lemon extract
2 to 4 drops vegetable food coloring
Gum drops to contrast

Halloween:
2 tablespoons frozen orange juice
2 drops yellow vegetable coloring
2 drops red vegetable coloring
Black gumdrops
Black shoestring candy

Confetti Ice Cream

Scoop in the form of a ball any ice cream or sherbet of your choice. Place balls on baking sheet and freeze until needed. Just before serving, sprinkle heavily with multicolored fancies or sugar seed.

2 quarts ice cream or sherbet
Multicolored fancies
or sugar seed

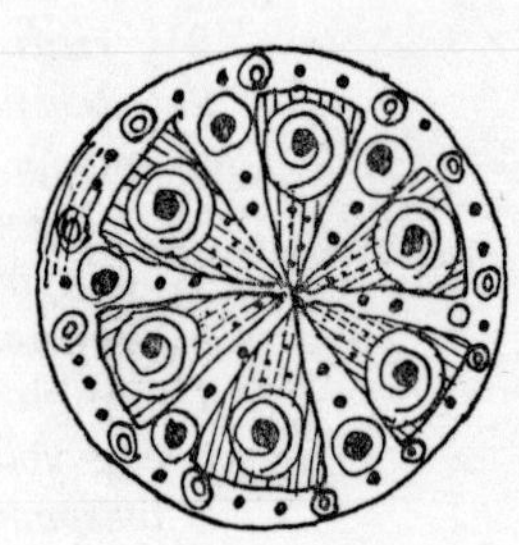

9

Teen-Agers Entertain for Ten—Summer

HERO SANDWICHES
APPLES ON A STICK
BUTTERSCOTCH BROWNIES *
CHOCOFFEE OR BLACK COWS

Is the name, Hero Sandwich, descriptive of its heroic size or the heroic appetite that would dare tackle it? We haven't pinned this down—but we do know that the appetite of a teen-ager will match that of any hero.

And, when it comes to *what* they like to eat, remember that this is not the age for subtlety. Keep the soufflés and delicate sauces for *your* friends and cater to your youngster's crowd with plenty of rib-sticking provender, topped off with an outrageously sweet dessert.

If you comment as you read this that we don't know what we're talking about, and you have in mind two or three youngsters who like nothing better than those very sauces and soufflés, we know them too. But with those young ones, it's a case of gastronomic precocity—they're just knowledgeable before their time, and it's unlikely you'll ever have ten of them in the house at once.

Candy the apples a day or two before the party and keep them in a cool place, but not in the icebox or they will get too sticky. A candy thermometer is a great help. If you don't have one, test for the soft-ball stage by dropping a bit of the boiling syrup into cold water. It's ready when you can pick it up between your fingers and make a ball that almost holds its shape.

Bake the brownies the morning of the party or tap the reserve supply in your freezer. (We have teen-agers in our homes, too, and brownies, both butterscotch and chocolate, are a staple freezer item.)

Have all the sandwich ingredients ready to arrange on the bread just before serving, and all the drink makings ready, too. Either make the drinks

* see Index

yourself, or put everything for both drinks out on the table and let each one be his own soda jerk. You'll probably see a few added touches invented that you would never even dream of.

Hero Sandwiches

Buy 5 to 8 small loaves of Italian bread, depending upon whether guests are boys or girls; ½ loaf is enough for a girl but not for most boys. Lengthwise, remove top slices from loaves of bread, leaving ⅔ of bread for bottom slice. Spread bottom slices thickly with Mustard Mayonnaise, and over it place alternately leaves of Boston lettuce and romaine. Over greens, place slices of turkey at one end of sandwich, then 3 slices of tomato next to them, then sliced hard-boiled egg, then chili beans, then roast beef, then chow-chow pickles, then salami at far end of sandwich. Garnish with bits of pimiento and small onion rings. Arrange open sandwiches on checkered or gaily printed napkins, on a large tray. Spread top slices lightly with Mustard Mayonnaise, and place on their sides next to each sandwich. Let guests put the lids on their sandwiches and halve them just before eating.

5–8 loaves Italian bread
2 cups Mustard Mayonnaise (see Index)
2 heads Boston lettuce
2 heads romaine
1 pound cold sliced turkey
6 tomatoes
6 hard-boiled eggs
1 cup chili beans
1 pound cold sliced roast beef
1 jar chow-chow pickles
1 pound salami
½ cup pimiento strips
Onion rings

Apples on a Stick

Select 10 firm red apples and insert orange sticks from drug counter in place of stems. Into a large saucepan pour 2 quarts water, add 7 cups granulated sugar, boil, and bring to the soft-ball stage (234°–238° on candy thermometer). Stir in ½ small bottle red food coloring, then dip each apple in the syrup. Remove quickly and hold by stick until syrup hardens. Repeat procedure twice for each apple to get a high glaze. Cool on a greased baking sheet.

10 red apples
10 orange sticks
2 quarts water
7 cups granulated sugar
½ small bottle red food coloring

Chocoffee

Fill 10 parfait glasses one third full with cold coffee, add 2 scoops chocolate ice cream, and top with whipped cream, shaved chocolate, and 1 glacéed cherry per glass.

1½ quarts cold coffee
2 quarts chocolate ice cream
2 cups cream, whipped
½ cup shaved chocolate
10 glacéed cherries

Black Cows

Fill 10 stemmed water glasses two thirds full with root beer, add 2 scoops vanilla ice cream, and top with whipped cream, a sprinkling of crushed peanut brittle, and ½ preserved kumquat per glass.

3 quarts root beer
2 quarts vanilla ice cream
2 cups cream, whipped
½ cup crushed peanut brittle
5 preserved kumquats

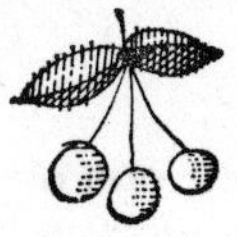

10

Teen-Agers Entertain for Ten—Winter

CORN CHOWDER
RAILSPLITTERS
WINNI'S FRUIT SALAD
FRUIT MARLOW
MINTED CHOCOLATE FUDGE
SOFT DRINKS

A meal in a soup pot generally helps to fill up the bottomless pit that exists inside almost every teen-ager. It seems to satisfy hunger pangs that otherwise voice themselves every hour on the hour. And, it satisfies the hostess, because she can provide *food* within minutes after the clamor for same gets too insistent.

The Chowder and the Railsplitters, made early in the day, only need reheating—the soup over low heat for about fifteen minutes, and the cornsticks in a 400° oven for five minutes. Lacking the cornstick pans, use small muffin tins. You should then change the name, because Railsplitter indicates a long, thin shape, but this is a minor technicality. Your guests are interested in food, not semantics. If you have the celery, nutmeats, and grapes ready for the salad, it won't take more than a few minutes to cut the rest of the fruit and toss them all together. In fifteen minutes at the outside, you can sound the supper bell.

While everyone is concentrating on soup and salad, you have ample time to unmold the frozen fruit creams. Stack and slice them, and put them on a platter and into the freezer; you may even do this earlier if it's more convenient.

We can imagine serving this meal right from the kitchen, providing traffic in and out is practical. Leave the soup pot on the stove and use a kitchen ladle. Have the chowder mugs and the basket of Railsplitters close at hand, and let the junior hostess do the honors, with the line forming to the right.

Set the fruit salad just beyond, on one of the counter tops, with a stack of plates and napkins (paper for both is fine) and the necessary number of spoons and forks. Do the same with the Fruit Marlow when they're ready for it. As a safety measure, you might set out a bowl of popcorn in addition to the chocolate candies—many youngsters have an allergy to chocolate and nuts. (For kitchen service, have the Fruit Marlow sliced on the platter and ready in the freezer, as suggested above; the simplest things can be hard to manipulate with everyone all around you.)

They'll all find a place to sit and eat. Don't worry about making formal provision for it—this is the age when floors look comfortable, and a log fire in the living room or library is the best centerpiece. Schedule this menu for early supper around six, or later in the evening, after the movies or whatever, at ten or ten thirty. And, if you're of a mind that growing boys must have meat, too, for an early supper add a platter of sliced cold turkey or chicken —it won't be amiss.

Corn Chowder

Dice ½ pound country-smoked bacon. In a skillet, over medium heat, fry to a golden brown. Add 6 cups stock and 6 cups diced potatoes, and boil until potatoes are soft. Add 4 cups corn, ⅛ teaspoon freshly ground pepper, a dash of Tabasco, 8 cups scalded top milk (or 4 cups each scalded light cream and milk), then stir in 1 cup cracker crumbs. Serve in mugs.

½ pound country-smoked bacon
6 cups stock
6 cups diced potatoes
4 cups corn
⅛ teaspoon freshly ground pepper
Dash Tabasco
8 cups scalded top milk
or 4 cups each scalded light cream and milk
1 cup cracker crumbs

Railsplitters

Preheat oven to 400°. Fry three slices of bacon until crisp, drain on absorbent paper, crumble to very small bits, and reserve. Melt ¼ pound butter and cool. In a large bowl beat 2 eggs with 2 tablespoons sugar and 2 teaspoons salt. Add 2 cups yellow cornmeal and cooled melted butter, and mix thoroughly. Pour in 2 cups buttermilk or sour milk and beat. Then sift in 2 cups flour with 1 teaspoon baking soda and 2 tablespoons baking powder, and beat for 2 minutes. Mix in crumbled bacon. Grease iron cornbread-stick pans, pour in batter, and bake for about 15 minutes.

3 slices bacon
¼ pound butter
2 eggs
2 tablespoons sugar
2 teaspoons salt
2 cups yellow cornmeal
2 cups buttermilk or sour milk
2 cups flour
1 teaspoon baking soda
2 tablespoons baking powder

Winni's Fruit Salad

Wash 12 to 16 stalks Pascal celery. Cut each stalk 3 or 4 times lengthwise, then crosswise into ⅜-inch slices. Place celery in salad bowl, press 2 cloves garlic over it, and toss together lightly. Wash 2 large rosy apples, quarter and core, but do not peel; then cut into ¼-inch dice. Peal 4 firm bananas, slice lengthwise 6 times and cut crosswise into ¼-inch dice. Wash 2 small bunches white grapes, cut grapes in half, remove seeds, and cut again. Chop coarsely 1 cup pecan meats. Add fruits and nuts to celery, sprinkle with 1 teaspoon lemon juice, add ¼ teaspoon salt, and toss together lightly. Decorate with 16 to 20 unbroken pecan halves. Serve within half hour after preparation to retain freshness and color.

12 to 16 stalks Pascal celery
2 cloves garlic
2 large apples
4 bananas
2 small bunches white grapes
1 cup pecans, plus 16 to 20 unbroken halves
1 teaspoon lemon juice
¼ teaspoon salt

Fruit Marlow

To make layers of pineapple marlow, melt in top of a double boiler, over hot water, 1 pound marshmallows with 1 cup canned crushed pineapple and 2 teaspoons lemon juice. To make layers of strawberry marlow, melt in same way 1 pound marshmallows with 1½ cups crushed strawberries. When both mixtures are cold and slightly stiffened, whip 2 pints heavy cream and fold half of cream into each mixture. Freeze separately in 4 ice trays. Serve pineapple and strawberry layers stacked alternately on top of each other and sliced through like a cake.

2 pounds marshmallows
1 cup canned crushed pineapple
2 teaspoons lemon juice
1½ cups crushed strawberries
2 pints heavy cream

Minted Chocolate Fudge

Bring 1 cup light cream to boiling point with 2 cups granulated sugar. Stir until sugar is melted. In a quart-size bowl place 4 ounces unsweetened chocolate and cover with boiling water, 2 cups more or less. Cover and leave undisturbed for 5 minutes. Pour off water; chocolate will be melted. Stir chocolate into cream-and-sugar mixture, and add ¼ cup honey and ¼ cup Garnier green *crème de menthe.* Cook to soft-ball stage (240°). Add 2 tablespoons butter, and remove from heat. Let stand until lukewarm, then beat until creamy. Add 1 cup chopped nuts, pour into a buttered pan, and dust with blanched grated pistachio nuts. Cool in refrigerator. When firm, cut into squares.

1 cup light cream
2 cups granulated sugar
4 ounces unsweetened chocolate
Boiling water
¼ cup honey
¼ cup Garnier green crème de menthe
2 tablespoons butter
1 cup chopped nuts
¼ cup blanched grated pistachio nuts

11

Card Party for Eight Women

Jelly Pinwheels

Prune-Bread Sandwiches

Raspberries au Vin *

Spritz Cookies

Tea or Coffee

Be it Casino or Canasta, the major attraction at the ladies' card table is generally conversation, served with a cup of coffee and a few tasty tidbits both edible and verbal. "Light refreshments" are in order for an afternoon or evening game; you will find additional suggestions for sandwiches and cookies on the menu for teas (see p. 17).

The recipes are self-explanatory and need little comment. Make the sandwiches ahead, arrange them on the platters, and cover them with waxed paper and a damp towel to keep them perfect for several hours. Heap the Prune-Bread Sandwiches in the center of the platter and circle around with the Jelly Pinwheels, overlapping them a bit. You might want to make a double batch of the Prune Bread while you're at it. Wrapped in foil and stored in a tightly covered tin, it keeps well; make it ahead in any case, because it develops flavor after several days and slices better, too.

The Spritz Cookies are a mainstay of the Scandinavian cooky jar. Delicate in flavor and not overly sweet, they keep for weeks in a covered tin—if your family stays away from them that long. Both the cookies and the Prune Bread freeze well, too.

Prepare the Raspberries *au Vin* (see Index) several hours in advance to allow the flavor of the wine to permeate them; they should be well chilled, and double the recipe for eight people. If you were smart enough to save one of your grandmother's cut-glass bowls that supposedly went out of fashion years ago, serve the berries in it. The shining red fruit and the faceted crystal are right for each other.

* see Index

Jelly Pinwheels

Blend together in small bowl of electric mixer 4 ounces currant jelly and 8 ounces cream cheese. If necessary, add one drop red food coloring to give mixture a pale rose color. Cut all crust from unsliced loaf of bread so as to make a perfect oblong loaf. Spread longest side generously with cream-cheese mixture, then, with serrated knife, cut off spread side in a thin even slice. Roll like a jelly roll, press together, and repeat to end of loaf. Wrap in a damp cloth and chill for 2 hours; then slice each roll into thin sandwiches. Count 2 to 3 sandwiches per guest.

4 ounces currant jelly
8 ounces cream cheese
Red food coloring (optional)
Loaf white bread

Prune Bread

Make two days ahead, since bread slices better after 48 hours.

Preheat oven to 350°. Sift 1¼ cups flour with 1 cup granulated sugar, ½ teaspoon salt, 1 teaspoon baking powder, and 1 teaspoon baking soda. Stir in 1 cup graham flour and ¾ cup broken walnut meats. Beat 1 egg with 1 cup sour milk. (A drop or two lemon juice will curdle sweet milk.) Add ½ cup prune juice, 2 tablespoons melted butter, ⅓ cup chopped cooked prunes, and 1 tablespoon grated orange rind. Combine this mixture with dry ingredients, beating at low speed in electric mixer for 1 minute. Pour into well-buttered loaf pan and bake 55 to 60 minutes. Cool, wrap in foil, and store in cool place.

To make tea sandwiches, spread lightly with whipped butter or cream cheese, and cut into triangles. Count 2 to 3 sandwiches per guest.

1¼ cups flour
1 cup granulated sugar
½ teaspoon salt
1 teaspoon baking powder
1 teaspoon baking soda
1 cup graham flour
¾ cup broken walnut meats
1 egg
1 cup sour milk
½ cup prune juice
2 tablespoons melted butter
⅓ cup chopped cooked prunes
1 tablespoon grated orange rind

Spritz Cookies

Preheat oven to 350°. In small container of electric mixer, at low speed, blend together ½ pound softened butter and ½ cup Vanilla Sugar. Add 1 egg, turn speed of mixer to high, and beat until mixture is fluffy and light in color. With a spatula, gradually fold in 2⅓ cups sifted flour. Place this soft dough in a pastry tube and press through fluted nozzle directly onto lightly buttered baking sheet into outlines of rings, hearts, and diamonds. Bake until golden.

1 cup butter
½ cup Vanilla Sugar (see Index)
1 egg
2⅓ cups sifted flour

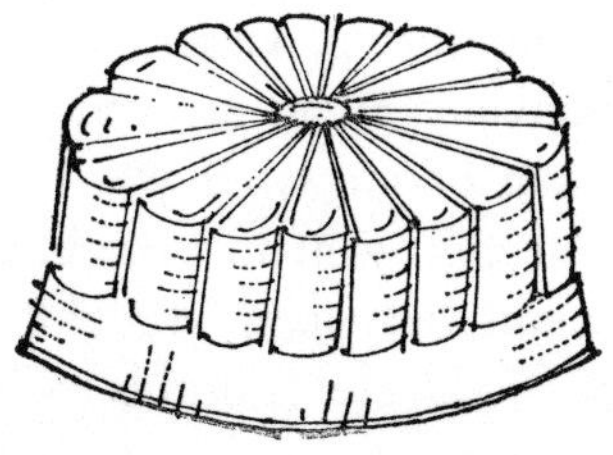

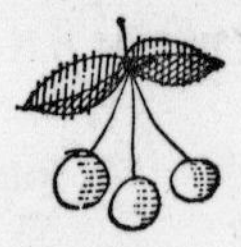

12

Card Party for Eight Men

SAUCISSON EN CROÛTE

OLD-FASHIONED PINEAPPLE CHEESE *

KUGELHOPF

SESAME CRACKERS OR IMPORTED ENGLISH BISCUITS

BEER AND COFFEE

You would give odds that men playing cards are oblivious to everything around them. But if you think they won't even notice the difference if you give them dry crusts of bread, beware. Suddenly the hand is over, the outside world breaks through—and they're hungry!

An afternoon game on a weekend might start off with this menu for lunch; on weekdays, an evening game with a late snack is more likely. They will enjoy demolishing this kind of meal anytime—as long as it doesn't arrive just in time to interfere with a grand slam or a royal flush.

When we bake this *Kugelhopf,* we generally double the recipe. One we use, the other goes into the freezer. To use it at a later date, unwrap it still frozen and reheat it in a 350° oven for 25 to 30 minutes. Serve it almost any time: with midmorning coffee or afternoon tea, as a dinner dessert or an evening snack. This is a particularly easy and a particularly good recipe. Unlike most yeast doughs, this one rises only once, yet the texture is excellent. (We have punched it down after the first rising and let it rise a second time, to see if there was any improvement. The texture was identical, so we leave well enough alone.)

The particular sausage we suggest for the *Saucisson en Croûte* is not mandatory. There are any number of varieties—Hungarian, Polish, Italian, Spanish, German, Scandinavian. Some are milder, some spicier, made of beef, pork, or a combination of meats. If you have access to a shop that specializes in sausages, you will want to experiment with several. We are particularly fond of German *bratwurst,* a light, delicately flavored veal sausage, the size of a large frankfurter. For this recipe, we order it especially

* see Index

in a large size. Some sausages are not precooked; parboil any uncooked sausage, remove the skin, and cool it before you wrap it in the pastry. Serve the *Saucisson* warm, on a hotplate if it has to wait until the men tear themselves from the card table. To go with it, two or three types of mustard—Bahamian, English, or a Dijon white-wine mustard are all good.

Prepare the *Saucisson* ahead and put it in the icebox on a cooky sheet, ready for the oven. Plan your baking schedule so that the *Kugelhopf* comes out of the oven just in time to put the *Saucisson* in; the cake will be slightly warm when you serve it, just as a yeast cake should be.

Saucisson en Croûte

Into a chilled mixing bowl sift together 2 cups flour and 1 teaspoon salt. With a pastry blender cut ¼ pound plus 3 tablespoons chilled sweet butter into flour until butter is the size of peas. Moisten with ¼ cup ice water and toss with a fork until mixture holds together, but no more; minimum handling is important. If more water is needed, add a teaspoon at a time. Chill dough 10 minutes. Place between sheets of waxed paper and roll out into rectangle large enough to enclose sausage.

Preheat oven to 375°. Cut a 3-pound Danish Summer Sausage * in half crosswise, and reserve half for other uses. With a sharp knife make several long incisions in casing of sausage and peel off. Brush sausage with ¼ cup Riesling and wrap in crust. Brush edges of crust on top and at both ends with beaten egg, press edges together, and seal and crimp with a fork or flute with fingers. Bake on a greased jelly-roll pan for 30 minutes, or until crust is well browned. Serve warm, cut in 1-inch slices.

2 cups flour
1 teaspoon salt
⅔ cup sweet butter
¼ cup ice water
Danish Summer Sausage *
¼ cup Riesling
1 egg

Kugelhopf

Dissolve 1 package dry yeast and 1 teaspoon sugar in ½ cup lukewarm milk. Cream together ½ cup butter with ¼ cup sugar. Add to butter-sugar mixture 4 egg yolks, 2 cups flour, 1 teaspoon cardamon, ¼ cup raisins, 1 teaspoon grated orange peel, ¼ cup milk, and the yeast mixture. Beat with back of a large wooden spoon until the dough blisters. Grease a *Kugelhopf* or *Bundkuchen* form thoroughly, and sprinkle with ¼ cup slivered almonds. Spoon batter into form, filling no more than two thirds, then cover with a cloth and set in a warm place to rise to top of pan, about 2½ hours. Preheat oven to 350° and bake 40 to 45 minutes. Turn out on cake rack to cool. Dust generously with confectioners' sugar.

1 package dry yeast
1 teaspoon sugar
½ cup milk
½ cup butter
¼ cup sugar
4 egg yolks
2 cups flour
1 teaspoon cardamon
¼ cup raisins
1 teaspoon grated orange peel
¼ cup milk
¼ cup slivered almonds
Confectioners' sugar

* May be ordered from Hickory Farms of Ohio, 1021 N. Reynolds Road, Toledo, Ohio.

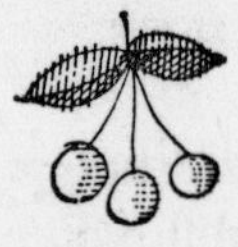

13

Late Supper for Two

Crème St. Germain

Poulet Docteur

Steamed Rice

Adam and Eve Salad

Petits Coeurs à la Crème with Strawberries *

French Bread

Coffee

WINES

Inexpensive: Almadén Grenache Rosé

Medium-priced: Agneau Rosé Baron Philippe de Rothschild

Lest you skip lightly over this menu thinking that the glamor of a late supper for two has no part in your life, we must set you straight right away. Though we admit to being taken with the charm of such a situation, this supper need not necessarily be late, nor just for two. It is also for any crowded day when you might wish you had an Aladdin's lamp to summon dinner in the nick of time before you.

As we have set the stage, this menu is for after the theatre or a concert. You return home, the table is laid, and supper is ready. Aladdin's genie would be just as welcome, though, when you have invited someone to dinner at seven, and suddenly find yourself called to an emergency meeting that, with luck, will have *you* home barely by then. Or, you have out-of-town visitors coming to dine, and who is expected to spend the afternoon showing them the sights? You guessed it. This can present problems.

Magic being on the whole undependable, you have to be your own little genie the day before and in the morning, but the point is to come up with an Aladdin effect in the evening. The day before, mold the individual *Coeurs*

* see Index

à la Crème in 2½- to 3-inch cooky cutters lined with cheese cloth. (One sixth of the recipe, see Index, will make two hearts.) The next day, wash and hull a cup and a half of firm, ripe strawberries and let them dry thoroughly. Unmold the hearts on two plates, put the berries around the hearts, and keep them in the refrigerator; dust the berries with powdered sugar later, when you serve dessert. Cook the chicken in the morning, and put it in a stove-to-table pot, so you won't have to arrange it on a platter later. While the chicken is simmering, attend to soup, rice, and salad ingredients. Finally, put the wine in the refrigerator, set the table, and line up the coffee pot and all the necessary dishes and serving adjuncts in the kitchen.

Now, you've gone to theatre, or the emergency meeting, or whatever, and the time has come. Simply turn on the heat under the rice and the chicken, preheat the oven to 350°, and then devote your attention to having someone else give you a drink. (The chicken should be on an asbestos mat over very low heat.) When you go into the kitchen to ladle out the chilled soup, toss the salad, and put the bread in the oven. Bring the wine to the table, light the candles and, abracadabra, you're ready.

Crème St. Germain

Pressure-cooker and electric-blender method: Place 1 package frozen peas in pressure cooker, add 1 tablespoon monosodium glutamate, salt and pepper to taste, and ¼ cup water. Cover, bring up the pressure, then cook 1 minute under pressure. Without tilting it at all, remove cooker from heat, take to the sink, and pour a steady stream of cold water over the top until a distinct whispering noise releases all steam pressure. Open cooker. Place peas in electric blender. Add enough cold chicken broth to juice from peas to make up 1 cup. Add this to blender, cover, and blend until smooth. Add ½ cup heavy cream, and blend 3 seconds longer. Taste and correct seasoning. Pour into individual cups, chill, and serve ice cold.

1 package frozen peas
1 tablespoon monosodium glutamate
Salt, pepper
¼ cup water
Chicken broth
½ cup heavy cream

Poulet Docteur

In a Dutch oven, over medium heat, melt 2 tablespoons butter. In it brown evenly, a few pieces at a time, a 2- to 2½-pound broiler chicken, first cut into serving pieces. Remove pieces as they are browned then add more, and add 2 more tablespoons butter. Return pieces of chicken to pot, cover, reduce heat, and cook for 15 minutes. Then add ½ cup Port and 1 cup chicken broth, and cook, uncovered, for 20 minutes.

Meanwhile, check ¼ pound chicken livers for any trace of gall (green); halve them. Cut into julienne strips ¼ pound veal cutlets first pounded very thin by butcher. In a skillet, over medium heat, sauté veal and chicken livers together in 2 tablespoons butter until livers are brown on the edges but still pink on the inside. Season with pepper and salt and 1½ teaspoons crumbled dried tarragon. When done, remove livers and veal strips to shallow heated platter or a heat proof serving casserole. Top with pieces of chicken. Over high heat, boil juices in the pan, uncovered, and reduce to three quarters of original volume. Taste and correct seasonings, and pour over chicken.

6 tablespoons butter, in all
2- to 2½-pound broiler chicken
½ cup Port
1 cup chicken broth
¼ pound chicken livers
¼ pound veal cutlet
Salt, pepper
2 teaspoons dried tarragon

Steamed Rice

To make 2 servings: Use a tall pot into the top of which you can fit a sieve. Bring 4 cups water with 1 tablespoon salt to a rolling boil, and throw in ½ cup unwashed rice all at once. Boil for 8 minutes at a rolling boil. Pour contents of pot into sieve (add a little cold water to the pot to catch the last grains), then place sieve with rice in it under cold running water to wash away extra starch. Boil 2 cups of hot water in the same pot, and place sieve with rice over it; rice must not touch water. Cover with a clean kitchen towel, folded several times, and gently steam rice for 45 minutes over low heat. Rice can be done this way the morning of a party, left in sieve after steaming, and reheated in the same manner 30 minutes before serving. It will be perfect.

4 cups boiling water
1 tablespoon salt
½ cup rice, unwashed

To multiply this recipe, count: for four, *1 cup rice, 6 cups water;* for six, *1½ cups rice, 7 cups water;* for eight, *2 cups rice, 8 cups water.*

Adam and Eve Salad

Wash and pare 2 heads endive. Cut it in strips lengthwise. Quarter and core 1 medium red Delicious apple. Cube apple with the peel, and reserve a few red cubes for decoration. Mix together endive, apple, and 3 tablespoons Italian-Style Dressing. Place in serving bowl and decorate with reserved cubes of apple.

2 heads endive
1 medium red Delicious apple
3 tablespoons Italian-Style Dressing (see Index)

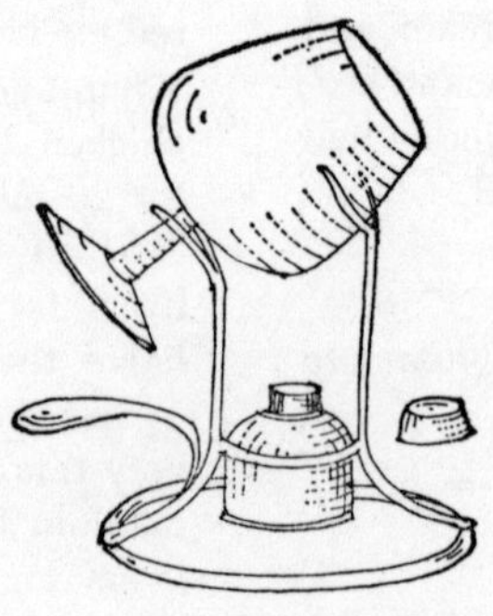

14

Election-Night Open House for Twenty

BAKED BEANS
BOSTON BROWN BREAD
BAKED VIRGINIA HAM ELAINE
COLESLAW WITH FENNEL
SPECIAL APPLE PIE
OLD-HARTFORD ELECTION CAKE
BLACK VELVET
COFFEE

Some years ago the county historical society put a bronze plaque on Elaine's house that reads: "This house was built 1766 by Captain Samuel Crawford who here on or about October 23, 1775 entertained at luncheon General George Washington on his way to White Plains. 1790–1810 it was the home of Richard Morris Chief Justice of the Supreme Court of the State of New York."

The plaque was just about the only part of the house still in one piece when the Rosses bought it. Someone suggested brightly that Elaine's husband, as general in charge of restoration, might as well change his name from Cornelius to Cornwallis. No War of Independence could expose a man to more ignominious defeat than the Blandings-in-Scarsdale he was about to face. Elaine maintains that the first time she read *Mr. Blandings Builds His Dream House,* she was vastly amused by Mr. Blandings' struggles to restore his old house. Her reaction when she reread it during the Ross campaign was quite different. Blandings, she now knows, grossly underestimated. The matter of putting dampers in the fireplaces, for instance—a very minor matter, the contractor said, even though there were nine fireplaces. He started in the living room and that evening, when the Rosses went to inspect the day's progress, they found the whole fireplace wall in a heap on the floor. The contractor began a long-winded explanation about unexpected layers of brick, the Rosses saw unexpected inroads into the finances—and at the present writing only four of the fireplaces have dampers.

The Rosses weren't the only ones who supervised the remodeling. They bought the house from the estate of an eighty-year-old spinster, a direct descendant of Justice Morris. Though she had no immediate family, the roster of nieces and nephews and friends was enormous, and they all proved to be vitally interested in what was happening to Miss Theodora's house. Weekly visits became the rule, and there was scarcely a time when Elaine didn't find a friend or relation at the scene of operations. Most of them assured her that Dora would have *loved* what she was doing.

One of Dora's cronies stepped up her visits and managed to stop by at least twice a week. She told wonderful tales about the house and the family such as the one about the gentleman, in the late 1800's, who was so concerned that nobody would make a proper coffin for him that he made it himself. It was finished long before he was, so, in the interim, he installed it in the living room and used it as a humidor. Her finest moment, though, came one day when she drew Elaine aside confidentially to tell her about the bronze plaque. "Don't tell anyone," she said, "but that part about Washington's stopping here isn't true!" One of Miss Theodora's nieces neatly confused the issue later on by pointing out the very spot in the dining room where Washington had enjoyed his lunch.

If the Rosses' gastronomic connection with the father of our country is somewhat vague, history nevertheless was made in their house, since the reconstruction did not quite defeat them after all. Elaine's husband feels himself far more of a Washington than a Cornwallis; the victory is clearly his, dampers and all, though he doesn't necessarily propose, now, to go on to be president. With peace declared and things in order, better to stay home, as General Washington himself would have preferred to do, and continue the tradition of hospitality started right here by Captain Crawford and his famous lunch.

In this early-American setting, Elaine has dreamt up a flock of ideas for entertaining with an Americana theme, from a barbecue in the huge fireplace in the original downstairs kitchen, to a Fourth of July picnic dinner on the lawn, with village fireworks to watch later on. But the most fun of all has been on Election Day, which, after all, the man who came to lunch made possible.

The guest list deliberately includes both political camps—no fear that conversation at *this* party will lag—and the heated discussions seem to build up tremendous appetites. The menu is always predominantly American, like this one, and everyone relishes food and argument with equal gusto.

Politics aside, the main thing to work out is the baking schedule. Elaine has two ovens, but this is the way she would plan it with just one (note, however, that with a freezer you can make the Brown Bread and the Election Cake weeks before if you want):

Soak the beans *two* days before, and bake them the day before, until they are almost done. (She likes them on the dry side, but if you don't, shorten the baking time an hour or two.) While the beans are in the oven, steam the Brown Bread, and put it in the oven when the beans come out. On Election-Day morning, put the ham in to bake first, then set the yeast dough for the cake to rise, and get the pie ready for the oven. (For big eaters, double the recipe and make two pies.) Bake it next, while you finish the cake preparation. The cake can go in last, since it is frosted warm. An hour before dinner, put the beans back in the oven (they generally need more water by then).

The buffet is set on the dining-room table. Small folding tables supplement those already in the living room and library to ensure comfortable eating for everyone. The buffet table is decidedly patriotic, with blue-and-white china, a navy-blue cloth, and, for the centerpiece, a bright-red toy drum filled with the old-fashioned flowers that bloomed in early-American gardens.

The dinner hour stretches over two or three. Your embattled friends will eat wherever they please and whenever the thought of food becomes more fascinating than talk or TV. As the evening wears on, returns start to come in, the trend is established, excitement mounts, eventually the election is conceded. Heaven only knows what time it is by then—but time for a final round of Black Velvet and a toast to wish the winning candidates Godspeed.

Baked Beans

Soak 3 pounds yellow-eyed beans * overnight in cold water. Drain, then cover with fresh water and boil ½ hour. Add 2 teaspoons baking soda and boil 15 minutes longer, then drain once more and rinse with boiling water. Cut 2 pounds lean salt pork (jowl butt is best) in thin strips and fill bean pot with alternate layers of beans and pork, leaving some strips of pork for top. For seasoning, dissolve ¾ cup granulated sugar, ¼ cup light molasses, and 2 teaspoons salt in 1 cup boiling water. Add 1 teaspoon ground pepper, 3 tablespoons dry mustard, 1 very large minced onion, and pour this mixture over beans, adding enough water to fill the pot. Cover and bake at least 7 hours at 250°. Remove lid after 3 hours and bake uncovered, adding boiling water occasionally if the beans appear too dry. Add no water last hour of baking, as sauce must thicken.

3 pounds yellow-eyed beans *
2 teaspoons baking soda
2 pounds lean salt pork

* If unavailable, use navy beans.

¾ cup granulated sugar
¼ cup light molasses
2 teaspoons salt
1 cup boiling water
1 teaspoon ground pepper
3 tablespoons dry mustard
1 large minced onion

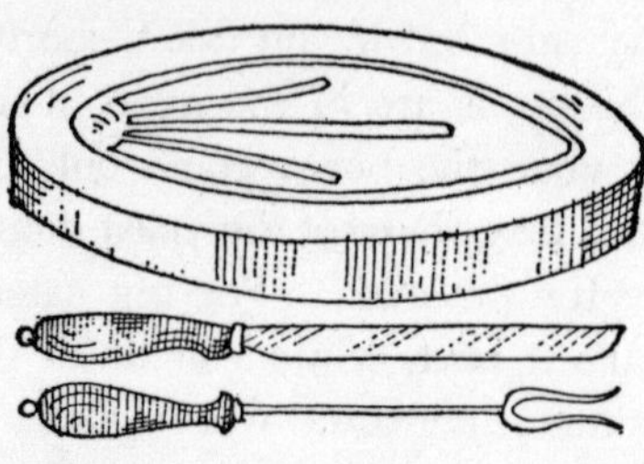

Boston Brown Bread

Dissolve 2 teaspoons baking soda in 2 cups buttermilk, and add 4 tablespoons dark molasses or honey, 4 tablespoons dark-brown sugar, and ½ teaspoon salt. Beat in 4 cups (approximately) graham flour until mixture makes a stiff batter; then add 4 tablespoons melted butter and beat until smooth. Fill 2 coffee cans with batter and cover tightly. Steam for 3½ hours, then dry out for ½ hour in 250° oven. Slice when cold, and serve with sweet butter.

2 teaspoons baking soda
2 cups buttermilk
4 tablespoons dark molasses or honey
4 tablespoons dark brown sugar
½ teaspoon salt
4 cups graham flour
4 tablespoons butter

Baked Virginia Ham Elaine

Preheat oven to 350°. Place a skinned 15-pound precooked ham in a roasting pan, baste it with 1½ cups Guinness stout, and bake for 40 minutes. For glaze, combine 1 cup granulated sugar, 2 teaspoons dry mustard, 1 teaspoon ground ginger, and 1 teaspoon cardamon, and add enough stout to make a smooth paste. Remove ham from oven and baste with drippings. Score fat diagonally in two directions to make diamond pattern, spread glaze over ham, stud with cloves, and bake another 35 minutes.

15-pound precooked ham
1½ cups Guinness stout
1 cup granulated sugar
2 teaspoons dry mustard
1 teaspoon ground ginger
1 teaspoon cardamon
Guinness stout for glaze
Cloves

Coleslaw with Fennel

Remove outer leaves and hard cores of 2 medium heads of cabbage, and soak heads in salted water for 10 minutes. Peel, core, and dice 6 tart apples. Slice thinly 8 stalks fennel * and chop enough of fennel tops to make 2 tablespoons. Drain cabbage, chop finely, combine with apples and fennel, and add 1 cup white raisins. Then toss with ¾ cup Italian-Style Dressing, below.

2 medium heads cabbage
6 tart apples
*8 stalks fennel **
2 tablespoons chopped fennel tops (optional)
1 cup white raisins
¾ cup Italian-Style Dressing

Italian-Style Dressing

Blend together:
½ cup olive oil
¼ cup wine vinegar
½ clove garlic, pressed
1 tablespoon tomato ketchup
⅛ teaspoon Tabasco

* Celery stalks and 1 tablespoon crushed dried fennel seed may be substituted.

Special Apple Pie

?reheat oven to 350°. Sift 2 cups flour vith ¾ teaspoon salt, and cut in a ;enerous ½ cup shortening. With fin;ertips mix in lightly 1 cup grated :heddar cheese, then add enough vater to hold pastry together, but no nore (6 to 8 tablespoons). Place on wo overlapping sheets of waxed pa›er (arrange waxed paper so there is 'oom enough to roll out an 11-inch ›ie crust). Cover with more waxed ›aper and roll out lightly until pastry s ½ inch thick. Remove top waxed ›aper. Fold pastry in three, then fold n three again in opposite direction, ınd divide in half. Place halves be:ween fresh sheets of waxed paper, ınd roll out each one to an 11-inch :ircle. Peel off top papers, invert one :ircle into a 10-inch pie plate, and 'emove second paper. Brush with 1 :ablespoon melted butter, put in fillng, below, and invert second circle ›ver filling. Pinch edges together and :rimp. Then make two criss-cross ılashes to vent steam, and bake 40 ninutes.

Filling: Peel and core 6 large ap›les, slice them in thin wedges, ar'ange in pie shell, and add ½ cup ugar, ½ cup raisins, 1 teaspoon cinıamon, and 1 tablespoon lemon juice.

? cups flour
¾ teaspoon salt
½ cup shortening
l cup grated cheddar cheese
3–8 tablespoons water
l tablespoon melted butter

3 large apples
½ cup sugar
½ cup raisins
1 teaspoon cinnamon
1 tablespoon lemon juice

Old-Hartford Election Cake

Dissolve ½ yeast cake in ½ cup lukewarm water, and add 1 tablespoon butter or other shortening, 1 tablespoon granulated sugar, ¼ teaspoon salt, and 1¼ cups flour. Mix well, and set aside in warm place to rise until double in bulk, about 1½ hours.

Cream together ½ cup butter and 1 cup sugar, and beat until light. Add 2 eggs, well-beaten, 1 cup raisins, ¼ cup sliced citron, 1 teaspoon grated lemon rind, and 1½ teaspoons lemon juice. Sift together ¾ teaspoon soda, ¾ cup flour, and ½ teaspoon nutmeg, and add, alternately with ½ cup brandy, to first mixture.

Combine this cake batter with the raised dough, and pour into a well-greased bread pan. Let rise again in a warm place for about 1 hour. Bake in a preheated 350° oven for 1 hour. While still warm, ice with Royal Icing, below.

½ yeast cake
½ cup lukewarm water
1 tablespoon butter or other shortening
1 tablespoon granulated sugar
¼ teaspoon salt
1¼ cups flour

½ cup butter
1 cup sugar
2 eggs
1 cup raisins
¼ cup sliced citron
1 teaspoon grated lemon rind
1½ teaspoons lemon juice
¾ teaspoon soda
¾ cup flour
½ teaspoon nutmeg
½ cup brandy
Royal Icing

Royal Icing

Onto waxed paper sift 1 pound confectioners' sugar twice. In a bowl mix 2 egg whites lightly with juice of 1 lemon. With a wooden spoon gradually mix sugar into egg-white mixture. Add only enough sugar to make a creamy, smooth, thinly spreadable icing. Use metal spatula dipped in water to spread icing over cake. Then, to obtain a high glaze, let first layer of icing dry, and ice cake a second time.

1 pound confectioners' sugar
2 egg whites
1 lemon

Black Velvet

Chill ten 12-ounce bottles Guinness stout and 5 bottles of Almadén brut champagne. Pour both champagne and stout at the same time in a steady stream into stemmed water glasses.

10 bottles Guinness stout
5 bottles Almadén brut champagne

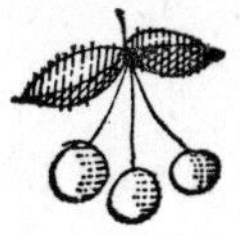

15

Christmas Eve Open House for 100 or More

Terrine of Duck Bristol *
Syrian Koufté in Tomato Sauce
Fish Pâté a la Russe
Barbecued Pineapple and Cocktail Frankfurters
Scotch Shortbread *
Special Cheese Dip *
Nürnberger Lebkuchen
Christmas Cream Puffs
Flaming Pudding
Mulled Wine or Mulled Cider

So many people in and around Purchase were at loose ends the one Christmas Eve that Juliette couldn't have her usual open house. In the course of almost twenty years, an annual party does become an institution.

Following family custom in Belgium, Juliette opens the holiday season the Sunday before Christmas—or a week before that, if Christmas falls on Monday or Tuesday. Every neighbor with a strong right arm and a saw is invited to join the tree-hunting safari in her pine woods. Sounds of "Timber!" mingle with the vociferous encouragement of dogs and children, the whole crew hauls the trees back to the house—and, as usual, Juliette's is too tall and must be trimmed down. Then into the living room, where a blazing fire and mulled cider will soon warm the inner man and loosen up vocal chords for a round of Christmas carols.

Christmas is the time for sharing. Starting with decoys with which she flanks her doorway to attract the birds to sheaves of wheat and balls of

* see Index and make 3 recipes.

suet, Juliette has a Yuletide treat for all the animals that might come by—salt licks for the deer, catnip and marrow bones where they apply—for bird and beast must be remembered at Christmas.

Invitations for Christmas Eve itself read from 9 P.M. till midnight, but, like children who are afraid they will miss something, the first guests are there before the hour strikes. The boxwood in front of her century-old white country house has been strung with lights, the shining black door bears its usual gleaming-white Della Robbia wreath, the sounds of music and family laughter within anticipate Juliette's "Welcome to our home."

And then, you are on your own, for Juliette favors a true spirit of informality which leaves her free to enjoy her guests, and the guests free to come and go as they please, to meet old acquaintances and make new ones. Almost everyone she invites already knows at least half a dozen others, and no one will have that left-out feeling, for two or three of her close friends take special charge for her of newcomers to the neighborhood.

Juliette's welcome is seconded at the hall table by a bowl of mulled wine kept hot over a brass candle warmer and dozens of punch cups inviting you to help yourself. She has enormous numbers of these inexpensive glass cups, because someone is always forgetting one in a corner and she wants plenty of fresh ones around. (She counts on three times as many cups as there are people in case there isn't any help to keep washing up, and the virtual carload she bought years ago still does annual duty.) To simplify bartending, she prepares huge quantities of the wine early in the day and, although she has her usual bar setup in the living room, almost everyone seems to patronize the mulled-wine table that night.

She carries her favorite blue-and-silver color scheme right through the house, accenting it here and there with American-beauty red. Chandeliers and wall brackets are festooned with silver garlands and hung with shining blue balls, the Christmas tree is a blue-and-silver wonder in a corner of the living room. In sharp contrast to the informal mood of the party is the elegant formality of the dining table. The almost floor-length damask cloth, (she dyed it blue in the washing machine), has its corners caught up with silver-bowed nosegays of tiny red artificial roses and tiny blue balls. At either end of the table, tall candelabra are wound with Christmas greens and trimmed with more roses and baubles. Instead of the candelabra, several times she has used a row of silvered pineapples, each holding a tall candle and each on an alabaster stand, the base of the fruit ringed with tiny roses. She still hasn't made up her mind which motif she prefers, but all the other decorations are the same each year and Juliette's friends expect her Christmas trademark.

Juliette makes it a point to post several friends with voracious appetites near the table, knowing their example will keep the others nibbling. Every-

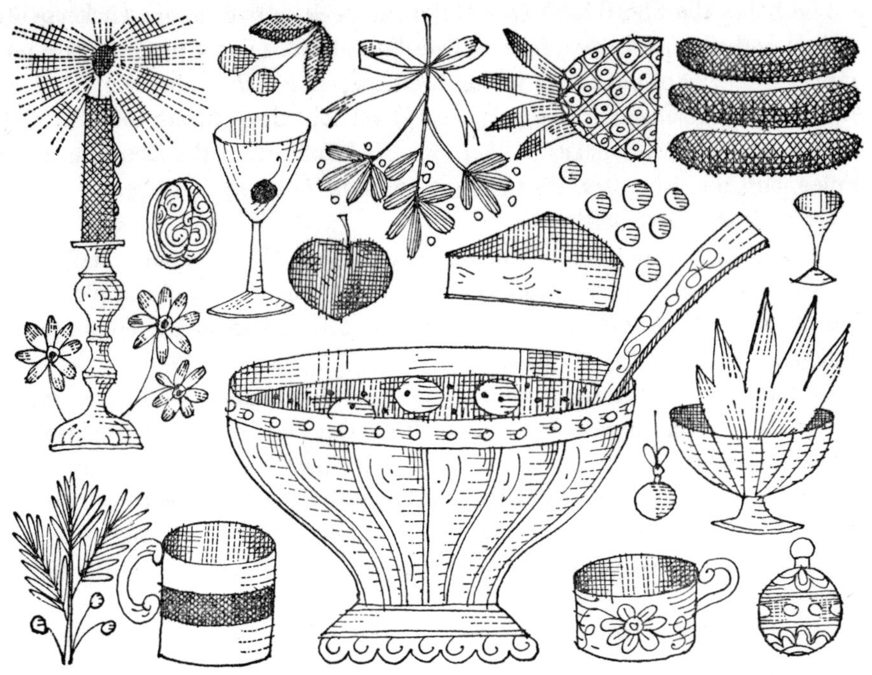

thing is finger food except the pudding, so that cutlery and plates (paper plates for the pudding) are kept to a minimum. She says, only partly joking, that this is her party for over one hundred people, with no dishes to wash. At one end of the table, an over-sized French-bread basket holds an assortment of breads: crisp Buttery Rye (see Index), small chunky pieces of braided egg bread, squares of light and dark pumpernickel. At one side of the basket is the lavish *Terrine* of Duck Bristol (see Index), and at the other, a crock of Special Cheese Dip (see Index), and a basket of water biscuits and toasted sesame crackers. The *Koufté* in a chafing dish and the fish pâtés on a marble slab occupy the opposite end of the table, and, dominating the center, the platter of pineapple and frankfurters keeps hot over a large candle warmer. In between, the small cakes on silver plates fill in all the empty spaces.

Preparation started a month ahead, when Juliette made her Christmas pudding and the little cream puffs, and put them both in the freezer. (In pre-freezer days, she made them the day before, stored the puffs in a tin, and unmolded the pudding and kept it in the icebox. Either way, to reheat the pudding, put it back in the mold and steam for an hour and a half.) If it's more convenient, steam the pudding in 8 coffee tins and cut the cooking time to two hours, but use the one large bowl if you can—it produces a pudding that is straight out of Dickens.

She bakes the Shortbread (see Index) a week or two before (it keeps in a tin), and the *Lebkuchen* four or five days ahead. (Put a piece of raw potato or apple, or of rye bread, in the tin to keep *Lebkuchen* chewy.) The *Terrine* and the Cheese Dip are prepared about four days ahead, too. The day before the party, she makes the *Saté* for the frankfurters, the *Koufté* in their sauce, and the fish pâtés. It's been a busy time, but only in stages, and now there's not too much left to do.

On *the* day, Juliette sets the table, decorates the fish pâtés, boils the frankfurters and drops them in the *Saté,* and marinates the pineapple. Then she transfers the *Koufté* to the chafing dish, fills and frosts the cream puffs, and arranges the plates of cakes.

Generally, she has someone to help, mainly to empty ashtrays, wash glasses, and make coffee, but also to broil the pineapple and frankfurters when they are needed. On occasion, Juliette has broiled the pineapple in a roasting pan herself and put the frankfurters on the broiler tray, both an hour before her guests arrived. No one noticed that she slipped out later for a few minutes to reheat the pineapple in the oven and to broil the frankfurters.

Christmas Eve at Juliette's is a storybook party, where everyone recaptures a childhood thrill when young Peter is awakened and brought down to chat with a volunteer Santa, and when, at 11:30, everyone comes into the dining room to watch the hostess bear in the flaming pudding with all due ceremony. The carollers take over for a bit, and everyone lingers to say "Merry Christmas" many times over.

Syrian Koufté in Tomato Sauce

To make 200 cocktail *Kouftés,* have the butcher put 3 pounds top round through the grinder twice. Work into it 3 tablespoons chopped parsley, salt, pepper and 3 eggs. Roll between your palms into balls the size of walnuts. Fry in deep oil at 390° until brown.

To make sauce: Dip 3 pounds tomatoes one by one in boiling water, then in cold water, then peel and quarter them. Add 12 medium onions, chopped, and 1 tablespoon ground cumin, ¼ teaspoon black pepper, 2 tablespoons prepared mustard, and ½ cup water. Bring to a boil over high heat, then reduce heat and simmer for 15 minutes. Remove from heat and add ½ cup chopped parsley, 4 eggs, and 2 tablespoons vinegar, stirring vigorously all the while. Pour over the meat balls and serve from top pan of a chafing dish, over hot, not boiling, water.

3 pounds top round
3 tablespoons chopped parsley
Salt, pepper
3 eggs

3 pounds tomatoes
12 medium onions
1 tablespoon ground cumin
¼ teaspoon ground black pepper
2 tablespoons prepared mustard
½ cup water
½ cup chopped parsley
4 eggs
2 tablespoons vinegar

Fish Pâté à la Russe

Poach 3 pounds fillet of sole and 1 pound salmon, cut in thin steaks, for 4 to 6 minutes in *Court-Bouillon* for Fish to cover, and cool in the cooking liquid. Meanwhile, shell 14 hard-cooked eggs; mince separately the yolks and whites of 6 of the eggs, and reserve. Mash the remaining whole eggs to a paste with the meat from salmon steaks. Moisten paste with 1 cup *Sauce Russe.* Taste and correct seasoning, which must be on the peppery side.

Drain fillets of sole on absorbent paper. Oil two loaf pans. Place layer of sole in bottom of pans, spread with a layer of salmon-egg paste, and repeat until pans are full, finishing with a layer of sole. Invert on serving platter. Decorate each loaf with a cross of grey or black caviar, going down sides, too, and make a border of caviar around bases and tops of loaves. Fill in top rectangles so delineated alternately with reserved minced egg whites and yolks, spread thinly. Chill thoroughly before serving. Serve with buttered pumpernickel or buttered Russian rye squares.

3 pounds fillet of sole
1 pound salmon
Court-Bouillon for Fish (see Index)
14 eggs
1 cup Sauce Russe (see Index)
8 ounces grey or black caviar
1 loaf pumpernickel or rye bread
½ pound butter

Barbecued Pineapple

Cut 1 medium-size pineapple lengthwise into 8 sections. Remove core from each section, and with a serrated knife remove meat from shell. Cut each piece in three, making 24 tidbits. Marinate them in 1¼ cups honey for ½ hour, then broil 6 inches from heat until edges are brown. Serve hot, with canned cocktail frankfurters that have been dipped in *Saté* Sauce and broiled 4 inches from heat until brown.

1 medium pineapple
1¼ cups honey
24 canned cocktail frankfurters
Saté Sauce (see Index)

For 100 guests, you will need 5 pineapples, 125 cocktail frankfurters, and 4 recipes *Saté* Sauce.

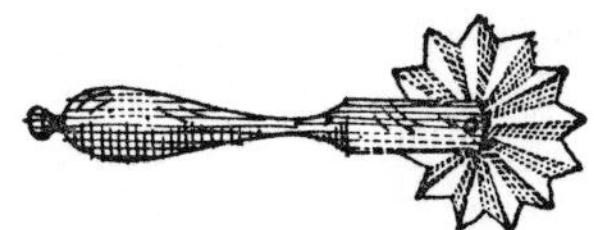

Nürnberger Lebkuchen

Preheat oven to 325°. In large bowl of an electric mixer, beat 2 eggs and ⅞ cup sugar until light and thick. Mix together 1½ cups ground almonds, 1½ cups ground hazelnuts, ⅛ teaspoon cloves, 1 teaspoon cinnamon, 2½ ounces candied orange rind, finely ground, and 2 tablespoons cocoa. Fold into egg mixture, then with wet hands roll into about 30 balls. Place 1½ inches apart on a buttered baking sheet, and bake 15 to 17 minutes. While *Lebkuchen* are baking, melt 2 ounces semisweet chocolate in top of double boiler. Frost cookies while warm with the melted chocolate.

2 eggs
⅞ cup sugar
1½ cups ground almonds
1½ cups ground hazelnuts
⅛ teaspoon cloves
1 teaspoon cinnamon
2½ ounces candied orange rind
2 tablespoons cocoa
2 ounces semisweet chocolate

For 100 guests, multiply recipe by four (120 *Lebkuchen*).

Christmas Cream Puffs

Triple this Basic *Pâte à Chou* recipe to make 100 *profiterole*-size puffs:

Place 1 cup hot water in a large saucepan with ¼ pound butter and bring to a boil over high heat. As soon as mixture comes to a boil, add 1 cup flour all at once, reduce heat, and stir vigorously until mixture leaves sides of the pan (about 1 or 2 minutes). Remove from heat, place mixture in largest bowl of electric mixer, then beat in 5 eggs, one at a time, beating each one about 1 minute (2 minutes by hand). After all eggs have been added, beat 2 minutes more. Chill dough in refrigerator for 1 hour. Preheat oven to 450°. Drop dough by heaping teaspoonfuls onto greased cooky sheets. Bake 15 minutes at 450°, then 20 to 25 minutes at 350°.

Note: This basic recipe will make 30 to 35 *profiterole*-size Christmas Cream Puffs. Or, it will make 60 tiny cocktail puffs, which are baked 15 minutes at 450°, then about 7 minutes at 350°; or, 12 dessert-size puffs, which are baked 15 minutes at 450°, then 30 to 35 minutes at 350°. It will also make 2 *Gougères Bourguignonne* (see Index).

1 cup hot water
¼ pound butter
1 cup flour
5 eggs

For 100 Christmas Puffs, whip 4 cups of heavy cream with ½ cup Vanilla Sugar. With a pastry tube, fill puffs with whipped cream, inserting tube in bottom of puff. Make an icing with 6 tablespoons butter melted in ½ cup milk, and add 2 tablespoons kirsch and about 6 cups confectioners' sugar to make a spreadable icing. To one half the icing add red food coloring and to the other half, add either nothing, or green coloring, depending on your color scheme. Work fast in icing puffs. Should the icing get too stiff, thin it out carefully with hot milk.

4 cups heavy cream
½ cup Vanilla Sugar (see Index)

6 tablespoons butter
½ cup milk
2 tablespoons kirsch
6 cups confectioners' sugar
Green and red food coloring

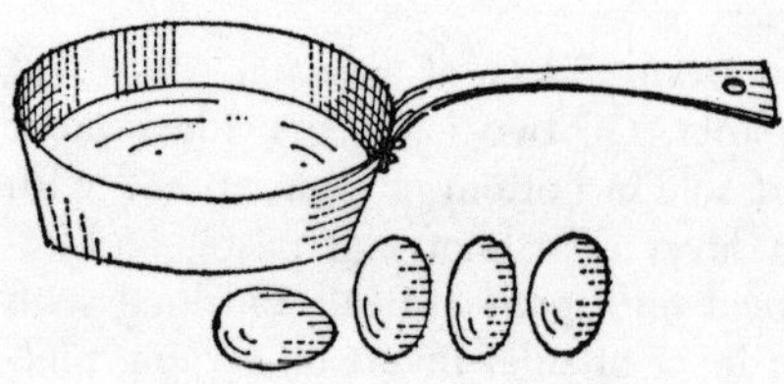

Flaming Christmas Pudding

Dry 2 loaves sliced white bread in a 200° oven; discard end crusts. Soak 2 cups black raisins, 2 cups white raisins, and 2 cups currants in boiling water until plump. Place dry bread in a large mixing bowl with 9 egg yolks, 1½ cups dark brown sugar, and ⅔ cup rum. Scald 1 quart milk and pour it slowly over bread, eggs, and sugar, mixing and mashing to form a paste. When paste is smooth, drain raisins and currants, and beat into paste with 1 cup assorted chopped candied fruit and 1 cup glacéed cherries. Flavor with ½ teaspoon ground pepper, ½ teaspoon ground ginger, and 2 tablespoons grated orange peel. Then fold in 9 egg whites beaten stiff but not dry.

Rub a 6-quart stainless-steel mixing bowl heavily with butter. Pour mixture into it to within 3 inches of top. Cover with 2 thicknesses of foil and tie foil securely; then place in a large roasting pan and fill pan with hot water to within 3 inches of rim of bowl. Cover pan and cook over low heat for 4 hours. Invert pudding on platter. Warm 1 cup dark rum, set aflame at the table, and pour over pudding. Serve with Hard Sauce, below.

2 loaves sliced white bread
2 cups black raisins
2 cups white raisins
2 cups currants
9 egg yolks
1½ cups dark brown sugar
⅔ cup rum
1 quart milk
1 cup assorted chopped candied fruit
1 cup glacéed cherries
½ teaspoon ground pepper
½ teaspoon ground ginger
2 tablespoons grated orange peel
9 egg whites
Butter
1 cup dark rum
Hard Sauce

Hard Sauce

Beat 1 pound softened butter at high speed in small bowl of electric mixer, gradually adding 1 pound confectioners' sugar, 2 egg whites, and 2 tablespoons rum. Continue beating until butter becomes frothy and white, about 12 minutes.

Heap in a silver bowl and stud with crystallized violets or candied cherries. Chill in refrigerator for at least 3 hours.

1 pound butter
1 pound confectioners' sugar
2 egg whites
2 tablespoons rum
Crystallized violets
or candied cherries

Mulled Wine

To make 10 punch-cupfuls, combine 2 cups water, 4 cups claret, and 1 cup sugar or 1 cup honey, and add 1 thinly sliced lemon with the rind, 6 cloves, 4 berries allspice, crushed, and 2 small sticks cinnamon. Heat to boiling point. Count 3 punch cups per guest.

2 cups water
4 cups claret
1 cup sugar or honey
1 lemon
6 cloves
4 berries allspice
2 small sticks cinnamon

For 100 guests you will have to multiply this recipe by 30. Calculate liquids by the quart, but remember when ordering wine that one bottle averages only about one fifth of a quart.

Mulled Cider

To make 8 punch-cupfuls, combine 1 cup bourbon and 4 cups cider, and add 1 thinly sliced lemon with the rind, 6 cloves, 4 berries allspice, crushed, and 2 small sticks cinnamon. Heat to boiling point. Count 3 cups per guest.

1 cup bourbon
4 cups cider
1 lemon
6 cloves
4 berries allspice
2 small sticks cinnamon

For 100 guests you will have to multiply this recipe by 35. Calculate liquids by the quart.

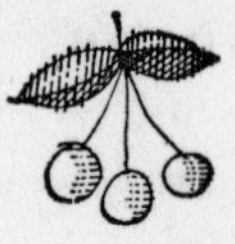

16

New Year's Eve Supper for Twelve

Elaine's Pâté Maison
Seafood Crêpes Smitane
Poppy Seed Roll-Ups
Peaches Ablaze
Almond Butter Slices
Coffee
Forbidden-Fruit Champagne Punch

CHAMPAGNES

Inexpensive, for Punch: New York State Great Western
Medium-priced: Mumm's Cordon Rouge

For our New Year's Eve celebration, we are imagining an evening spent with a small group of close friends; an evening of good music, good conversation, culminating in a midnight buffet of a certain elegance to fit a mellow mood. If it's a whoop-it-up, large party you're thinking of, pick another menu. Simpler, more down-to-earth fare will prove better then. Furthermore, this menu is not geared for quantity cooking unless you have lots of help, for it does take time. Be courageous, however, because you can put in most of that time the day before.

The pâté and the cookies, of course, should be completely finished ahead. The *crêpes* may be made, filled, rolled, placed in the baking dish, and covered loosely with foil during the afternoon. A half hour before serving, place them in a 425° oven for 10 minutes. Then remove the foil, spoon the sauce over the *crêpes,* and bake them for another 15 minutes. (Diced cooked chicken may be substituted for the seafood, in which case eliminate the anchovy paste.) The Poppy Seed Roll-Ups can also be made ahead, refrigerated right on the baking sheet, then put in the oven with the *crêpes* for 10 minutes.

The preparation of the Peaches Ablaze is a matter of very few minutes. If everything is set out, the actual cooking is nothing at all. If you don't have a chafing dish, try to borrow one, and prepare them in front of your audience. You can't really call it work and they'll enjoy watching.

Despite the elegance of this menu, it adapts well to several kinds of service. For a buffet, with the guests eating wherever they please, just be sure you have enough tables, (sets of little individual ones are a boon). Any meal can lose savor if you have to juggle a plate and a glass and yearn for a third hand when coffee is served. Or set your dining room table for twelve and go all out for formality. Either way, take your choice, and in setting the table or buffet, do it with glitter and sparkle. Heap one or two shallow bowls with mounds of Christmas-tree ornaments in lieu of flowers. Have as much candlelight and as little electric light as possible, and pay no attention to the men who inevitably complain they can't see too clearly what they're eating. This evening feminine romanticism should win out.

To arrange this party still another way, invite your guests for a late supper, say at 9 o'clock. Serve the *crêpes* with a hot vegetable or Artichoke and Truffle Salad (see Index) and Poppy Seed Roll-Ups. Finish off with the peaches and cookies. Reserve the pâté for after midnight, adding thinly sliced dark bread and some gaily decorated *petits fours* from a good bakery.

With all three of these arrangements, we would prefer using a good champagne, served before dinner with Cheese Cookies (see Index) and throughout dinner and the evening. But, of course, if you expect extra people to drop in to hear the clock strike twelve, it's more practical to switch later to Champagne Punch. Even on New Year's Eve, we might as well be practical!

Elaine's Pâté Maison

Preheat oven to 350°. Blend together 1¼ pounds ground lean veal, 1 pound ground lean pork, 2 eggs, and 2 teaspoons Lowry's Seasoned Salt. Cut ¾ pound ham into julienne strips. Slice 1 cup pitted black olives. Cover ¼ cup pistachio nuts with boiling water to blanch them, then take out of the water and slip off skins. In bottom of a loaf pan place one quarter of the meat mixture. Cover with half the ham, pressing strips lightly into ground meat. Spread with another quarter of meat mixture. Sprinkle with olive slices and pistachio nuts, reserving a few for garnishing. Spread with third quarter of meat mixture, repeat layer of ham, and top with remaining ground meat.

Wrap pan completely with foil, overlapping foil underneath, and folding under securely at both ends. Bake for 1½ hours. Unwrap, cool in pan, then chill. Turn out on serving platter, and garnish with reserved olives and pistachios.

1¼ pounds ground lean veal
1 pound ground lean pork
2 eggs
2 teaspoons Lowry's Seasoned Salt
¾ pound boiled ham, in 2 thick slices
1 cup pitted black olives
¼ cup pistachio nuts

Seafood Crêpes Smitane

Make batter 2 hours before frying *crêpes,* and let it stand at room temperature: Sift together ⅔ cup flour and ¼ teaspoon salt. Beat 4 eggs, preferably with an electric beater, add dry ingredients, and beat again. Gradually pour in 1¾ cups milk, 2 tablespoons melted butter, and 1 tablespoon cognac, and continue beating until batter is silky smooth.

Over high heat, heat a 6-inch griddle or frying pan with low edges until a speck of butter sizzles at the touch of it. Put in ½ tablespoon butter, and shake and tilt pan to spread butter. Ladle about 2 tablespoons of batter into pan; hold handle while doing this and tilt pan to coat bottom. Fry until gold on bottom and dry on top. Turn with a spatula. To get an even golden color on reverse side, shake pan from side to side with wrist movement so that *crêpe* slides back and forth. When done, slide onto a hot platter. Repeat, adding ½ tablespoon of butter each time, until there are 24 *crêpes.* Pile *crêpes* on top of each other, and keep warm in 225° *open* oven.

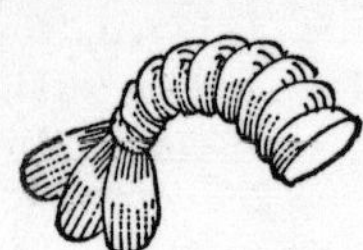

Gently heat 1 pound each cooked crab meat and lobster meat in 4 tablespoons melted butter for 3 minutes. Blend together 3 cups sour cream, 3 lightly beaten eggs, ¾ cup minced capers, ⅓ cup grated imported Parmesan cheese, and 1 tablespoon anchovy paste. Combine seafood and one third of sour-cream mixture. Remove *crêpes* from oven and turn up heat to 425°. Spoon filling down center of each *crêpe,* roll them up, and place side by side in a shallow buttered baking dish. Pour remaining sour cream mixture over *crêpes,* and sprinkle with another ⅓ cup grated Parmesan. Dot with 2 tablespoons butter, and sprinkle with ⅓ cup fine bread crumbs. Bake for 15 minutes.

⅔ cup flour
¼ teaspoon salt
4 eggs
1¾ cups milk
2 tablespoons melted butter
1 tablespoon cognac
⅜ pound butter, about

1 pound crabmeat
1 pound lobster meat
6 tablespoons butter
3 cups sour cream
3 eggs
¾ cup capers
1 tablespoon anchovy paste
⅔ cup grated imported Parmesan
⅓ cup fine bread crumbs

Poppy Seed Roll-Ups

Trim crusts from 24 thin slices white bread. Flatten each slice with rolling pin. Spread with ¼ pound butter and sprinkle with 3 tablespoons poppy seeds. Roll up, secure with toothpicks, and place on buttered cooky sheet. Bake in 425° oven for 10 minutes, until light gold. Remove toothpicks before serving.

24 thin slices white bread
¼ pound butter
3 tablespoons poppy seeds

Peaches Ablaze

Drain syrup from 24 canned Elberta peach halves. In top pan of large chafing dish melt ¼ pound butter over direct flame. Add ¼ cup sugar and peaches, and simmer for 4 minutes. Pour ⅓ cup each cognac, peach brandy, kirsch, and Grand Marnier over peaches, and ignite. When flames die out, pour in 1 cup orange juice, and serve immediately. If you have

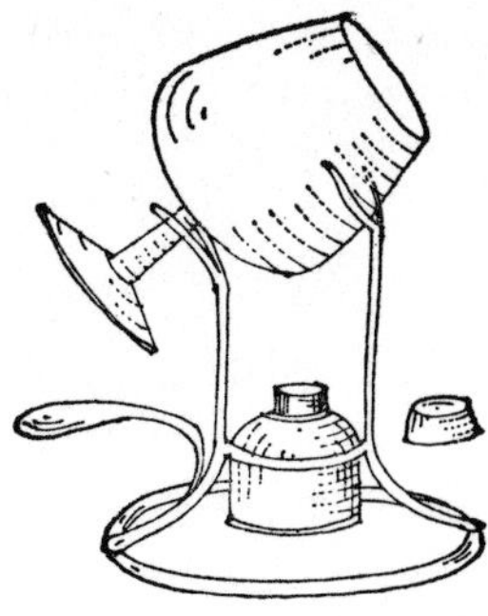

no chafing dish, use decorative enamel skillet, prepare peaches in kitchen, and serve directly from skillet.

¼ pound butter
¼ cup sugar
24 canned Elberta peach halves
⅓ cup each cognac, peach brandy, kirsch, Grand Marnier
1 cup orange juice

Almond Butter Slices

Preheat oven to 300°. Chop or grind finely 24 almonds. Blend together with hands to make a smooth dough ½ pound less 2 tablespoons butter, 7 tablespoons sugar, 2 cups plus 2 tablespoons flour, ½ teaspoon baking powder, ½ beaten egg, and ½ teaspoon almond extract. Divide dough in half. Shape each half into a roll about 1¼ inches in diameter. Roll these in chopped almonds and slice ⅓ inch thick. Place slices on greased cooky sheet and bake 25 to 30 minutes, until pale gold.

24 almonds
½ pound less 2 tablespoons butter
7 tablespoons sugar
2 cups plus 2 tablespoons flour
½ teaspoon baking powder
½ beaten egg
½ teaspoon almond extract

Forbidden-Fruit Champagne Punch

The day before the party, select a metal mixing bowl or pot about half the diameter of your punch bowl. Put in 12 lady apples, or any pretty small red apples, stem side up, arranging them very neatly. Cover with water, leaving room in container for ice to expand. Freeze.

To serve, place frozen block of apples in punch bowl. Pour in 3 quarts New York State Great Western champagne and 1½ quarts domestic vodka, and stir gently to blend.

12 lady apples or small red apples
3 quarts New York State Great Western champagne
1½ quarts domestic vodka

BRUNCHES AND LUNCHEONS

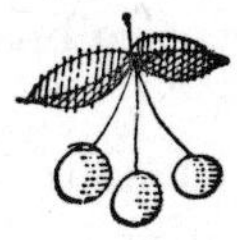

17

Summer Brunch for Twelve

Pink Ladies and Screwdrivers

BLUEBERRIES ARAGONAISE
SCRAMBLED EGGS FINANCIÈRE
COEUR À LA CRÈME WITH BAR-LE-DUC JELLY
LUCY'S CROISSANTS
COFFEE OR TEA

Why is it that women shy away from yeast dough with an, "Oh, I wouldn't dare," or, "It takes so long—I don't have time."? And, when you mention puff paste, you might as well talk about the mysteries of outer space.

Here we are suggesting that you try not only one, but both, *and* in a single recipe. We are not fooling when we say that yeast dough is *not* difficult, *nor* time-consuming, and that puff paste is well within the ken of ordinary mortals. And, just picture the result—flaky, tender, butter-rich *Croissants*, served hot from the oven with fresh coffee? Is your mouth watering—are you willing to try?

Certainly, there are things to know. Puff paste will puff only when the butter is sealed between the layers of dough. In extremely hot weather, when it is difficult to keep the butter firm, it might be wise to bake Hilda's *Brioches* (see Index), instead. The preparation of puff paste encompasses several hours of alternate chilling and rolling, but the actual working time is short. Anyway, there are always things to be done in between. With available freezer space, make the *Croissants* any time. To serve, put them, still frozen, in a 375° oven for 15 minutes.

If you make the *Croissants* just in time for the brunch, complete the dough and place them on cooky sheets the day before. Keep them in the icebox overnight, and take them out to rise in the morning. Whip up the cottage cheese the day before, too. A heart-shaped basket is traditional for

Coeur à la Crème, but any inexpensive bread basket from the 5-and-10 will do as well.

Morning preparations are not complex. Wash the berries, let them drain and dry thoroughly. You can substitute strawberries for blueberries, or use a combination of both. To flavor them try a light, orange-flavored honey instead of sugar; it gives an especially subtle sweetness. Start with ½ cup and add more until it suits you; honey is sweeter than sugar.

Whether you handle this yourself or not depends on the formality of the occasion. It's very easy, but you, or someone in to help, must scramble the eggs at the very last. If you don't have a mammoth pan, do them in two batches. The first will keep hot for a few minutes on a well-heated platter, but be quick anyway.

Serve buffet style on the porch, with a long table set to seat everyone, or don't set a table at all and let them all sit where they please. Don't hesitate, though, to press this menu into use for the most gilded, four-star occasion. It lends itself to formal, seated service with all the table trappings and the hostess dressed in her best.

Blueberries Aragonaise

Pour juice of 1 lemon over 6 pints washed and well-drained ripe blueberries. Add 2 tablespoons grated orange peel, 2 tablespoons grated lemon peel, and 1 cup granulated sugar, and mix well. Serve chilled, in individual bowls, and pass a pitcher of heavy cream separately if desired.

6 pints blueberries
Juice 1 lemon
2 tablespoons grated orange peel
2 tablespoons grated lemon peel
1 cup granulated sugar
Heavy cream (optional)

Scrambled Eggs Financière

Over very low heat, in a heavy saucepan, melt 2 tablespoons butter, and add 2 tablespoons Madeira, the meat of 12 cooked and shelled lobster claws (or 12 large prawns), and ½ pound ham cut in julienne strips. Heat gently without browning. Break 24 eggs into a bowl and add 2 tablespoons butter cut in small bits. Season with pepper and salt and stir with a fork sufficiently to blend whites and yolks. Mince 3 truffles finely and add to eggs. Over very low heat, in a very large

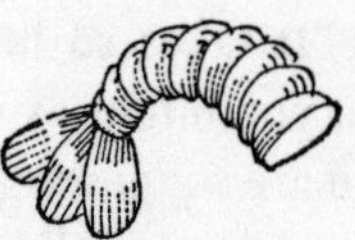

heavy skillet, melt 6 tablespoons butter and pour in eggs. Stir continually as eggs cook on bottom and around edges of skillet, blending liquid and solid until mass has become firm but is still shiny and moist. Stir in ¼ cup cold heavy cream and transfer immediately to heated serving platter. Garnish with lobster claws and ham.

2 tablespoons butter
2 tablespoons Madeira
12 cooked lobster claws or large prawns
½ pound ham
24 eggs
¼ pound butter
Salt, pepper
3 truffles
¼ cup cold heavy cream

Coeur à la Crème

Line a sieve with 2 thicknesses of cheese cloth, and through it force 1½ pounds of cottage cheese. In large bowl of electric mixer, place cottage cheese, 1½ pints sour cream, and 3 tablespoons Vanilla Sugar. Beat at low speed for 8 minutes. Line a heart-shaped basket with cheesecloth and pour mixture into it. Refrigerate 24 hours, with a plate underneath to catch the dripping whey.

Unmold on crystal or silver platter. Trim with border of *Bar-le-Duc* jelly, and serve more jelly separately.

1½ pounds cottage cheese
1½ pints sour cream
3 tablespoons Vanilla Sugar (see Index)
Bar-le-Duc jelly

Lucy's Croissants

With a knife or pastry blender, cut ¾ pound butter into ⅓ cup flour. Place between 2 sheets of waxed paper and roll to a 7-by-12-inch rectangle; then chill while making yeast dough.

Dissolve 2 packages yeast in ¼ cup lukewarm water, and add 1 cup cold milk, 1 teaspoon granulated sugar, 1 egg, 2 teaspoons salt, and 3¾ cups unsifted flour. Mix well, then turn out on lightly greased and floured board, and knead dough until smooth. Roll out to a rectangle 13 by 15 inches (and always roll to a rectangle subsequently).

Peel waxed paper off chilled butter dough. Place it on lefthand half of rolled-out yeast dough. Fold right half over left, then press edges together to seal in butter dough. Roll out to ⅓-inch thickness. Fold top third of dough toward center, then fold bottom third over that, to make three layers, and chill 30 minutes.

Turn dough so open end is facing you. Roll out again to ⅓-inch thickness, and fold in three as before; turn dough once more so that open edge is facing you, roll out, fold again, and chill 30 minutes. Repeat this double turn-fold procedure twice more, chilling both times. Then roll out to ¼-inch thickness in a large rectangle. From this, cut 20 to 24 squares and divide into 40 to 48 triangles. Starting from the widest side, roll each *croissant* loosely. Bend ends slightly into a crescent, and place on buttered baking sheets, 1½ inches apart. Let rise in a warm place until double in size (about 3 hours). Preheat oven to 375°, and bake for 15 minutes, until golden.

⅓ cup flour
¾ pound butter
2 packages yeast
¼ cup lukewarm water
1 cup cold milk
1 teaspoon granulated sugar
1 egg
2 teaspoons salt
3¾ cups flour

18

Shore Brunch for Six

Citrus Cup in Cantaloupe
Petits Soufflés Henri IV
Oatmeal Bread
Gingered Pear Jam
Coffee or Tea

You would think that with all this writing and talking about food, we'd get a bit blasé about the whole matter. Maybe we will some day, but that day hasn't come yet. We've looked over these menus dozens of times, and every time the same thing happens: We read one again, and the first thing you know, one of us is in the kitchen putting theory into practice. Think a moment of a delicate fish soufflé anointed with buttery Hollandaise and moist home-baked bread heaped with homemade jam. The very idea is a call to action. Before you take off into the kitchen, line up several hungry people for brunch this coming weekend.

Since you would have to be up at daybreak to make the bread by noon the same day, it's more sensible to bake it right away when the spirit moves you. If it's the day before, wrap it in foil; it's a moist bread and will stay fresh. Or, you can bake it a week or two ahead and freeze it. In either case, while the bread is rising or baking, cook the jam.

With these out of the way, your morning schedule can be concentrated into one session in the kitchen: Prepare the fruit, arranging the orange and grapefruit sections alternately in the melons; poach and flake the fish and make the *Béchamel* (this could wait until an hour before your friends come); prepare the potatoes and make the nests in individual baked-egg or onion-soup dishes; and set out the ingredients for the Hollandaise.

When your guests have all arrived, light the oven, then join them for a drink. The disappearing hostess's last preparation should take no more than twenty minutes: Put the fish in the potato nests, whip the egg whites stiff, fold them into the *Béchamel,* and spoon this sauce over the fish; sprinkle the cheese on top. Then make the Hollandaise. Set the melons at each place, the bread and jam on the table, and, as your guests find their places, put the soufflés in the oven.

You can enlarge this brunch to the extent of your oven space—as many soufflés as will fit on one shelf. You may well want more than six people, since there's little extra work involved and service is simple. You only have to get up from the table to clear the fruit plates and bring in the soufflés, and later to bring in the coffee. Whether you're at the seashore or not, eat outdoors at one long table, using shells and flowers (see p. 218) for decoration.

Citrus Cup in Cantaloupe

Halve 3 cantaloupes and remove seeds. Fill cavities first with grapefruit and orange sections, arranged clockwise, and then with orange juice, and chill. Immediately before serving, dust with sifted confectioners' sugar.

3 cantaloupes
6 oranges
4 grapefruit
Confectioners' sugar

Petits Soufflés Henri IV

Make 6 Potato Nests, but do not bake too brown. Prepare a *Court-Bouillon* for Fish. In it poach 6 fillets of haddock for 8 minutes, or until just cooked through, and reserve. Make a Béchamel Sauce with 1 cup of the fish stock; add 1/4 cup heavy cream and 3 egg yolks, and cool.

Preheat oven to 450°. Beat 6 egg whites with 1/8 teaspoon salt until stiff, and fold into sauce. Flake fish and place a generous portion of it in each potato nest. Cover fish entirely with sauce-and-egg-white mixture, and smooth out surface with rubber spatula. Sprinkle soufflés with 1/2 cup grated Parmesan, then bake 12 minutes, or until puffed and golden brown. Serve at once, with Hollandaise Sauce, below.

6 Potato Nests (see Index)
Court-Bouillon for Fish (see Index)
6 fillets of haddock
1 cup Béchamel Sauce (see Index)
1/4 cup heavy cream
3 egg yolks
6 egg whites
1/8 teaspoon salt
1/2 cup grated Parmesan
Hollandaise Sauce

Hollandaise Sauce

Blender method: Preheat glass container of electric blender in boiling water. Melt 1/4 pound butter, separate 4 egg yolks, and measure 2 teaspoons lemon juice. Place all ingredients in heated blender. Season with pepper and salt, and blend at high speed for 20 seconds. Keep hot in hot-water bath until soufflés are ready.

1/4 pound butter
4 egg yolks
2 teaspoons lemon juice
Salt, pepper

Oatmeal Bread

Dissolve 2 envelopes yeast in 1/3 cup lukewarm water. In a saucepan, over high heat, scald 1 1/2 cups milk, add 1 cup quick-cooking oatmeal, and cook 3 minutes. Then add 2 tablespoons butter, 1 1/4 cups light cream, 1/2 teaspoon salt, and 1/2 cup sugar. Cool mixture, then add yeast, and beat well with back of a wooden spoon for 5 minutes. Add 2 cups flour and 3 cups whole-wheat flour to form a soft dough, and knead until smooth. Let rise until double in bulk, or about 1 hour. Punch down, shape into 3 loaves, place in buttered loaf tins, and let rise again until double in bulk. Preheat oven to 375° and bake for 50 minutes. Serve with sweet butter and Gingered Pear Jam, below.

2 envelopes yeast
⅓ cup lukewarm water
1½ cups milk
1 cup quick-cooking oatmeal
2 tablespoons butter
1¼ cups light cream
½ teaspoon salt
½ cup sugar
2 cups flour
3 cups whole-wheat flour

Gingered Pear Jam

Peel, core, and cube 12 ripe pears. Measure pears, and measure an equal amount of granulated sugar. Mince very finely 3 pieces of preserved ginger. Place all together in a deep pot, and add juice of 2 lemons, ⅓ cup syrup from ginger jar, and 1 cup water. Bring slowly to a boil, stirring often while juice from pears melts sugar; ripe pears should make enough liquid to cover—but, if necessary, gradually add water. Cook at a rolling boil for about 20 minutes, stirring from time to time. Drop jam from skimmer, and when it falls in flakes, remove from heat, cool a little, and skim very carefully. Pour into sterile jars and cap, or cover with paraffin.

12 ripe pears
Equal measure granulated sugar
3 pieces preserved ginger
Juice 2 lemons
⅓ cup ginger syrup
1 cup water

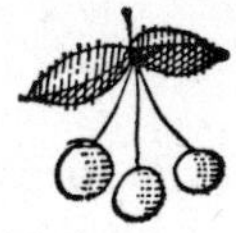

19

Malayan Brunch for Ten

*Bitterballen,** and Bols Genever with Angostura Bitters*

NASI GORENG

SATÉ WITH PEANUT SAUCE

KROEPEK

PINEAPPLE HONG KONG

MALAYAN COFFEE

Heineken's Beer

If you want a brunch that is delicate and ethereal, designed for the listless appetite, don't consider this one. It is a typical Malayan menu, served at about noon to the Dutch tea planters and merchants who have already done the better part of a day's work. Up at dawn, they are off to their offices or plantations in the cool hours of the morning and gather at their clubs around eleven to drink a glass of genever and bitters, munch on *Bitterballen,* and exchange local gossip.

So consider this brunch when you want a meal of substance. Stevedore activity is not a prerequisite to appreciate it fully, but appetites whetted by a round of golf or a morning's sailing will do more justice to it than appetites that have just rolled out of bed.

With this many people on your hands so early in the day, plan to do as much as you can ahead so that you won't be snowed under at the last minute. The previous day, fry the *Kroepek* and store them in a tin; make the pineapple sauce, the coffee concentrate, the *Bitterballen* (see Index), the Peanut Sauce, and the pork marinade.

In the morning, marinate the pork, steam the plain rice, which will be reheated later (see Index), and cook the *Nasi Goreng,* which will also be reheated. This leaves you free to set your table and just sit back until about an hour before servingtime. Then start roasting the pork, reheating the rice, the *Nasi Goreng,* and the *Bitterballen.* If you cook outdoors, you will have to remember to light the fire an hour before you roast the pork.

Time now for genever and bitters before final preparations. Since brunch

* see Index

really should be a relaxed affair, even for you, maybe you can blow yourself to a little help in the kitchen to take care of finishing touches—not really necessary, but the last few minutes are fairly busy: keep turning the pork, make the omelettes for the *Nasi Goreng* and arrange the whole dish, warm the Peanut Sauce, and you're all set.

A few of the ingredients may be new to you. *Sambals* are hot seasoning spices with a base of chili pepper and vinegar; some *sambals* are more scorching than others. It is safer to put a minimum in the *Nasi Goreng* and have more on the table for those who want it. (Crushed, hot Italian pepper may be substituted.) *Kroepeks* are also known as shrimp wafers. They are crisp and crunchy, made of rice flour and pulverized dried shrimp, and do not have their counterpart in Western cookery. You shouldn't have trouble, though, getting either *sambals* or *Kroepek* through a fine food shop.

This is a menu for either indoor broiler or outdoor barbecue. If you are outdoors, reheat the *Nasi Goreng* at one side of the barbecue. In either case, heat and serve in an enameled cast-iron casserole—it keeps food hot, which is important for a rice dish; if you don't have one, use any Dutch oven. Swathe it in two or three bright kitchen towels, knotted together, to bring it to the table.

Nasi Goreng

In a Dutch oven, melt 4 tablespoons chicken or bacon fat over medium heat. Add 4 sliced onions and 4 cups unwashed raw rice, then stir constantly until about half the grains are edged with brown. Moisten with 4 cups chicken broth, season lightly with salt, and add 2 tablespoons *sambal oelek* and 2 tablespoons *sambal brandal*. Reduce heat and simmer, covered, for 20 minutes; then, if rice looks dry on top, add another cup or more of broth but do not stir. Cover and cook 20 minutes longer.

Meanwhile, steam 2 cups white rice and keep warm over hot water. Make two 3-egg omelettes: Beat 6 eggs with 2 tablespoons water and season with pepper and salt. In a 9-inch skillet, over medium heat, melt 1 tablespoon butter, pour in half the egg mixture, and rotate the pan with wrist motion to spread the egg and make a very flat omelette. Cook until bottom is solid but top is still glossy, then remove to a board. Repeat with remaining egg, then cut both omelettes into 1-inch strips and reserve.

Drain three 4-ounce cans small pink shrimp and add to *sambal* rice, stirring in to heat shrimp. Transfer to a heated serving casserole, arrange *Saté,* below, around the edge, and decorate with a lattice of omelette strips. Serve with individual bowls of plain steamed rice to mix with the spiced, and serve small bowls of *sambal oelek* and *sambal brandal* for those who like their food very highly spiced.

4 tablespoons chicken or bacon fat
4 sliced onions
4 cups unwashed raw rice
4–6 cups chicken broth, as needed
Salt
Sambal oelek
Sambal brandal

Steamed rice (*see Index*)
6 eggs
2 tablespoons water

Salt, pepper
2 tablespoons butter
3 cans small pink shrimp
Saté with Peanut Sauce

Saté with Peanut Sauce

Trim fat from 4 pounds boned loin of pork and cut meat into cubes. Mix together 3 cups orange juice, juice of 2 lemons, 6 pressed cloves garlic, 1½ teaspoons sugar, and 3 tablespoons soy sauce, and marinate meat in this mixture for 3 hours or more. Thread meat on skewers, then broil 8 to 10 inches away from coals, or 5 inches from slow broiler, for 40 minutes. Turn meat frequently and brush with Peanut Sauce.

Combine 2 tablespoons butter, 3 tablespoons soy sauce, 4 tablespoons peanut butter, 4 teaspoons lemon juice, and 1 tablespoon *sambal brandal.* Simmer over low heat for 5 minutes, then blend in ½ cup cream. Because of high fat content, sauce separates easily; an ice cube dropped into it will restore its smoothness.

4 pounds boned loin of pork
3 cups orange juice
2 lemons
6 cloves garlic
1½ teaspoons sugar
3 tablespoons soy sauce

2 tablespoons butter
3 tablespoons soy sauce
4 tablespoons peanut butter
4 teaspoons lemon juice
1 tablespoon sambal brandal
½ cup cream

Kroepek

Kroepek chips come in colors: deep red, orange, pink, and white. You will need 6 dozen. Deep fry briefly, 2 or 3 chips at a time at 400°, until they finish expanding and become light in color, a few seconds in all, how many depending upon the size of the chip. Drain on absorbent paper, and serve at room temperature.

6 dozen kroepek chips
Fat for deep frying

Pineapple Hong Kong

Cut 1 very large, ripe pineapple in two lengthwise. With a sharp knife, remove core, then scoop out meat, dice and crush, and mix with ½ cup sugar and ¼ cup kirsch. Marinate this sauce in refrigerator for several hours or overnight. Decorate fronds of pineapple with fresh cherries or strawberries, kumquats, and grapes. When ready to serve, fill pineapple shells with 2 quarts of pineapple and/or orange sherbet. Serve sauce in a bowl.

1 very large pineapple
½ cup sugar
¼ cup kirsch
2 quarts pineapple and/or orange sherbet
Kumquats, grapes, and cherries or strawberries for decoration

Malayan Coffee

Grind to a powder in an electric blender 3 cups regular-grind American coffee. Do this 1 cup at a time. Add as much cold water as the coffee will absorb to make a very heavy syrup. Pour into a jar with a tight-fitting cover and refrigerate for 24 hours. Strain through 8 thicknesses of cheesecloth or a fine muslin to obtain about 2 cups strong extract.

Scald 5 cups milk. For average demitasse, use 2 tablespoons extract in each cup and fill with hot milk (roughly one part coffee, two parts milk). Serve sugar on the side.

3 cups coffee, regular grind
Cold water
5 cups milk
Sugar

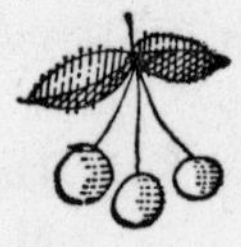

20

Winter Brunch for Twelve

Whiskey Sours and Bloody Marys

GLAZED APPLES

RED-FLANNEL HASH WITH POACHED EGGS

BUTTERY RYE

MELON ALASKA

COFFEE OR TEA

The simplest things are often the trickiest—and two of them are on this menu. We tend to think of poached eggs and baked apples as elementary cooking, and, in a way, that's true; they aren't difficult—*if* you know how.

We have been dealing with food for a long time and trust that we know a good deal about it, but we wouldn't dare count up the fruit we used until we finally produced the perfect baked apple—shining, plump, and of just the right tenderness. We don't actually bake the apples at all now. In the beginning we did, but when we kept them in the oven until they were tender, the skins were wrinkled as prunes', and, if we took them out when they still looked beautiful, they were too hard. An old cook book furnished the clue; now that we poach them and glaze them under the broiler, we make apples as they should be. You have to use the right fruit, too. Many of them disintegrate, others are not flavorful. One variety of Rome Beauty is cultivated especially for baking, and it's perfect.

Poach eggs in the usual whirlpool of water, as we suggest, to keep the whites together and prevent them from floating away in threads and scraps. But there's another way to poach eggs successfully, and to do several at a time: Fill a shallow 9-inch saucepan with water to a depth of 1½ inches. Heat the water until it is scarcely simmering. Break an egg into a saucer, bring the saucer close to the level of the water, tip the egg *quickly* into the water (this is the trick), and poach it for 3 minutes. You can poach three or four eggs at a time this way. If you don't have anyone in the kitchen to do them at the last minute, poach them just before your guests come and keep them in a pot of very hot (but not boiling) water. If the eggs have to wait a long time, carefully drain off the water and replace with more hot water.

The fruit Alaska needs last-minute attention, and should be eliminated if you plan to do this brunch alone. Don't have any first course in that case, use the apples for dessert, and with them bring out an Edam or a Wisconsin beer cheese with water biscuits. You can make the rye toasts the day before, keep them in a tin, and reheat them while you brown the hash. It will take 8 to 10 minutes to finish the hash, providing you've assembled it ahead. Your guests can spare you that long while they finish building up their appetites with conversation and the good things their host is pouring for them in the living room.

Glazed Apples

To make a syrup, over high heat dissolve 1 cup sugar in 2½ cups boiling water. Add ½ cup orange juice and 3 tablespoons lemon juice. Core 12 large Rome Beauty baking apples and peel no more than two thirds of skin from top. Place them peeled side down in two heavy skillets, over high heat, and pour syrup over them. Bring to a boil, reduce heat, then simmer apples, covered, for 15 minutes. Turn them over and simmer approximately 10 minutes more. Then place apples under broiler; baste with pan juices every 5 minutes for 20 minutes, or until glazed. Serve at room temperature, in bowls, with last drop of glaze poured over tops.

1 cup sugar
2½ cups water
½ cup orange juice
3 tablespoons lemon juice
12 large Rome Beauty baking apples

Red-Flannel Hash with Poached Eggs

Chop together 12 boiled potatoes, 14 small cooked beets, and 2 medium onions. Dice ¾ pound salt pork (jowl butt is best); divide into two equal portions, and sauté in two heavy skillets, over medium heat, until golden. Then, to each skillet add 1½ cups ground cooked corned beef and half the potatoes, beets, and onion. With a fork, pack hash firmly into skillets and cook, uncovered, over medium heat until brown and crusty on bottom. To turn hash, place a plate on top of skillet, invert skillet onto plate, then slide uncooked side of hash into skillet and cook until crusted. Transfer to heated platter, and garnish each cake of hash with 6 poached eggs.

While hash is browning, boil 1 cup salted water in a small shallow pan. Break 1 egg into a cup. Stir water in pan until it forms a small whirlpool in the center. Drop egg in the whirlpool, reduce heat at once, and poach egg for 3 minutes. Remove from water, place on paper towel, and trim edges. Repeat 11 more times, adding salt water to pan as it boils down. Place eggs on hash and serve at once.

12 boiled potatoes
14 small cooked beets
2 medium onions
¾ pound salt pork
3 cups cooked ground corned beef
12 eggs

Buttery Rye

Trim crusts from 2 rectangular loaves of sliced rye bread. Flatten each slice with rolling pin, then trim edges again if necessary and cut each slice into triangles. Cream together ¼ pound butter and 1 large pressed clove garlic. Spread slices lightly with it, then place on cooky sheet and bake at 250° for 25 minutes. Serve hot.

2 loaves rye bread
¼ pound butter
1 large clove garlic

Melon Alaska

Preheat broiler to maximum heat. Cut 6 small cantaloupes in half and remove seeds. Scoop out pulp with melon-ball cutter and trim remaining meat from shell. Marinate melon balls for 1 hour in ½ cup Grand Marnier mixed with ½ cup water, stirring frequently. Fill shells half full with well-drained melon balls, then cover with hard-frozen orange sherbet.

Make a Meringue Norvégienne: Beat 8 egg whites until stiff and glossy, gradually adding 1 cup granulated sugar. Beat 2 egg yolks with ½ cup Vanilla Sugar, until light and pale yellow. Fold yolks into whites, and cover top of filled melons with the meringue. Set melons in a pan of crushed ice and place on middle shelf of broiler to brown meringue. Serve at once.

6 small cantaloupes
½ cup Grand Marnier
½ cup water
2 quarts orange sherbet

8 egg whites
1 cup granulated sugar
2 egg yolks
½ cup Vanilla Sugar *(see Index)*
Crushed ice

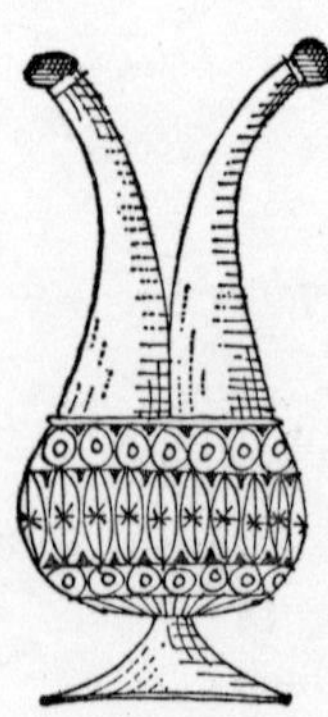

21

Informal Summer Luncheon for Four—I

SALADE PARISIENNE
RASPBERRIES AU VIN
LANGUES DE CHAT
COFFEE

WINE

Charles Krug Cabernet Sauvignon, en carafe

Dollars to doughnuts, the chef who created America's all-time chef salad was French! It's Gallic thrift that takes a smidgin of this, an end of that, tastes and seasons, arranges the whole to please the eye—*et voilà*. But by now, we've had it, it's been too much of a good thing. Not that we don't hold with Gallic or any other thrift. It's just that we're weary of being thrifty with exactly the same ham, cheese, and chicken, and we propose beef for a change.

By and large, Sunday's roast ends up as Monday's hash, and beef that comes out of the soup kettle lingers on in the icebox. The chef who dreamed up *Salade Parisienne* conceived a worthier *dénouement*. Worthy enough, even, for us to recommend that you imitate it quite extravagantly by buying a thick slice of roast beef at the delicatessen if you didn't have roast the day before. Or be very sensible and, a day ahead, boil 1½ pounds of soup meat (the meat will shrink) in 1½ quarts of water, with a leek, a carrot, 2 pieces of celery, a handful of parsley, a few veal bones and a veal knuckle, 1 teaspoon of monosodium glutamate, and salt and pepper to taste. Cover and simmer for 1¾ hours, or until the meat is tender. Remove vegetables, beef, and bones, and reduce the stock to 1 quart. Replace the meat in the stock; when it cools, take out the meat and set it aside. Skim the fat from the stock, correct the seasoning, and chill (the veal bones will make it jell). Two for the price of one—Jellied Beef Consommé plus beef for the salad. Any housewife, or chef, for that matter, must approve such practicality.

If you time yourself providently in the morning, you can cook and cool the vegetables and eggs for the salad, and still allow two hours for the beans to marinate. If you foresee a tight schedule, cook them all the day before. Chill the salad ingredients separately until just before friends are expected. Then, toss the salad with the mayonnaise and arrange the platter. Put the berries in a glass bowl and pour the wine over them at least an hour before serving.

Langues de Chat keep for several days in a tightly covered tin, but in hot, humid weather they might get soft. Bake them ahead and freeze them, or bake them just the day before. They, too, will remind you to be practical: If you've stored extra egg whites in your freezer, use some for the cookies; if not, start your stockpile of extra yolks right now with those you have left over (see p. 247).

Salade Parisienne

Marinate 1 cup cooked string beans for 2 hours or more in ½ cup Basic French Dressing to which has been added 1 tablespoon minced onion and 1 tablespoon chopped parsley. Cube 4 cold cooked potatoes and slice 4 hard-cooked eggs. Wash, drain, and dry heart of 1 small head chicory. Cube 1 pound cold roast beef or soup meat. Drain string beans, mix together meat, vegetables, and 2 of the sliced eggs, and toss with 1 cup Mayonnaise. Grind a little black pepper on top of salad, and garnish with remaining egg slices. Serve well chilled.

1 cup cooked string beans
½ cup Basic French Dressing (see Index)
1 tablespoon minced onion
1 tablespoon chopped parsley
4 cooked potatoes
4 hard-cooked eggs
1 small head chicory
1 pound cold roast beef or soup meat
1 cup Mayonnaise (see Index)
Pepper

Raspberries au Vin

Wash and drain well 1 quart very ripe raspberries. Place in a glass bowl and cover with same red wine as used at the meal. Heat another ¼ cup wine, and dissolve ½ cup granulated sugar in it. Cool and add to raspberries. Serve well chilled.

1 quart raspberries
Red wine
½ cup granulated sugar

Langues de Chat

Preheat oven to 450°. In small bowl of electric mixer, cream ¼ pound softened butter with ½ cup Vanilla Sugar until light and fluffy. Add 4 egg whites, one at a time, beating 1 minute after each addition. Sift ½ cup flour onto waxed paper and fold it into mixture a little at a time with a rubber spatula. Force batter through a plain pastry tube onto a buttered baking sheet, making strips 2 inches long, the width of a pencil, and 2 inches apart. Bake about 5 minutes until edges are golden. With a spatula remove quickly from baking sheet, and cool on absorbent paper. Makes about 2½ dozen cookies.

¼ pound softened butter
½ cup Vanilla Sugar (see Index)
4 egg whites
½ cup flour

22

Informal Summer Luncheon for Four—II

RADISHES AND SAUCISSON
PIPÉRADE BASQUAISE
FRENCH BREAD
TRAY OF ASSORTED CHEESES: STILTON, BRIE, BEL PAESE
PEARS
COFFEE

WINE
Widmer's Isabella, en carafe

One of the most successful books ever published is a cook book that says on the cover, "The way to a man's heart." We'd like our cook book to have a fair degree of success and, if this is the key, let's not forget the men (not that we do anyway)! This is a man's lunch, or one for mixed company, but not the best choice for ladies' day.

In fact, we think of one man in particular, a doctor with an enormous zest for living and eating. We recall his taking us into the kitchen where he had hung sausages from hooks in the ceiling, in the manner of his European forebears. He sniffed each sausage in turn—and with each sniff a rapturous "Ah." Nothing would do but that we taste on the spot; then a lively discussion on the merits of each, with a final conclusion that they're all good, it's a matter of taste. So, pick your own favorite for this lunch, or, in line with our thinking, ask your host to choose.

Serve the first course *à la française*. Everything is on the table; the sausage on a cutting board with a razor-sharp knife, the bowl of radishes, the bread and butter, the wine decanted into a *carafe*. You won't have to invite them to dig in.

Just before everyone is finished with this course, go out to the kitchen to complete the *Pipérade*. (Plan to prepare the ham and vegetable mixture during the morning; arrange the cheese platter then too, and leave it at room temperature.) Reheat the *Pipérade* mixture over low heat while you scramble the eggs, and then combine the two. When you bring the pears and cheeses in for dessert, leave the bread and butter on the table.

This menu should have a merit badge for being easy to produce. You can extend it to serve eight people with no difficulty, and it's handy for serving just two. And it accommodates all kinds of midday appetites, from the nibbling to the ravenous.

Pipérade Basquaise

Seed 1 green pepper, 1 sweet red pepper (or use 1 canned pimiento), and ½ hot pepper (or use 1 teaspoon dried Italian pepper), and mince all together. Chop 1 large onion. Dip 2 ripe tomatoes in boiling water, then quickly in cold water, and peel, seed, and chop them. In a heavy skillet, heat 2 tablespoons olive oil to sizzling point, add onions and 1 small pressed clove garlic, then, almost at once, add the rest of the vegetables and let mixture simmer over reduced heat for 6 minutes. Cut 3 slices boiled ham into julienne strips. Add to skillet and continue simmering. Taste, and correct seasoning with salt and pepper and ¼ teaspoon monosodium glutamate.

Mix 6 eggs with ¼ cup heavy cream, and scramble in 2 tablespoons butter in another skillet. When they are still very soft and glossy, combine with vegetable mixture and serve at once.

1 green pepper
1 sweet red pepper
or canned pimiento
½ hot pepper
or 1 teaspoon dried Italian pepper
1 large onion
2 tomatoes
2 tablespoons olive oil
1 small clove garlic
3 slices boiled ham
Salt, pepper
¼ teaspoon monosodium glutamate
6 eggs
¼ cup heavy cream
2 tablespoons butter

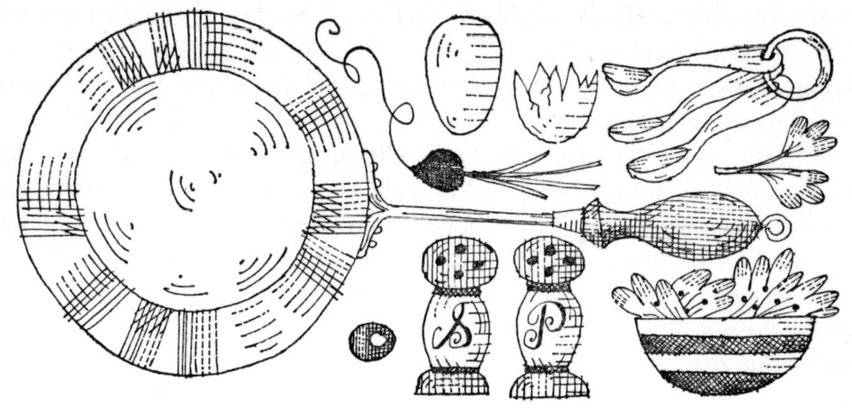

23

Informal Summer Luncheon for Four—III

SIMPLE OMELETTE
HEARTS OF LETTUCE WITH TARRAGON DRESSING
DROP BISCUITS
CURRANT JELLY
ICED COFFEE OR TEA

WINE
Widmer's Elvira, en carafe

Few people mean *exactly* what they say *all* the time, but this time we do. The heading of this menu is to be taken seriously; it's for a small group and for people you know well. Save the proverbial grain of salt for the specifications on some other, possibly more complicated menu. The pristine simplicity of this one demands your close attention to succeed. It won't if you have too many people to cook for, or if these are not friends who will overlook your disappearance for twenty minutes before you feed them.

Aside from the salad dressing and the jelly, which you can make days ahead, almost everything is last minute, though you can do several things in the morning: Wash and drain the lettuce; mix the biscuit dough, but don't add the cream until you're ready to bake them; set out the eggs, large measuring cup, and omelette pan; butter the baking sheet—and that's as far as you can go at the moment.

So, after you settle everyone down with an *apéritif* or a drink, off with you to the kitchen to get the biscuits in the oven, finish the salad, and make the omelettes. If these are really good friends, however, possibly their place is right in the kitchen with you. We have a special affection for our kitchens and mean it as a compliment when we ask people to join us there. And, we've noticed, the production of a perfect omelette fascinates an audience; no flaming *crêpes Suzette* in a formal dining room can match it.

Simple Omelette

Preheat oven to 300°. Break 8 eggs into a quart-size measuring cup. Add ¼ cup cold water, salt and pepper, and 2 tablespoons butter cut into small pieces. Beat enough to mix thoroughly but not to make a foam. Heat a skillet or omelette pan over medium heat, then melt 1 tablespoon butter in it. Pour one quarter of eggs into skillet and with a rotating movement of the wrist spread eggs in pan. As edges begin to cook, use fork to bring cooked parts gently toward center. Reduce heat and do not let bottom of omelette brown. It is cooked when the thinnest glossy film remains on top. With a rubber spatula, roll omelette and slide onto heated individual plate. Place in *open* oven to keep warm. Make 4 omelettes and serve with side dishes of salad.

8 eggs
¼ cup cold water
Salt, pepper
6 tablespoons butter, in all

Hearts of Lettuce with Tarragon Dressing

Choose 2 firm heads of Boston lettuce. Reserve outer leaves for other uses; wash, drain, and dry hearts. Chop 1 tablespoon parsley, and soft-boil 1 egg

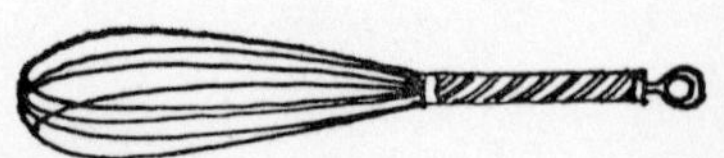

for 2 minutes. Break egg into salad and cut into big pieces with a fork to make yolk run. To 6 tablespoons Basic French Dressing, add 1 teaspoon monosodium glutamate, parsley, and about 2 dozen fresh tarragon leaves or 1 tablespoon crushed dried tarragon. Pour over salad, toss, and serve at once.

2 heads Boston lettuce
1 tablespoon chopped parsley
1 egg
6 tablespoons Basic French Dressing (see Index)
1 teaspoon monosodium glutamate
2 dozen fresh tarragon leaves or 1 tablespoon dried tarragon

Drop Biscuits

Preheat oven to 400°. To make 9 to 10 biscuits, sift 1 cup flour into a bow with ½ teaspoon salt and 1 teaspoo double-action baking powder. Wit fingertips lightly blend in 2 table spoons softened butter. Stir in ⅓ cu heavy cream to make a soft dough Drop on greased baking sheet with tablespoon, flatten tops a little, an bake from 12 to 15 minutes. Split an serve warm with a pat of butter in center.

1 cup flour
½ teaspoon salt
1 teaspoon double-action baking powder
2 tablespoons butter
⅓ cup heavy cream

Currant Jelly

To make 10 to 12 six-ounce glasses: Rinse and pick any bad berries from 5 quarts red currents. Place them, still on stems, in jelly bag. Squeeze fruit *lightly* over jam basin or over stainless steel pot. Measure juice, and add 1 cup sugar per cup of juice. Over high heat and stirring to dissolve sugar, bring to a rolling boil. Keep it rolling for 20 minutes, skimming occasionally. When a few drops of jelly left on skimmer flake off rather than run, jelly is ready. Cool a little, then skim very carefully, and pour into sterile glasses. When cold, cover with paraffin or vacuum-seal covers.

5 quarts red currants
1 cup sugar per cup of juice
Paraffin

24

Informal Summer Luncheon for Six

Portuguese Salad
Rhubarb and Strawberry Compote
Coconut Bars
Iced Coffee or Tea

WINE

Chilean Riesling, or Spanish Vino Verde, en carafe

All of a sudden, some of us have *discovered* rice salads. We've learned what our Continental cousins have known for years; that rice is equally good cold or hot; that cold rice blends beautifully with cold cooked meats, poultry, and fish, and with vegetables, both cooked and raw; that you can create beautiful effects by combining its pristine whiteness with colorful food; and (we don't know whether this should have been first or last on the list), you can take practically any odd bits of leftovers, toss them with cold cooked rice, add a tasty dressing, and arrange and garnish the salad to great effect on a serving platter. The end result is a far cry from the usual concept of leftovers. The combination we suggest in the Portuguese Salad is only one of many. You'll think of all sorts of possibilities.

Complete the salad any time in the morning; it won't suffer from standing. (If you don't have ham and tongue in the house, buy them at a delicatessen and have the meats sliced ¼ inch thick.) Stew the fruit and bake the cookies the day before, or early in the morning.

Though this is a perfect light lunch for a summer day, it's substantial enough for hot-weather dinners too. Add stuffed Eggs Romanoff (see Index), and slices of ham cut ⅛ inch thick and rolled up. Press the rice salad in a mixing bowl, and unmold it in the center of a large round platter. Arrange the filled tomatoes, the stuffed eggs, and the ham rolls around it; mince an extra tablespoon of green pepper and sprinkle it over the rice.

A parting thought, don't forget this salad platter when you need a handsome cold buffet dish.

Portuguese Salad

Season ¾ cup chopped raw mushrooms with freshly ground pepper, salt, and 1 tablespoon chopped parsley. Add 1 tablespoon olive oil, 1 egg yolk, and 2 tablespoons toasted bread crumbs. Mix all together and reserve. Preheat oven to 350°. Wash 6 small tomatoes, cut off one third from smooth ends, and remove meat and seeds from rest of tomatoes. Fill with mushroom mixture, cover with top slice, bake 30 minutes, then chill.

Mix together 4 cups cooked rice, 1 cup cooked peas, 1 cup raw diced celery, ¼ cup minced green pepper, and 1 cup grated carrots. Season with ⅔ cup Basic French Dressing to which has been added ¼ teaspoon dried marjoram. Toss the salad with 1½ cups each julienne strips of boiled ham and boiled tongue. Garnish with filled tomatoes and serve very cold.

¾ cup minced raw mushrooms
Salt, pepper
1 tablespoon chopped parsley
1 tablespoon olive oil
1 egg yolk
2 tablespoons toasted bread crumbs
6 small tomatoes
4 cups cooked rice
1 cup cooked peas
1 cup raw diced celery
¼ cup minced green pepper
1 cup grated carrots
⅔ cup Basic French Dressing (see Index)
¼ teaspoon dried marjoram
1½ cups julienne strips boiled ham
1½ cups julienne strips boiled tongue

Rhubarb and Strawberry Compote

Peel stalks of 2 pounds rhubarb and cut in 2-inch pieces. Over high heat bring to a boil ½ cup water and 1 cup granulated sugar. Add rhubarb, bring back to a boil, then reduce heat, and simmer for about 5 minutes or until rhubarb is tender. Remove from fire, and add 1 pint hulled, halved strawberries, or 1 package frozen strawberries, not defrosted. Cool, stir strawberries through the compote, and chill.

2 pounds rhubarb
½ cup water
1 cup granulated sugar
1 pint strawberries
or 1 package frozen strawberries

Coconut Bars

Preheat oven to 375°. In small bowl of electric mixer, cream ¼ pound butter, add gradually ½ cup well-packed brown sugar, and beat until fluffy, about 5 minutes. Sift 1 cup flour; with a rubber spatula, fold flour into butter-sugar mixture. Spread in ungreased 8-inch-square pan, and bake for 20 minutes. Meanwhile, beat 2 eggs with ½ cup each brown sugar and Vanilla Sugar. Stir in ½ cup chopped walnuts and ¾ cup canned flaked coconut. Spread this batter quickly over baked crust and bake for another 20 minutes. Cool, then sift confectioners' sugar on top, and cut into bars.

¼ pound butter
½ cup brown sugar
1 cup flour
2 eggs
½ cup brown sugar
*½ cup Vanilla Sugar (see **Index**)*
½ cup chopped walnuts
¾ cup canned flaked coconut
Confectioners' sugar

25

Spanish Summer Luncheon for Four

Ramos Golden Oloroso Sherry

Olives à la Sévillane

Gaspacho

Rosemary Bread

Edam or Cheddar Cheese

Suspiros

Demitasse

Are you in the mood for salad or soup? *Gaspacho* is both—you might say it's a soupy salad, or you might call it a salady soup—it's all in the point of view. Next question: Do you like your vegetables purèed in soup, or do you favor the crunchy texture of finely diced raw vegetables? No matter, *gaspacho* is still your dish—it has both.

It's as much a part of Spain as *paella*, flamenco, or sherry. Just as there are many varieties of sherry or *paella*, and many nuances of flamenco, there are innumerable versions of *gaspacho*. They range from a simple combination of vegetables to an elaborate recipe of the Hotel Ritz in Barcelona. Their chef uses the same vegetables we do, but he cooks and purées them, then chills the purée, and blends in a few tablespoons of mayonnaise to make it creamy; the Hotel Ritz *gaspacho* then calls for the addition of finely chopped cucumbers, tomatoes, and green peppers before serving, and a sprinkling of croutons on top.

Unless you're willing to start the Rosemary Bread almost before you have morning coffee, it won't be finished in time for lunch. It's wiser to bake it a day, or many days, ahead. Bake it for only half the baking time, then cool and freeze it. When you need it, preheat the oven to 400°, and bake the still-frozen loaf for 30 minutes. (This is the principle of brown-and-serve bread and rolls. If the pan of boiling water puzzles you, it's the steam that makes the crust crisp.)

Bake the *Suspiros* the day before, too, and while they're in the oven, prepare the marinade for the olives. Serve the olives and sausage with the sherry as a first course or outdoors before lunch. But why not set the table in the cool shade of a tree in the first place? Bring the food out on a tray, and enjoy a leisurely meal in true Spanish fashion. Two hours for lunch, and none of this pointless American rushing about. Don't worry, everything will get done—besides, there's always *mañana*.

Olives à la Sévillane

Drain 1 large can small black olives, place them in a shallow bowl, and cover with sherry. Press 2 cloves of garlic over the olives, stir, and marinate overnight. Serve on small individual plates with a sprig of parsley and 2 slices *chorizo* sausage or Italian *peperone*. Serve with sherry.

1 large can small black olives
Sherry
2 cloves garlic
Parsley
8 slices chorizo sausage
or Italian peperone

Gaspacho

Rinse 4 tomatoes and 1 cucumber, and dice them finely, unpeeled. Add 1 minced pimiento *morrón*, which can be bought in a Spanish-American grocery store or replaced with 2 canned red pimientos. Place vegetables and their juice in a china bowl, add 1 very finely minced red onion, and press 1 clove garlic over all. Take out ½ cup of vegetables and blend 3 seconds in electric blender, or rub through food mill, and return to bowl. Add 2 tablespoons olive oil, 1 tablespoon wine vinegar, freshly ground pepper, and some salt. Chill 3 hours or more, and serve in individual soup plates, garnished with a diamond-shaped piece of toast and an ice cube.

4 tomatoes
1 cucumber
1 minced pimiento morrón
or 2 canned red pimientos
1 red onion
1 clove garlic
2 tablespoons olive oil
1 tablespoon wine vinegar
Salt, pepper
Toast
Ice cubes

Rosemary Bread

Dissolve 1 envelope dry yeast in 1/4 cup lukewarm water. Over high heat scald 1/2 cup milk with 1 tablespoon butter, 1 tablespoon sugar, 1 1/2 teaspoons salt, and 1 teaspoon dried powdered rosemary. When sugar and salt are dissolved, remove from heat and cool in a large mixing bowl. When mixture is lukewarm, add 1 1/4 cups water of same temperature, and stir in yeast. Gradually mix in 5 cups flour, or enough to make a dough that pulls away from sides of bowl. Turn out dough onto lightly floured board and knead for 10 minutes, or until it is smooth and elastic. Place dough in buttered bowl, cover, and let rise in warm spot for about 1 hour, or until double in bulk. Punch dough down, and let rise again for 3/4 hour, or until double in bulk. Turn out on floured board and knead 1 minute.

Preheat oven to 400°. Divide dough in half and shape into long narrow loaves like French bread. Place on a greased baking sheet, cover, and let rise in warm spot for about 3/4 hour, or until double in bulk. Cut diagonal slits 1/4 inch deep in top of loaves and brush surface with milk, then bake on middle shelf of oven 45 to 50 minutes, or until golden brown. Place a large flat pan filled with boiling water (add a sprig of rosemary) on bottom shelf of oven. Serve cool, with cheese.

1 envelope dry yeast
1/4 cup lukewarm water
1/2 cup milk
1 tablespoon butter
1 tablespoon sugar
1 1/2 teaspoons salt
1 teaspoon dried powdered rosemary
1 1/4 cups water
5 cups flour
Sprig of rosemary

Suspiros

Preheat oven to 300°. Boil together 3 cups Vanilla Sugar and 1 cup water until a drop of syrup forms a soft ball in cold water, or until candy thermometer registers 234° to 238°. Beat 6 egg whites until stiff but not dry. Gradually beat syrup into egg whites to make an Italian meringue. Beat 3 egg yolks until fluffy and light, and fold into meringue. Stir in 3 cups blanched chopped almonds, 1 tablespoon curaçao or Triple Sec, and 2 teaspoons grated orange peel. Spoon into 18 fluted paper cupcake cups, and top each little cake with an almond. Bake 40 minutes. Store in airtight container.

3 cups Vanilla Sugar *(see Index)*
1 cup water
6 egg whites
3 egg yolks
3 cups blanched chopped almonds
1 tablespoon curaçao or Triple Sec
2 teaspoons grated orange peel
18 whole almonds

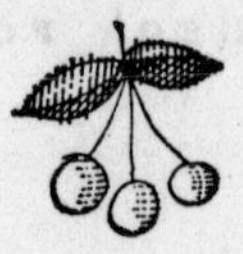

26

Formal Luncheon for Four—I

CHILLED CLAM-JUICE COCKTAIL
OR
GREEN-TURTLE SOUP WITH SHERRY
ENGLISH MIXED GRILL
LIME CHIFFON PIE
IRISH COFFEE

WINES

Inexpensive: Inglenook Cabernet Sauvignon, Napa Valley
Medium-priced: Saint-Estèphe, Château Cos-d'Estournel
Expensive: Château Smith-Haut-Lafitte

The leading character in *Jacobowsky and the Colonel* maintains that, given any situation, there are always two possibilities. And so with lunch; there is the lettuce-leaf-*garni* possibility, as opposed to the none-of-this-rabbit-food approach. But given a lunch situation involving male guests or people who have come a distance to see you, rabbit food is *not* the thing.

You don't need much advance notice for this luncheon, though it is easier to make the pie the day before; but if you are an early riser, you can manage it the same day. An alternate suggestion if time is short is to eliminate the crust and convert the recipe to Lime Cream: Make up the recipe for the filling. Whip ½ cup of heavy cream until stiff. Fold most of the whipped cream into the custard when you fold in the egg whites. Pour into a crystal serving bowl or individual serving dishes, and decorate with the remaining whipped cream and a teaspoon of grated lime rind. (When you buy limes, look for those with a yellowish cast; they are riper and more flavorful.) Since this dessert is light, the thick layer of cream on the Irish Coffee is not amiss. Have the whipped cream in a bowl at the table, and spoon it onto the surface of the coffee as you are about to serve it. You don't want the liquids to mingle, and you do want the coffee *hot,* the cream *cold.* Special Irish-coffee cups are to be had at a very reasonable price. They are tall and slender, like old-fashioned chocolate cups, which you may use instead; or use punch cups.

We haven't given a recipe for Green-Turtle Soup, since it is one of those luxuries that is simplicity itself: To 2 cans of hot green turtle soup, add ¼ cup of medium-dry sherry. Start the mixed grill about twenty minutes before lunch. Because it needs almost constant attention for thirty-five minutes, you should have someone in the kitchen to help. Even if you leave your guests for that length of time, you are faced with the problem of eating your soup at one go or not at all. If you have a fairly formal occasion in mind, the hostess shouldn't act like a jack-in-the-box, so you probably had better look for a more accommodating menu to tackle unaided. However, it does lend itself beautifully to outdoor cooking, in which case you can rule out the help problem and manage the cooking singlehanded while you are with your guests. For a summer lunch out-of-doors, you will want to eliminate the soup and serve the Clam-Juice Cocktail instead. Or, serve the menu with soup for an informal winter dinner indoors, on an occasion when you don't mind hiking to and fro from the kitchen.

Because the mixed grill makes such an attractive picture on individual plates, you will want to serve it that way. You will find that service is faster, too. Arrange the meats and vegetables as quickly as possible on *heated* plates. This is food that must be eaten fresh and hot.

Clam-Juice Cocktail

To 1 bottle clam juice add an equal quantity tomato juice, 1 drop Tabasco, juice of ½ lemon, and a pinch celery salt. Chill well.

1 bottle clam juice
Tomato juice
1 drop Tabasco
Juice of ½ lemon
Pinch celery salt

English Mixed Grill

Boil 4 links pork sausage over medium heat for 10 minutes, then drain. Prepare a sauce with ¼ cup bottled Escoffier Sauce Robert blended with ¼ cup salad oil. Pour sauce over the pork sausage and 4 two-inch-thick English lamb chops with kidneys, 4 slices Canadian bacon cut 1 inch thick,

and 4 large mushroom caps; mix until all are well coated with sauce. Place sausage on broiler rack 6 inches from heat; turn often to cook evenly. Eight minutes later, put lamb chops on; broil 12 minutes. Then add Canadian bacon, turn all meats at once, and allow 12 minutes on second sides; turn bacon in about 5 minutes. Add towards center of heat and grill for 4 minutes the mushrooms (cap sides down) and 4 halved tomatoes (cut sides down); season vegetables with salt and pepper. Divide into individual portions and arrange on plates with bunches of water cress.

¼ cup bottled Escoffier Sauce Robert
¼ cup salad oil
4 links pork sausage
4 English kidney lamb chops, 2 inches thick
4 slices Canadian bacon, 1 inch thick
4 large mushroom caps
4 tomatoes
Salt, pepper
Water cress

Lime Chiffon Pie

Prepare a Baked Pie Shell. Soften 1 envelope gelatin in ¼ cup water. Place 3 egg yolks, ½ cup granulated sugar, and a pinch of salt in top of a double boiler, over boiling water, and stir constantly until thickened. Add gelatin to hot custard and stir until dissolved; then stir in ½ cup lime juicc and 1 teaspoon grated lime rind, and cool. Beat 3 egg whites with ½ cup granulated sugar until they stand in soft peaks, and fold into cooled custard. Turn into pie shell, chill, and garnish with sweetened whipped cream if desired.

Baked Pie Shell (see Index)
1 envelope gelatin
¼ cup water
3 egg yolks
½ cup granulated sugar
Pinch salt
½ cup lime juice
1 teaspoon grated lime rind
3 egg whites
½ cup granulated sugar
Whipped cream (optional)

Irish Coffee

In a heated stemmed 7-ounce goblet, or an Irish coffee cup, put 1 jigger Irish whiskey and 1 to 2 teaspoons sugar. Fill to within ½ inch of top with strong hot coffee. Stir until sugar is dissolved. Top to brim with chilled whipped cream, so that cream floats on top; do not stir after adding cream. For 4 cups:

4 jiggers Irish whiskey
4–8 teaspoons sugar
1 pint strong hot coffee
½ cup cream, whipped

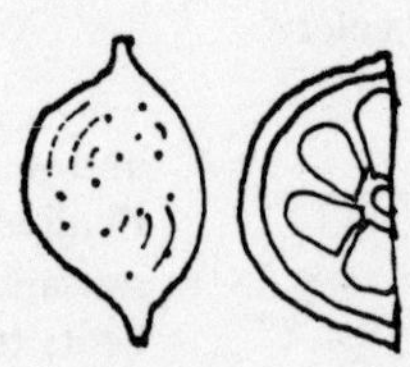

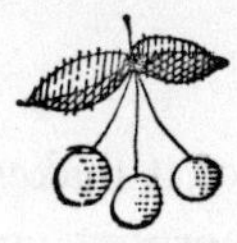

27

Formal Luncheon for Four—II

EGGS PRINCESSE DE CARAMAN-CHIMAY
FRENCH BREAD
TAORMINA SALAD
MRS. WALTER COWEN-KORN'S STRAWBERRY PIE

WINES
Inexpensive: California Riesling
Medium-priced: Wente Brothers New York State Riesling
Expensive: Kanzemer Altenberg, Riesling Vintage, Estate-bottled Priesterseminar

The recipe for the baked eggs—no less than its resounding title—tells you this is a dish fit for a princess. Follow through to the ingredients of the salad and you find peasant fare. All of which leads up to our feeling that the caste system doesn't exist in the kitchen; that the unexpected combination of the regal and the rustic adds spice to the meal.

Naturally, you don't just pick at random from your recipe files and invite any two dishes to share the honors. One must offset the other with complementary flavor or texture or color. And, in this menu, you will serve them as separate courses: first the eggs, delicate, rich, and golden; then the salad, highly seasoned, crisp, and colorful. To go with both, a crusty French loaf, as bakery fresh as you can manage. The dessert reverts again to elegance. It is obviously too large a pie for four people (it will serve eight to ten), but there's method in the seeming madness. If you are fortunate enough to hide it from after-school pantry prowlers, you will have dessert ready for dinner. No fear that you won't be able to face it twice in one day; the question is, will you be able to resist two *big* helpings?

There is almost no last-minute preparation. Two days ahead, remember to make the *Sachiacciate* mixture for the salad. We think you will agree, once you have tried it, that it should be made in double or triple quantities and stored for future use. (A jar of it makes a wonderful gift when you go visiting.) Any time during the morning, arrange the salad ingredients in the bowl as directed. Put in the dressing, then the olive mixture as support, so that the greens are kept free of the liquid and retain their crispness—a good point to remember with other salads—and put the bowl in the refrigerator.

You will want to see to the pie fairly early in the day to allow time for chilling. Don't forget that the pie shell must have time to cool after baking before it is filled. Fill and arrange the eggs in the baking dish beforehand. Prepare the Mornay sauce ahead, too. Reheat the sauce, or keep it hot over simmering water, and pour it over the eggs just before they go under the broiler.

If you have individual baking dishes, substitute them for the one large dish; they keep food beautifully hot. There are some charming white ones available, made with a cover in the shape of a chicken sitting on a nest. In both individual and large sizes they are reasonably priced and useful for serving baked eggs or any recipe involving diced chicken in a sauce. We see in our mind's eye a solid-red cloth on the table, milk-glass or plain white china, and milk-glass goblets; in the center a small, stylized pyramid of red carnations alternating with red-flecked white ones; and the chickens nesting cozily at each place as you call your guests in to lunch.

Eggs Princesse de Caraman-Chimay

2 tablespoons butter
¼ pound chopped mushrooms or chopped mushroom stems
1 tablespoon minced onion
½ clove garlic
1 tablespoon chopped parsley
1 teaspoon powdered tarragon
4 hard-cooked eggs
2 tablespoons bottled Escoffier Sauce Robert
2 cups Sauce Mornay (see Index)
½ cup bread crumbs
½ cup grated Parmesan

Sauté together lightly in 2 tablespoons butter ¼ pound chopped mushrooms, or chopped mushroom stems, and 1 tablespoon minced onion. When mushrooms are semisoft, add ½ clove garlic, pressed, 1 tablespoon finely chopped parsley, and 1 teaspoon powdered tarragon. Remove from heat. Cut 4 hard-cooked eggs in halves lengthwise. Remove yolks and mash with 2 tablespoons bottled Escoffier Sauce Robert. Combine sautéed mushrooms and yolks, and with a fork pile into egg whites. Place in shallow buttered baking dish, cover with 2 cups hot *Sauce Mornay*, and sprinkle with ½ cup each bread crumbs and grated Parmesan. Brown 5 inches from preheated broiler for 4 minutes.

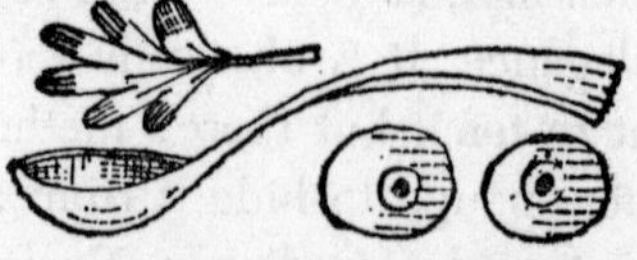

Taormina Salad

Two days ahead, prepare Olives *Sachiacciate:* Drain a 7- or 8½-ounce can small green olives. Pound olives

until broken up, with the pits showing, but do not remove the pits. Add 1 small celery heart, sliced finely, leaves and all, ¼ cup capers, 1 clove garlic, pressed, 1 minced shallot, ½ cup Italian olive oil, ½ teaspoon ground pepper, 1 small chili pepper, sliced, ½ teaspoon crushed fennel seed, and 1 tablespoon white Chianti or 1 tablespoon lemon juice. Store this mixture in covered glass jar in refrigerator for 48 hours. (It may be used in many other Italian-style salads and keeps indefinitely.)

In the bottom of a wooden bowl pour ¼ cup Italian Dressing and add ½ cup Olives *Sachiacciate*. On top of this place leaves of 1 small head Boston lettuce; 4 leaves romaine, shredded; ¼ seeded green pepper, cut into thin strips; ½ heart chicory, shredded finely; if available, 1 heart fennel, threads removed, sliced finely; and 8 cherry or small plum tomatoes, whole. Be sure all greens are well dried after washing. Toss just before eating.

1 7- or 8½-ounce can small green olives
1 small celery heart
¼ cup capers
1 clove garlic
1 shallot
½ cup Italian olive oil
½ teaspoon ground pepper
1 small chili pepper
½ teaspoon crushed fennel seed
1 tablespoon white Chianti or 1 tablespoon lemon juice

¼ cup Italian Dressing (*see Index*)
1 small head Boston lettuce
4 leaves romaine
¼ green pepper
½ heart chicory
1 heart fennel
8 cherry or small plum tomatoes

Mrs. Walter Cowen-Korn's Strawberry Pie

Melt ½ pound marshmallows in a double boiler with 3 tablespoons sour cream (taken from a ½ pint jar). Beat 3 egg whites stiff. Add marshmallows and rest of sour cream to beaten whites. Spread filling over a 10-inch cooled Baked Pie Shell, below. Refrigerate about an hour.

Cover filling with 1 quart hulled fresh strawberries, neatly arranged, stem ends down. Press 1 glass currant jelly through a very fine strainer to thin it, then spoon a light layer over the berries. Edge pie with finely grated pistachio nuts. Serves eight.

½ pound marshmallows
½ pint sour cream
3 egg whites
10-inch Baked Pie Shell
1 quart strawberries
1 glass currant jelly
Pistachio nuts

Baked Pie Shell

Into a chilled mixing bowl sift together 1 cup flour and ½ teaspoon salt. With a pastry blender or two knives cut 5½ tablespoons chilled sweet butter or other shortening into flour until butter is the size of peas. Moisten with 2 tablespoons ice water and toss with a fork until mixture holds together, but no more; minimum handling is important. If more water is needed, add half a teaspoon at a time. Chill dough 10 minutes, then place between sheets of waxed paper and roll out into a circle 11 inches in diameter. Ease into pie plate, prick well with a fork, crimp edges, and chill again. Preheat oven to 450°. Cover bottom of shell with raw rice or dried beans, and bake for 15 minutes, or until golden brown.

1 cup flour
½ teaspoon salt
5½ tablespoons sweet butter or other shortening
2 tablespoons ice water
Rice or dried beans

28

Informal Winter Luncheon for Four—I

Almadén Solera Cocktail Sherry

Chicken and Okra Gumbo

Spoon Bread

Citrus-Fruit Salad with Honey Dressing

Rum Pecan Cookies

Coffee

This luncheon from south of the Mason and Dixon line includes regional specialties a Southern belle might serve when she's dispensing that famous hospitality. Yankees and other outlanders will recognize the names, but if you're not quite sure what they mean in actual practice, a gumbo is a soup that is more of a stew, and spoon bread is really a soufflé.

It's best to start the cooking with the dessert and work backwards. Mix the cooky dough and, while it chills, peel and slice the fruit and make the the Honey Dressing. Then bake the cookies, and on to the Gumbo, the rice, and the Spoon Bread. Prepare the Spoon Bread to the point where you incorporate the egg whites, but don't beat or fold them in until thirty five minutes before lunch is served. Or, you can do most of the preparation the day before: Cook the gumbo, bake the cookies, and prepare the fruit and its dressing. That leaves only the rice and the Spoon Bread for the morning, and the gumbo to be reheated for half an hour over very low heat on an asbestos mat.

Cook and serve the chicken in a stove-to-table enameled iron pot or casserole, or serve it from a tureen. Put a spoonful of rice (you don't need much) in each soup plate and ladle the chicken and soup over it. Have additional small plates for the Spoon Bread.

Each of us has a special spoon-bread recipe. They're practically identical, and both came from Southern butlers. We tossed a coin to decide which to use. Sam's won—but if you want to make David's Spoon Bread, add a tablespoon of grated cheddar to the batter. Unorthodox, but very good.

Chicken and Okra Gumbo

In Dutch oven, sauté a whole 2½- to 3-pound chicken in 2 tablespoons of butter and 2 tablespoons of salad oil until golden. With poultry shears, cut in approximately 2-inch pieces, removing large bones, and reserve. Stir 2 tablespoons butter and 2 tablespoons flour into juices in Dutch oven, and add 2 large sliced onions and 1 pound wiped and sliced okra. Stir often to prevent burning and cook until juice from okra ceases to rope; then add pieces of chicken, 2 tablespoons chopped parsley, ½ bay leaf, pepper and salt, and 5 cups boiling water, and simmer until chicken is tender, about 35 minutes. Just before serving, sprinkle with 1 tablespoon filé powder.* Do not boil again, and serve at once with Steamed Rice.

2½- to 3-pound chicken
4 tablespoons butter, in all
2 tablespoons salad oil
2 tablespoons flour
2 large onions
1 pound okra
2 tablespoons chopped parsley
½ bay leaf
Salt, pepper
5 cups boiling water
1 tablespoon filé powder *
Steamed Rice (see Index)

Spoon Bread

Preheat oven to 350°. Gradually stir ½ cup white water-ground corn meal into 2 cups boiling water. Reduce heat and continue stirring until mixture is smooth. Add 3 tablespoons melted butter and 1 scant teaspoon salt, and pour in slowly 1¼ cups scalded milk. Remove pan from heat. Beat 3 egg yolks until light and fluffy, stir into corn-meal mixture, and let cool. Beat 4 egg whites until stiff and fold into batter. Bake in a buttered baking dish for 30 minutes, until brown and well puffed. Serve with a spoon.

½ cup white water-ground corn meal
2 cups boiling water
3 tablespoons melted butter
1 teaspoon salt
1¼ cups scalded milk
3 egg yolks
4 egg whites

Citrus-Fruit Salad with Honey Dressing

Peel 1 seedless grapefruit and 4 seedless oranges and carefully remove bitter white skin. Slice fruit, discard end slices, and quarter the grapefruit slices. Slice thinly 6 kumquats, fresh or preserved. Chill thoroughly. Toss in a glass bowl with Honey Dressing: Combine ⅔ cup olive oil, ¼ cup lemon juice, ¼ cup orange-blossom honey, and ¼ teaspoon salt.

* Filé powder is a mixture of herbs with sassafras leaves as a base; it is a thickening and may be bought at herb and specialty shops.

1 seedless grapefruit
4 seedless oranges
6 kumquats

⅔ cup olive oil
¼ cup lemon juice
¼ cup orange blossom honey
¼ teaspoon salt

Rum Pecan Cookies

Preheat oven to 350°. Into a bowl sift together 2 cups flour and ½ teaspoon double-action baking powder. Add 1 cup brown sugar, well-packed, ¼ cup ground pecans, ¼ pound softened butter, 1 egg, beaten, and ½ cup dark rum. Work with fingers until paste feels like clay. Roll into a sausage and chill in freezer or ice compartment for 15 minutes. Then cut in slices ¼ inch thick, and bake on a greased baking sheet, 2 inches apart, for 10 to 12 minutes. Store in an air-tight container.

2 cups flour
½ teaspoon double-action baking powder
1 cup brown sugar
¼ cup ground pecans
¼ pound butter
1 egg
½ cup dark rum

29

Informal Winter Luncheon for Four—II

Louis Martini Pale Dry Sherry
MANHATTAN CLAM CHOWDER
SEA TOAST CRACKERS, OR NEW ENGLAND PILOT CRACKERS
TOSSED SALAD WITH ROQUEFORT DRESSING
RICHMOND BUTTER COOKIES
COFFEE

One of us spent a summer on Martha's Vineyard, in the little fishing village of Menemsha. Fish was on the menu at least four times a week—fish bought late in the afternoon when the day's catch was brought in, or lobster straight from the pot, or crabs, the haul of a family crabbing party. It was bound to happen—just once; the pail slipped while the crabs were en route to their doom in a cauldron of boiling water. For a hilarious and frightful five minutes, the kitchen floor was alive with skeetering claws.

In this piscatorial paradise, this stronghold of food from the sea, you do as the Romans—you make New England clam chowder and contemplate no deviations, or you're likely to overhear a comment about summer people and why it's so *long* until Labor Day. After Labor Day, back in the suburbs of New York, you're in the other chowder camp. Which is better? We really can't take sides—we like them both.

If you don't have a native prejudice against it, we believe you'll enjoy our version of Manhattan clam chowder. An hour and a quarter, early in the morning, or before lunch, should give you time to do everything except the cookies. If you haven't baked them ahead, add another half hour to the morning's stint. Prepare the vegetables, and start simmering the soup. If you're going to reheat it just before lunch, don't add the clams until then, or they will be tough. While the soup is on the stove, attend to the salad and its dressing, and butter the crackers. When you add the clams and heat the chowder, put the crackers in a 400° oven for five or six minutes, and toss the salad.

A final bit of advice—if your friends hail from any point between Rhode Island and Maine, just pick another menu.

Manhattan Clam Chowder

Dice 1/4 pound salt pork (jowl butt is best). Fry it lightly in a deep kettle. Reduce heat, and add 1 large onion, minced, 2 leeks, halved lengthwise and finely sliced, 2 stalks celery, finely sliced, 1/2 small green pepper, minced, 3 medium potatoes, cubed, 1/2 bay leaf, and 1/2 teaspoon thyme. Dip 3 tomatoes in boiling water, then quickly in cold water, peel, seed and chop, then add to kettle with 4 cups water. Drain liquor from 1 quart shucked clams, add it to the pot, and season lightly with salt and pepper. Cover kettle, bring to a boil over high heat, then reduce heat and simmer for 30 minutes.

Meanwhile, in a wooden bowl, mince the raw clams. Add to kettle and poach over medium heat for 4 minutes. Stir in 1/2 tablespoon chopped chives and 1/2 tablespoon chopped parsley. Serve at once with toasted and buttered Sea Toast crackers, or New England pilot crackers.

1/4 pound salt pork
1 large onion
2 leeks
2 stalks celery
1/2 small green pepper
3 medium potatoes
1/2 bay leaf
1/2 teaspoon thyme
3 tomatoes
4 cups water
Salt, pepper
1 quart shucked clams
1/2 tablespoon chopped chives
1/2 tablespoon chopped parsley

Tossed Salad with Roquefort Dressing

Combine equal amounts of romaine, Boston lettuce, chicory, and water cress, and add enough diced celery

and julienne beets to make good contrast of color and texture. Toss with Roquefort Dressing: To 6 tablespoons salad oil add 2 tablespoons Garlic Vinegar. Season with coarse salt and freshly ground pepper. Stir in ½ cup finely crumbled Roquefort cheese and ½ teaspoon monosodium glutamate.

Romaine
Boston lettuce
Chicory
Watercress
Diced celery
Julienne beets

6 tablespoons salad oil
2 tablespoons Garlic Vinegar (see Index)
Coarse salt
Pepper
½ cup crumbled Roquefort
½ teaspoon monosodium glutamate

Richmond Butter Cookies

Preheat oven to 325°. Sift together onto waxed paper 1 cup flour, ½ teaspoon baking soda, and ¼ teaspoon salt. In large bowl of electric mixer, cream together ¼ pound softened butter and ½ cup honey. Gradually add ½ cup granulated sugar and beat 2 minutes. Add flour mixture and beat 1 more minute. Drop by teaspoonfuls onto a greased baking sheet, and bake 15 to 20 minutes. Store in an airtight container. Makes about 3½ dozen cookies.

1 cup flour
½ teaspoon baking soda
¼ teaspoon salt
¼ pound butter
½ cup honey
½ cup granulated sugar

30

Informal Winter Luncheon for Four—III

Dry Sack Sherry

Scotch Broth

Salade Belle Aurore with French Dressing

Alfoldi Squares*

Coffee

Some day we may actually get around to testing a soup according to the old-fashioned directive to cook until it's so thick a spoon will stand up in it. That's almost the consistency a Scotch Broth should have, though perhaps not quite—our spoon might possibly topple over after a second and

* see Index

a half. In any event, you get the point—this is not a weak, anemic affair.

If you don't have the left-over leg of lamb, forget the whole thing and turn to the luncheon menus with Chicken and Okra Chowder or Manhattan Clam Chowder (see Index). If you do have the meat, and if it's a cold, blustery day, don't turn the page, you're in the right place. Since half the purpose of a roast is to stretch it over more than one meal, it doesn't take too much forethought to remember to get the vegetables for the broth when you buy the meat; you'll be prepared for a spur-of-the-moment luncheon (or supper) anytime during the following week. You only need three hours warning, but get out the kettle and start the soup right away if you're just now drinking morning coffee and want this ready for lunch.

The fresh, crisp texture of the salad is a good complement to the soup. Be sure to keep it crisp; don't mix it with the dressing until you serve it. And if this is a last-minute affair you really don't have time to bake Alfoldi Squares; they should be done the day before. Viennese Crescents or Scotch Shortbread (see Index) are much quicker.

Scotch Broth

Place the bone and 2 cups cubed left-over meat from a leg of lamb in a soup kettle, cover with 2 quarts water, and bring to a rolling boil. Season with salt and pepper, and add ½ cup barley, ½ bay leaf, ¼ teaspoon dried thyme, and 2 cloves. Reduce heat and simmer for 2½ hours. Then add 1 package frozen lima beans, 1 package frozen Brussels sprouts, 2 cups sliced carrots, 1 cup sliced celery, 4 small whole onions, and 4 sliced leeks. Turn up heat and boil vegetables for ½ hour. Remove large pieces of bone, add 1 tablespoon chopped parsley, and serve in heated plates.

Bone from leg of lamb
2 cups cubed cooked lamb
2 quarts water
Salt, pepper
½ cup barley
½ bay leaf
¼ teaspoon dried thyme
2 cloves
1 package frozen lima beans
1 package frozen Brussels sprouts
2 cups sliced carrots
1 cup sliced celery
4 small onions
4 leeks
1 tablespoon chopped parsley

Salade Belle Aurore

Core and cube 2 McIntosh apples; do not peel. Wash, drain, and dry 1 medium head Boston lettuce. Combine, add 1 cup coarsely chopped walnut meats, and toss with 6 tablespoons Basic French Dressing. Use walnut oil in dressing if available.

2 McIntosh apples
1 medium head Boston lettuce
1 cup walnut meats
6 tablespoons Basic French Dressing (see Index)
Walnut oil (optional)

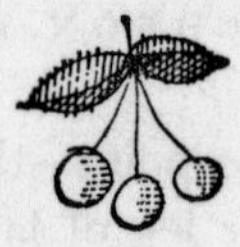

31

Informal Winter Luncheon for Four—IV

Coquilles Gratinées
Endive and Field Salad with Mustard Mayonnaise
Spritz Cookies
Coffee

WINE
Gold Seal Charles Fournier Nature, en carafe

We know of a sound investment for about three dollars. Buy a dozen scallop shells at a hardware store or gift shop and use them for *Coquilles Gratinées* or any baked seafood, and for seafood cocktails, such as Shrimp in the Pink (see Index). They're just as practical as they are decorative.

For this very simple luncheon, get everything ready in the morning for the *Coquilles,* paying special attention to the cooking of the shrimp (see Index), but don't add the sauce and fill the shells until just before you expect the doorbell to ring. (The seafood gives off water and thins the sauce.) Wash and drain the endive and the field salad; and, when we say wash the field salad, we do mean *thoroughly.* It must grow in very sandy, gritty fields, for if it weren't so delicately flavored, the job would hardly be worth it; nonetheless, it remains one of our favorite greens.

We purposely chose Spritz Cookies to serve with coffee because they can be made ahead. They keep a good while in a cooky jar. Just how long, we can't exactly say—our families have never given us a chance to test.

Almost every little restaurant in France serves both a red and a white wine *en carafe.* These are pleasant *vins ordinaires* of no great consequence, particularly not to your purse. Restaurateurs buy them in large casks, and your dealer will gladly advise you on a choice of comparable wines in standard-size bottles or the larger gallon or half gallon. A simple decanter or *carafe* is an attractive way to serve a *vin ordinaire,* and it's also an invitation to your guests to help themselves. You needn't be ashamed to serve a small wine if it has an agreeable bouquet. Not every menu should have a great wine. Your taste buds need a rest and a change—even caviar and truffles would not wear well if you had them every day.

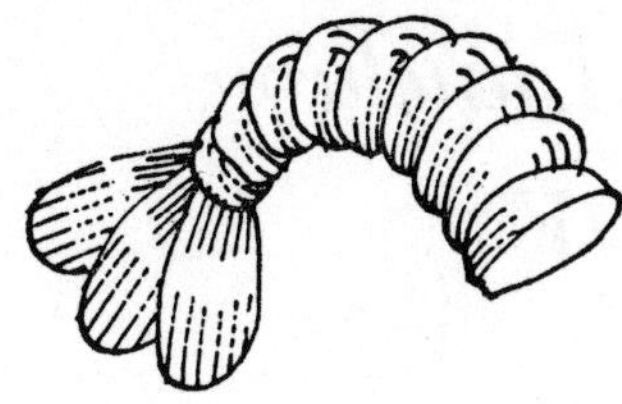

Coquilles Gratinées

Cook 1 cup *pasta* shells in boiling salted water with 1 tablespoon salad oil for 18 minutes; drain. Meanwhile, prepare 1 recipe Gratin Sauce, below.

Preheat oven to 400°. Slice ¼ pound mushrooms and sauté in 1 tablespoon butter over medium heat. Reduce heat, season with pepper, salt, and 1 teaspoon lemon juice, and simmer 4 minutes longer, until mushrooms are tender. Chop ½ pound shelled, deveined, cooked shrimp, and add ½ pound lobster meat, cut in pieces. Mix mushrooms and their juice, *pasta* shells, and seafood with Gratin Sauce, and heap into large individual *coquilles* or ramekins. Melt 2 tablespoons butter over medium heat. Stir in ½ cup toasted bread crumbs, and sprinkle mixture lightly over *coquilles.* Bake 15 minutes.

1 cup pasta shells
1 tablespoon salad oil
1 recipe Gratin Sauce
¼ pound mushrooms
1 tablespoon butter
Salt, pepper
1 teaspoon lemon juice
½ pound cooked shrimp
½ pound cooked lobster meat
2 tablespoons butter
½ cup toasted bread crumbs

Gratin Sauce

Bring 1 cup Béchamel Sauce made with fish-stock or consommé base just to boiling point. Remove from heat, and stir in ½ cup freshly grated imported Swiss cheese and 2 tablespoons dry white wine.

Use over fish, vegetables, macaroni, poultry, or poached eggs in recipes which require glazing in the oven.

1 cup Béchamel Sauce (*see Index*)
½ cup grated imported Swiss cheese
2 tablespoons dry white wine

Endive and Field Salad

Trim roots and yellow leaves from ¼ pound field salad (often called Burnett or corn salad); wash, drain, and dry well. Wash and pare 4 heads endive, and remove hard cores. Halve endive lengthwise, then cut in chunks 1 inch long. Toss greens together with ½ cup Mustard Mayonnaise.

¼ pound field salad
4 heads endive
½ cup Mustard Mayonnaise (*see Index*)

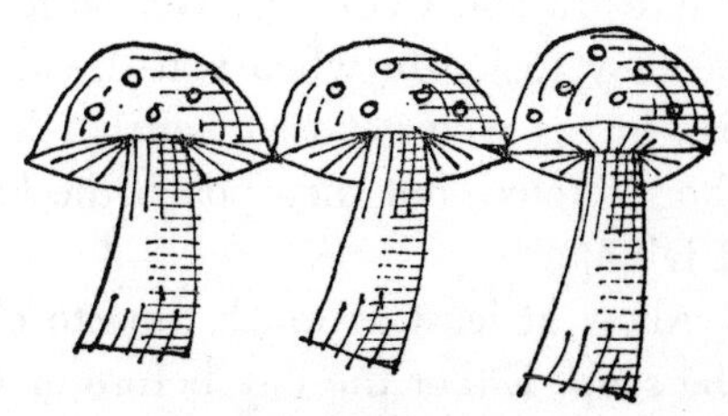

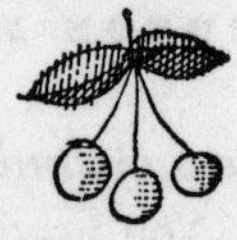

32

Informal Winter Luncheon for Four—V

BOUILLABAISSE
TOSSED GREEN SALAD WITH ITALIAN DRESSING
PORT DU SALUT—FROMAGE D'OKA
FRENCH BREAD, OR TOASTED EUPHRATES BREAD
COFFEE

WINE

Rosé Château Ste. Rosaline

There are certain dishes that can make your reputation as a cook. True, some of them require advanced standing as a *cuisinière*. You needn't be a chef but you do need practice to make perfect puff paste or *quenelles*. But other recipes that will impress the public require little more than patience. What we're leading up to is that *Bouillabaisse* is just such a dish.

The list of ingredients may look formidable—and it is, rather. But, between the fish market and the frozen food counter at the supermarket, you can readily gather together what you need unless you live in a part of the country where people simply don't take any interest in fish anyway. Nowadays this has become fairly rare. However, if you can't find the fish we specify, use more cod or substitute halibut. (The only one we've ever had difficulty with in the East is snapper, so, when we do see a good piece, we buy extra and freeze it.) Get large fish bones to make the stock, so they'll be easy to locate when you discard them. For landlubbers and would-be fish lovers who get that worried look unless fish is boneless, order everything filleted, but then poach the fish very gently in the *Bouillabaisse,* lest it fall apart.

Allow at least as much time to chop and cut the ingredients as to cook the soup. Either the day before or during the morning, prepare the *Bouil-*

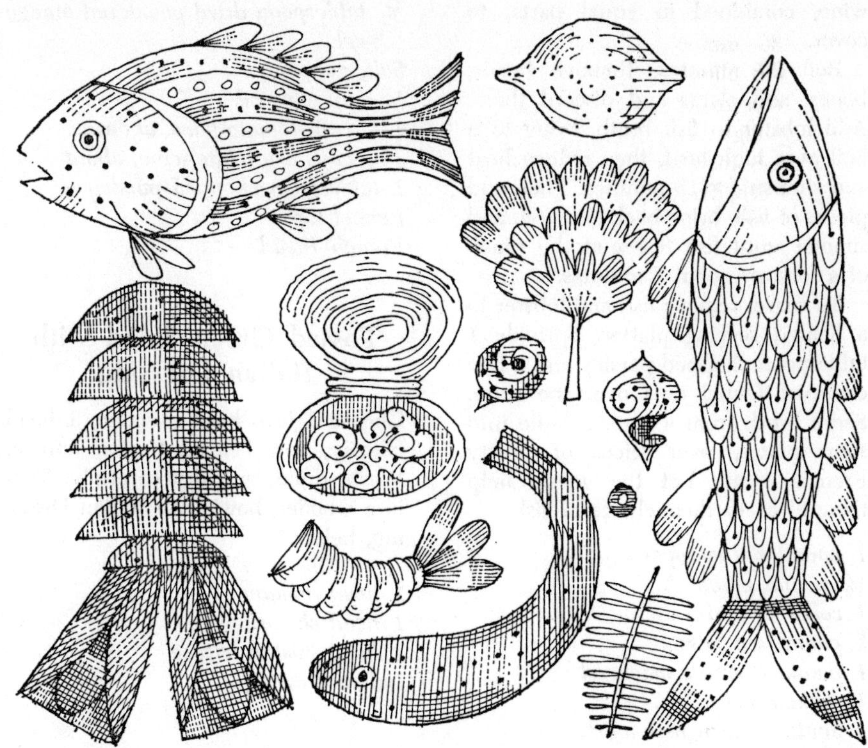

labaisse to the point where you add the lobster; don't finish it until your friends arrive. Several hours before lunch, wash the lettuce and put it in a salad bowl in the icebox, and take the cheeses out to warm to room temperature.

There's no necessity to limit this to a luncheon menu, nor to four people. Just remember to allow extra preparation time for large quantities. Give the men a break—and yourself too—by inviting them to share the informality and marvelous aromas of a *Bouillabaisse* dinner. The men we know will always vote for a party that isn't best bib and tucker—and this one assuredly isn't—it's largely bib.

Bouillabaisse

Cut into slices 1 inch thick 1 pound red snapper, ½ pound perch, 1 collar of cod, 1 pound sea bass, 1 pound Spanish mackerel, ½ pound eel, and 2 South African rock-lobster tails, shell and all. Ask fish market to give you fish heads and fish bones. Buy also 12 clams, and scrub well.

Peel and chop 3 leeks, 2 medium onions, and 2 carrots, and place them in a large kettle. Press 3 cloves of garlic over vegetables, and add 1 teaspoon saffron, ½ bay leaf, ⅛ teaspoon thyme, ½ tablespoon dried powdered orange peel, salt and freshly ground pepper, fish heads, fish bones, and clams. Then add ½ cup olive oil and enough tomato juice and dry white wine, combined in equal parts, to cover.

Boil 20 minutes. Remove heads, bones, and clams and discard them. Add lobster to fish broth, bring to a boil over high heat, then reduce heat and simmer for 15 minutes. Then add pieces of fish, bring back to a boil, and simmer until fish flakes at the touch of a fork, or about 8 minutes.

To serve, remove fish and lobster to a heated serving platter. Sprinkle 1 tablespoon chopped parsley and a few chopped fennel tops over the soup. Serve broth from a tureen; ladle into soup plates, over slices of crusty French bread. Let the guests help themselves to their choice of fish.

1 pound red snapper
½ pound perch
1 collar of cod
1 pound sea bass
1 pound Spanish mackerel
½ pound eel
2 South African rock-lobster tails
Fish heads and bones
12 clams
3 leeks
2 medium onions
2 carrots
3 cloves garlic
1 teaspoon saffron
½ bay leaf
⅛ teaspoon thyme
½ tablespoon dried powdered orange peel
Salt, pepper
½ cup olive oil
1½ cups tomato juice, about
1½ cups dry white wine, about
1 tablespoon chopped parsley
Fennel tops
French bread

Tossed Green Salad with Italian Dressing

Choose 1 firm head romaine, 1 head chicory, and 1 head Boston lettuce. Wash, drain, and dry carefully. Toss in a wooden bowl with Italian Dressing, below.

1 head romaine
1 head chicory
1 head Boston lettuce
Italian dressing

Italian Dressing

Combine:
6 tablespoons olive oil
2 tablespoons lemon juice
1 tablespoon Italian tomato paste
½ teaspoon coarse salt
¼ teaspoon freshly ground pepper
1 small clove garlic, pressed

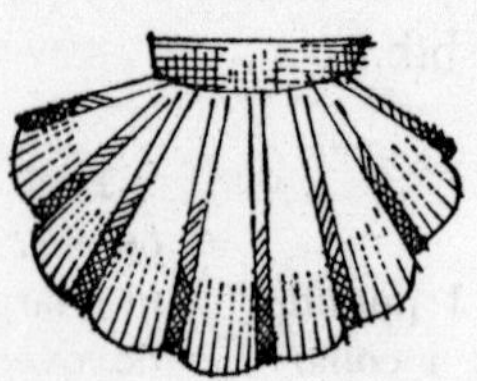

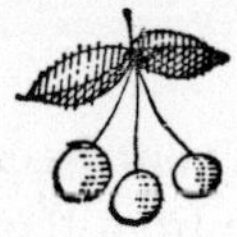

33

Low-Calorie Luncheon for Six

Consommé Bordelaise
Tossed Lobster Salad
Sour-Cream Dressing
Salzburger Nockerl

WINES

Inexpensive: Widmer's Lake Niagara
Medium-priced: Muscadet
Expensive: Pouilly Blanc Fumé, Estate-bottled, Lucien Marchand

Memories of ladies' luncheons as recent as three decades ago recall feasts of banquet proportions. The ladies staggered home to face their evening meal with hardly enough appetite for a cup of tea. Today, eating contests are no longer the rule except at country fairs. It is not fashionable to serve a luncheon consisting of a whole fillet of beef, elaborate platters of vegetables bathed in hollandaise sauce, and a macaroon bisque veiled in spun sugar. It is neither fashionable, wise, nor wanted.

To the average woman, whether guest or hostess, lighter lunches are a necessity if she expects to avoid the Stylish Stouts. Generally, she hoards the bulk of her day's calories for the evening meal with her family. Yet there are occasions when you do want to make a bit of a midday show. You can manage this and still be merciful to the waistlines of all concerned.

Get your salad ingredients ready first, so the greens will be chilled and crisp when you toss them with the lobster for serving. Mix your dressing now, too. The Austrian *Salzburger Nockerl* may be prepared an hour before serving. Stow it, unbaked, in your freezer and put it in the oven when you start to clear the main course from the table. A spectacular soufflé-like dish, *Salzburger Nockerl* is a specialty of Salzburg which appears on all the restaurant menus and is made in every home. Everyone has a personal version; as a native put it, "There are about 30,000 women in Salzburg, so there must be 30,000 recipes for *Salzburger Nockerl.*" If you don't have a freezer, or if you want to make it just before serving, have the eggs separated in two bowls beforehand, the sugar and flour added to the yolks, and the baking dishes buttered. After the lobster salad, while your friends enjoy a cigarette and tomorrow's gossip, you can have it ready to pop into the oven in two shakes.

Salzburger Nockerl is also a fine main course for lunch, accompanied by fruit and muffins, and equally good served with midmorning coffee. (When you serve it as a main dish allow two eggs for each portion.) Pass extra powdered Vanilla Sugar (see Index) at the table, in a pretty sugar shaker if you have one. This is customary, since some people want to add more sweetening as they get beneath the sugared surface.

A few minutes before servingtime, heat your bouillon cups by filling them with boiling water. Meanwhile, assemble the salad. When the cups are thoroughly heated, spill off the water, pour in wine and soup, and quickly to table.

Consommé Bordelaise

Preheat 6 consommé cups. Combine:

2 cans jellied consommé madrilène
1 teaspoon lemon juice
2 drops Tabasco
½ teaspoon Worcestershire

Heat to boiling point. Remove from heat and add:

¾ cup claret

Fill heated cups with consommé, and serve at once.

Tossed Lobster Salad

Score skins of 2 chilled, unpeeled cucumbers with a fork. Slice cucumbers and 8 radishes very thin, and combine. Sprinkle with 1 teaspoon salt and chill in refrigerator for an hour, then press out all liquid. Wash and drain very thoroughly 1 large or 2 small heads Boston lettuce. Tear into bite-size pieces and chill. In a salad bowl, combine lettuce, cucumber and radish slices, 1 cup cooked and chilled french-cut string beans, and 1 pound cooked chilled lobster meat, cut in bite-size pieces. Pour ½ cup Sour-Cream Dressing over all, toss lightly, and sprinkle with 1 tablespoon minced chives.

1 large or 2 small heads Boston lettuce
2 cucumbers
6–8 radishes
1 teaspoon salt
1 cup cooked, french-cut string beans
1 pound cooked lobster meat
1 tablespoon minced chives
Sour-Cream Dressing

Sour-Cream Dressing

Blend together:

2 tablespoons sour cream
2 tablespoons catsup

¼ cup skimmed milk
½ teaspoon lemon juice
1 teaspoon salt
⅛ teaspoon white pepper

Salzburger Nockerl

Preheat oven to 450° at least 20 minutes before servingtime. Beat 6 egg whites very stiff. Beat 6 yolks with 2 tablespoons granulated sugar and 1 tablespoon flour. Pour yolk mixture over whites and fold in lightly. Butter 6 individual baking dishes or one very large shallow ovenproof dish. Spoon batter into dishes, shaping one mound in each small dish with a spatula, or 6 mounds in the large dish. Bake individual *Nockerl* 4 minutes, or the large one 5 minutes. Dust very generously with confectioners' sugar.

6 eggs, separated
2 tablespoons granulated sugar
1 tablespoon flour
Butter
Confectioners' sugar

34

Danish Sandwich Luncheon for Six

Smoked Salmon with Mushrooms
Portuguese Sardines with Anchovies and Oysters
Corned Brisket of Beef with Horseradish
Potato Salad with Herring Tidbits and Beet Salad
Beef Tartar with Smoked Oysters and Caviar
Bombay Toast
Vera's Apples with Vanilla Sauce
Mumma

Many things are the same the whole world over, but a sandwich is not one of them. Triple deckers, Dagwoods, and plain old ham-on-rye's bear not the least resemblance to Danish sandwiches—those 3D, out-size canapés that are virtually knife-and-fork meals on thin slices of bread. Moreover, bread is only incidental to the net result; a flimsy foundation for an imposing structure. The ingredients are arranged in sections or layers on a well-buttered slice of white or dark bread—and, we do mean arranged. Many of the productions you see in Copenhagen look as though they must require a blueprint as well as a recipe.

These sandwiches are neither made nor eaten in a hurry, though some, like the corned beef, take much less time to make than others—the tartar steak, for instance, which is a pretty fair test of patience. Should you wonder if the game is worth the candle—emphatically, yes, they're as beautiful to eat as to behold.

There are two ways to plan this lunch: Either make all six sandwiches, put them on a platter, and let each person make a choice (or draw lots to see who gets which); or, make three each of two kinds, or two each of three, or all six the same. Preparing all six different kinds involves a good deal more work (with only one, it's assembly-line production), but it's more fun to make the complete variety, and we trust that everyone will make a selection amicably. If you have healthy male appetites to cope with, count on an extra sandwich for each man.

Preparation for this luncheon includes considerable marketing if you decide to make all six sandwiches. You'll have quite a few leftovers, which needn't cause any real concern: Toss extra beets with greens in a salad for dinner that evening or the following day; if you have guests again during the next few days, use the herring, caviar, oysters, anchovies, and sardines for Assorted Canapés (see Index); or, treat just your husband and yourself to these special tidbits with cocktails; there's nothing wrong, either, with a Simple Omelette (see Index), filled with caviar or oysters and topped with sour cream.

Allow an hour to prepare the full assortment of sandwiches, and don't make them too far ahead. Hard-boil a few eggs, cook the macaroni and the potatoes, and marinate the potatoes and beets for the sandwiches early in the morning, while the apples are in the oven. (The recipe makes eight portions of apples, just in case.) Cook the Vanilla Sauce and chill it, then fold the cream into it after you've finished the sandwiches.

It takes two minutes to mix the *Mumma,* so wait till you're ready to serve it. Swedish friends who gave us this recipe (there are many versions of *Mumma*) couldn't enlighten us as to the meaning of the name.

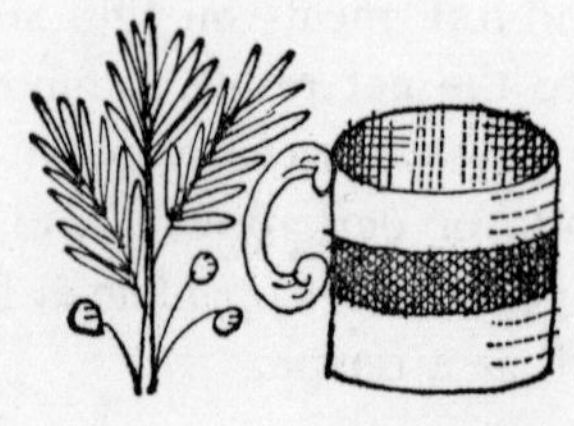

Danish Knife-and-Fork Sandwiches

Smoked Salmon with Mushrooms

Butter heavily a slice of dark pumpernickel, and spread sliced smoked salmon on it generously. Diagonally across, place 3 medium-size sautéed mushroom caps. Under each mushroom slide a small frill of chicory leaf or parsley.

Dark pumpernickel bread
Smoked salmon
Medium mushroom caps
Chicory leaves
or parsley

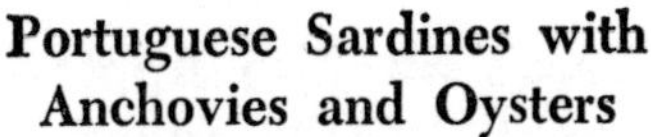

Portuguese Sardines with Anchovies and Oysters

Butter heavily a thin slice of firm white bread, and on it spread leaves from hearts of Boston lettuce. Place 2 large Portuguese sardines side by side diagonally in center. On one side, place 3 Italian rolled anchovies with pimiento centers; on other side, 3 smoked oysters. Sieve hard-cooked egg yolk over oysters and anchovies.

White bread
Hearts of Boston lettuce
Portuguese sardines
Italian rolled anchovies with pimiento centers
Smoked oysters
Hard-cooked egg yolk

Corned Brisket of Beef with Horseradish

Boil, then slice thinly 2 small potatoes, and marinate in ½ cup Basic French Dressing to which has been

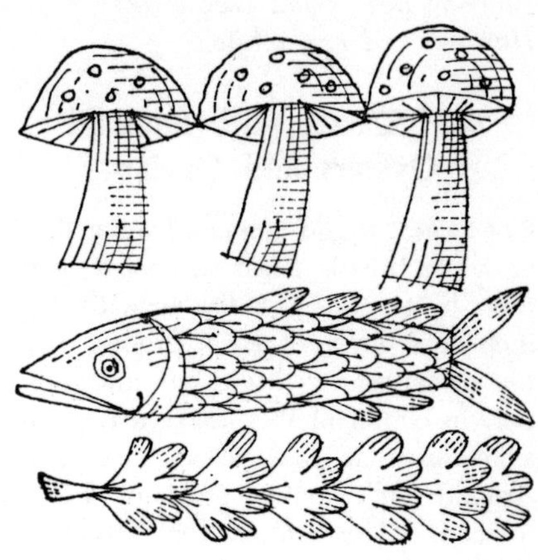

added 1 teaspoon chopped dill. Drain carefully on absorbent paper. Butter heavily a slice of rye bread and on it place lettuce leaves, a thin layer of marinated potatoes, and a generous slice of corned beef. Decorate with grated white and red horseradish.

2 small potatoes
½ cup Basic French Dressing (see Index)
1 teaspoon chopped dill
Rye bread
Lettuce leaves
Corned beef
White and red horseradish

Potato Salad with Herring Tidbits and Beet Salad

Butter heavily a thin slice of light pumpernickel. Cover with potato salad (see above). Over this, place herring tidbits in sour cream on one side and julienne Beet Salad on the other, making the dividing line diagonally across the sandwich. Sieve hard-cooked egg white over all.

Light pumpernickel
Potato salad
Herring tidbits in sour cream
Julienne Beet Salad (see Index)
Hard-cooked egg white

Beef Tartar with Smoked Oysters and Caviar

Cut largest round you can from a slice of white bread. Toast it, cool it, and then butter heavily. Cover with ½-inch-thick layer of twice-ground raw top sirloin seasoned with salt and pepper. In center of this, make a depression and in it place a raw egg yolk. Around yolk make circle of finely minced onion, around that circle of capers, then one of finely chopped parsley, then one of minced smoked oysters, and finish with border of black caviar. Over all, grind a little black pepper. To make another way, stir egg yolk and part of all ingredients into ground meat, season, and merely decorate with remainder of ingredients. This would, however, not be as authentic as first method.

White bread
Top sirloin
Salt, pepper
Egg yolk
Onion
Capers
Chopped parsley
Smoked oysters
Black caviar
Black pepper

Bombay Toast

Boil ½ cup elbow macaroni, drain, and cool. Mince 1 chicken giblet. Add ½ teaspoon curry powder to ½ cup Mayonnaise, and mix all ingredients together. Toast 1 slice white bread, cool, then butter heavily. Place above mixture on it, and top with a rolled slice of smoked salmon. Place a frill of chicory leaf under salmon, and sieve hard-cooked egg yolk over the macaroni.

½ cup elbow macaroni
1 chicken giblet
½ teaspoon curry powder
½ cup Mayonnaise (see Index)
White bread
Butter
Smoked salmon
Chicory leaf
Hard-cooked egg yolk

Vera's Swedish Apples with Vanilla Sauce

Make about 2½ cups Vanilla Sauce: In a small pot, blend 3 egg yolks, 4 tablespoons Vanilla Sugar, and 1 cup hot milk. Cook over very low heat, stirring constantly, until thickened. Set aside to cool thoroughly.

Preheat oven to 350°. Peel and core 8 medium-size firm baking apples, but do not bore all the way through the bottom. Mix ⅓ cup ground almonds and 4 tablespoons sugar with about ½ tablespoon water to make a paste. Put a portion of paste in cavity of each apple. Melt 2 tablespoons butter in a shallow pan, and crush enough vanilla cookies to make ½ cup crumbs; roll apples in butter, then in crumbs. Place in shallow baking pan and bake about 30 minutes, or until just tender.

Just before serving, whip ⅔ cup heavy cream and fold into cooled Vanilla Sauce. Serve apples in individual dishes, at room temperature, and serve Vanilla Sauce in a separate sauceboat.

3 egg yolks
4 tablespoons Vanilla Sugar (see Index)
1 cup hot milk
⅔ cup heavy cream
8 medium baking apples
⅓ cup ground almonds
4 tablespoons sugar
½ tablespoon water
2 tablespoons butter
½ cup vanilla-cooky crumbs

Mumma

Chill thoroughly and mix together in a large pitcher 2 bottles of Löwenbräu, 2 of Tuborg and 2 of Seven-Up. Stir in ½ cup Port.

2 bottles Löwenbräu beer
2 bottles Tuborg beer
2 bottles Seven-Up
½ cup Port

35

Formal Winter Luncheon for Eight

OYSTERS ON THE HALF SHELL
WHALER'S JAGASEE
BEET SALAD WITH GARLIC DRESSING *
BRANDIED APPLE PAN DOWDY
DEMITASSE

WINES

Inexpensive: Inglenook Traminer, Napa Valley
Medium-priced: Alsatian Riesling Hanhart

In the days of sailing ships, when it took weeks to cross the ocean, men brought strange souvenirs from distant ports of call to their womenfolk at home. In many a New England sea captain's house, oriental and European treasures still remain, oddly at home in their severe eighteenth-century settings. In the same fashion, sailors brought back tales of foreign dishes. Among the familiar recipes for chowders and pan dowdies in old handwritten family cook books, there appeared others that bore exotic names.

Jagasee, for instance, is a corruption of *jagacita,* the Portuguese fisherman's staple dish, and the recipe, as we have it, is undoubtedly a corrup-

* see Index

tion of the original, too. It comes from an old lady in New Bedford, Massachusetts, whose family for generations back were whalers and seafaring men.

This isn't a hard menu, but neither is it one that will give you time to twiddle your thumbs if you've only the morning to prepare it. We've used it as a dinner menu, too, and for twice as many people—but then you should pamper yourself and have someone to help serve and do the dishes. Prepare the Jagasee to the point where you add the liquid, and set it aside until forty minutes before you serve it; then, add the liquid, and let it simmer while you have a cocktail and the first course. If you have a waitress in, she'll check the liquid as it cooks away and, when it's finished, put it in a serving casserole to pass it at the table.

After you've started the Jagasee, bake the Apple Pan Dowdy; it will be just the right temperature by lunchtime. Then marinate the beets (you could do this the night before), and transfer them to a serving bowl when you're ready to sit down.

If you want to approach this formal luncheon, without help, in an informal manner, it's easy to handle if you revise the service. Cook and serve the Jagasee in an enameled iron casserole, and make a mental note to check the liquid yourself after twenty minutes. Put the covered casserole on a sideboard with the salad, dinner plates, and small salad bowls, for self-service. Set the oysters at each place before the guests sit down (this for either formal or informal service), and clear the oyster plates while they help themselves to the main course.

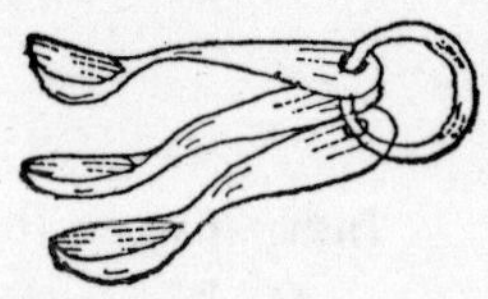

Whaler's Jagasee

In a heavy skillet, over medium heat, sauté 8 pork cutlets until golden in 1 tablespoon lard or bacon fat. Cut into bite-size pieces and reserve. Mince 2 large onions. In a Dutch oven, over medium heat, melt 3 tablespoons butter, and add the onions and 2 cups rice. Stir until onions are delicately browned and most grains of rice have golden edges. Add 2 cups fresh or frozen lima beans, the pork, and vegetable stock to cover generously. Reduce heat to low, and season with salt and pepper, ¼ bay leaf, 2 cloves, and 1 teaspoon nutmeg. Cover pot and simmer for 35 minutes. Remove cover once after 20 minutes, check liquid without stirring, and add more stock if necessary. Fluff rice with a fork when done, and transfer to heated serving casserole.

8 pork cutlets
1 tablespoon lard or bacon fat
2 large onions
3 tablespoons butter
2 cups rice
1–1½ quarts vegetable stock
2 cups fresh or frozen lima beans
Salt, pepper
¼ bay leaf
2 cloves
1 teaspoon nutmeg

Brandied Apple Pan Dowdy

Preheat oven to 300°. Peel and core 6 to 8 McIntosh apples and cut them into chunks. Mix together 1 cup light brown sugar, ½ teaspoon nutmeg, ½ teaspoon cinnamon, ½ teaspoon salt, and 1 tablespoon lemon juice, and sprinkle over apples. Warm ¼ cup Calvados or apple brandy, ignite, and pour over apples. When flames subside, place mixture in a buttered baking dish.

With tips of fingers work together ¾ cup unsifted flour, ½ cup Vanilla Sugar, and ⅜ pound softened butter until mixture holds together. Spread over apples, and bake 50 to 60 minutes. Serve warm, from the baking dish.

6 to 8 McIntosh apples
1 cup light brown sugar
½ teaspoon nutmeg
½ teaspoon cinnamon
½ teaspoon salt
1 tablespoon lemon juice
¼ cup Calvados or apple brandy
¾ cup flour
½ cup Vanilla Sugar (see Index)
⅜ pound butter

36

Formal Luncheon for Twelve

Hors-d'Oeuvre Variés

Veal Birds à la Parisienne

Royal Ice-Box Cake

WINES

Inexpensive: Paul Masson Gamay Beaujolais, Napa Valley

Medium-priced: Beaujolais

Expensive: Côte Fleurie, Vintage

A menu for francophiles, sure to awaken nostalgic yearnings if you have been to France. It may send you running to the nearest French restaurant for a meal—or, we hope, to the telephone to extend invitations for Sunday dinner *à la française*, at home.

You can use this menu for formal, seated service with a waitress, or arrange it all as a buffet. For seated service, put the dishes of *hors-d'oeuvre* on a rolling cart; your waitress will offer it to each guest in turn. If you don't own the oblong French porcelain dishes, get a dozen shallow fruit dishes in the 5-and-10. Should your dining room be too crowded for rolling-cart service, set the *hors-d'oeuvre* and a stack of plates on a sideboard as you would for buffet, and let people help themselves before sitting down.

The list of *hors-d'oeuvre* may seem long. But when you get right down to it, none of them is very rich, two thirds use the same basic dressing, and a good part of the preparation is done the previous day—all sensible virtues that French home cooks appreciate. So, on what will probably be Saturday, make the *Gourilos;* put the vegetables in their French-dressing marinades; cut the celery root and mix the Rémoulade Sauce; cook the beans and potatoes for the *Salade Niçoise;* and peel all the tomatoes and boil all the eggs you will need. Lastly, make the dessert.

The next morning there won't be too much left to do: Marinate the tomatoes and the celery root in their respective sauces; assemble the *Salade Niçoise;* and fill the Eggs Romanoff. Have plenty of French bread and sweet butter—both have a way of disappearing with *hors-d'oeuvre.*

Cook the rice (see Index) in the morning and keep it hot or reheat it later. Prepare the veal birds ahead, but don't thicken the sauce. Reheat them and finish the sauce just before you start eating; keep them hot, covered, over a pot of simmering water or in a very low oven.

For formal service, the size of your table will dictate the number of guests. For a buffet, the number is practically limitless. This is a very easy menu to double for a big party. A wonderful centerpiece for a buffet table is a huge basket filled with a variety of breads and rolls. There won't be any centerpiece left after the *hors-d'oeuvre* except the basket, but that suits Gallic practicality too.

With the main project attended to, the thrifty Frenchwoman would approve saving the juice of the canned mushrooms, asparagus, and beets for excellent quick soups. Mushroom Bisque: Add enough chicken stock (or water plus ½ teaspoon chicken concentrate or ½ chicken-bouillon cube) to the mushroom juice to make 1 cup, and heat to the boiling point. Melt 1 tablespoon butter, blend in ½ tablespoon flour, and add the hot liquid gradually, stirring constantly until thickened. Add 2 tablespoons heavy cream, heat but do not boil, pour into two bouillon cups, and dust with nutmeg.

Cream of Asparagus Soup: Follow the same directions with the asparagus juice, but dust the top of each portion with finely chopped parsley.

Quick Borscht: Add enough beef consommé (or water plus ½ teaspoon beef concentrate or ½ beef-bouillon cube) to the beet juice to make 1 cup. Add 1 teaspoon lemon juice and ¼ teaspoon sugar. Put ¼ cup sour cream in a bowl, and add beet juice gradually, beating with a whisk. Correct seasoning and chill. Before serving, boil 2 new potatoes, and peel. Pour cold soup into two small soup bowls, put one hot potato into each bowl, and dust with minced chives.

 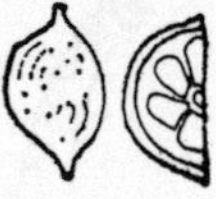  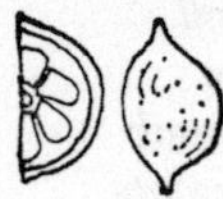 

Céleri Rémoulade

Prepare *Rémoulade* as follows: To ¾ cup Mayonnaise add ⅛ teaspoon white pepper, 1 tablespoon prepared mustard, and 1 tablespoon lemon juice.

Peel 2 celery knobs (celeriac) and cut into julienne strips or shred coarsely with a vegetable grater. Place in a colander, douse with 2 cups boiling water, and drain on absorbent paper. Marinate 2 hours in the *Rémoulade* before serving. Garnish with chopped parsley or paprika.

¾ cup Mayonnaise (see Index)
⅛ teaspoon white pepper
1 tablespoon prepared mustard
1 tablespoon lemon juice
2 celery knobs (celeriac)
2 cups boiling water
Chopped parsley or paprika

Eggs Romanoff

Halve 6 hard-cooked eggs crosswise and take a little slice from bottom of each half so they will stand up. Remove the yolks and mash them with 3 tablespoons soft butter, 1 teaspoon onion juice, and 3 tablespoons black caviar. Fill the egg-white cups with yolk mixture forced through pastry tube. Chill well before serving.

6 hard-cooked eggs
3 tablespoons butter
1 teaspoon onion juice
3 tablespoons black caviar

Gourilos à la Grecque

Prepare day ahead if desired. Wash and pare 12 heads endive. Remove small bitter cores from bottoms with pointed knife, cut off tops so endives are 1½ inches high, and trim bottoms evenly so they will stand upright. Arrange in an enamelware * saucepan and cover with 1½ cups hot lamb or beef broth. Add ½ bay leaf, a dash powdered rosemary, 1 clove, salt and pepper to taste, and shell of ½ lemon. Bring to a boil, then reduce heat and simmer, uncovered, for 18 minutes. Remove from heat, drain, and cool.

Meanwhile, prepare 1 cup tomato purée: Peel and seed 3 or 4 small tomatoes, chop coarsely, and simmer, covered, for 20 minutes with 2 tablespoons butter, 1 slice onion, ½ bay leaf, and salt and pepper to taste. Force through a sieve; purée should not be too thick.

In a small skillet heat 2 tablespoons olive oil to smoking point. In it sauté quickly ½ cup minced onion, ½ cup ground raw lamb, and ½ cup raisins or dried currants. Reduce heat and cook until onion is soft. Make a cavity in each endive by pushing down center leaves with finger. Fill with sautéed mixture, place upright in a small casserole, and cover with tomato purée. Reheat just before serving.

12 heads endive
1½ cups lamb or beef broth
½ bay leaf
Dash powdered rosemary
1 clove
Shell of half lemon
Salt, pepper

3 or 4 small tomatoes
2 tablespoons butter
1 slice onion
½ bay leaf
Salt, pepper

* Metal pans have a tendency to blacken endive.

2 tablespoons olive oil
½ cup minced onion
½ cup ground raw lamb
½ cup raisins or currants

To serve cold: Omit tomato purée. Marinate stuffed cooled endive in 1 cup Basic French Dressing (see below) for 2 or 3 hours, then drain and serve arranged upright in a shallow dish.

Basic French Dressing

For a green salad to serve 4 people, blend together well 1 tablespoon red wine vinegar, 3 tablespoons olive oil or other salad oil, 1 teaspoon salt, freshly ground pepper to taste, and 1 teaspoon prepared mustard. Or, to make larger quantities, mix together 1 part vinegar and 3 parts oil, and for each cup of dressing add 4 teaspoons salt, 1 teaspoon pepper, and 4 teaspoons mustard. To make the seven *hors-d'oeuvre* salads that follow, you will need 3½ cups of dressing in all to serve 12.

Red wine vinegar
Olive or other salad oil
Salt
Pepper
Mustard

Beet Salad

Prepare day ahead. To ½ cup Basic French Dressing add 1 pressed clove garlic, 1 teaspoon chopped parsley, 1 teaspoon chopped chives, ½ teaspoon salt, and ⅛ teaspoon pepper. Drain 1 No. 2 can sliced beets and marinate overnight in dressing.

½ cup Basic French Dressing (see above)
1 clove garlic
1 teaspoon chopped parsley
1 teaspoon chopped chives

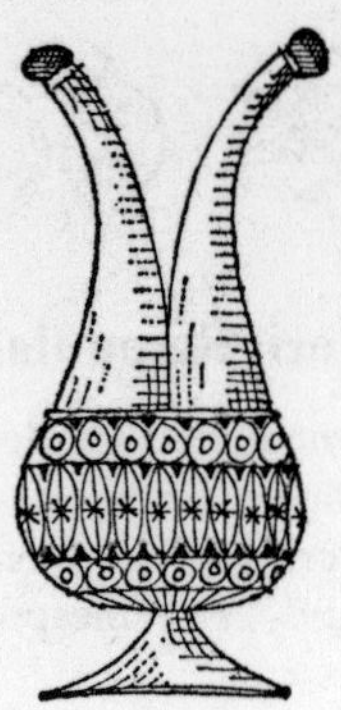

½ teaspoon salt
⅛ teaspoon pepper
1 No. 2 can sliced beets

Button-Mushroom Salad

Prepare day ahead. To ½ cup Basic French Dressing add 1 tablespoon prepared mustard and ½ pressed clove garlic. Drain two 8-ounce cans button mushrooms and marinate overnight in dressing.

½ cup Basic French Dressing (see above)
1 tablespoon prepared mustard
½ clove garlic
2 8-ounce cans button mushrooms

Asparagus Salad

Prepare day ahead. To ½ cup Basic French Dressing add 1 tablespoon lemon juice, 1 tablespoon chopped chives, and 1 teaspoon chopped parsley. Drain 2 No. 2 cans white or green asparagus and marinate in dressing overnight. Place in serving dish. Sieve 2 hard-cooked egg yolks over tips of asparagus, and garnish with ribbons of red pimiento.

½ cup Basic French Dressing (see above)
1 tablespoon lemon juice
1 tablespoon chopped chives
1 teaspoon chopped parsley

2 No. 2 cans white or green asparagus
2 egg yolks
Red pimiento

Kidney-Bean Salad

Prepare day ahead. To ½ cup Basic French Dressing add 1 teaspoon onion juice, 1 tablespoon lemon juice, 1 teaspoon chopped parsley, and ⅛ teaspoon ground pepper. Drain 1 No. 2 can kidney beans and marinate overnight in dressing. Place in *hors-d'oeuvre* dish and garnish with additional teaspoon chopped parsley and paper-thin onion rings.

½ cup Basic French Dressing (see above)
1 teaspoon onion juice
1 tablespoon lemon juice
1 teaspoon chopped parsley
⅛ teaspoon ground pepper
1 No. 2 can kidney beans
1 teaspoon chopped parsley
Onion rings

Ceci or Chick Pea Salad

Prepare day ahead. To ½ cup Basic French Dressing add 1 pressed clove garlic, 1 tablespoon chili sauce, and 1 tablespoon chopped parsley. Drain 1 No. 2 can chick peas and marinate in dressing overnight. Toss before placing in serving dish, and garnish with green-pepper rings.

½ cup Basic French Dressing (see above)
1 clove garlic
1 tablespoon chili sauce
1 tablespoon chopped parsley
1 No. 2 can chick peas
Green pepper rings

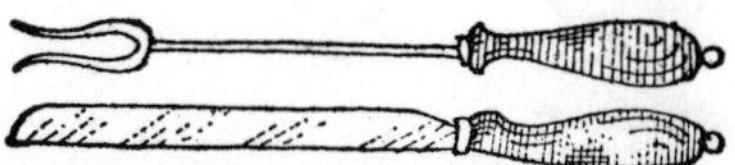

Tomato Salad

Dip 6 small ripe tomatoes in boiling water, quickly rinse with cold water, peel, and slice. Marinate for 1 hour, more or less, in ½ cup Basic French Dressing to which has been added 2 tablespoons minced shallots and 1 tablespoon chopped parsley.

6 small tomatoes
½ cup Basic French Dressing (see above)
2 tablespoons minced shallots
1 tablespoon chopped parsley

Salade Niçoise

Dip 4 ripe tomatoes in boiling water, rinse quickly with cold water, peel, and cut in eighths. Place half the tomatoes in a bowl with: ½ cup cooked whole green beans; 3 sliced boiled potatoes; 15 small Italian black olives; 1 can French or Italian tuna fish, drained of its olive oil and coarsely flaked with a fork; 1 green pepper, seeded and cut in julienne strips; and 1 sweet red pepper, seeded and cut in 1-inch squares. Toss with ½ cup Basic French Dressing to which 1 pressed clove of garlic has been added. Arrange salad in *hors-d'oeuvre* dish and decorate with reserved tomatoes, 2 sliced hard-cooked eggs, and 8 to 12 anchovy fillets crisscrossed over the salad.

4 tomatoes
½ cup cooked green beans
3 boiled potatoes
15 Italian black olives
1 can French or Italian tuna fish in olive oil
1 green pepper
1 sweet red pepper
½ cup Basic French Dressing (see above)
1 clove garlic
2 hard-cooked eggs
8 to 12 anchovy fillets

Veal Birds à la Parisienne

Season ¾ cup sausage meat with 1 tablespoon chopped parsley, ¼ teaspoon dried powdered tarragon, ⅛ teaspoon dried powdered thyme, 1 pressed clove garlic, and ⅛ teaspoon nutmeg. With a rolling pin pound well 24 very thin veal scallops (about 5 by 3 inches). Place 1½ teaspoons sausage mixture on each scallop. Roll meat around stuffing and tie with string. In Dutch oven, sauté "birds" over medium heat in 3 tablespoons corn oil until golden. Pour off oil and add 3 tablespoons butter, 1 cup dry white wine, 12 mushroom caps, and 12 peeled whole shallots. Bake, covered, in a preheated 350° oven for 45 minutes. Remove birds from pot to a heated serving dish.

Measure the sauce. For each cup of liquid blend 1 tablespoon butter with 1 tablespoon arrowroot or cornstarch. Bring sauce to a boil over high heat. Add butter mixture to sauce and stir until it thickens (process is almost instantaneous). Pour sauce over veal birds and serve with steamed white or brown rice (see Index).

¾ cup sausage meat
1 tablespoon chopped parsley
¼ teaspoon dried powdered tarragon
⅛ teaspoon dried powdered thyme
1 clove garlic
⅛ teaspoon nutmeg
24 thin veal scallops
3 tablespoons corn oil
3 tablespoons butter
1 cup dry white wine
12 mushroom caps
12 shallots
Butter
Arrowroot or cornstarch

Royal Ice-Box Cake

In small bowl of electric mixer, cream together ½ pound each butter and confectioners' sugar for 15 minutes, or until very light and white. Add 3 whole eggs and 3 egg yolks, one at a time, beating all the while. In the large bowl, beat 3 egg whites until stiff but not dry. With a rotary beater, beat ½ pint heavy cream, flavored with 1 tablespoon kirsch, until it stands in peaks; then gently fold egg whites and cream into first mixture. Line a 9-inch springform pan with 12 split ladyfingers, round side out. Crush and crumble 12 medium-size macaroons and spread half these crumbs over bottom of pan. Cover with half the filling, add rest of macaroon crumbs, and top with rest of filling. Decorate with candied cherries and pineapple. Cover, and refrigerate for 24 hours.

½ pound butter
½ pound confectioners' sugar
3 whole eggs
3 egg yolks
3 egg whites
½ pint heavy cream
1 tablespoon kirsch
12 ladyfingers
12 macaroons
Candied cherries and pineapple

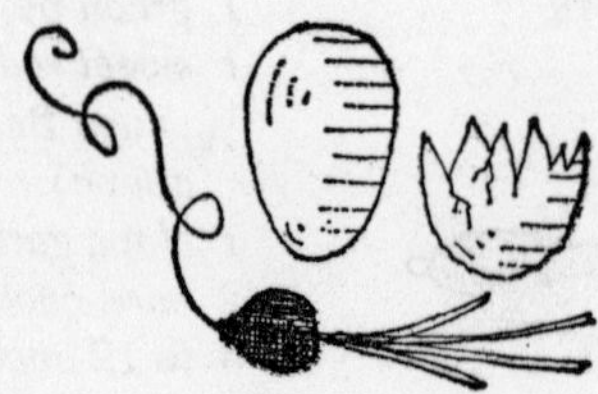

37

Formal Summer Luncheon for Twelve

ICED CREAM OF ALLIGATOR PEAR
FILLET OF BEEF STRASBOURGEOISE
ARTICHOKE AND TRUFFLE SALAD WITH CHAMPAGNE DRESSING
VIENNESE STRAWBERRY TORTE
DEMITASSE

CHAMPAGNES

Inexpensive: Almadén, Brut
Medium-priced: Madame Pinot, Brut, or Martin Ray, Saratoga, California
Expensive: Bollinger, Brut

"Elegant simplicity" generally needs one word tacked on to it—*expensive;* somehow, that's the way it turns out. So, take time out before you read further to consult the exchequer. Once you've looked over the recipes, you needn't actually pawn the family jewels to produce them, but still, truffles and champagne, goose-liver pâté, fillet of beef and caviar—they're all here. Even if you don't buy the most outrageously superior quality, things have a way of adding up.

If you're still reading, either the budget is in good repair or you have decided on a bread-and-water diet for a few days to make up for this elegant feast. It will be worth it. You can see at a glance that it *is* elegant, and we'll show you just how simple. Believe it or not, it isn't a difficult dinner to cook, and the plan of attack is easy if you devote time to it the day before.

Start off with the beef and the aspic. After you cook the meat and put the aspic in the icebox, make the *Torte*. Then prepare the soup, up to the addition of the cream and caviar. (The smaller-grain caviar will do nicely, but make sure it's only lightly salted.) Once the beef is well chilled, spread it with *pâté,* cover the whole with aspic, and return it to the icebox. (Rest easy about handling the aspic; there's enough gelatine in it so you can pull it away from the tin very easily.) The next thing on the agenda is to wash and drain the lettuce and put it in the refrigerator, but don't make the dressing ahead unless you're *really* in a spendthrift frame of mind; remember you have to use champagne for it. (On second thought, if you're looking for a good excuse to open a bottle the evening before the party, this is as good a reason as any.)

All this sumptuousness calls for formal service with two waitresses for a dozen people. (After the food bills you've just paid, there's nothing you can't swing!) If they come an hour and a half ahead, they can set the table, take care of last-minute jobs, and still be ready to serve champagne and hors-d'oeuvres before lunch. (Cheese Cookies, see Index, and Macadamia nuts, heated a few minutes beforehand to crisp them, would be good choices.) One of the waitresses should slice the beef, arrange the slices on a platter, and garnish them. The other can spread the cream on the *Torte* and decorate it with berries. (We use a new precision hand-eggbeater for small whipping jobs; it costs about five dollars, but how it increases the volume of cream or egg whites!)

If the waitresses come only in time to serve hors-d'oeuvres, they can nevertheless take care of the soup and salad dressing. You can handle the other jobs in the morning and still be ready to greet your guests beautifully turned out—the very picture of elegant simplicity.

Iced Cream of Alligator Pear

In a large wooden bowl, using a wooden potato masher or a pestle, pound ½ teaspoon Italian red pepper with 2 teaspoons coriander seeds until very fine. In same bowl, mash 4 large peeled and seeded alligator pears, and force mixture through a fine sieve or purée in electric blender. Place over hot but not boiling water in top of double boiler, add 4¼ cups chicken broth and a pinch of chili powder, and heat through. Cool, then add ½ pint heavy cream, and chill thoroughly. Just before serving, stir in 6 ounces black caviar. Taste and correct salt content, and pour into chilled soup cups.

½ teaspoon Italian red pepper
2 teaspoons coriander seeds
4 large alligator pears
4¼ cups chicken broth
Chili powder
½ pint heavy cream
6 ounces black caviar
Salt

Fillet of Beef Strasbourgeoise

Trim off flat end of a fillet of beef and reserve for other uses. Wrap fillet in thin slices of larding fat and tie it securely. Drive a long thin knife lengthwise through center of fillet; then, with handle of a wooden spoon, push 12 to 15 small truffles or truffle pieces into the slit and down length of meat. Place in a heavy skillet or oblong roasting pan, rub with salt and pepper, and sear on all sides over high heat, turning several times. Di-

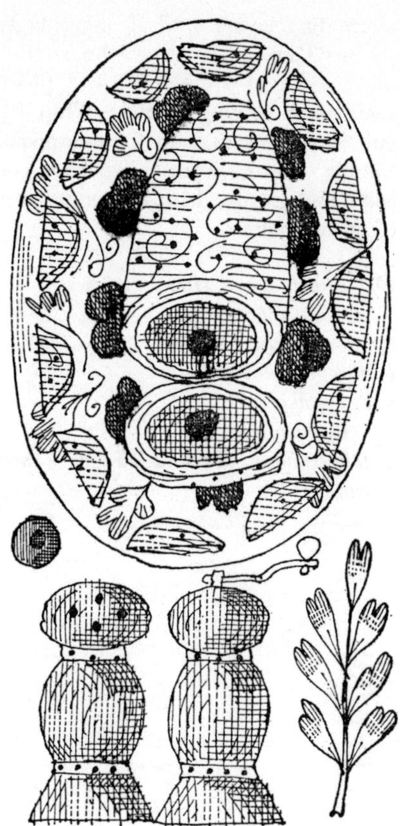

ameter of fillet must be guide for top-of-stove cooking; the fillet ends which are exposed show progress of cooking. When meat is seared, reduce heat to medium and continue cooking, turning slowly so all sides will cook evenly, until ends are done (approximately 8 to 12 minutes per pound for medium rare). When done, remove string and fat, and chill in refrigerator.

Make a sheet of aspic: Soften 2 envelopes gelatin in ½ cup Madeira or port. Heat 3 cups beef consommé (or 2 cans) and dissolve gelatin in it. Pour into jelly-roll tin and place in refrigerator until set.

Spread entire surface of fillet with approximately 8 ounces goose-liver pâté, then place on a long serving platter. Chop the aspic and sprinkle on top of fillet. Then slice, and garnish with more aspic alongside fillet, and with truffle cut-outs and little bunches of watercress.

4½- to 5-pound prime fillet of beef
Larding fat
12 to 15 small truffles or truffle pieces
Salt, pepper
2 envelopes gelatin
½ cup Madeira or port
3 cups beef consommé
8 ounces goose-liver pâté
Truffle cut-outs
Watercress

Artichoke and Truffle Salad with Champagne Dressing

Rinse, drain, and dry 4 hearts of Bibb lettuce. Rub a wooden salad bowl with a piece of garlic, and arrange lettuce in bowl. Cut 12 artichoke bottoms into julienne strips, slice 4 large truffles, and arrange on top of lettuce. Toss with Champagne Dressing, below, at the table.

4 hearts Bibb lettuce
Garlic
12 artichoke bottoms
4 large truffles
Champagne Dressing

Wine or Champagne Dressing

Mix 6 tablespoons walnut oil * or French olive oil with ¼ cup champagne or wine served with the meal, and a little salt and pepper to taste.

6 tablespoons walnut oil
or French olive oil
¼ cup champagne or wine
Salt, pepper

* Some delicacy stores carry this most delicate of all salad oils.

Viennese Strawberry Icebox Torte

Hull, rinse, and drain 1½ quarts small strawberries, and set aside 1 cup. Split 3 packages ladyfingers and with some of them, round side out, line bottom and sides of a 9-inch springform pan. Cream ⅜ pound sweet butter with 1 cup granulated sugar, add 4 egg yolks, and beat until fluffy and light in color. With rubber spatula, spread some of mixture over ladyfingers on bottom of springform. Cover with a layer of strawberries, then a layer of ladyfingers, and again spread with butter mixture. Continue alternating layers until all ingredients are used up. Chill several hours. Remove sides of springform and place cake on a serving platter. Whip ½ cup heavy cream with 2 tablespoons Vanilla Sugar, spread over top of cake, and garnish with remaining cup of strawberries.

1½ quarts small strawberries
3 packages ladyfingers
⅜ pound sweet butter
1 cup granulated sugar
4 egg yolks
½ cup heavy cream
2 tablespoons Vanilla Sugar (see Index)

PICNICS, BARBECUES AND PATIO DINNERS

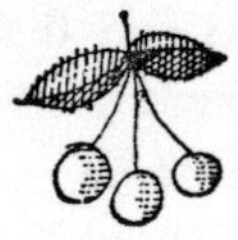

38

Pique-Nique à la Française for Four

RADISHES
SAUCISSON
TERRINE OF DUCK BRISTOL
FRENCH BREAD
TOMATOES
ASSORTED CHEESES
FRESH FRUIT
COFFEE

WINES
Inexpensive: Widmer's Seibel-Rosé
Medium-priced: Rosé d'Anjou
Expensive: Tavel

There is a story irrevocably associated in our minds with roadside picnics. It concerns a linguist friend of ours and her husband on a motor trip through France. In Poitiers, late one morning, they found market day in full swing. Hypnotized by a display of foods such as they had never before seen, they decided to forego a restaurant lunch in favor of a *déjeuner sur l'herbe.* Palest pink ham, creamy white cheese, cloud-textured bread and home-churned butter found their way into our friend's shopping bag. To the nearest wine shop for a fine bottle, a nearby *pâtisserie* for some pastries, and they were off. On their way out of the city, they realized that they had forgotten to buy a knife. It had just turned noon and they could hardly wait to begin their feast. But it was also lunchtime for all the shopkeepers, who couldn't wait either and who lock their doors on the stroke of twelve. They had just decided to settle for Henry the Eighth table etiquette when they spied a shop and the rotund, aproned *patron* out in front. Our friend summoned up her best French.

"*Est-ce-qu'on vend des couteaux içi?*"

The *patron* bowed low. "Yes, *Madame*, we sell knives; we sell anything you might desire." Our friend claims she refused to utter a word of French for the next three days.

Nevertheless, the picnics became a daily ritual, and one that it is easy to fall into at home if you have the time. Or occasionally, when you're on the road traveling or just away from the house for a few hours, the break from everyday routine is infinitely refreshing. What's more, it is easy to assemble this picnic, since you buy everything on the way save the *Terrine*. (If you were shopping in the market place at Poitiers, you could even buy that.) Once you have enjoyed this duck pâté, you will probably start making two or three at once, as we do, so that it is always available. We almost consider it a staple. It's invaluable for a last minute dinner or to serve with cocktails. Protected by its top layer of fat, an unopened pâté keeps beautifully for several weeks in a cool place.

Use an insulated bag or bucket with a can of synthetic ice to carry the *Terrine*, butter, and cheese, if your cheese should be kept cool. (Camembert or Brie may get too runny and Cheddar or Swiss develop an unpleasant fatty surface in the heat.) Fruits and vegetables are best dead ripe. If you know that you will pass a good farm stand *en route*, wait to buy them there; they will have that sun-warmed flavor. The fresher the better is also true of bread and the coffee you put in the thermos.

Terrine of Duck Bristol

Pâté crocks or *terrines* come in many sizes. The best, those that conduct heat most evenly, are made of ovenproof, glazed porcelain or pretty ovenproof bronze bisqueware that portray on the lid a hare or a game bird's head.

Size Number 1 will make a 2-cup pâté which will serve six to eight people for snacks generously, or yield 6 slices to serve with a tossed salad. Unless you are preparing for a large party, this and the next size are the most convenient, for, once opened, a conserve pâté *has* to be finished off by the next day. Most people love pâté once, but it is rich and appetites may not keep up with leftovers in large quantities. So it is better to make several smaller conserve pâtés than one large one.

Note: Whatever the game or game fowl used in a recipe, to detach the meat easily from the carcass it must be poached in *Court-Bouillon* for Meat, below, until almost but not quite tender.

Preheat broiler to highest heat; quickly sear a 5- to 6-pound duck under broiler until brown on all sides, then poach in approximately 3 quarts *Court-Bouillon* for Meat for 1 hour. Remove duck, reserve cooking liquid, and remove skin and meat from carcass. Discard skin, reserve carcass for other uses, and set meat aside for pâté. Sauté ½ pound unpeeled chopped mushrooms until tender in 1 tablespoon butter; set aside with meat. To same pan add 1 tablespoon butter. In it sauté ½ pound chicken livers, plus the duck liver, until very lightly browned. Marinate all the meats and the mushrooms for 15 minutes in ½ cup orange juice and ½ cup Madeira. Place small portions of this mixture in an electric blender and blend to a paste, moistening as needed with just enough reserved *Court-Bouillon.* Or put through finest blade of food chopper and moisten afterwards. Pâté should be smooth and rich in texture, but should hold its shape.

Preheat oven to 375°. For this quantity of meat, line 2 pint-size or 1 quart-size *terrine* with sliced fatback. Pack pâté paste into the *terrine* to within ¼ inch of top, cover with layer of fatback, top with bay leaf, and cover with lid. Bake in a pan of hot water for 1¼ hours. The lid should then be sealed to the *terrine* with melted fat to make it airtight. Store in a cool place. Pâtés will keep, unopened, for two or three weeks.

1 duck, 5–6 pounds
3 quarts Court-Bouillon for Meat
½ pound mushrooms
2 tablespoons butter
½ pound chicken livers
1 duck liver
½ cup orange juice
½ cup Madeira
½ pound fatback, about
Bay leaf

Court-Bouillon for Meat

Use enough water to cover meat. For each quart water add 1½ cups or 1 can beef or chicken consommé (chicken for white meat and beef for dark), 2 carrots, 3 sprigs of parsley, ¼ bay leaf, 2 crushed peppercorns, 1 small onion, 2 cloves, ⅛ teaspoon thyme, and ½ teaspoon salt. Bring to a boil all together, reduce heat, then simmer for 20 minutes before poaching meat.

1 quart water
1½ cups or 1 can beef or chicken consommé
2 carrots
3 sprigs parsley
¼ bay leaf
2 peppercorns
1 small onion
2 cloves
⅛ teaspoon thyme
½ teaspoon salt

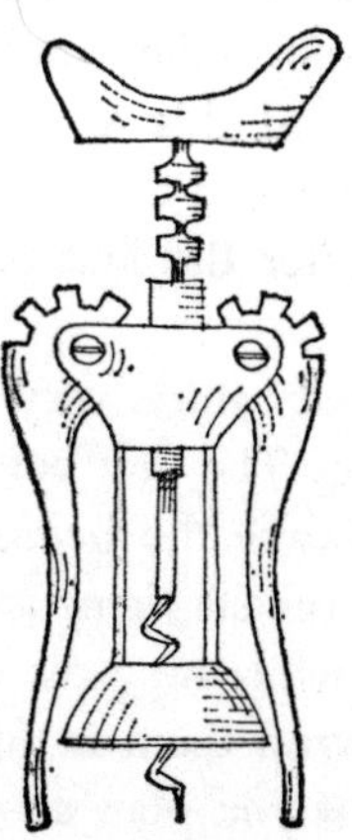

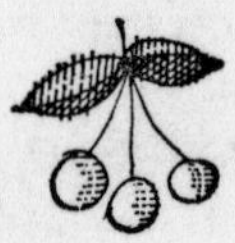

39

Picnic for Six

CARROTS, CELERY, ZUCCHINI AND CHERRY TOMATOES
HAMBURGERS À LA DIABLE
MEXICAN BEANS
CORN IN THE HUSK
PEACH SHORTCAKE
COFFEE

WINES

Inexpensive: Beringer Brothers Gringnolino, Napa Valley
Medium-priced: Valpolicella, Cantina Sociale

The Superior Male likes nothing better than to prove the lyrics of that popular song, "I can do anything you can do better"; and the smart woman is wise enough to help him prove it. She does all the advance preparation, packs the hampers and the car, then unpacks the food at the picnic site and quietly fades into the background. And, His Highness, Master Chef, takes over. With fanfare and showmanship, he lights the fire, unwraps the packages, and starts to cook—the whole accompanied by a running commentary on how he *invented* this or that cooking technique. Finally, a come-and-get-it announcement and the moment of triumph as he watches the expression on each face after the first taste. There's nothing like it to build up an ego!

Your behind-the-scenes activity starts very briefly two days before, when you must soak the dried beans. The day before the picnic, cook them and bake the shortcake biscuits. Leave the beans in the pot to take along the next day. The boss man will reheat them and roast the corn at the same time. They will both stay hot while he grills the hamburgers. Cut the vegetable strips the day before, wrap them in foil, and store them in the icebox. Soak the corn overnight if you plan an early start.

In the morning, make the hamburger patties. Stack with pieces of waxed paper between them, wrap the whole thing in foil, and put it in an oversized ice bucket, or in an insulated plastic bag with one or two cans of synthetic ice. (Special padded bags and ice are available at hardware stores; the Scotch Koolers are excellent buckets.) Put the butter, cream, and vegetables on the ice, too. Fill one or two thermos bottles with hot coffee, and wrap the corn in a terry-cloth towel to hold the moisture. Check your supplies—pepper, salt, sugar, cinnamon; onion rolls, sauce to brush the meat; peaches for the shortcake, bowl and egg beater for the whipped cream; plates, cups, and napkins; corkscrew, forks, knives, and spoons; asbestos glove, charcoal or briquets, and a commercial fire-lighting preparation if the Superior Male has trouble starting fires; and a portable barbecue if there aren't outdoor fireplaces at your destination.

That's about it and you're off. His Highness is at the wheel, already assuming his role of King for a Day.

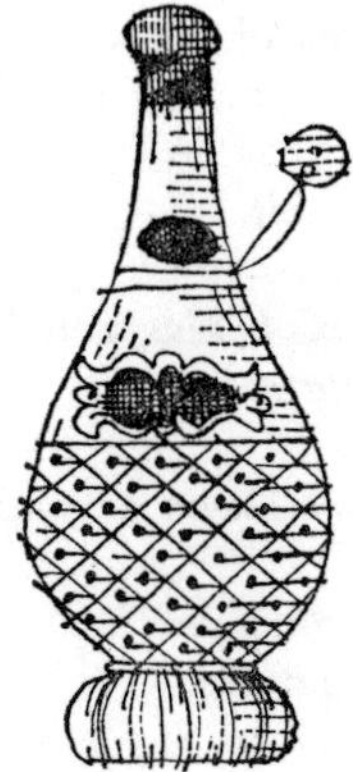

Hamburgers à la Diable

Mix lightly 3 pounds ground beef (top round), 2 eggs, beaten, 3 tablespoons bottled Escoffier Sauce Diable, and 1 teaspoon salt; form into 16 patties ½ inch thick. Mix together ½ large minced onion, 6 tablespoons mashed capers, and another 3 tablespoons Sauce Diable. Place a little of mixture in the center of 8 patties, cover with remaining 8 patties, and seal edges. Brush hamburgers on one side with ⅓ cup melted butter mixed with an additional 2 tablespoons Sauce Diable.

Grill about 2 inches from glowing coals for 2 to 3 minutes, buttered side down; then brush top side with some of the sauce left in bottle, turn hamburger over, and grill 2 to 3 minutes longer. Serve on split and toasted onion rolls.

3 pounds ground top round of beef
2 eggs
8 tablespoons bottled Escoffier Sauce Diable, plus enough for basting
1 teaspoon salt
½ large onion
6 tablespoons capers
⅓ cup melted butter
8 onion rolls

Mexican Beans

Wash 1 pint red beans and soak for 12 hours, then boil gently for 2 hours. Drain and rinse. Melt 1 tablespoon bacon fat or other fat in a skillet, and add 2 chopped medium onions, 1½ pressed cloves garlic, 3 chopped green peppers, 2 teaspoons salt, and ½ teaspoon black pepper. Cook 5 minutes, then add to beans in pot with enough water to cover. Boil slowly until thoroughly soft, but not mushy. Add hot water if necessary during the cooking.

1 pint red beans
1 tablespoon bacon fat or other fat
2 medium onions
1½ cloves garlic
3 green peppers
2 teaspoons salt
½ teaspoon black pepper

Corn in the Husk

Choose 12 slightly underripe, freshly picked ears of corn. Trim stems from husks, wash under running water, then soak in lightly salted water for 1 hour. Drain, but do not dry husks.

Place on side of grill about 5 inches away from glowing coals, turn frequently, and grill for 8 to 10 minutes, depending on size of ears. Husks should be dry and very lightly charred. Wearing an asbestos glove, remove husks with a sharp knife, and serve corn with butter and freshly ground pepper.

12 ears of corn
Salted water
Butter
Pepper

Peach Shortcake

Preheat oven to 425°. Sift 2¾ cups flour with ¾ teaspoon salt, 1 tablespoon sugar, and 1½ teaspoons baking powder. Melt ¼ pound butter and mix in 6 tablespoons of it. Beat 1 egg in a measuring cup and add enough heavy cream to make ¾ cup. Stir into flour mixture, then pat out dough into 2 rounds to fit a 9-inch pie plate. Put one round in the plate, brush generously with remaining butter, then place second round on top, and bake for 25 minutes. Cool. If necessary, separate two rounds with a knife.

Fill with 5 large freshly peeled and sliced freestone peaches. Whip 1 pint heavy cream with ¼ cup granulated sugar and 1 teaspoon cinnamon. Place ½ the cream over peaches, cover with second round of shortcake, and dribble rest of cream over top and sides of cake.

2¾ cups flour
¾ teaspoon salt
1 tablespoon sugar
1½ teaspoons baking powder
¼ pound butter
1 egg
plus heavy cream to make ¾ cup

5 large freestone peaches
1 pint heavy cream
¼ cup granulated sugar
1 teaspoon cinnamon

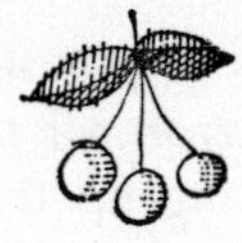

40

Hamper Picnic for Six

Martinis

MACADAMIA NUTS

CREAM OF ASPARAGUS SOUP

OLD-ENGLISH OYSTER PIE

COLD CHICKEN JOSÉPHINE

CAESAR SALAD

CHEESECAKE

COFFEE

WINES

Inexpensive: White—Christian Brothers White Pinot
Red—Louis Martini Mountain Zinfandel
Medium-priced: White—Wente Pinot Blanc
Red—Bardolino

Six tickets on the fifty-yard line for *the* game of the season—or, six seats, third row center, for a pre-Broadway summer tryout—there's only one fly in the ointment: From past experience you know the best restaurants near the stadium are never at their best the day of the big game, and the usually charming inns close to the playhouse are somewhat less than charming when everyone's racing against curtaintime. But, there's no alternative, so you might as well make the best of it—or, is there?

It comes as no great surprise that we have a very good alternative to suggest, or we wouldn't have brought up the subject in the first place; but the menu will be a surprise. This—a picnic? It sounds more like Wedgwood-and-Waterford than plastic-and-paper service—and indeed it can be served at home as formally and elegantly as might you wish. But this dinner travels well, too.

It takes a bit of doing and will tie you up a good part of the day before if you're to leave in the morning; or all morning if you plan an evening picnic. But, you won't mind giving up the time if you've done battle in a restaurant *en route* before and not fared nearly as well as we propose. Our one word of warning—get to your chosen picnic spot early; there's even less point in having to rush through this meal than having to do the same in a restaurant.

Broil the chicken first, and get the Oyster Pie ready in the meantime. Once the pie is in the oven, wash the lettuce, and make the dressing, the croutons, and the eggs for the salad. (For the picnic, put the dressing in a jar, pack the croutons and the eggs in foil, chill the greens in a towel, and don't forget the anchovies.) By that time, the oven will be free for you to bake the Cheesecake. Finally, start the soup, but don't add the eggs and butter until just before you leave, when you will reheat the soup and finish it.

Picnic or not, this is elegant eating, and, while it doesn't require Wedgwood and Waterford, it involves a good deal of paraphernalia; you may have to borrow here and there, or ask one of your guests to tap her resources. A mammoth basket is perfect to carry things in: Six mugs for soup and six for coffee, glasses for martinis and wine; forks, knives, and spoons, and plenty of paper, or preferably plastic, plates; a simple cloth and napkins (this menu deserves *that* much formality, even if the table is only a grassy bank); a salad bowl, pepper mill, and salt shaker; and a thermos for soup and one for coffee. Mix the martinis at home, pour them into a bottle, and pack it and the white wine in ice in a bucket. We don't suggest expensive wines, even for so grand a picnic, because this would be a waste; they shake up too much in transit. A large insulated bag, with two cans of synthetic ice, is a perfect traveling refrigerator for the cake, Oyster Pie, salad greens, chicken, and cream for coffee. (These bags are handy even to save steps for backyard picnics.)

There's no gainsaying that this mounts up to a formidable job of packing, but give your host just a hint of what's in store, and he might volunteer his help where a strong arm is needed. And there's reason to hope, after you've done this once, that he will come home with *season* tickets for summer stock or the football season, as the case may be. Take it as a compliment and don't be surprised, however, if he decides instead that a spell of magnificent weather is good and sufficient reason for a trip up-country and a repeat performance of *Hamper Picnic.*

Cream of Asparagus Soup

Scrape 2 pounds asparagus to about 1 inch from tips, removing more peel at the bottom of stalk than at top. Place flat in an oblong pan, and add water to cover generously and a little salt. Bring to a boil over high heat and cook until tender but still a little crisp, about 8 to 10 minutes. Purée asparagus in a food mill, and mix with 1½ cups hot Béchamel Sauce and 1½ cups hot chicken consommé or stock. Scald 1 cup heavy cream, stir it into mixture, and remove from heat. Beat 2 egg yolks into soup with a wire whisk, and add 2 tablespoons butter for a smooth finish. Rinse a large thermos with boiling water and pour soup into it. Serve in small mugs.

2 pounds asparagus
or 2 packages frozen asparagus
Salt
1½ cups Béchamel Sauce (see Index)
1½ cups chicken consommé or stock
1 cup heavy cream
2 egg yolks
2 tablespoons butter

Old-English Oyster Pie

Preheat oven to 375°. Simmer 2 quarts shelled and bearded oysters with their liquor and 4 tablespoons butter until the edges begin to curl. Drain all liquor from them. Make ¼ pound Anchovy Butter; incorporate in it 4 tablespoons toasted bread crumbs, 1 tablespoon minced parsley, and ⅛ teaspoon grated nutmeg. Make a Simple Pie Crust, and roll it out in two rectangles—one slightly larger than the top of a loaf pan, the other big enough to line the pan. Dot pastry-lined pan with Anchovy-Butter mixture. Add half the oysters, rest of Anchovy Butter, then rest of oysters. Sprinkle with 1 tablespoon lemon juice and a little freshly ground pepper. Cover with smaller crust, crimp edges, and make two steam vents in top. Bake 35 to 40 minutes. Cool in pan, and wrap in foil. Keep pie cold, and unmold and slice at the picnic.

2 quarts shelled oysters
or equivalent in frozen oysters
4 tablespoons butter
¼ pound Anchovy Butter (see Index, Fish Butters)
4 tablespoons bread crumbs
1 tablespoon minced parsley
⅛ teaspoon grated nutmeg
1 tablespoon lemon juice
Pepper
Simple Pie Crust

Simple Pie Crust

Chill a mixing bowl and a rolling pin. Into bowl sift 2¼ cups flour with 1 teaspoon salt. Cut 6 tablespoons shortening into flour with a pastry blender, or with 2 knives, until mixture looks like coarse corn meal. Cut in 6 more tablespoons shortening until particles are like peas. Add 4 to 5 tablespoons ice water, blending with a fork until dough gathers together. Chill dough well and divide. Roll out larger part for lower crust, gauging size by holding pan over it. Lift crust into ungreased pan, prick with a fork to remove air bubbles which sometimes form underneath, and brush with 1 tablespoon melted butter. Roll out remaining dough for upper crust and lay it on waxed paper; chill both crusts for 10 minutes in refrigerator, then fill according to directions above.

2¼ cups flour
1 teaspoon salt
12 tablespoons shortening
4–5 tablespoons ice water
1 tablespoon melted butter

Cold Chicken Joséphine

Preheat broiler to medium heat. Split three 2-pound broilers, rub inside and out with a damp cloth, and season cavity with freshly ground pepper and very little salt. Place skin side down in broiling pan, and place 1 tablespoon Tarragon Butter in each cavity. Broil 4 to 5 inches from heat until well browned, or about 12 minutes. Turn chicken, brush skin generously with pan juices, and broil again for 8 to 10 minutes, or until skin is well browned. Reduce heat to 350°, add ½ cup dry white wine, and bake in oven for 12 minutes. Cool, wrap in foil, and store in refrigerator until time to pack for picnic.

To serve hot at home, remove chicken to heated serving platter after baking. Deglaze pan with ½ cup cold stock or water. Knead together to a paste 2 tablespoons each arrowroot and butter, stir into pan juices, add a little more liquid if necessary to bring sauce to perfect consistency, and pour over chicken.

3 2-pound broilers
Salt, pepper
⅜ pound Tarragon Butter (see Index)
½ cup dry white wine
½ cup cold stock or water
2 tablespoons arrowroot
2 tablespoons butter

Caesar Salad

Make 2 cups garlic croutons: Remove crusts from 3 slices white bread and cube bread. Rub a heavy iron skillet with garlic and ⅛ teaspoon salt. In the skillet, over medium heat, bring ½ cup olive oil to a sizzle, and in it fry the bread cubes until golden, adding more oil if necessary. Coddle 2 eggs 2 minutes in boiling water, and reserve. To ½ cup Basic French Dressing add ¼ teaspoon dry mustard, 1 small pressed clove of garlic, and ½ cup grated Parmesan. Place dressing in a wooden bowl, and over it tear 2 heads romaine into medium-size pieces. Cut 4 anchovy fillets into tiny pieces and lay them over greens. Break the soft-cooked eggs over salad and toss all together. Sprinkle with croutons and toss again very lightly just before serving. For a picnic, prepare ingredients ahead, but assemble salad at serving time.

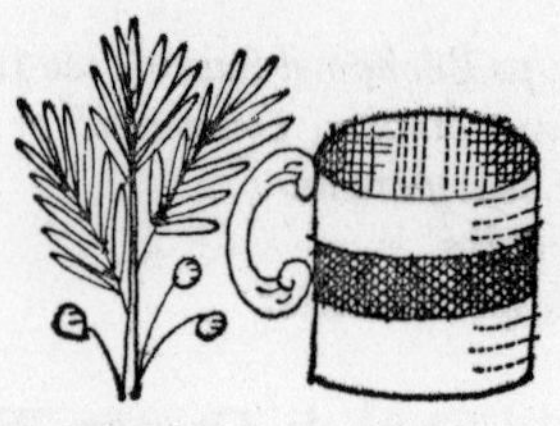

3 slices white bread
Garlic
⅛ teaspoon salt
½ cup olive oil
2 eggs
½ cup Basic French Dressing (see Index)
¼ teaspoon dry mustard
1 small clove garlic
½ cup grated Parmesan
2 heads romaine
4 anchovy fillets

Cheesecake

To make crust, crush ¾ package Zwieback to fine crumbs with a rolling pin, and mix with ¾ cup sugar, ½ teaspoon cinnamon, and 6 tablespoons melted butter. Pack on bottom and around sides of an 8-inch spring-form pan, reserving a handful of crumbs to sprinkle over top of cake.

To make filling, beat 3 eggs well, using electric mixer or detachable egg beater. Add ¾ cup sugar, ½ cup sifted all-purpose flour, 1½ pounds creamed cottage cheese, 1½ cups unbeaten heavy cream, 1 teaspoon vanilla, and the juice and grated rind of 1 lemon. Pour into lined springform, sprinkle with remaining crumbs, and bake at 300° for 1½ to 2 hours, or until set. Open oven door and let cake cool in the oven for 1 hour before removing. Carry to picnic in springform pan.

¾ package Zwieback
¾ cup sugar
1 teaspoon cinnamon
6 tablespoons melted butter
3 eggs
¾ cup sugar
½ cup sifted flour
1½ pounds creamed cottage cheese
1½ cups heavy cream
1 teaspoon vanilla
1 lemon

41

Fourth of July Patio Dinner for Twelve

BARBECUED OYSTERS
TURKEY WITH TARRAGON
TARRAGON BUTTER
TARRAGON LOAF
SWEET POTATOES CONGOLESE
SPINACH SALAD
WATERMELON BASKET
BRANDY BLACK-BOTTOM PIE

WINES

Inexpensive: New York State Sauterne
Medium-priced: Barsac
Expensive: Pouilly-Fuissé, Vintage

Not so many years ago, someone rediscovered outdoor cooking. Whether this was a carry-over in full-fledged adults from their Boy Scout and Girl Scout days, or an honest yearning to get back to nature, the craze assumed epidemic proportions. Grilling a steak or a hamburger or a chicken became

definitely the thing to do. The happy hostess needed no persuasion to adopt this new kind of party: It outlawed formality in a day when help was hard to come by, made entertaining something she could cope with herself, and pried more culinary assistance from the man of the family than she had ever had before. If she had salad fixings on hand, potatoes or corn, and an ice-cream dessert, she was all set. Now, a fine steak, a well-dressed salad, and country-fresh corn are magnificent, but when they or a reasonable facsimile become the standard menu, it's time to do a little shaking up. This has become too much of a good thing!

Outdoor cooking can and should remain simple. Even so, there need be no holds barred if you want to raise your menu to the highest level of sophistication. We've explored the possibilities extensively and have had great success with the widest variety of foods. A case in point, this menu which we used one Fourth of July. We think it evoked even more comment than it would have done served in the confines of the dining room. Perhaps it was the appeal of the unexpected, but it did seem, too, that sitting leisurely about midst the barrage of enticing aromas heightened our anticipation of wonderful food to come.

The work is well taken care of hours ahead if this is to be an evening dinner. You can manage it for a holiday midday dinner too, however, as part of it is done the day before. Oysters are ready on skewers. (Naturally, there wasn't a fresh oyster to be had in July, so we resorted to the smoked kind which is always available tinned. We'll never again care which months have an R in them.) The turkey, too, is ready and foil-wrapped, to be blanketed in coals an hour or more before dinner. Just be sure to start your fire an hour before cookingtime; you'll want a good bed of glowing coals, not a roaring fire. The salad is chilling in the refrigerator. So is the pie, made the day before. The half hour before dinner takes care of assembling the watermelon basket and putting the salad together.

The only last minute chore involved, and we can't rightly say it is a chore, is to fry the Potatoes Congolese. We have our electric deep fryer plugged into an outlet on the terrace. The sweet potatoes have been marinating and now are batter-dipped and fried to be served as they're ready. The only trouble is that enough of them never seem to get to the table at once. Second, third, and fourth helpings are the rule. While you fry them, the host can carve the turkey.

Our color scheme took its cue from the holiday itself and from the watermelon basket which did double duty as dessert and centerpiece. We invested in a few yards of inexpensive watermelon-red cotton, zipped around it with pinking shears—and there we were, cloth and napkins for a very few dollars. As we sat down to dinner, one appreciative man said, "Everything looks good enough to eat!" He was right, too.

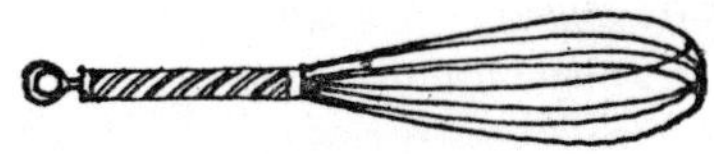

Barbecued Oysters

Shell and drain 24 oysters. Season with a little salt and pepper. Wrap each oyster in a thin strip of bacon and pin securely with wooden toothpicks. Place blanketed oysters in hinged, double-wire rack. Barbecue quickly about 6 inches above a hot, glowing bed of coals, turning often. Oysters are ready when bacon is broiled to your fancy.

Melt 1/4 pound butter and add 1 bottle of A-1 Sauce. Keep warm and use as a dip for oysters.

24 oysters
Salt, pepper
24 strips bacon
1/4 pound butter
1 bottle A-1 Sauce

Turkey with Tarragon

Order 2 young 6-pound turkeys. Have them split like broilers. Place halves in a shallow pan and sprinkle with salt and pepper. Add 1 cup dry white wine, 1 cup olive oil, and 1/4 cup minced fresh tarragon leaves. Marinate overnight.

Next day, place each turkey in double thickness of heavy foil. Pour marinade over turkeys, and fold foil securely so no juices can escape. Place packages on a bed of ash-covered coals and place more coals on top. Occasionally add new coals, and bake for 1 3/4 hours. Unpack on a platter, preserving the juices. Slice and serve, and add Tarragon Butter, below.

2 young 6-pound turkeys
Salt, pepper
1 cup dry white wine

1 cup olive oil
¼ cup minced fresh tarragon leaves or 2 tablespoons dried tarragon
Tarragon Butter

Tarragon Butter

Blend all together with a fork:

¼ pound softened butter
¼ cup minced fresh tarragon leaves or 2 tablespoons dried tarragon leaves

At servingtime, mix with juices on turkey platter, and spoon over helpings of meat. Make 1½ recipes if butter is also to be used for Tarragon Loaf.

Tarragon Loaf

Cut 2 loaves Italian bread in half lengthwise and spread with 4 tablespoons Tarragon Butter. Toast lightly, buttered side down, over hot coals. Cut in pieces and serve from a basket.

Sweet Potatoes Congolese

Blanch 10 medium-size sweet potatoes 5 minutes in boiling water. Peel, and slice ½ inch thick. Marinate for 1 hour in mixture of ½ cup honey, ½ cup brandy, and 2 teaspoons grated lemon rind. Blend 3 cups flour with 1½ pints light beer to make a smooth batter. Take slices from marinade and, without drying them, dip in batter and fry in deep fat at 390° until golden brown. Serve very hot.

10 medium-size sweet potatoes
½ cup honey
½ cup brandy
2 teaspoons grated lemon rind

3 cups flour
1½ pints light beer

Spinach Salad

Wash, dry, and refrigerate 2 pounds fresh young spinach leaves. Fry ¼ pound sliced bacon until crisp, then drain on a paper towel. Tear spinach into bite-size pieces, crumble bacon, and slice 3 hard-cooked eggs; toss all together. Pour over salad dressing made of ⅔ cup olive oil, ⅓ cup wine vinegar, 1 tablespoon coarse salt, ½ teaspoon ground pepper, 1 clove garlic, pressed, and 1 teaspoon monosodium glutamate, and toss well.

2 pounds fresh young spinach leaves
¼ pound bacon
3 hard-cooked eggs
⅔ cup olive oil
⅓ cup wine vinegar
1 tablespoon coarse salt
½ teaspoon ground pepper
1 clove garlic, pressed
1 teaspoon monosodium glutamate

Watermelon Basket

Use ½ watermelon. With an ice-cream scoop, make large watermelon balls, discarding as many seeds as possible and leaving only the shell of the watermelon. Make smaller balls from a cantaloupe. With a sharp knife trim the edge of the watermelon shell. Cut 1-inch triangles out of it all the way around, making a decorative saw-tooth edge. Insert the knife slantwise, and make an incision one inch deep; right next to it, make another incision slanted in the opposite direction to finish the triangle point. Repeat all around, cutting one triangle out and leaving one standing up.

Fill the shell with the watermelon

and cantaloupe balls, and add 1 quart each strawberries, blueberries or blackberries, and cherries; reserve a few beautiful strawberries and cherries to place in strategic spots on top. Pile the fruit high in the shell, decorate with 3 quartered limes and a few mint leaves, and pour 2 cups domestic port over all. Chill for 15 minutes.

½ watermelon
1 cantaloupe
1 quart strawberries
1 quart blueberries or blackberries
1 quart cherries
3 limes
Mint leaves
2 cups domestic port

Brandy Black-Bottom Pie

In a 10-inch Pyrex pie plate make a crumb crust with 40 ginger snaps, crushed, and ¼ pound butter. Bake 5 minutes at 300°.

Soften 1 envelope gelatin in 2 tablespoons cold water and 1 tablespoon brandy, (takes about 10 minutes), and reserve for top filling.

Bottom filling: Beat 4 egg yolks until light; gradually add ½ cup dark brown sugar, 3¾ teaspoons cornstarch, and ¼ teaspoon salt. Then stir in 1½ cups scalded milk and 5 tablespoons brandy. Cook this mixture in top of 2-quart double boiler over hot water until thick and smooth, beating constantly with rotary or electric beater. Remove from heat.

Now melt 1½ squares bitter chocolate in a bowl by covering with 2 cups boiling water for 3 minutes, then quickly pouring off the water. Stir 1 cup of the hot custard into softened chocolate. Cool chocolate custard, and pour into pie shell.

Top filling: Add reserved gelatin to rest of hot custard, mixing well. Cool mixture slightly in refrigerator, but remove before it sets. Beat 4 egg whites stiff with ¼ teaspoon cream of tartar, and beat in ½ cup Vanilla Sugar. Fold egg-white mixture into cooled yellow custard. Pour this over chocolate filling in pie shell.

Chill pie at least 3 hours. To serve: Sprinkle pie with shaved sweet chocolate. Beat ½ cup heavy cream with 1 tablespoon Vanilla Sugar. With a pastry tube, make a border of whipped cream around outer rim of pie, and serve chilled.

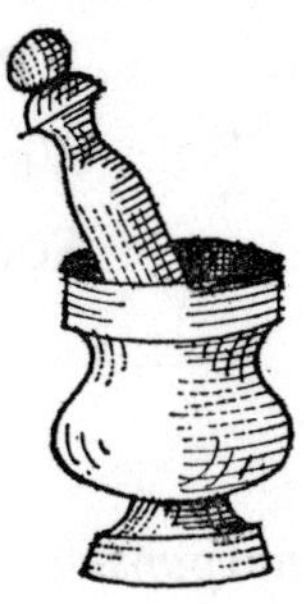

40 ginger snaps, crushed
¼ pound butter

4 egg yolks
½ cup dark brown sugar
3¾ teaspoons cornstarch
¼ teaspoon salt
1½ cups scalded milk
5 tablespoons brandy

1½ squares bitter chocolate
2 cups boiling water
1 cup hot custard, above

1 envelope gelatin
2 tablespoons cold water
1 tablespoon brandy
Remaining hot custard
4 egg whites
¼ teaspoon cream of tartar
½ cup Vanilla Sugar (see Index)

Shaved sweet chocolate
½ cup heavy cream, whipped
1 tablespoon Vanilla Sugar

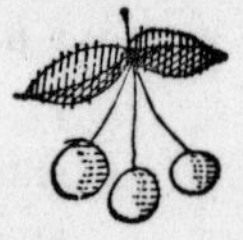

42

Patio Luncheon for Eight—I

BARBECUED VEAL KIDNEYS EN BROCHETTE

GRILLED TROUT WITH DILL BUTTER

POTATOES BAKED IN FOIL

WEST COAST ORIENTAL SALAD

SOUFFLÉ GLACÉ AUX FRAISES

DEMITASSE

WINES

Inexpensive: Louis Martini Johannisberg Riesling, Napa Sonoma Valley

Medium-priced: Piesporter Güntherslay Dünweg

Expensive: Erdener Treppchen, Estate-bottled Priesterseminar

The toss of a coin decided the fate of this menu; patio luncheon or patio dinner, it can be either. No question, though, that it must be outdoors; the charcoal barbecue gives an indefinable last touch to the kidneys and the trout that a kitchen range can't match. Double-check with the weatherman before you call the butcher and the fishmonger.

If you plan an evening barbecue, wait until morning to make the soufflé; there will be plenty of time for it to chill. But if it's midday you're aiming for, you'll have to make it the night before. If the weather goes back on you in the morning, do your shopping for some other menu entirely, and use the soufflé anyway. It would be a fitting conclusion to the *Poulet Normand* menu (p. 244), for instance, and this, too, is fine for noon or night.

You can comfortably handle the rest of the preparation in the morning. Buy frozen Danish trout, if fresh fish is unavailable in your neck of the woods, and set them out to defrost. Then trim the kidneys (unless the butcher will oblige), and put them in their marinade. Wash the salad greens, make the dressing, and boil the onions for the *brochettes*.

About two hours before servingtime, light the fire so the coals will be ready in plenty of time to bake the potatoes. During that hour, wrap them in foil, and mix the Dill Butter for the trout. Slice the cucumber and water chestnuts for the salad and arrange it in the bowl. Thread the kidneys and vegetables on the skewers, and set up the coffee pot. Then keep an eye on the clock for the moment to bury the potatoes in the coals.

There will be time for the hostess to collect herself in the meanwhile. We like to think of this as a leisurely meal for the cook (that's you, and you won't need outside help). Relax with your friends over drinks around the fire, and put on the *brochettes* when the clamor for food gets just insistent enough. Shortly before the last of the kidneys disappears, start the trout. It's impossible to specify just how long they will take (it depends on the size of the fish and the heat of the coals), but remember this is the meal you're not going to rush through. After you've turned the fish, bring out the salad and toss it at the table; unwrap the potatoes, add the butter, and the chances are the fish will be ready. On your last trip to the kitchen, make the coffee and garnish the soufflé.

When we say you don't need help for this barbecue, we picture an informal group—Bermuda shorts on all those who can get away with it, and no one feeling too much the lady to give the hostess a hand to clear the table and wash a dish or two. If the guest list includes ladies who are terribly *grandes dames,* they'll enjoy the menu no less for that, but then we'd suggest you do have someone to help serve and clean up.

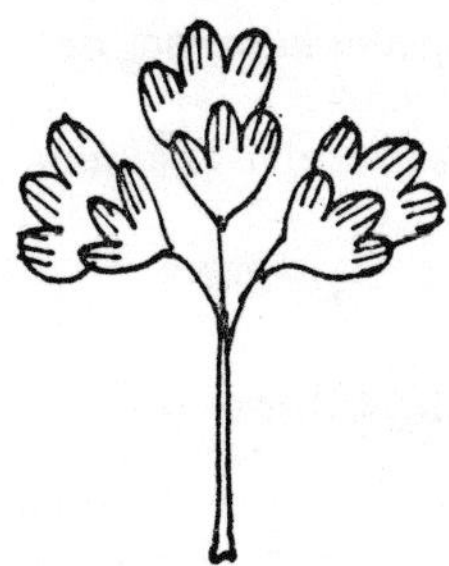

Barbecued Veal Kidneys en Brochette

Trim all but a very thin layer of fat from 8 veal kidneys, split them, and season with salt and pepper. Then marinate at least 1 hour in a mixture of 1 tablespoon lemon juice, 2 tablespoons bottled Escoffier Sauce Diable, and 2 tablespoons corn oil. Quarter 4 tomatoes and wrap each piece in a slice of bacon. Mix together ½ tablespoon crushed dried tarragon, ⅛ teaspoon freshly ground pepper, ¾ teaspoon salt, and 4 tablespoons corn oil; brush 8 large mushroom caps and 16 cooked onions with mixture. Divide meats and vegetables into 8 portions on *kebab* skewers: Start with a mushroom cap, then skewer half a kidney so it stays flat, and continue, alternating vegetables and meats. Broil 8 minutes, 5 to 6 inches from glowing coals. Turn once, and grill 8 minutes more. Serve at once.

8 veal kidneys
Salt, pepper
1 tablespoon lemon juice
2 tablespoons bottled Escoffier Sauce Diable
2 tablespoons corn oil

4 tomatoes
16 slices bacon
½ tablespoon dried tarragon
⅛ teaspoon pepper
¾ teaspoon salt
4 tablespoons corn oil
8 large mushroom caps
16 cooked onions

Grilled Trout with Dill Butter

Ask fishmonger to clean and split 8 trout, leaving them whole. Season with freshly ground pepper, salt, and 1 teaspoon lemon juice each. Place on ungreased grill, 8 to 10 inches from ash-covered coals. When fish stops sticking to grill, that side is done; turn, and repeat for other side. Place 1 tablespoon Dill Butter inside each trout and serve at once.

8 trout
Salt, pepper
8 teaspoons lemon juice
¼ pound Dill Butter (see Index, Herb Butters)

Potatoes Baked in Foil

Scrub 8 medium-size Idaho potatoes, and rub skins with ½ teaspoon butter each. Wrap in double thickness of aluminum foil, and place packages on outer edge of barbecue, among the coals. Bake 50 minutes, turning 4 times. Unwrap, split, and season each with 2 tablespoons salt butter and freshly ground pepper.

8 medium-size Idaho potatoes
4 teaspoons butter
½ pound salt butter
Pepper

West Coast Oriental Salad

Rinse, drain, and dry thoroughly yellow inner leaves of 3 heads chicory and 1 head Iceberg lettuce. Wrap in a towel and crisp in refrigerator. To ¾ cup Basic French Dressing add 2½ teaspoons curry powder, and beat with rotary beater to blend well. Rub a wooden salad bowl with a clove of garlic and pour in dressing; drain 1 small can water chestnuts. Slice 1 unpeeled cucumber and the water chestnuts, and arrange greens, cucumber, and water chestnuts in a pretty pattern on top of dressing. Crumble finely ¼ pound Roquefort, sprinkle over salad, and toss just before serving.

3 heads chicory
1 head Iceberg lettuce
¾ cup Basic French Dressing (see Index)
2½ teaspoons curry powder
Garlic
1 small can water chestnuts
1 cucumber
¼ pound Roquefort

Soufflé Glacé aux Fraises

Rub inside edge of a 1-quart soufflé dish with enough butter to make a waxed-paper collar stick to it; collar should extend 1 inch above rim. Stick ends together with more butter.

Over low heat, melt 1 cup Vanilla Sugar in ½ cup hot water with ¼ teaspoon cream of tartar. Boil rapidly until syrup spins a thread when dropped from spoon (242° on a candy thermometer). When syrup begins to boil, beat 5 egg whites very stiff in a metal bowl. As soon as syrup has begun to thread, pour in a thin, steady stream into beaten whites. Continue to beat until the mixture stands in peaks. Cool meringue at once by turning the bowl in a larger bowl filled with cracked ice.

In another bowl, beat 6 egg yolks until light in color and fluffy, gradually adding 1½ cups granulated sugar. Drain juice from 2 containers frozen strawberries; purée berries in electric blender (or in a food mill), adding just enough juice to blend with ease. Soften 1½ envelopes gelatin in ½ cup strawberry juice, then dissolve in top of double boiler over hot water, and add to strawberry purée. Stir 1 cup sour cream into purée, then fold cream-and-strawberry mixture into beaten egg yolks. Finally, fold this into cooled meringue. Pour at once into prepared soufflé dish and chill overnight in refrigerator. Just before serving, remove paper collar and decorate top with small fresh strawberries.

Butter
1 cup Vanilla Sugar (see Index)
½ cup hot water
¼ teaspoon cream of tartar
5 egg whites
Cracked ice
6 egg yolks
1½ cups granulated sugar
2 containers frozen strawberries
1½ envelopes gelatin
1 cup sour cream
Fresh strawberries

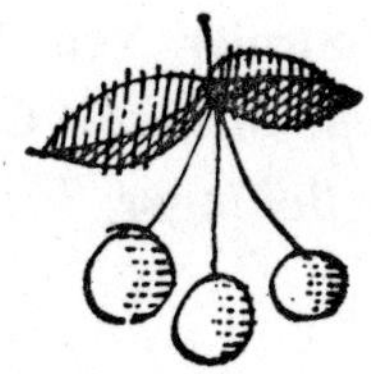

43

Patio Luncheon for Eight—II

Blinis and Caviar
Shashlik
Wheat Pilaff Véronique
Artichoke Bottoms en Brochette
Peaches in Champagne

WINES

Inexpensive: Charles Fournier New York State Champagne
Medium-priced: Mumm's Cordon Rouge
Expensive: Bollinger, Brut, Vintage

This luncheon we shall compare to an impeccably dressed woman; everything chosen with care, nothing *de trop,* the whole effect one of effortless perfection. We know better than to think it just happened that way—it took plenty of effort—but let's indulge in a little harmless play-acting and shrug it off with an I-can-do-this-anytime look.

In the morning, early, the first effort is to make the marinade and put the lamb in it, and to chill the champagne. Then make the *Blinis,* put them in a heavy pan, and wrap the whole thing in foil. Sauté the mushroom caps and artichoke bottoms, and place them on skewers. And sauté the wheat Pilaff and onions in a stove-to-table pot. A few more small chores: Mix the caviar and sour cream for the *Blinis* in a small bowl; stem the grapes or soak the raisins for the Pilaff; peel the peaches, dust them with sugar, and sprinkle with lemon juice; and lay the fire.

The next effort is for appearance sake—the dining table's and yours. This can be a special-occasion menu, and even if it isn't, it warrants your most glamorous appointments and an extravagant floral centerpiece. Next, an effort in your own direction; the hostess must look impeccable, too.

An hour before cookingtime, light the fire. A little later, thread the lamb on skewers and you're ready to greet your guests as though you'd done nothing but loll about the whole morning; it shall be your secret pleasure to know that this simply isn't true. If this really is a special occasion, you'll want someone to do the serving and last-minute cooking, though you can manage it yourself without too much damage to the leisurely illusion, since there's no rush about getting one course ready after the other in quick succession. Settle everyone outside with a drink before you go to the kitchen to add liquid to the Pilaff and start it simmering. Bring back the bowl of caviar and cream and the pan of *Blinis,* and set the pan well to one side of the barbecue to heat slowly. (When you serve them discard the bottom *blini;* it will be dry.)

By the time you've sipped your drink, the Pilaff will be finished; add the grapes or raisins, and carry it outside. It will stay hot in the covered pot. Bring out the skewers of lamb and the vegetable *brochettes* at the same time. Once you have the *Blinis* and caviar on plates and are about to set them at each place, put the lamb on the fire. Turn the meat and start the artichoke bottoms after you eat the first course; then clear the table, and have a little champagne while you wait. Then after the Shashlik and vegetables, a final trip to the kitchen to clear the table once again and to fetch the peaches.

You see, it is possible to manage alone, though it's only fair to say that it's a great deal easier to have help at the last. The finishing touch to all this perfection is to persuade *yourself* when it's all over that it really was effortless. For that you just will have to have help.

Quick Blinis

Preheat griddle over low heat while mixing batter. In a bowl, beat together ½ cup heavy cream, 2 tablespoons corn oil, and 4 eggs. Add ½ cup unsifted buckwheat pancake mix and ½ cup unsifted regular pancake mix. Blend lightly together (a lumpy batter makes light, fluffy pancakes), and add ½ cup light beer. Test griddle for heat; a few drops of water on it should bounce a second before evaporating. Brush griddle with melted butter. Pour about 2 tablespoons batter from a small ladle to make each *blini.* Turn *blinis* when tops are covered with bubbles and edges look cooked. Serve hot, with a dab of sour cream mixed with grey or black caviar.

½ cup heavy cream
2 tablespoons corn oil
4 eggs
½ cup buckwheat pancake mix
½ cup regular pancake mix
½ cup light beer
Butter
1 cup sour cream
4 ounces grey or black caviar

Shashlik

Cut 2½ pounds of meat from a leg of lamb into pieces about 1½ inches thick and 2 inches square; trim off excess fat. Place cubes in a bowl with 1 large chopped onion and 1 pressed clove of garlic, and mix well. In a saucepan, combine ¾ cup vinegar, ¼ cup water, ¼ teaspoon each cloves and cinnamon, and 6 crushed peppercorns. Over high heat, bring the mixture to a boil and add ½ cup red wine. Pour over meat and vegetables, and marinate at least 4 hours at room temperature. Then remove meat, dry each piece carefully, and brush with olive oil. Thread on long skewers, and put a cube of bread brushed with oil at end of each skewer to prevent meat from slipping off. Place skewers on grill 4 to 6 inches from glowing coals and broil, turning to brown on all sides. Salt the Shashlik lightly before serving, and arrange on a heated platter around Wheat Pilaff, below. Slip the meat off the skewers onto individual plates.

2½ pounds meat from leg of lamb
1 large onion
1 clove garlic
¾ cup vinegar
¼ cup water
¼ teaspoon cloves
¼ teaspoon cinnamon
6 peppercorns
½ cup red wine
Olive oil
8–10 bread cubes
Salt

Wheat Pilaff Véronique

In a heavy skillet, over medium heat, bring 4 tablespoons butter to sizzling point. In it sauté 2 cups packaged "wheat for pilaff" and 4 tablespoons minced onion. Moisten with 4 cups chicken broth, and stir in 1 to 2 tablespoons seasoned powdered chicken-broth base. Cover, reduce heat, and simmer 15 minutes. Add 4 cups green seedless grapes (or 1½ cups white raisins soaked in boiling water until plump).

4 tablespoons butter
2 cups packaged "wheat for pilaff"
4 tablespoons minced onion
4 cups chicken broth
1–2 tablespoons powdered chicken-broth base
4 cups green seedless grapes or 2 cups white raisins

Artichoke Bottoms en Brochette

Scrub 16 medium-size fresh mushroom caps. Drain 2 No. 2 cans artichoke bottoms, or use 16 fresh cooked ones. Sauté mushroom caps and artichoke bottoms in 2 tablespoons butter for 5 minutes, stirring frequently with a wooden spoon. Drain and season with salt and pepper. Thread mushrooms and artichoke bottoms alternately on 8 skewers, using two of each per skewer. Brush *brochettes* with ½ cup olive oil seasoned with 4 teaspoons lemon juice, and place on grill 6 inches from glowing coals for 6 minutes, turning twice. Serve at once, with Shashlik.

16 medium-size mushroom caps
2 No. 2 cans artichoke bottoms or 16 fresh cooked artichoke bottoms
2 tablespoons butter
Salt, pepper
½ cup olive oil
4 teaspoons lemon juice

Peaches in Champagne

Peel 8 very ripe freestone peaches and leave them whole. Dust with ½ cup granulated sugar, sprinkle with 1 tablespoon lemon juice, and place in refrigerator. Just before serving (individually, in champagne glasses, or from a large crystal bowl), cover with well-chilled champagne.

8 ripe freestone peaches
½ cup granulated sugar
1 tablespoon lemon juice
1 bottle New York State champagne

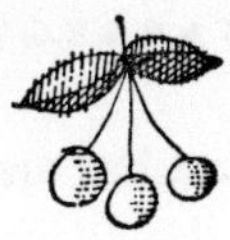

44

Patio Dinner for Six—I

POLISH COLD CREAM OF CUCUMBER SOUP
SWORDFISH STEAKS
DOMASTELLI PILAFF
INDIAN EGGPLANT ON THE SPIT
PEACHES PRINCESS MARGARETHA

WINES

Inexpensive: Inglenook Traminer
Medium-priced: Niersteiner Glöck, Estate-bottled Verwaltung der Staatsweingüter
Expensive: Schloss Johannisberger Grünlack, Estate-bottled, Von Metternich

It used to be that men vied with each other demonstrating their carving skill on the Sunday roast. Along came the age of cook-outs, and arguments among weekend chefs waxed hot and heavy on how to grill the perfect steak. And now the genial host has something new with which to prove his prowess. Flaming swords and flaming desserts have ushered in the *flambéed* era. The boys are playing with fire.

If your host is really in a show-off mood, let him don the chef's apron to grill the swordfish (sorry, no pyrotechnics yet) and keep the basting spoon going over the eggplant. If your barbecue pit doesn't boast a spit, set the eggplant on the grate and turn it every few minutes. Cooking time depends on the heat of the coals (not too intense, if you put them on the grate), but estimate anywhere from 20 to 30 minutes on either grate or spit.

With the host as co-chef, your work load is considerably lightened. Make the soup in the morning, but wait till the last minute to add the chopped chives, parsley, and fennel. Brown the rice and onions for the pilaff ahead of time in a stove-to-table pot or casserole, and add the liquid and let it simmer on the grate when everyone has arrived. (Don't forget to check the liquid as the pilaff simmers.)

Poach the peaches early in the day, and assemble all the dessert equipment on a tray: cooked peaches, the jam, jelly, and preserve in a heavy pan, a bottle of brandy and one of kirsch, a bowl for the ice cream, and a saucer of toasted almonds. When the time comes, fill the bowl with ice cream, bring the tray to the chef, and he can perform with the peaches while you dutifully clear the table.

With all this help to look forward to and so little to do at the last minute, you may feel like a guest at your own party and wish you had asked more people to join you. By all means, do. The menu should be easy to multiply for eight or ten, especially with a willing partner on the cooking team.

Polish Cold Cream of Cucumber Soup

Rinse well ½ pound young beet tops. Cook as quickly as possible, in the same way as spinach, with only the water that clings to the leaves; then drain, chop, and cool. Chop finely enough peeled cucumber to make 2 cups. Mix vegetables together in a large bowl with 1 quart chilled sour cream, and dilute with about 1 cup well-skimmed chicken broth; season to taste, and chill. Then add 1 teaspoon parsley, 1 tablespoon chives, and 1 teaspoon fennel tops, all minced, and serve in chilled individual bowls, topped with a few slices unpeeled cucumber.

½ pound beet tops
3–4 medium cucumbers
1 quart sour cream
1 cup chicken broth
Parsley
Chives
Fennel tops (optional)

Swordfish Steaks

Season two 1½-pound swordfish steaks with juice of 1 lemon, pepper, salt, and paprika, and let them stand at least 1 hour. Place on ungreased barbecue grill, 5 inches from ash-covered coals. When fish stops sticking to grill, that side is done; turn, and grill other side. Serve with 1 tablespoon Parsley Butter on each portion.

2 1½-pound swordfish steaks
1 lemon
Salt, pepper
Paprika
6 tablespoons Parsley Butter (*see Index, Herb Butters*)

Domastelli Pilaff

Chop 2 medium onions. In a heavy skillet, over medium heat, lightly sauté onions and 2 cups rice in 3 tablespoons butter, stirring constantly. Cover with 2 cups chicken broth, season with salt and freshly ground pepper, and stir in 3 tablespoons tomato paste. Reduce heat, cover, and simmer 40 minutes in all; after 25 minutes add water or broth to cover, without stirring, if rice looks dry on top.

2 medium onions
2 cups rice
3 tablespoons butter
2–3 cups chicken broth

Salt
Pepper
3 tablespoons tomato paste

Indian Eggplant on the Spit

Cut small caps from tops of two 1-pound eggplants and scoop out flesh, leaving shells ½ inch thick. Chop eggplant and mix with ¼ pound ground raw meat. Chop 3 onions and fry in 2 tablespoons butter until soft; then add meat-and-eggplant mixture, 2 teaspoons cumin, salt to taste, and 1 teaspoon black pepper, and mix well. Cook 5 minutes and stuff inside the eggplant shells. Replace caps, fastening with toothpicks. Arrange eggplants on spit and cook about 10 minutes; baste with mixture of 1 pint plain yogurt, 4 tablespoons melted butter, and 2 teaspoons turmeric, and cook another 10 minutes, or until tender. Baste with 2 tablespoons melted butter just before serving. Serve sliced.

2 1-pound eggplants
¼ pound ground meat
3 onions
¼ pound butter (in all)
2 teaspoons cumin
Salt
1 teaspoon black pepper
1 pint plain yogurt
2 teaspoons turmeric

Peaches Princess Margaretha

Poach 6 ripe peaches with a piece of vanilla bean in lightly sugared boiling water to cover for 6 to 8 minutes. Remove with a ladle and take off skins. In a heavy pan put 2 tablespoons each green-gage plum preserve, the best procurable red-currant jelly (preferably *Bar-le-Duc*), and strawberry jam. Heat all three together on the grill. Then add peaches, and pour on ½ cup each brandy and kirsch. Do not stir. Put 6 servings vanilla ice cream on dessert plates, then flame the peaches. To each plate add one peach and a portion of flaming sauce. Sprinkle with toasted and slivered almonds and serve immediately.

6 ripe peaches
Vanilla bean
2 tablespoons green-gage plum preserve
2 tablespoons red-currant jelly
2 tablespoons strawberry jam
½ cup brandy
½ cup kirsch
1½ quarts vanilla ice cream
¼ cup almonds

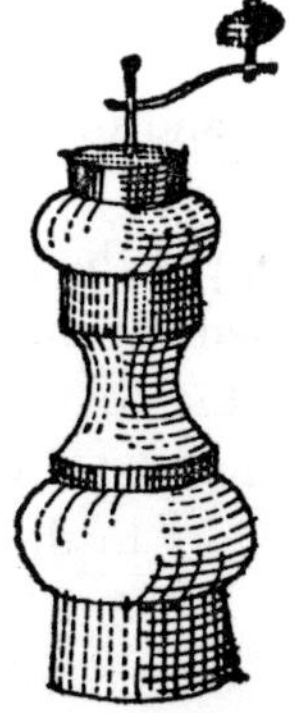

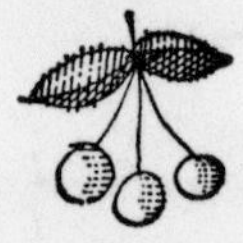

45

Patio Dinner for Six—II

COSTILLAS CON SALSA BARBACOA
HAITIAN RICE SALAD
LOBSTER TAILS GRAND MAÎTRE ESCOFFIER
VIENNESE CHOCOLATE ROLL
Sangria

Wouldn't you know, we worked out *this* menu when the snow was a foot and a half deep outside and all the magazines in the house were choked with ads for West Indies cruises. Escapist fashion, we planned dinner for a lush tropical night on a moonlit terrace—the hostess in a Caribbean mood, complete with flower in her hair. If such is your mood also, then call this only technically a barbecue, and don't breathe the word when you invite your friends—they might show up in shorts and jeans and spoil the whole effect. Tell them simply that it's a party, and, if we know women, they will all be looking marvellous and will have seen to it that their men are dressed to match. (Just incidentally, however, note that since that winter's day, we've also done this dinner shorts-and-jeans style, with lots of audience participation, mostly male, at the barbecue. The effect is different, but good.)

Getting back to the tropics, since a beautiful summer's night generally means a scorcher of a day, we planned the work for early morning and late afternoon, as they do in the tropics. First thing then, make the cake for the chocolate roll. While it bakes, boil the rice and the eggs for the Haitian Salad, and prepare the Chocolate Sauce and the sparerib marinade. And that's all there is to do at the moment.

Two hours before cookingtime, put the spareribs in the marinade, fill the cake, and assemble the salad. Then cut the lobster tails and mix their basting sauce. (If you are put off by the combination of cherries and chocolate in the Viennese Roll, make a Chocolate Nut-Cream Roll: Add ½ cup of coarsely chopped pecans or walnuts to the whipped cream instead of the cherry jam, and add another ½ cup of chopped nuts to the chocolate sauce. Substitute rum for Cherry Heering in the sauce.)

Pineapple, capers, and mayonnaise are standard ingredients in Haitian Rice Salad, but the seafood garnish may vary; any shellfish or cold poached fish would do, but we think you will agree that nothing could equal the broiled lobster tails.

The *Sangria* we suggest with this meal is the hot-weather drink of Spain and Latin America, but you might prefer the Haitian *Clairène au Miel,* served in chilled coconut shells and sipped through a straw. You need fresh coconuts to make it. (See a strong man and directions in some other book for opening coconuts!) Add 2 tablespoons of honey to 1 cup of lukewarm coconut milk. Pour into a martini mixer half filled with cracked ice. Add 2 cups of light rum and stir. Serve either the *Sangria* or *Clairène* with dinner and throughout the evening.

For this, as for any barbecue, have someone light the fire for you an hour before cooking time. It should be almost ready when your guests arrive. Bundle up the spareribs in their foil packages, then go off and make yourself glamorous. Serve the first round of *Sangria* as you wait for the spareribs to cook. They will be ready to eat with the second round (about time, too—the aromas are tantalizing beyond belief!) Twenty minutes before dinner, put the lobster tails on the grill.

If you're reading this menu when there's snow a foot and a half deep outside *your* door and you, too, feel thwarted by it all, you can do something about it if you have a Japanese *hibachi.* These inexpensive stoves are efficient, and neat enough to permit charcoal cooking right in the living room. The small ones won't perform for a party of six, but, when there are just two of you, have a tête-à-tête barbecue, scaling down the amounts given in the recipes. And, even if you're wearing slacks and a sweater, tuck a flower in your hair.

Costillas con Salsa Barbacoa

Combine 1 cup Madeira or Malaga wine, juice of 3 lemons, 1 cup bottled Escoffier Sauce Diable, 3 cloves garlic, crushed, ½ tablespoon imported paprika, ¼ teaspoon salt, and ⅛ teaspoon freshly ground black pepper. Cut 5 pounds lean spareribs into small serving pieces of 2 to 3 ribs each. Place in the Madeira marinade for 2 hours. When ready to grill, divide ribs into 6 portions, place on double thicknesses of foil, cup the foil, and baste each portion with 3 tablespoons of marinade. Seal foil around ribs, place packages among hot but ash-covered briquettes, and place more hot briquettes on top. Cook for 30 minutes. Open packages, remove ribs, draining off fat, and transfer to a heated platter. If some of the ribs are not brown enough when you open foil, turn them and cook with the foil open for 5 to 10 minutes, until nicely colored.

1 cup Madeira or Malaga wine
3 lemons
1 cup bottled Escoffier Sauce Diable
3 cloves garlic
½ tablespoon imported paprika
¼ teaspoon salt
⅛ teaspoon black pepper
5 pounds spareribs

Haitian Rice Salad

Mix ½ cup tarragon or garlic wine vinegar with 1 teaspoon dry mustard, ¼ teaspoon Tabasco sauce, and 1 teaspoon salt. Toss 4 cups cold steamed rice with this dressing, and mound rice in center of large earthenware platter.

Dip 2 tomatoes in boiling water, then quickly in cold water, peel, and cut into eighths. Peel and quarter 4 hard-cooked eggs. Peel, quarter, and core 1 small fresh pineapple, then cut meat into 8 sticks about 5 inches long. Slice enough green or black olives to make ¼ cup. Decorate rice with vegetables, eggs, and fruit. Over everything, with a pastry tube, press a latticework of Mayonnaise, and sprinkle with ⅓ cup capers. Edge platter with Lobster Tails Grand Maître Escoffier, below. Warm ¼ cup brandy, ignite, and pour flaming over hot lobster tails.

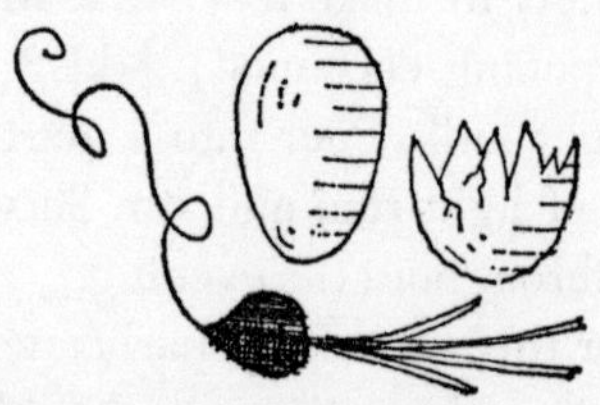

½ cup tarragon or garlic wine vinegar
1 teaspoon dry mustard
¼ teaspoon Tabasco
1 teaspoon salt
4 cups cold steamed rice (see Index)
2 tomatoes
4 hard-cooked eggs
1 small pineapple
Green or black olives
Mayonnaise (see below)
⅓ cup capers
Lobster Tails Grand Maître Escoffier
¼ cup brandy

Mixer Mayonnaise

Rinse the small bowl of an electric mixer with hot water and dry thoroughly. In it place 2 egg yolks, 1 tablespoon salt, ½ teaspoon white pepper, and 1 teaspoon prepared mustard. Beat well at medium speed. Pour in olive oil, a few drops at a time, then, as sauce stiffens, in a thin stream, until 1 cup oil is incorporated. Add 1 tablespoon white wine vinegar to thin the sauce. Continue beating, adding gradually 1 more cup oil and 3 more tablespoons vinegar. Makes 2 cups.

2 egg yolks
1 tablespoon salt
½ teaspoon white pepper
1 teaspoon prepared mustard
¼ cup white wine vinegar, in all
2 cups olive oil
or 1 cup each salad and olive oil

Lobster Tails Grand Maître Escoffier

Place 12 defrosted South African rock-lobster tails on a board, and with a sharp pointed knife, slit undershells lengthwise for about 3 inches to prevent curling. Make 1½ cups barbecue sauce: Blend ¾ cup bottled Escoffier Sauce Robert with ¾ cup salad oil and 1 tablespoon Tabasco sauce. Brush tails with this barbecue sauce, and place tails, shell side down, on grill; you may also thread them on skewers for grilling. Grill 4 inches from ash-covered coals for 15 minutes. Brush again with barbecue sauce and grill 3 minutes more, or until shells are bright red. Serve flambéed with ¼ cup brandy, around Haitian Rice Salad above.

12 South African rock-lobster tails
¾ cup bottled Escoffier Sauce Robert
¾ cup salad oil
1 tablespoon Tabasco
¼ cup brandy

Viennese Chocolate Roll

Preheat oven to 400°. Sift together twice ¼ cup sifted flour, ½ teaspoon salt, 4 tablespoons cocoa, and 1 cup confectioners' sugar. Beat 5 egg yolks until thick, and fold the sifted ingredients into them. Beat 5 egg whites until stiff, add 1 teaspoon vanilla, and fold them into the egg-yolk mixture. Spread in a greased jelly-roll pan, and bake for 15 to 20 minutes. With a sharp knife, cut edges off cake, loosen with spatula, and turn out on a damp cloth. Roll up cloth and cake like a jelly roll. Store in refrigerator until ready to use.

When the cake is cold, unroll, spread with 1 cup heavy cream, whipped, into which ½ cup sour-cherry jam has been folded, and roll up again. Slice, and serve with 1 cup hot Chocolate Sauce flavored with ¼ cup Cherry Heering.

¼ cup sifted flour
½ teaspoon salt
4 tablespoons cocoa
1 cup confectioners' sugar
5 eggs, separated
1 teaspoon vanilla
1 cup heavy cream, whipped
½ cup sour-cherry jam
1 cup Chocolate Sauce (*see Index*)
¼ cup Cherry Heering

Sangria

Combine following ingredients and serve ice cold:

1 can frozen lime juice
3 cups water
2 cups red wine
Ice to fill a 2-quart pitcher

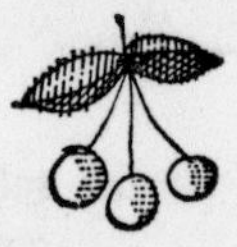

46

Patio Dinner for Eight—I

VITELLO TONNATO WITH SICILIAN TOMATOES
CHICKEN CECI
BROCCOLI AND ASPARAGUS SALAD
SESAME GRISSINI
CHILLED ZABAGLIONE

WINES

Inexpensive: American White Chianti, en carafe
Medium-priced: Ruffino White Chianti
Expensive: Soave, or Cortese Bianco

We have a friend who swears by *The Farmer's Almanac.* Whether she has just been lucky or whether such blind faith must be rewarded, we cannot say, but she abides by their predictions and always has perfect weather for her barbecues. Most of us are too sceptical and operate on the principle that the best laid plans of mice and men, etc. For us, it is safer to choose two-faced barbecues that function well either indoors or out. We are also in favor of menus that we can serve at noon or at night; this menu is flexible on both counts—this time, with an Italian accent.

Start the *Vitello Tonnato* two days in advance. The meat itself is bland and absorbs a wonderful flavor standing in the sauce. There are many recipes for this traditional dish that use the same basic ingredients in varying proportions. We like this one which is neither too rich nor too intense in flavor. Another thought for *Vitello Tonnato* is to serve it for lunch one summer's day, with the tomatoes and the breadsticks and followed by the *Zabaglione* for dessert.

Make the *Zabaglione* and prepare the salad ingredients the day before, or get them ready early in the morning. Once you have prepared the chicken and wrapped it in the foil, there is nothing further on your schedule until you light the fire. The recipe for the Italian Chicken *Ceci* came to us quite unexpectedly one summer via the gardener, who was watching us spit roast some chickens outdoors. His description of his way of cooking chick peas with chicken furnished enough clues for us to fill in the gaps and come up with this recipe. Apparently, we followed his train of thought, because he sampled our first trial run, washed it down with a glass of Chianti, and accorded it his approval. We like to believe that the Chianti did not influence his decision.

If you have picked this menu only the day you want to use it, you will have to skip the veal. Or, you may feel that three courses are more food than you want. Then use the Broccoli and Asparagus Salad as a first course, and serve the herb-flavored tomatoes with the chicken.

Convert this barbecue to indoor cooking and service just as you do the Persian Chicken (see p. 156). Put a handful or so of the *Grissini* bread sticks in two tumblers, place one at each end of the table, and the bottles of wine on the table, too. If you can find the tiny red and yellow cherry or egg-shaped tomatoes, as well as the pear-shaped tomatoes that you use with the veal, combine them all heaped in a bowl to make a wonderful centerpiece. It invariably attracts nibblers and you may find that the bowl is empty even before you announce dinner.

Vitello Tonnato and Sicilian Tomatoes

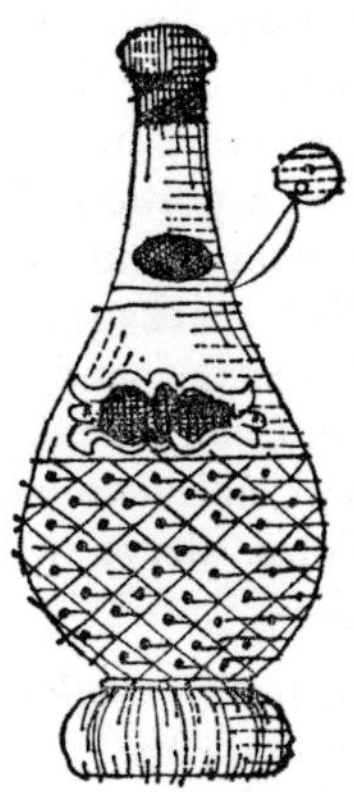

Remove fat and tendons from 2 pounds veal (leg round or head of round). Place 2 anchovy fillets in slit in meat, and tie well to hold shape. Poach 1½ hours, or until tender, in enough *Court-Bouillon* for Meat to cover. Remove meat from pot, drain, and cut into bite-size cubes.

In electric blender or electric mixer, purée together 4 ounces Italian tuna fish in olive oil, 6 anchovy fillets, 2 teaspoons lemon juice, 1 tablespoon capers bottled in vinegar, and ¼ to ½ cup olive oil; blend until sauce is smooth and fluid. Combine meat and tuna-fish sauce and store, covered, in refrigerator.

Marinate 1 pint cherry or pear-shaped tomatoes for 12 hours in 1 cup Basic French Dressing to which has been added ¼ teaspoon dried powdered orégano and ¼ teaspoon dried powdered basil. Drain dressing from tomatoes and reserve for other uses. Heap veal with its sauce on a round platter, border with tomatoes, and sprinkle 1 tablespoon chopped parsley over all.

2 pounds veal, leg round or head of round
8 anchovy fillets, in all
Court-Bouillon for Meat (see Index)
4 ounces Italian tuna fish
2 teaspoons lemon juice

1 tablespoon capers in vinegar
¼–½ cup olive oil
1 pint cherry or pear-shaped tomatoes
1 cup Basic French Dressing (*see Index*)
¼ teaspoon orégano
¼ teaspoon basil
1 tablespoon chopped parsley

Chicken Ceci

Drain 3 No. 2 cans Italian chick peas. Split four 2½-pound broilers and wipe inside and out with a damp cloth. In a bowl, combine ½ cup bottled Escoffier Sauce Robert with ½ cup olive oil. Mince 2 large red onions and chop 2 stalks celery with tops. Add onions, celery, and chick peas to sauce, and season with 1½ teaspoons Italian seasoning, ½ teaspoon salt, ¼ teaspoon freshly ground black pepper, and 2 tablespoons vinegar. Place each half broiler on a double thickness of foil large enough to wrap it securely. In cavity of each chicken place a portion of sauce and vegetable mixture, and wrap chicken securely. Place packages on glowing coals of barbecue, and drop more coals on top. Cook 35 minutes. Open packages and slide contents onto individual plates. Serve with Sesame *Grissini,* below.

3 No. 2 cans Italian chick peas
4 2½-pound broilers
½ cup bottled Escoffier Sauce Robert
½ cup olive oil
2 large red onions
2 stalks celery
1½ teaspoons Italian seasoning
½ teaspoon salt
¼ teaspoon black pepper
2 tablespoons vinegar

Asparagus and Broccoli Salad

Trim stems from 3 bunches very fresh broccoli. Boil, uncovered, for 8 minutes in salted water, then drain and cool. Marinate in Italian Dressing for 2 hours. Drain 2 No. 2 cans white asparagus and marinate in the same way. Chop separately yolks and whites of 2 hard-cooked eggs. Lift asparagus out of dressing, place in center of shallow salad bowl and arrange broccoli bouquets all around. Sprinkle egg yolk on asparagus and decorate broccoli with egg white. Serve well chilled.

3 bunches broccoli
2 No. 2 cans white asparagus
Italian Dressing (*see Index*)
2 hard-cooked eggs

Sesame Grissini

Melt 4 tablespoons butter and brush 24 *grissini* (Italian bread sticks) with it; then roll in sesame seeds and toast lightly for 5 minutes on side of barbecue grill.

4 tablespoons butter
Sesame seeds
24 grissini

Cold Zabaglione

In top pan of a 2-quart double boiler, beat together with electric or rotary beater 6 egg yolks and ½ cup sugar until thick and pale in color. Gradually beat into mixture ⅔ cup Marsala. Place over boiling water and continue beating until mixture foams up and begins to thicken. Place pan in a bowl of cracked ice and continue beating until cold. Whip ¾ cup heavy cream and fold into cooled *zabaglione.* Pour into cups and chill in icebox.

6 egg yolks
½ cup sugar
⅔ cup Marsala
¾ cup heavy cream

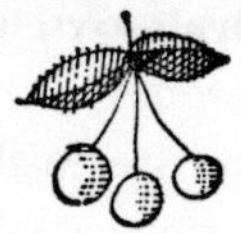

47

Patio Dinner for Eight—II

Iced Melon
Persian Chicken
Steamed White Rice *
Persian Saffron Rice
Vegetables en Brochette
Peaches Sultana
Turkish Coffee

WINES

Inexpensive: Wente Pinot Blanc, Livermore Valley
Medium-priced: Meursault
Expensive: Montrachet

Persian cookery relies on the most delicate flavorings rather than strong spices to achieve its subtle, sophisticated taste. Persian Chicken is as old as the Hanging Gardens of Babylon. Envoys from Egypt in the eleventh century B.C., came back to their Pharaoh with tales of a most wonderful bird that laid an egg each day. No one might slaughter the chicken until it had stopped laying, but then, they went on to relate, the Persians cooked it and bathed it in one of a number of exquisite sauces. Even at present, the natives of primitive sections of Iran follow the ancient recipe. They barbecue the bird over a charcoal pit, baste it with the juice of the bitter orange and cook the saffron-almond rice in round earthenware cauldrons in their cliff ovens.

We use essentially the same procedure in preparing the chicken today. Light your barbecue an hour ahead, so that you will have a bed of glowing coals about three layers deep when it is time to place the foil-wrapped packages of chicken on the fire. Spend that hour getting the orange-butter sauce, orange rind, almonds, rice, and vegetables ready.

* see Index

If it is more convenient, boil and steam the rice hours ahead (see Index). Turn off the heat and leave the rice, covered with a towel, in a colander over a pot of water. Thirty minutes before you want it, bring the water to a boil, turn down the heat, and let the rice steam again over simmering water. Because rice is starchy, bread is not traditionally served with this menu. We need not be such purists, though sesame-seed crackers would probably be better here than bread.

Depending on weather and whim, this is an outdoor or indoor barbecue. For indoor cooking, your broiler replaces the barbecue pit. Preheat the broiler for 10 minutes, wrap the chicken in foil as directed and place 3 to 4 inches away from the heat. Allow 30 minutes for an electric broiler, 45 minutes for gas. Turn the packages when they are half cooked.

Best poach the peaches for the dessert the same day to retain the fresh taste; for maximum flavor, buy fully ripened fruit. In winter, you could use pears instead.

Serve the barbecue for either a midday or evening meal. Indoors, you will have to limit your guests to eight people, unless you have two broilers; for outdoor cooking, you can probably accommodate many more.

Naturally, the dressiness of your table depends on the where and when of service. A decorative scheme that you could carry out in any setting: a muted tangerine cloth, brass candlesticks (if it's evening), and an arrangement of oranges or peaches and unshelled almonds in a leaf-lined brass bowl.

Iced Melon

To select perfectly ripe melons, feel the stem end with your thumb; it should yield slightly to pressure. Then take a deep breath through one nostril, with mouth half open, holding the melon close to your face; a strong aroma of melon should be conveyed to you. If a melon has no smell, chances are that it has been picked too soon and never will reach perfect maturity.

Cut 1 Persian melon or 2 cantaloupes into 8 wedges, scrape out seeds, and pour ½ cup fresh lime juice over wedges. Chill thoroughly before serving.

1 Persian melon
or 2 cantaloupes
½ cup fresh lime juice

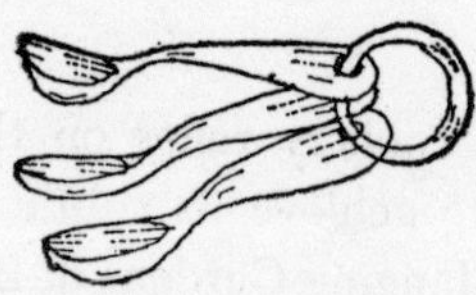

Persian Chicken

Heat 2 cups orange juice, in it melt ¼ pound butter, and mix well. Split four 2½-pound broiler chickens and rub inside and out with a damp cloth. Place each half on two thicknesses foil large enough to wrap chicken securely. Season with pepper and salt, cup foil, and baste each half chicken with ¼ cup butter-orange-juice mixture. Close the packages and place in barbecue pit on a bed of glowing coals; heap more hot coals on top, and cook 35 minutes.

Meanwhile, prepare Steamed White

Rice and Persian Saffron Rice, below, or reheat if prepared ahead. When chicken is ready, place white rice on bottom of large heated serving platter; unwrap chicken, lay it on white rice, then heap Saffron Rice on top of it all. Serve with Vegetables *en Brochette,* below.

2 cups orange juice
¼ pound butter
4 2½-pound broiler chickens
Salt, pepper
1 recipe Steamed White Rice (see Index)
1 recipe Saffron Rice

Persian Saffron Rice

To 6 cups boiling water add 2 tablespoons Spanish saffron, and boil together for 5 minutes. Water will be bright yellow. In it boil 2 cups unwashed rice at a rolling boil for 10 minutes with 1 tablespoon salt, then proceed as for Steamed Rice (see Index).

While rice steams, remove rind from 2 oranges and cut into fine julienne strips. (Extract juice from oranges and use in basting sauce for Persian Chicken, above.) Boil orange rind rapidly in water for 2 minutes to remove bitter oils, and drain. Make a syrup by boiling together 1 cup granulated sugar and ½ cup water for 5 minutes. Cook drained orange rind in syrup over medium heat for 5 more minutes, and add 10 drops orange-flower water.*

When rice is done, mix into it the orange rind plus 3 tablespoons of its syrup, and ¾ cup slivered blanched almonds. Heap on top of Persian Chicken.

6 cups boiling water
2 tablespoons Spanish saffron
2 cups rice
1 tablespoon salt
2 oranges
1 cup granulated sugar
½ cup water
10 drops orange-flower water *
¾ cup slivered blanched almonds

Vegetables en Brochette

In a large shallow pan, in a single layer, place 8 drained canned artichoke hearts, 8 fresh mushroom caps, 4 small firm ripe tomatoes, halved, 8 peeled pieces of cucumber, 8 pieces of eggplant, and 1 small green pepper, cut into squares. Combine ¾ cup salad oil, ¼ cup lemon juice, and 1 teaspoon salt, and pour over the vegetables. Let them stand, basting often, for 2 to 3 hours, then drain and reserve marinade.

On 8 skewers thread 1 piece of each kind of vegetable. Grill 5 inches away from glowing coals, basting often with marinade, for about 10 minutes, or until cooked through.

8 canned artichoke hearts
8 mushroom caps
4 small tomatoes
8 pieces cucumber
8 pieces eggplant
1 small green pepper
¾ cup salad oil
¼ cup lemon juice
1 teaspoon salt

* Orange-flower water may be bought at most pharmacies.

Peaches Sultana

Peel 4 large peaches and leave them whole. Boil 1½ cups water with 1 cup granulated sugar until syrup is reduced to 1 cup. Flavor with 1 tablespoon or more rose water.* Place peaches in syrup, reduce heat, and simmer fruit until tender. Drain and cool on absorbent paper. Reduce liquid to heavy syrup, almost a glaze, by boiling it over high heat. Roll peaches in this glaze. Place 1 quart pistachio ice cream in silver or crystal bowl, place peaches on ice cream, and pour rest of glaze, cooled, over all. Garnish with pistachio nuts and crystallized rose petals.*

8 large peaches
1½ cups water
1 cup granulated sugar
*1 tablespoon or more rose water **
1 quart pistachio ice cream
Pistachio nuts
*Crystallized rose petals **

Turkish Coffee

Put 8 tiny coffee cupfuls water and 8 teaspoons sugar into a *kanika* or a small pan and bring to boil; then pour off half and reserve. Add 8 heaping teaspoons finely ground Turkish coffee, and boil. Tap pan gently three times; boiling will subside. Repeat this two more times and, when it boils up the third time, add reserved liquid and pour coffee at once into tiny cups.

8 cupfuls water
8 teaspoons sugar
8 heaping teaspoons Turkish coffee

* Rose water may be bought from most pharmacies. Crystallized rose petals are more difficult to find. They are made in southern France and sold as candy in some delicacy shops. Pink sugar fancies may be substituted. It is all right, however, to use just the pistachios.

COCKTAIL PARTIES

The Cocktail Party

A successful cocktail party requires strategic planning. A small party for an intimate group of a dozen or so serves one purpose, and one so large that you almost (but only almost) fill all the available space with standees serves another. The logistics of serving cocktails and hors-d'oeuvres will differ in each case, so be clear in your mind which kind of occasion this is to be: a small party where your guests can mostly help themselves to hors-d'oeuvres, and where your host can easily handle all the serving of drinks; or a big one where hors-d'oeuvres will have to be passed to avoid a traffic jam, and where help will be needed in mixing and serving cocktails.

Some sort of a combination of the two can also be practical, but these are still the basic situations, and they influence your choice of hors-d'oeuvres first of all. We have divided our recipes accordingly, into two lists, one for the small and one for the large party. Before you glance ahead and turn pale at their length, we hasten to say that from these suggestions you will pick only a relevant few to suit the occasion. From both lists, also, pick what strikes your fancy for the cocktail hour before a dinner party, for the menus in this book do not include the pre-prandial hors-d'oeuvres. We believe in a *very* modest array of these to precede a dinner, to pique and not spoil the appetite.

The cocktail party runs anywhere from four or six in the afternoon to seven or eight in the evening, at which point everyone supposedly leaves for dinner. Therefore, especially in the suburbs, where you may invite people from a nearby metropolis as well as the neighborhood, it may be wise to arrange a third kind of party, a cocktail-buffet that follows up the hors-d'oeuvres with more substantial food, so your guests will go on their way remembering a gesture of hospitality that truly repays their trip.

You, as hostess, are the general in charge of commissary, so see to it that the bar accessories are in order and that you have an adequacy of food and a plan for serving it. But this is the occasion to yield the post of commander-in-chief to your host. While he takes over the center of the stage and dispenses good cheer, both literal and figurative, you can relax and maybe even let someone else wait on *you* for a change.

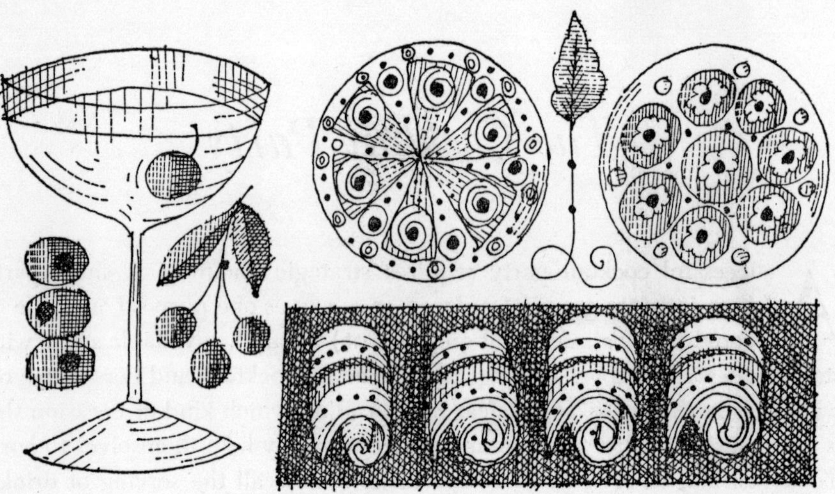

Bar equipment should include a roomy tray, a cocktail shaker and a martini mixer, a long bar spoon and a long muddler, a bottle opener, small strainer and small, sharp knife, ice tongs, a large pitcher for water and several smaller ones for fruit juices and tomato juice if there are to be mixed drinks. You should have a standard jigger, a bottle of bitters, one of bar syrup, several small dishes for the cocktail onions, cherries, twists of lemon peel, wedges of lime, and cocktail olives, and a simple cocktail recipe book that your host both understands and approves of. Plenty of cocktail napkins and coasters are important. On-the-rocks glasses have supplanted highball glasses in popularity, though some people still prefer a long drink. You should also have a supply of martini glasses, a lesser number of two-ounce stemmed glasses for sherry or Dubonnet, and a few wine glasses.

Basic items for the liquor closet include scotch, bourbon and rye, Italian vermouth, gin and dry vermouth, a light Jamaican rum, vodka for the sophisticates, Dubonnet and sherry for those who shun hard liquor; or, as a novel *apéritif,* either a domestic, fruity, white varietal wine such as Widmer's Niagara Lake, or one of the light, dry European vermouths, served with a cube of ice, such as a Chambéry. And check your supply of drink mixings:

club soda, tonic, and ginger ale; and orange, lemon, lime, and tomato juice if your host requests them.

With this equipment you are prepared for highballs and whisky on the rocks; whisky sours, Old-Fashioneds, and Manhattans; martinis, gibsons and vodka martinis; daiquiris, screwdrivers, bloody Marys, gin or vodka and tonic, and rye and ginger ale; and you have a choice of four *apéritifs*—surely a substantial list of the better-known cocktail-hour potions, from which your host will choose only as many as suit the occasion. We leave it to his bar book to supply the ideas for anything more exotic than these current stand-bys.

Mixing drinks is as precise as chemistry. Accuracy and the finest ingredients produce the best cocktails, and no drink can be better than the liquor it contains. It helps to know, too, that there are seventeen 1½-ounce drinks in a fifth bottle, or roughly two hundred drinks to a case, and that you can figure on an average of three drinks per person. No host, hostess, fortune-teller, or astrologer has ever found a way to predict exactly who is going to drink what at a party, however, so be provident, within reason.

If you have available freezer space, start collecting ice cubes one or two days before the party. Empty the ice into large plastic bags and stow them in the freezer. We all know that a cocktail party lasts only as long as the ice cubes!

And last but not necessarily least, perhaps you should be prepared for the appearance of non-drinkers. We have observed a strange phenomenon among maiden aunts and very proper ladies which would seem to belie their supposedly unbending characters. Those we have come across down their whisky straight and drink their Burgundy *bien chambré*. Still, for those who prefer non-alcoholic drinks, there are excellent fruit and vegetable juices on the market, as well as clam juice or beef consommé, to be served chilled. And you can make a number of old-fashioned drinks that anyone would enjoy. We have selected three that we consider particularly good:

Orgeat

Raspberry or Dewberry Acid

Honey Water

Orgeat

To make 3 quarts: Pulverize in an electric blender (or pound in a mortar) 3 cups blanched almonds and 30 blanched bitter almonds. Combine almonds with 4 cups boiled water (hot, but below boiling point) and 5 cups milk. Let stand for 10 minutes, then strain through 8 thicknesses of cheesecloth. Meanwhile, dissolve 1 cup granulated sugar in 2 cups water, boil over high heat, skim well, and mix with almond milk; then add 2 tablespoons orange-flower water.* Warm and ignite 1 cup good brandy. Allow to burn until flames subside and all alcohol has evaporated, leaving only the flavor. Add to rest of mixture, store in bottles in refrigerator, and serve in sherry glasses.

3 cups almonds
30 bitter almonds
4 cups boiled water
5 cups milk
1 cup granulated sugar
2 cups water
2 tablespoons orange-flower water
1 cup brandy

Raspberry or Dewberry Acid

To make 3 pints: Place 1 gallon raspberries or dewberries (a variety of blackberry) in a stone crock. Cover with water and stir in 1 ounce pulverized citric acid. Let stand 24 hours. Drain off liquid without squeezing berries. Measure liquid and add 1 pound granulated sugar for each pint of juice. Heat, stirring, to dissolve sugar. Strain through jelly bag or 4 thicknesses of cheesecloth. In a deep pot, bring strained juice to a rolling boil over high heat, and reduce by evaporation to one third original volume. Bottle while hot in pint-size ring-top ball jars. Serve three quarters diluted with soda or ice water. Once jar is opened, store it in refrigerator for further use.

1 gallon raspberries or dewberries
1 ounce pulverized citric acid
2 pounds granulated sugar, about

Honey Water

To 1 quart boiling water add one 8-ounce jar honey, the juice of 1 lemon, and 1 sliced lemon. Chill and serve.

1 quart boiling water
1 8-ounce jar honey
2 lemons

* Orange flower water may be bought at most pharmacies.

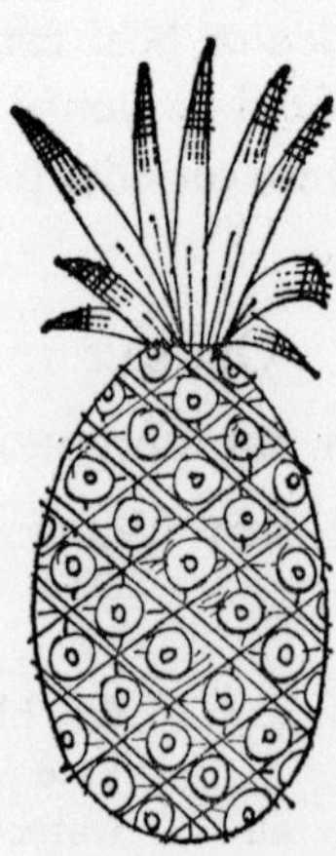

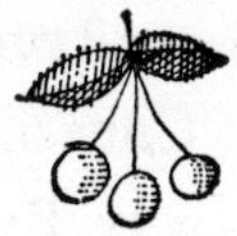

48

The Small Cocktail Party for Twelve or Less

We have noticed that the critics of cocktail parties as a social institution tend to get bogged down in their own generalities—quite often while they are *at* a cocktail party. For if the group promises to be a congenial one—and particularly if it is to be small—our critic seems to come as early and stay as late as the next fellow. His inconsistency is to be forgiven, for the small cocktail party is one of the happiest of social inventions. And for the hostess it imposes no stringent rule save one, that she enjoy her guests in uninterrupted relaxation. What could be more enchanting?

In accordance with the rule, have the bar tray nearby and set out the hors-d'oeuvres on one or two low tables within easy reach of everyone in the conversational circle. Have plates, forks, and napkins close at hand, and your job is done; now, it's up to everyone to help themselves—and to beg you for the recipes.

If you have an inkling that the members of this group are *so* congenial that they will be reluctant to part from each other and from you, you might have a casserole ready to serve later, perhaps Veal Birds *à la Parisienne* or a hearty soup, such as Corn Chowder (see Index). Salad greens crisping in the icebox, a brown-and-serve loaf, coffee and after-dinner mints will round out your supper. Should your intuition prove wrong, you will have supper ready for the following evening, so there's nothing lost.

Three selections from the next page should provide ample food and enough variety to please everyone. Choose one hot dish, unless you are sure you will serve a casserole later, and include in the assortment one fish, one cheese, and one meat. Shrimp Waikiki, one of Juliette's Cheese Spreads, and Peking Duck would be fine together. (Just remember that you must have the duck in the refrigerator two days ahead.) The Red Bean Sauce is, by itself, a wonderful dip for crackers.

Pissaladière, Old-fashioned Pineapple Cheese, and Liver Pâté are an-

Mock Goose-Liver Pâté
Juliette's Cheese Spreads
Mulligatawny Endive Dip
Italian Endive Dip
Pissaladière Niçoise
Peking Duck with Red Bean Sauce
Fondue Suprême
Shrimp Waikiki
Old-Fashioned Pineapple Cheese
Belgian Kip Kap with Mustard Mayonnaise
Brandade de Morue
Gougère Bourguignonne

other good combination. You can use a relatively inexpensive tinned liver pâté or a liver sausage, though naturally, the finer the liver, the better your pâté. You can bake the *Pissaladière* the day you need it or a day in advance. If you make it ahead, do not refrigerate it, but keep it in a cool place and reheat it in a 300° oven for 10 minutes before serving.

Besides being good with drinks, the *Pissaladière* and the *Kip Kap,* as well as the *Gougère* and the *Fondue,* are all excellent for lunch. Serve any one of them with a salad for a light meal. A domestic champagne is quite adequate for our very elegant *Fondue.* (You might as well make a point of telling your guests that this is a champagne *fondue;* if they are suitably impressed, this, too, adds a certain flavor!) When you prepare *Kip Kap,* chill the left-over broth, skim off the fat, and save the stock for a base for a split-pea or dried-bean soup. (You can easily make your own garlic wine vinegar for the *Kip Kap* or for salad dressings: Add 2 bruised garlic cloves and 4 pepper-corns to a pint bottle of wine vinegar; set it on a sunny window sill for a week to allow the heat of the sun to release the flavors.)

If you want something unusual and inexpensive (and who doesn't?), include the Italian Endive Dip, or the Mulligatawny Endive Dip, or the *Brandade. Brandade* is a dish for the gods and garlic-lovers, which, even in France where cooks are very patient, requires enough elbow grease so that it is not often made at home. The electric-blender method will change all that.

Mock Goose-Liver Pâté

Into small bowl of an electric mixer pour ½ cup heavy cream and whip lightly for 2 minutes at medium speed. Add 1 cup (8 ounces) of your favorite commercial liver pâté, and beat with cream at top speed for 1 minute. Warm ¼ cup cognac, add 2 medium truffles, minced, and ignite. When flames subside, blend cognac and truffles into liver-cream mixture. Chill 1 hour and serve on toast.

½ cup heavy cream
1 cup (8 ounces) liver pâté
¼ cup cognac
2 medium truffles

Juliette's Cheese Spreads

Have cheeses at room temperature. Mash to a smooth paste with a fork or beat with electric mixer:

1 Camembert, not too ripe
8 ounces Stilton cheese
8 ounces Hablé cheese
or
1 Camembert, ripe
1 Liederkranz
8 ounces Gorgonzola
8 ounces cream cheese
Dash cayenne pepper

Serve with toasted cheese biscuits, salty rye bread, or pumpernickel.

Mulligatawny Endive Dip

Wash and drain 6 heads Belgian endive, cut off bases, and separate leaves. Arrange on a platter around a bowl containing the following dip. Blend together until even in color:

¼ cup sour cream
¼ cup strained Junior-food peas
1 teaspoon curry powder
¼ cup finely minced cooked chicken
Salt to taste

Italian Endive Dip

For 6 heads endive prepared as in previous recipe, blend well a dip made of:

6 ounces cream cheese
⅓ cup Buitoni Spaghetti Meat Sauce
1 tablespoon House of Herbs Angel Dip Mix

Pissaladière Niçoise

Preheat oven to 375°. Line a 9-inch springform pan with 1 recipe of Salted *Sandtorte* Pastry. Slice 4 large onions paper thin and divide into rings. Sauté these gently over low heat in 2 tablespoons butter and 1 tablespoon olive oil until pale gold. Stir in 1 pressed clove garlic and salt and pepper to taste, and pour onions into pie crust. Dot with 18 small Italian-style black olives and 16 French-style rolled anchovies, and sprinkle with 3 tablespoons grated imported Parmesan cheese. Bake for 45 minutes and serve warm, cut in narrow wedges.

1 recipe Salted Sandtorte Pastry (see Index)
4 large onions
2 tablespoons butter
1 tablespoon olive oil
1 clove garlic
Salt, pepper
18 small Italian-style black olives
16 French-style rolled anchovies
3 tablespoons grated Parmesan

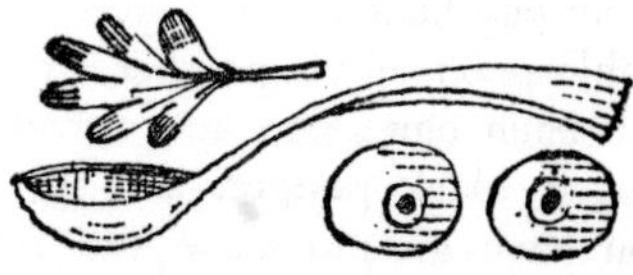

Peking Duck

Two days before the party, stuff a 5- to 6-pound duck with paper towels and let it stand uncovered on a rack in the refrigerator for at least 48 hours; change towels on second day. Then remove towels and let it stand at room temperature (if possible, in front of an electric fan) for about 3 hours.

Preheat oven to 450°. Rub skin of duck with 1 cup honey, then rub inside and out with a mixture of 1 teaspoon each cinnamon, cloves, black pepper, and ground anise and fennel seeds. Roast duck, breast up, in a deep roasting pan for 40 minutes.

Carve meat into bite-size pieces, and serve cold, Chinese-style, in the center of a platter, with toothpicks. Around meat place 2-inch pieces of scallion and heated butter-flake or fan-tan rolls separated into thin sections. The pieces of duck are dipped individually, by each guest, in Red Bean Sauce, below, and then placed with a piece of scallion in a sandwich made from two sections of the rolls.

1 duck, 5 to 6 pounds
1 cup honey
1 teaspoon cinnamon
1 teaspoon cloves
1 teaspoon black pepper
1 teaspoon ground anise seed
1 teaspoon ground fennel seed
Scallions
Butter-flake or fan-tan rolls
Red Bean Sauce

Red Bean Sauce

Grind 1 No. 2 can red chili beans through food mill, and beat purée with an egg beater. Mix together well 1 tablespoon chili powder, 1 teaspoon each cinnamon and cloves, ¼ teaspoon black pepper, and ⅛ teaspoon each ground anise and fennel seeds; add to ground chili beans. Mix well ⅓ cup water, 1 clove garlic, pressed, 1 cup plum jam, and 2 tablespoons soya sauce; boil, stirring constantly, for 5 minutes. Add bean mixture, and boil 10 more minutes.

This sauce keeps well in refrigerator and may be frozen; reheat in a double boiler and serve warm.

1 No. 2 can red chili beans
1 tablespoon chili powder
1 teaspoon cinnamon
1 teaspoon cloves
¼ teaspoon black pepper
⅛ teaspoon ground anise seed
⅛ teaspoon ground fennel seed
⅓ cup water
1 clove garlic
1 cup plum jam
2 tablespoons soya sauce

Fondue Suprême

Slice 2 truffles and reserve liquor in can. In a flameproof casserole, over medium heat, warm truffles in 1⅔ cups champagne. Add 1 pound coarsely grated imported Swiss cheese mixed with 2 tablespoons flour, and stir until blended to a smooth paste. Keep heat low and do not boil. Beat 2 egg yolks with truffle liquor, ⅓ cup champagne, and a dusting of white pepper. Stir into cheese mixture and heat thoroughly, but do not allow *fondue* to boil.

To serve, place casserole on a candle warmer. Guests spear cubes of French bread on a fork and dip into the common pot, using a circular motion which stirs the *fondue.*

2 truffles
2 cups champagne
2 tablespoons flour
1 pound imported Swiss cheese
2 egg yolks
White pepper
French bread

Shrimp Waikiki

Cook 1 pound shrimp. Halve a large pineapple lengthwise, scoop out meat, discarding core, and cut meat into bite-size pieces. Spear each shrimp on toothpick with a piece pineapple, and heap into one pineapple shell. In other shell place a dip made of ¾ cup sour cream, ¼ cup mayonnaise, and 1 tablespoon grated horseradish.

1 pound cooked shrimp
1 large pineapple
¾ cup sour cream
¼ cup Mayonnaise (see Index)
1 tablespoon grated horseradish

Belgian Kip Kap

In 2 quarts of water, cook 2 pounds pig's feet and 1½ pounds beef shank, with 1 onion, a few sprigs of parsley, and salt and pepper to taste, until tender (about 1½ hours). Remove meats from broth and cool. Cut meat from pig-feet bones and mince coarsely. Grind beef, or blend to a very coarse purée in electric blender, adding some of the cooking broth as needed. Place meats in large pot with enough additional broth to make 2 cups broth in all. Add ⅓ cup garlic-flavored wine vinegar, 1 bay leaf, and ⅛ teaspoon each dried thyme, cayenne pepper, powdered cloves, ground black pepper, and ground nutmeg. Bring mixture to a boil. Rinse a loaf pan with cold water, pour mixture into it, and jell in refrigerator for 12 hours. Serve cut in cubes, on toothpicks, and heaped around a bowl of Mustard Mayonnaise.

2 pounds pig's feet
1½ pounds beef shank
1 onion
Few sprigs parsley
Salt, pepper
⅓ cup garlic-flavored wine vinegar
1 bay leaf
⅛ teaspoon dried thyme
⅛ teaspoon cayenne pepper
⅛ teaspoon powdered cloves
⅛ teaspoon ground black pepper
⅛ teaspoon ground nutmeg
1½ cups Mustard Mayonnaise (see p. 170)

Old-Fashioned Pineapple Cheese

Cut off top quarter of a 6- to 8-ounce pineapple cheese. Scoop out cheese down to the rind in both top and bottom parts. In an electric blender, or by pounding in a mortar, make a paste of the cheese with ¾ cup very soft butter, 1 teaspoon celery salt, and ½ cup finest tawny port. Do this a small portion at a time, adding a little butter and a little port each time. Replace cheese mixture in shell, chill, and serve with sesame crackers or imported English biscuits for cheese.

1 pineapple cheese, 6 to 8 ounces
⅜ pound butter
1 teaspoon celery salt
½ cup tawny port

Blender Mayonnaise

In an electric blender place 1 whole egg, 1 egg yolk, 1 tablespoon salt, 1 teaspoon prepared mustard, and ½ teaspoon white pepper. Blend 1 second; then add in a steady stream, without stopping blender, 1 cup olive oil (or ½ cup each olive oil and corn oil), and ¼ cup your favorite vinegar. Makes 1½ cups.

To make Mustard Mayonnaise, use 1 tablespoon strong English-style mustard in the original egg mixture.

1 whole egg
1 egg yolk
1 tablespoon salt
1 teaspoon prepared mustard
or 1 tablespoon English-style mustard
1 cup olive oil
or ½ cup each olive and corn oil
¼ cup vinegar

Brandade de Morue

Soak 1 pound salt cod overnight in cold water. Change water at least once to remove salt. Poach fish in *Court-Bouillon* for Fish until soft. Place in a bowl or mortar with ¼ cup boiling olive oil, and work to a paste with pestle or wooden spoon. Add 1 pressed clove of garlic and another ¼ cup boiling oil, stirring vigorously. Bring ⅓ cup light cream to boiling point, incorporate into paste, and add ¼ teaspoon ground white pepper. Heap *Brandade* on a platter in the shape of half a melon. Smooth it out, and with a rubber spatula make a design like the ribs of a melon mold on mound. Serve either hot or chilled, with toast points.

1 pound salt cod
Court-Bouillon for Fish (see Index)
½ cup boiling olive oil, in all
1 clove garlic
⅓ cup light cream
¼ teaspoon ground white pepper

Blender method: Drain *Court-Bouillon* from steaming poached cod into glass container of electric blender to heat it thoroughly. Pour off liquid, and put half of remaining ingredients in blender. Blend at low speed until finely shredded but not pasty, or about 6 seconds. Repeat with other half of ingredients, and follow above serving directions.

Gougère Bourguignonne

Preheat oven to 450°. To ½ recipe Basic *Pâte à Chou* (use 3 eggs for a single *Gougère*) add 2 cups diced imported Swiss cheese. Spoon out in a ring on a greased baking sheet. Bake 8 minutes at 450°, then reduce heat to 350° and continue baking for 30 to 35 minutes, until golden. Serve hot.

½ recipe Basic Pâte à Chou (see Index)
2 cups diced imported Swiss cheese

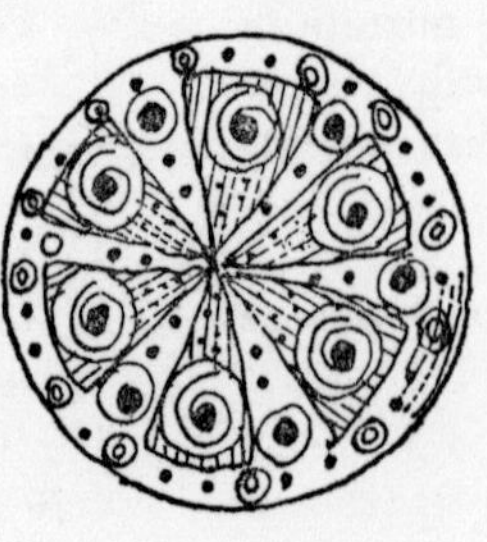

49

The Large Cocktail Party for Thirty or More

The critic mentioned before would not be so disagreeable about big cocktail parties if he always ate as well as he drank at them, and if his hosts always kept a reasonable relationship between the number of their guests and the available floor space.

With those two things taken care of, the supposedly cynical purposes of the cocktail party *en masse,* it seems to us, should become, instead, both gay and civilized. A flock of minor social obligations can be taken care of—because you are going to take care in doing this. You can invite people you have only met once, whom you would like to know better but so far hesitate to ask to a more intimate gathering; casual acquaintances or business acquaintances will fit in easily; and then there are the "characters," people who have intrigued you and who will no doubt intrigue others, but for whom just the right dinner-party group has never come to mind. The cocktail party is the perfect answer to all of this, personal only up to a point, but a friendly gesture.

There is a quite different, very personal reason for a large party, too—to celebrate an important occasion in your life. Then you might want to ask *everyone* you know. But neither time, space, nor even the mood of this event is right for serving a meal: solution—the cocktail party.

You can entertain the maximum number of people this way with the least amount of effort, though doing a good job of it will mean work just the same. Everything should of course be made beforehand. Count on three or four hours, though this is difficult to estimate exactly, since it depends on your deftness in making hors-d'oeuvres and on how much of a perfectionist you are about their appearance, as well as on how many of the recipes that follow you may decide to use.

All the canapés are first spread with a flavored butter to prevent the bread

Cold Hors-d'Oeuvres

Assorted Canapés
Assorted Cheese Cookies
Assorted Cheese Nuggets
King David Squash
Endive à la Diable
Endive Romanoff
Stuffed Raw Mushrooms
Liver-Pâté Aspics
Caviar and Cucumber Aspics
Miniature Stuffed Tomatoes
Cucumber Canapés
Cigarettes

from getting soggy. Flavorings for butter, not mentioned in the recipes, have been included for you to experiment with; you needn't be bound, either, by our directions for garnishing. Don't be frightened by a pastry tube; a little practice with it yields astonishingly good—and quick—results, and you will be so proud of yourself. Cover each platter of canapés with waxed paper and a damp towel, unless there are rosettes of butter or mayonnaise that would stick to the paper. In that case, envelop the whole platter loosely with foil. Set the finished platters in a cool place.

Make all the hot hors-d'oeuvres ahead, too. We suggest many that are deep fried especially because they can be made ahead and reheated. Place them on cooky sheets that have been covered with brown paper, and put them in a preheated 425° oven for 5 minutes, or until piping hot, and then serve *immediately*. Prepare *Tartelettes Florentine* in advance also, and reheat later. The rest of our hot hors-d'oeuvres can be organized well ahead, but cook them at the last minute.

Allow an average of 5 to 6 hors-d'oeuvres for each person. (Each recipe that follows makes 30 to 36, and you can multiply indefinitely.) This means that during the two hours or so that your party will last, platters should go around at intervals of about 20 minutes. If you don't have help, you will

Hot Hors-d'Oeuvres

MARTHA WASHINGTON'S TURKEY NIBBLES
CHINESE SHRIMP MARBLES
LOBSTER TEMPURA
TRUFFLE FRITTERS
EMPANADAS
BITTERBALLEN
TARTELETTES FLORENTINE
MALAYAN SHRIMP
SHRIMPS ON TOAST
PEPPERY CHEESE RAMEQUINS
FRIED MOZZARELLA
CROÛTES MAISON

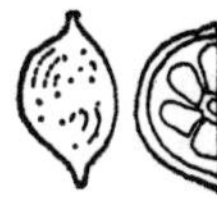

have to do a great deal of the passing yourself, particularly of the hot foods. Don't undertake too much without help, but we still know of no better prop to circulate a hostess among all her guests than a delectable platter of hors-d'oeuvres.

Assorted Canapés

The quantities given in each of the following recipes are for 30 to 32 canapés cut in the classic 1- to 1½-inch circles, or squares, rectangles, and triangles of approximately the same size. Trim off the crust and slice the bread thinly, of course.

Foundation Butters for Canapés

The basic recipe for spreading 30–32 canapés is ¼ pound butter plus one of the seasonings listed below. (Double the recipe if the same butter is to be used to border the canapés with a pastry tube.) Cream the soft butter in a bowl, add seasoning, and blend well. For quantities larger than ¼ pound, it can be more convenient to use an electric blender or mixer.

Fish Butters: 2 tablespoons commercial anchovy, lobster, salmon, or shrimp paste.

Cheese Butters: 2 tablespoons grated Parmesan, crumbled Roquefort, or Snappy-cheese spread.

Herb Butters: 2 tablespoons finely minced fresh herb—dill, garlic,

chives, parsley, fennel, mint, or tarragon.

Horseradish Butter: 2 tablespoons grated horseradish.

Spiced Butters: 1 tablespoon powdered spice—chili, gumbo filé, nutmeg, paprika, curry, or dry mustard.

Caviar Canapés

Foundation of plain butter on rounds of white toast. In center of each round place half the yolk of a hard-cooked egg, round side up. Make two borders around the yolk, first with 1 teaspoon minced onion, then with black caviar. Place a thin narrow strip of peeled lemon on one side, just long enough to reach from edge of canapé to center of yolk.

30–32 rounds white toast
¼ pound butter
15–16 hard-cooked egg yolks
10 small white onions
8 ounces black caviar
1 large lemon

Lobster Canapés

Foundation of lobster butter on white-bread rectangles or triangles, dab of Mayonnaise in center, small lobster claw or piece of pink meat on top, and border of lobster butter pushed through pastry tube.

30–32 white-bread rectangles or triangles
½ pound lobster butter
¼–½ cup Mayonnaise (*see Index*)
1 pound cooked lobster meat or 2 8-ounce cans lobster meat

Sardine Canapés

Foundation of dill butter spread on rye bread. Spread with contents of large can of imported sardines mashed to a paste with the juice of 1 lemon and ⅛ teaspoon ground black pepper. Garnish with paper-thin wedge lemon, unpeeled, and chopped parsley.

30–32 rye-bread rounds or assorted shapes
¼ pound dill butter
Large can imported sardines
Juice 1 lemon
⅛ teaspoon ground black pepper
1 lemon, cut in thin wedges
Chopped parsley

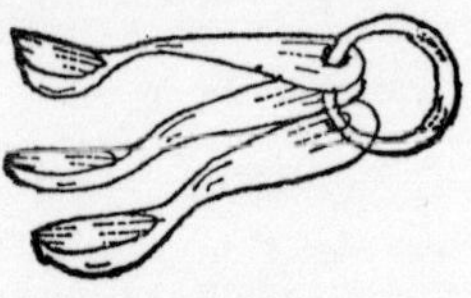

Shrimp Canapés

With a cooky cutter or 2-inch wine glass, cut 2-inch rounds of white bread. Spread with shrimp-paste butter, and cover with 2-inch circle of leaf lettuce. Arrange tiny Norwegian pink shrimp, neatly overlapping in a spiral, to cover lettuce. Top with mustard-butter rosette made with pastry tube.

30–32 rounds white bread
¼ pound shrimp-paste butter
Leaf lettuce
8 jars Norwegian pink shrimp
½ recipe mustard butter

Smoked-Salmon Canapés

Foundation of shrimp-paste butter on pumpernickel-bread rectangles with crust removed. Add a thin slice of smoked salmon, freshly ground black pepper, and 4 or 5 capers.

30–32 pumpernickel-bread rectangles
¼ pound shrimp-paste butter
1½ pounds smoked salmon
Black pepper
Small jar capers

Salmon Roll-Ups

Cut crust from loaf of white bread. Slice loaf lengthwise, spread with a thick coating salmon butter. Roll up slices from the narrow ends like a jelly roll. Wrap in foil, chill thoroughly, and slice into canapés ½ inch thick. Makes 30–32.

1 loaf white bread
½ pound salmon butter

Asparagus Canapés

Foundation of chive butter on white bread cut in finger-length strips 1-inch wide. Spread Mayonnaise down center, add single canned white asparagus tip, and garnish with strip of pimiento.

30–32 strips white bread, finger length, 1 inch wide
¼ pound chive butter
¼–½ cup Mayonnaise (see Index)
1 cans white asparagus tips
1 4-ounce can pimientos

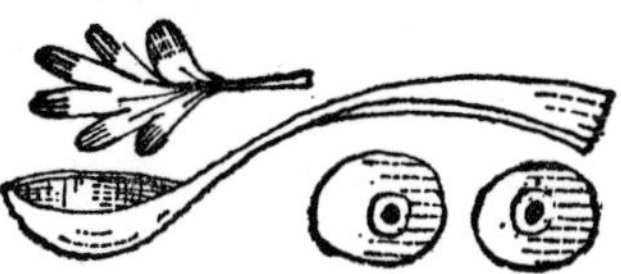

Olive Canapés

Foundation of anchovy butter on white-bread triangles. Top with slices of pimiento-stuffed olives, and finish with border of anchovy butter pushed through pastry tube.

30–32 white-bread triangles
½ pound anchovy butter
7-ounce jar pimiento-stuffed olives

Cheese Canapés

Foundation of Snappy-Cheese butter on salty-rye rounds. Add thin slice of American cheese cut with fancy cooky cutter, and center with chopped chives.

30–32 salty-rye rounds
¼ pound Snappy-Cheese butter
8 slices American cheese
Chives

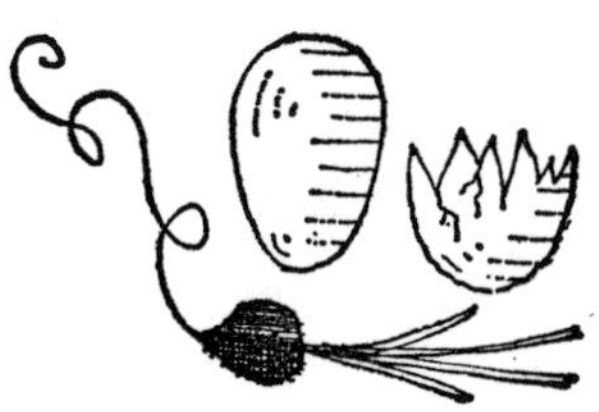

Egg Canapés

Foundation of salmon-paste butter on white-bread rounds. Center with coarsely chopped hard-cooked egg and border with salmon-paste butter pushed through pastry tube.

30–32 white-bread rounds
½ pound salmon-paste butter
6–8 hard-cooked eggs

Richmond Canapés

Soak 30–32 white or black raisins in boiling water until they get plump. Spread white-bread rounds with mixture of ⅔ cup crunch-style peanut butter and ⅓ cup Mayonnaise. Sprinkle with finely grated raw carrot and top each canapé with one raisin.

30–32 white-bread rounds
⅔ cup chunk-style peanut butter
⅓ cup Mayonnaise (see Index)
1 cup grated carrot
30–32 white or black raisins

Assorted Cheese Cookies

Preheat oven to 350°. Combine 1 cup grated aged Cheddar cheese and ½ teaspoon Tabasco sauce with double recipe Salted *Sandtorte* Pastry. Pat or roll to ½ inch thickness on pastry board. Cut with fancy cooky cutters. Make assortment of cookies by sprinkling some with celery seed, some with sesame seed, and some with poppy seed; or sprinkle 2 cups coarsely chopped peanuts over all. Bake 7 to 8 minutes on ungreased cooky sheets.

1 cup grated aged Cheddar cheese
½ teaspoon Tabasco sauce
Double recipe Salted Sandtorte Pastry (see Index)
Celery, sesame and poppy seeds or 2 cups coarsely chopped peanuts

Assorted Cheese Nuggets

Cream ¾ pound Roquefort cheese until soft. Blend in ⅜ pound salt butter, 4 tablespoons Scotch, and 1½ teaspoons dry mustard. Shape into 36 nuggets. Toast 12 ounces flaked coconut under broiler until edges are golden. Roll cheese nuggets in coconut, and spear with 36 pretzel sticks.

¾ pound Roquefort cheese
⅜ pound salt butter
4 tablespoons Scotch
1½ teaspoons dry mustard
12 ounces flaked coconut
36 pretzel sticks

Variations:
Substitute for butter and Scotch in above recipe:
¾ pound cream cheese
3 teaspoons Tabasco sauce
Roll cheese nuggets in:
¼ pound imported grated Swiss cheese

or

Substitute for first three ingredients:
¾ pound Camembert
¾ pound cream cheese
4 tablespoons sherry
Roll cheese nuggets in:
¼ pound grated yellow cheddar cheese

or

Substitute:
¾ pound Liederkranz
¾ pound cream cheese
4 tablespoons Scotch
Roll nuggets in:
¼ pound chopped peanuts

In all three variations, season mixture with 1½ teaspoons dry mustard and spear nuggets with pretzel sticks, as above.

King David Squash

Preheat oven to 350°. Parboil 2 long yellow squash 5 minutes in salt water. Cut off ends and hollow out center of squash with long serrated knife, leaving skin plus ¼-inch layer of meat intact all around. Over high heat in heavy skillet, fry 2 teaspoons cumin powder in 4 tablespoons butter. When the butter is golden, add 1½ cups cooked ground beef, 1½ cups cooked rice, and 1 tablespoon minced onion. Remove from heat immediately, co a little, and stuff mixture into squash. Bake squash in greased ovenproof dish for 15 minutes. Chill, then cut into slices ½ inch thick. Serve very cold.

2 long yellow squash
2 teaspoons cumin powder
4 tablespoons butter
1½ cups cooked ground beef
1½ cups cooked rice
1 tablespoon minced onion

Endive à la Diable

Chop ¾ cup walnut meats. Blend with 8 ounces cream cheese, 2 tablespoons bottled Escoffier Sauce Diable, and ½ teaspoon salt, until cheese is smooth and uniform in color. Stuff wider part of 36 small endive leaves with mixture, leaving tips empty. Serve well chilled for crispness and easy handling. (Reserve large leaves for a salad.)

¾ cup walnut meats
8 ounces cream cheese
2 tablespoons bottled Escoffier Sauce Diable
½ teaspoon salt
36 small endive leaves

Endive Romanoff

Cut 36 heads Belgian endive in half across the middle, and reserve tops for use in salads or soups. Trim bases and remove small bitter core at bottom of each. Stand endive upright in enamelware * pan large enough to accommodate them, and add hot chicken broth to cover. Cut 1 lemon in half, partly squeeze out juice, and add halves to broth. Simmer endive, uncovered, for 15 minutes, and drain. Using a small spoon, push a hollow in the top of each, and chill.

Season ½ cup Mayonnaise liberally with salt and pepper. With a fork, mash 4 hard-cooked eggs with the mayonnaise, and place a spoonful of mixture in hollow of each endive. Top half of them with a small spoonful of red caviar, the others with black caviar, using 4 ounces of each. Arrange on a platter, alternating red and black, and serve chilled.

6 pounds (36 heads) Belgian endive
Chicken broth
1 lemon
½ cup Mayonnaise (see Index)
Salt, pepper
4 hard-cooked eggs
4 ounces red caviar
4 ounces black caviar

Stuffed Raw Mushrooms

Wash, drain, and peel 36 raw mushroom caps. Fill with a well-blended mixture of 6 ounces crumbled Roquefort, 6 ounces Hablé cheese,† ¾ cup ground pecans, 1 tablespoon Worcestershire, and 1½ teaspoons curry powder.

36 raw mushroom caps
6 ounces Roquefort
6 ounces Hablé cheese †
¾ cup ground pecans
1 tablespoon Worcestershire
1½ teaspoons curry powder

Liver Pâté Aspics

Chill 3 plastic egg holders over an oblong pan of cracked ice. Meanwhile, soak 1 envelope gelatin in ¼ cup chicken broth, then dilute with 1¼ cups hot chicken broth, stirring until all crystals disappear. With a pastry brush, apply a thin coating of gelatin mixture to each egg holder, still over ice, and for a few seconds keep applying more gelatin, lightly, until set. Place a well-rounded teaspoon of Mock Goose-Liver Pâté in each hol-

* Metal pans have a tendency to blacken endive.
† Hablé is a rich Swedish cream cheese with a nutty flavor.

low, then fill hollow with rest of gelatin. Chill in refrigerator until set. Serve on rounds of white toast slightly larger than aspics.

3 plastic egg holders
1 envelope unflavored gelatin
1½ cups chicken broth
1 recipe Mock Goose-Liver Pâté (see Index)
36 rounds white toast

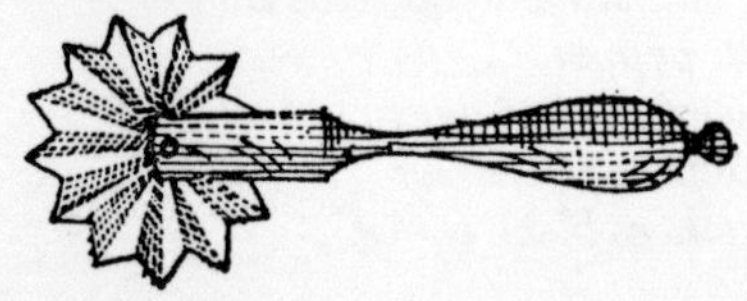

Caviar and Cucumber Aspic

Chill 3 plastic egg holders over an oblong pan of cracked ice. Meanwhile, soak 1½ envelopes gelatin in ⅓ cup chicken broth; season with dash of cayenne pepper. Peel and slice 1½ cucumbers. Parboil them, covered, in 1 cup boiling water with 1½ tablespoons wine vinegar, for 8 minutes. Place cucumbers and liquid in an electric blender. Add soaked gelatin, blend 10 seconds, and add 3 drops green vegetable coloring to purée. With a pastry brush, apply a thin coating of purée to egg holders, still over ice, and for a few seconds keep applying more gelatin, lightly, until set. Place a small teaspoon of red caviar in half of the hollows, one of black caviar in the others, then fill hollows with rest of cucumber-gelatin mixture. Chill in refrigerator until set. Place on pumpernickel rounds slightly larger than the aspics, and arrange on a platter, alternating red and black.

1½ envelopes gelatin
⅓ cup chicken broth
Dash cayenne pepper
1½ cucumbers
1½ tablespoons wine vinegar
1 cup water
3 drops green vegetable coloring
4 ounces black caviar
4 ounces red caviar
36 pumpernickel rounds

Miniature Stuffed Tomatoes

Mash to a granular paste the yolks and whites of 6 hard-cooked eggs with ⅛ pound creamed butter and ¼ pound ground or finely minced ham. Season with 2 tablespoons Mayonnaise, dash of Tabasco sauce, and ½ teaspoon salt. Cut off stem ends of 30 small plum tomatoes and scoop out pulp, leaving only the shell. With a serrated knife, cut just enough off smooth ends of tomatoes to make them stand upright, without piercing shells. Stuff with above mixture, and garnish tops with a little chopped parsley.

6 hard-cooked eggs
⅛ pound butter
¼ pound ground ham
2 tablespoons Mayonnaise (see Index)
Dash Tabasco sauce
½ teaspoon salt
30 small plum tomatoes
3 tablespoons chopped parsley

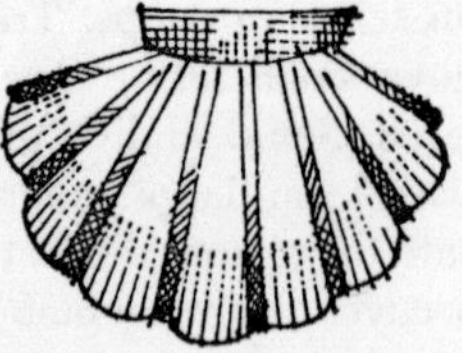

Variations:

Replace ham with tuna fish.

Replace ham with chicken; season with 1 teaspoon curry powder instead of Tabasco sauce.

Replace ham with 4 ounces chopped olives; increase Tabasco sauce to ¼ teaspoon.

Cucumber Canapés

With a fork, score skin of 2 chilled cucumbers. Cut in slices ¼ inch thick, and spread slices with 4 ounces cream cheese blended with 1 tablespoon minced fresh dill.

2 cucumbers
4 ounces cream cheese
1 tablespoon minced fresh dill

Cigarettes

In small bowl of an electric mixer, beat 8 ounces cream cheese with 1 tablespoon dried tarragon until creamy. Cut 8 slices of *prosciutto* in half crosswise, or use 16 slices chipped beef. With a spatula spread cream cheese evenly on *prosciutto* or beef, roll up, and chill for one hour. Cut rolls in half, and dip one end of each "cigarette" in very soft butter, then in finely minced truffle. Arrange on a small rectangular serving dish with bouquets of parsley.

8 ounces cream cheese
1 tablespoon dried tarragon
8 slices prosciutto
or 16 slices chipped beef
4 tablespoons soft butter
2 truffles
Parsley

Martha Washington's Turkey Nibbles

Make one day ahead: Poach ½ cup oysters in a little salted water for 3 minutes, then drain. In a wooden bowl, mince oysters finely with 1 cup cooked turkey meat, ½ teaspoon mace, ⅛ teaspoon freshly ground black pepper, and ¼ teaspoon seasoning salt. Add 3 tablespoons heavy cream, 1 tablespoon dry white wine or lemon juice, and 2 egg yolks, and stir until well blended. Store overnight in a covered jar in refrigerator. Shape into nuggets the size of large marbles. Roll nuggets in lightly beaten egg, then in a mixture made of ¼ cup each grated blanched almonds and toasted bread crumbs. Fry in deep fat at 390° until golden. Serve on toothpicks.

½ cup oysters
1 cup cooked turkey meat
½ teaspoon mace
⅛ teaspoon black pepper
¼ teaspoon seasoning salt
3 tablespoons heavy cream
1 tablespoon dry white wine
or lemon juice
2 egg yolks
1 egg
¼ cup blanched almond
¼ cup toasted bread crumbs
Deep fat for frying

Chinese Shrimp Marbles

Wash and shell 2 pounds fresh raw shrimp, and mince the meat. Add ¼ pound ground fat pork and season with 1 tablespoon soya sauce and ¼ teaspoon ground ginger. Beat 2 eggs until light and add to rest of ingredients. Chill. Roll the mixture into balls the size of large marbles, and fry in deep hot fat, preferably lard, until a golden brown. Serve on toothpicks.

2 pounds fresh shrimp
¼ pound fat pork
1 tablespoon soya sauce
¼ teaspoon ginger
2 eggs
Lard for deep frying

Lobster Tempura

Season 8 shelled cooked lobster tails with juice of 1 lemon and 2 tablespoons soya sauce. Let stand an hour, turning twice. Make a batter by adding gradually 1 pint *sake* * to 2 cups flour; mix until smooth. Cut each lobster tail in four or five bite size sections, dip in batter, then fry in deep fat at 390°. Drain on absorbent paper, and serve on toothpicks, around a container of soya sauce. On the same platter have an arrangement of hot onion rings fried in the same batter as the lobster, fringed scallions, and radish roses.

8 cooked shelled lobster tails
Juice of 1 lemon
2 tablespoons soya sauce
2 cups flour
1 pint sake *

Soya sauce for dipping
Scallions, radishes
2 large onions, cut into rings
Deep fat for frying

Truffle Fritters

Slice 16 large truffles into 6 slices each, reserving end pieces for other uses. Sprinkle center slices with salt and pepper. Spread one slice with 1 teaspoon Mock Goose-Liver Pâté, and place another slice on top, sandwichwise. Make a batter by adding gradually 1 cup light beer, 1 egg yolk, and 2 egg whites, stiffly beaten, to 1¾ cups flour. Dip truffle sandwiches in batter and fry in deep fat at 400° until golden.

16 large truffles
Salt, pepper
¾ cup Mock Goose-Liver Pâté (*see Index*)
1¾ cups flour
1 cup light beer
1 egg yolk
2 egg whites
Deep fat for frying

Empanadas

In a bowl, make a dough with 1½ cups flour, 3 tablespoons olive oil, ½ cup white wine, and ¼ teaspoon salt. Form dough into a ball and let it rise slightly with the ferments from the wine for 1 hour.

Meanwhile, mince finely enough boiled beef (or fry loose ground chuck) to make 1 cup meat. Then sauté over low heat 1 large onion, minced, and ¼ cup seedless raisins in 2 tablespoons olive oil until onion is pale gold. Add meat and season with pepper, salt, and 1 teaspoon chili powder.

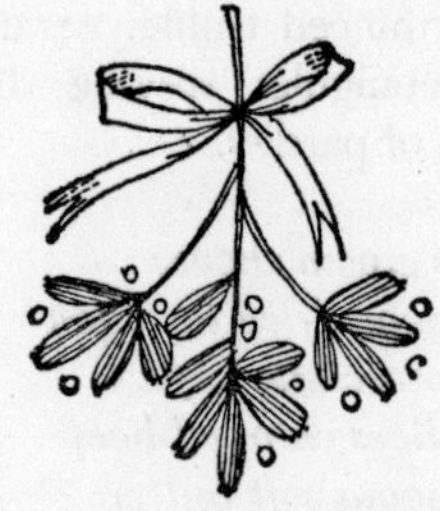

Roll out dough and cut with 2½- to 3-inch cooky cutter or glass. Place 1 teaspoon meat-and-onion mixture, slightly off center, on each round. Fold over side of circle to within ¼ inch of opposite edge. Moisten rim with a pastry brush dipped in milk, and fold rim back over stuffed side of *empanada* to seal in meat. Fry in deep fat at 390° until golden.

1½ cups flour
3 tablespoons olive oil
½ cup white wine
¼ teaspoon salt

* Japanese rice wine; if not available, use light domestic beer.

1 cup minced boiled beef
or 1 cup loose fried ground chuck
1 large onion
¼ cup raisins
2 tablespoons olive oil
Salt, pepper
1 teaspoon chili powder
1 cup or more milk
Deep fat for frying

Bitterballen

Place ½ pound of veal in 1¼ cups hot salted water, and bring to a boil over high heat. Skim, reduce heat, then simmer for ¾ hour with 1 small minced onion, ½ bay leaf, parsley, and salt and pepper. Meanwhile, soften 1 heaping teaspoon gelatin in ¼ cup cold water, then dissolve in ¼ cup hot stock from meat. Remove meat from stock and grind or mince finely.

Make ½ cup medium Béchamel Sauce with stock. Add gelatin, salt and pepper to taste, and juice of ½ lemon. Remove from heat and stir in vigorously 1 egg yolk. Add ground meat to sauce, then pour on a jelly-roll sheet to cool. Chill in refrigerator until set.

Cut jellied veal into 1½-inch squares, and roll each into marble-size ball. Roll in 1 cup toasted bread crumbs, dip in egg white lightly beaten with 1 teaspoon water, then roll again in bread crumbs. Fry in deep fat at 300°. Serve on toothpicks, around a container of mustard.

½ pound veal
1 small onion
½ bay leaf
Parsley
½ cup Béchamel Sauce (see Index)
Salt, pepper
1 teaspoon gelatin
Juice of ½ lemon
1 egg yolk

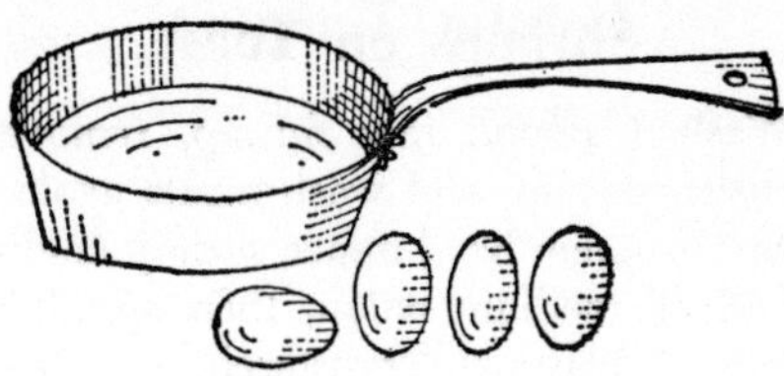

1 cup toasted bread crumbs
1 egg white
Deep fat for frying
Mustard

Tartelettes Florentine

Preheat oven to 375°. Into 30–32 small ungreased *brioche* molds or fluted tartlet molds, pat an even thin layer of Salted *Sandtorte* Pastry. Beat together 4 eggs, 1 tablespoon flour, ½ teaspoon salt, dash cayenne pepper, 2 cups light cream, ½ cup grated imported Swiss cheese, and ½ cup well-drained cooked chopped spinach. Fill tartlets with this mixture, and bake for 20 minutes, or until custard is set. Cool completely and tip out of tins. Reheat in 375° oven for 5 minutes before serving.

1 recipe Salted Sandtorte Pastry (see Index)
4 eggs
1 tablespoon flour
½ teaspoon salt
Dash cayenne pepper
2 cups light cream
½ cup grated imported Swiss cheese
½ cup cooked chopped spinach

Malayan Shrimp

Dip 2 pounds jumbo shrimp, boiled, shelled and deveined, in 1 recipe Saté Sauce. Broil 3 inches from heat in preheated broiler, turning them once, until golden on both sides. Serve at once on toothpicks.

2 pounds boiled shrimp
1 recipe Saté Sauce (see Index)

Shrimps on Toast

Wash 1 pound raw shrimp, remove shells, devein, and wash meats again. In a wooden bowl mince shrimp finely with 1 medium onion, then sprinkle with 1 teaspoon cornstarch, 1 tablespoon soya sauce, and add white of 1 egg, lightly beaten. With cooky cutter, cut out 30–32 rounds of thinly sliced white bread. Spread with a little shrimp mixture. In heavy skillet, over medium heat fry rounds, shrimp side down, in hot fat or lard ¼ inch deep. When golden brown, turn and fry other side. Drain, keep hot between layers of absorbent paper, and serve as soon as possible.

1 pound raw shrimp
1 medium onion
1 teaspoon cornstarch
1 tablespoon soya sauce
1 egg white
30–32 white-bread rounds
Fat or lard for frying

Peppery Cheese Ramequins

Mix together 1 cup grated imported Swiss cheese, ¾ cup finely crumbled Roquefort, and 8 ounces cream cheese. Add 5 well-beaten eggs and blend to a paste. Season with ¼ teaspoon Tabasco sauce. Turn into small, well-buttered ramequins. Bake in hot 375° oven for 7 minutes, or until well browned. Serve at once.

1 cup grated imported Swiss cheese
¾ cups crumbled Roquefort
8 ounces cream cheese
5 eggs
¼ teaspoon Tabasco sauce

Fried Mozzarella

Cut 1 pound *mozzarella* cheese in ¾-inch cubes. Roll in flour, dip in 4 eggs lightly beaten with ½ teaspoon salt, then roll in 2 cups bread crumbs. Dip again in egg and again in bread crumbs. Deep fry in olive oil at 390° until light gold. Serve at once.

1 pound mozzarella
1 cup flour, more or less
4 eggs
½ teaspoon salt
2 cups bread crumbs
Olive oil for deep frying

Croûtes Maison

With a cooky cutter, cut 30–32 2-inch rounds of white bread. Toast lightly on one side, and spread untoasted side thickly with Mayonnaise. Sprinkle each canapé with minced onion, and grated Cheddar, and broil until golden. Serve at once.

1 loaf white bread
¾ cup Mayonnaise (see Index)
½ cup minced onion
½ cup grated Cheddar

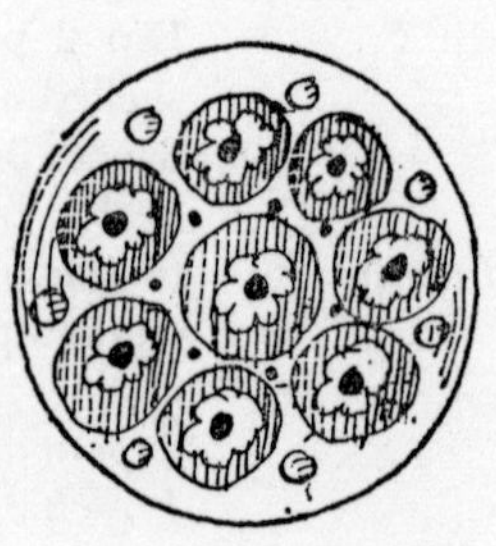

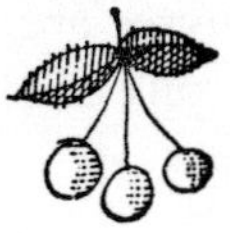

50

The Cocktail-Buffet

With suburbanites particularly in mind, we now suggest a pair of cocktail-buffets to go a shade further than the regulation cocktail party by providing additional sustenance for those who have a distance to travel. Four martinis plus four small hors-d'oeuvres could equal trouble!

These are not buffet dinners; enough food is available for the hungry and to promote the ounce-of-prevention theory, but the buffet table should not resemble the proverbial groaning board. The occasion is still essentially a cocktail party, but with a few well-chosen embellishments, a sweet or two, and a cup of coffee. Most of your guests will probably go on to dinner, though with good things to eat right where they are, you never can tell.

Choose from both the preceding large and small cocktail-party suggestions. Select first two hot and two cold hors-d'oeuvres to be passed and one or two dips to be placed on the buffet table. The handiest rule of thumb we know for varying their content is to include meat, fish, vegetable, and cheese, somewhat like a regular meal in miniature. Then plan, in addition, a substantial pâté or meat and a good table cheese or a smoked fish, appropriate breads, perhaps a salad, a sweet, and you are amply prepared.

To explain what we mean, here are two sample menus, but the possibilities are legion and the recipes listed under "Buffet Dishes" in the Index will give you many other ideas. However, we like this menu:

Cold hors-d'oeuvres: *Assorted Canapés* and *Liver-Pâté Aspics*

Hot hors-d'oeuvres: *Lobster Tempura* and *Peppery Cheese Ramequins*

Dips: *Mulligatawny Endive Dip* and *Brandade de Morue*

The center of attraction on the buffet table could be a Smithfield ham or a smoked turkey bought from a first-rate food shop. Add a basket of thinly sliced breads, Haitian Baked Pineapple and small wedges of Scotch Shortbread and coffee. The hors-d'oeuvres are so substantial to begin with, particularly the *Brandade,* that you won't need more food.

Another menu might be this one:

Cold hors-d'oeuvres: *Endive Romanoff* and *Stuffed Raw Mushrooms*

Hot hors-d'oeuvres: *Malayan Shrimp* and *Empanadas*

Dip: *Belgian Kip Kap with Mustard Mayonnaise*

Here, the *pièce de résistance* is a spectacular triple Omelette Cambacérès with its filling of pâté and garnish of *prosciutto.* With this, perhaps a green salad and a Brie cheese and, for the sweet-toothed, tartlets filled with Mocha Butter Cream, a bowl of fresh fruit, and coffee again.

A cocktail-buffet is fine for twenty guests or a hundred and twenty. Calculate quantities roughly as follows: 4 to 5 hors-d'oeuvres per person. In a small group, up to twenty, almost everyone *may* take a helping of the dishes on the buffet. The more people, the lower the percentage of hearty eaters; if you do reach a hundred and twenty, probably only a third of them will really get down to business.

Appraise your space, your time, and your inclination. Check your recipes for everything that can be done ahead, be realistic about whether or not you are going to need help—and have a good time.

Scotch Shortbread

Preheat oven to 300°. In large bowl of electric mixer, cream ½ pound butter, incorporating gradually 1½ pounds granulated sugar. Mix until butter is light and almost white, about 12 minutes. With a spoon, fold 5½ cups unsifted flour into mixture, then blend thoroughly with fingers until dough is waxy and feels like clay. Pat evenly to a thickness of ¾ inch in bottom of two 10-inch springform pans. With tines of a fork, make design around edge, and with a knife score top piewise, without cutting through, into sixteen sections. Bake 35 to 40 minutes or until delicately golden. Cool, remove springform edge, then cut along markings. Store between layers of waxed paper in airtight container.

½ *pound butter*
1½ *pounds granulated sugar*
5½ *cups flour*

Haitian Baked Pineapple

Preheat oven to 350°. Cut top from pineapple without spoiling frond and remove pulp from inside the top. With a grapefruit knife, remove core and pulp from rest of pineapple, taking care to leave ¼-inch layer on inside of rind to keep juices from running out while baking. Slice 1 banana thinly, dice pineapple pulp, and mix together with ¼ cup sugar. Warm and ignite ⅓ cup dark rum; when flame subsides, pour over fruit mixture. Fill pineapple bottom with fruit, replace top, moisten fronds and wrap them in foil, then secure top with a few wooden toothpicks. Bake pineapple, standing up in oven, for 25 minutes. Serve hot, first removing foil from fronds. One medium pineapple will serve 6 people and a sugar-loaf pineapple will serve 8 to 10.

1 pineapple
1 banana
¼ cup sugar
⅓ cup dark rum

Omelette Cambacérès

Break 18 eggs into three bowls, 6 to a bowl. To each bowl add 2 tablespoons cold water and 2 tablespoons butter cut into pea-size bits. Add pepper and salt, then beat with a whisk or fork until yolks and whites are well blended. In a 10-inch skillet or omelette pan melt 1 tablespoon butter over medium heat; when it sizzles pour in contents of one bowl, tilting pan to spread mixture evenly. Reduce heat, and with a fork, bring cooked edges gently toward center, tilting again to spread rest of uncooked egg. Bottom of omelette should remain pale yellow; if it starts to brown, reduce heat further. This is a large omelette; it should be as flat as possible and must therefore cook very slowly. When surface of omelette is still slightly glassy but bottom is firm, slide out of pan onto a flat dish and cool. Make 2 more omelettes. When cold, spread each omelette carefully and generously with either commercial goose-liver pâté or Mock Goose-Liver Pâté. Sprinkle 1 finely minced truffle over the omelettes, then roll each one loosely.

In the center of large oval serving platter place two omelettes side by side and top with the third. Blend together thoroughly 1 cup Mayonnaise and 2 tablespoons bottled Escoffier Sauce Robert. Spread mayonnaise over all three omelettes to mask them completely, and decorate lavishly with truffle cut-outs. Chill.

Dip 8 tomatoes, one at a time, in boiling water, then quickly in cold water, and peel. Quarter tomatoes, then marinate for 1 hour in 1 cup Basic French Dressing. Lift tomatoes out of marinade and drain thoroughly.

Just before serving, garnish one end of omelette platter with tomatoes and other end with 1½ pounds *prosciutto* or thinly sliced Virginia ham, extending rows of tomato and ham to meet on either side of omelettes. To serve, slice omelettes like jelly rolls and garnish with ham and tomato. Serves 30.

18 eggs
Salt, pepper
9 tablespoons butter
12 ounces goose-liver pâté or 1½ recipes Mock Goose-Liver Pâté (see Index)
4 large truffles
1 cup Mayonnaise (see Index)
2 tablespoons bottled Escoffier Sauce Robert
8 tomatoes
1 cup Basic French Dressing (see Index)
1½ pounds prosciutto or thinly sliced Virginia ham

Mocha-Cream Tartlets

You may prefer to buy about 20 tiny tartlet shells at a pastry shop. Or, make 1 recipe *Sandtorte* Pastry and bake it, in thin layers, in small ungreased *brioche* or fluted tartlet molds. Fill with Mocha Butter Cream, below, with a pastry tube with a plain nozzle. Top each with 2 or 3 silver fancies used for wedding-cake decoration, and chill thoroughly before serving.

20 tartlet shells, about
Mocha Butter Cream
Silver cake fancies

Blended Mocha Butter Cream

Put 2 ounces chocolate bits in dry container of electric blender. Cover and blend at high speed for 6 seconds. Turn motor off and scrape chocolate away from sides with rubber spatula. Add 6 tablespoons of triple-strength black coffee, cover, and blend 6 seconds. Then add 1 cup confectioners' sugar, 4 egg yolks, and ¼ pound soft butter, and blend 15 seconds. (If necessary, chill to spreading consistency when using for cake frosting.)

2 ounces chocolate bits
6 tablespoons triple-strength black coffee
1 cup confectioners' sugar
4 egg yolks
¼ pound butter

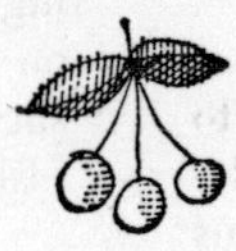

INFORMAL DINNERS

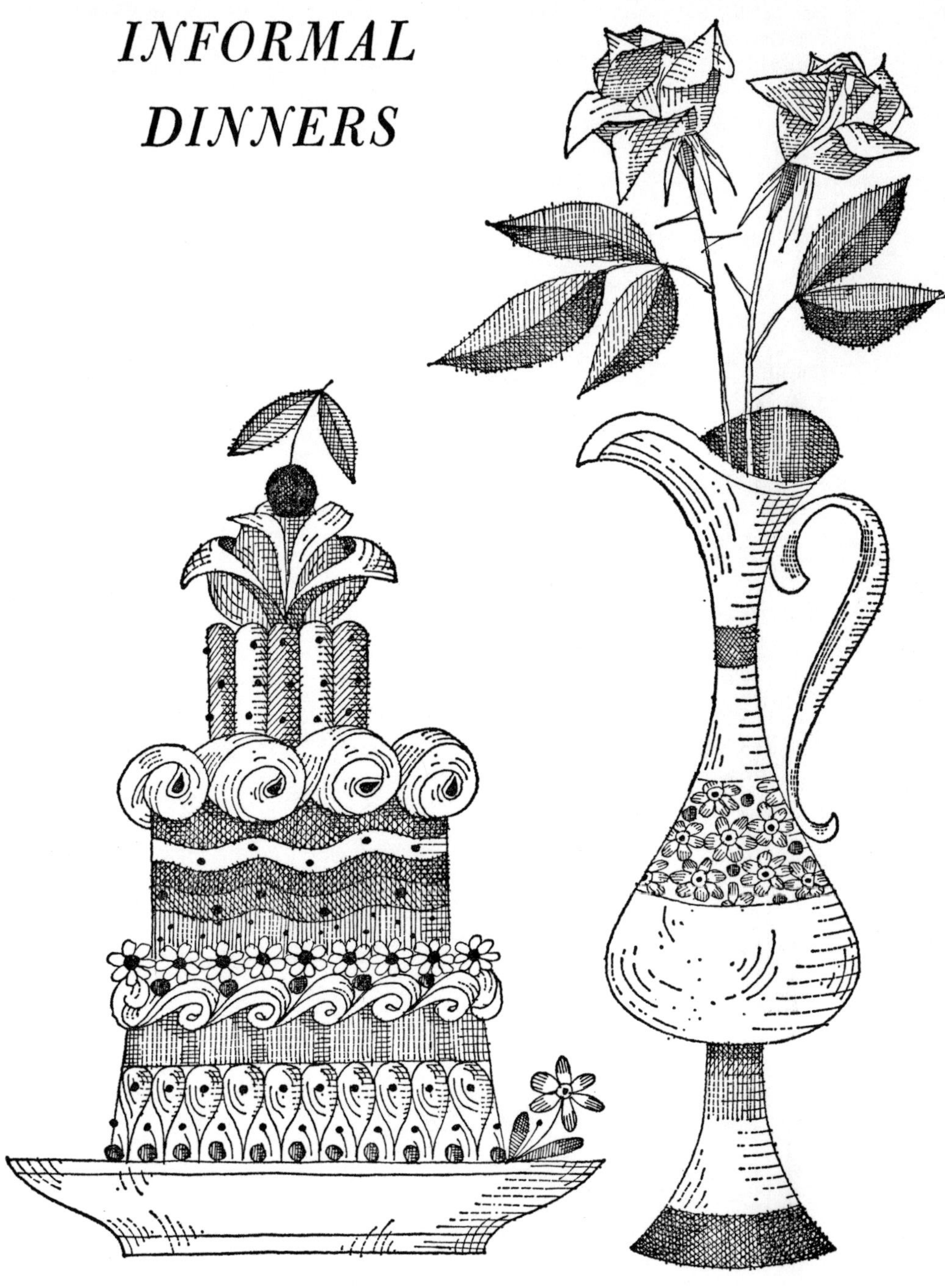

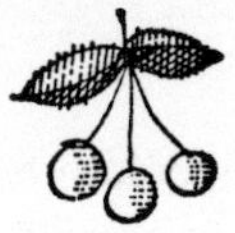

51

Informal Summer Dinner for Four

CUCUMBERS MARRAKECH
CUBE STEAK MINUTE
CURRIED GREEN BEANS
RYE BREAD AND SWEET BUTTER
MINTED CHOCOLATE RICE RING
COFFEE

WINES

Inexpensive: Beaulieu Cabernet Sauvignon
Medium-priced: Beaujolais

Potluck with forethought may be a contradiction of ideas, but it makes perfect sense to us. By our way of reasoning, it means keeping a few menus in mind for emergencies and being prepared to whip them up at the drop of an invitation.

Suppose, for instance, that you're headed for a cocktail party where you're bound to see old friends. It's more usual than not that no one has made plans for dinner, and the inevitable question comes up—where shall we eat? It's an old refrain; someone should write a song about it. You suggest potluck at your house with the calm of a woman with a staff of six. Home you go, your husband plays host in the living room, and you retire, staffless, to the kitchen. In no time at all you call them in to the table and serve a very creditable supper. Your husband, who has been doing his best to conceal his nervousness over the whole thing, beams at his clever little wife. Just do refrain from telling him that you planned it this way all along, or you'll dim your housewife's halo.

Apart from the morning's marketing, you really need forethought only for the Rice Ring on this menu, because you should make it early in the day (don't decorate it with cream, however, until dinnertime). While you're at it, you can make the Chocolate Sauce and prepare the cucumbers in the morning, too, though the sour cream for the cucumbers should wait until late afternoon. Before you leave the house, prepare the beans for cooking and leave them in a pot.

When you're ready to go behind the scenes, the props are all set. Whip the cream and decorate the Rice Ring. (Reheat the Chocolate Sauce at the last minute, and if you don't want to bother with a pastry tube, serve the whipped cream in a separate bowl.) Boil water in another pot, pour it over the beans, and let them cook. Allow about twenty-five minutes altogether, and sauté the steaks and the shallot for the beans last.

We planned this as a particularly good bet for casual company; the recipes can be conveniently increased to feed six or eight people, and they will do as well for everyday meal planning as for potluck entertaining since they don't involve a big production. For the same purpose, look over some of our simpler luncheon menus: The luncheon with Manhattan Clam Chowder (p. 94), the one with *Salade Parisienne* (p. 74), or the one with *Pipérade Basquaise* (p. 77) would all do beautifully as informal suppers, guests or no guests. The key point is to shop with the complete menu in mind, so you'll know just where you're at if you have to produce it, and so the larder will be stocked with something sensible for the family next day if you don't. Hang on to your halo—your admirable forethought mustn't be wasted if you do go out to dinner after all.

Cucumbers Marrakech

Peel and slice 4 cucumbers very thin. Place in a large shallow dish, sprinkle with 1 teaspoon salt and let stand ½ hour, then press out water and dry in a towel. Arrange in layers in a deep dish, sprinkling each layer with ½ teaspoon chopped mint and a touch of cayenne pepper. Cover with ½ pint sour cream or plain yogurt, and chill before serving.

4 cucumbers
1 teaspoon salt
1½ teaspoons chopped mint, about
Cayenne pepper
½ pint sour cream
or plain yogurt

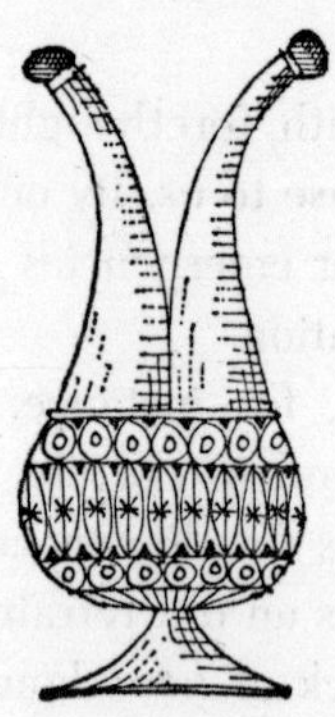

Cube Steak Minute

The trick for rare cube steak (and rare hamburgers) is to preheat a heavy iron pan until a drop of water evaporates at the touch of it. Sprinkle four 6-ounce cube steaks generously with paprika on both sides. Then melt 2 tablespoons butter in heated pan, add meat and sear for 1 minute on each side. Season with salt and freshly ground pepper and transfer at once to heated serving platter. To pan juices add ¼ cup wine served with the meal, and stir in 1 tablespoon chopped parsley, 1 teaspoon finely chopped chives or scallions, and 1 teaspoon butter. Pour over meat and serve at once.

4 6-ounce cube steaks
Paprika
2 tablespoons butter
Salt, pepper
¼ cup wine
1 tablespoon chopped parsley
1 teaspoon chopped chives or scallions
1 teaspoon butter

Curried Green Beans

Wash and snap 1½ pounds green beans and cook over high heat, uncovered, in rapidly boiling salted water until tender (about 10 minutes), then drain. Finely mince 1 shallot, and sauté over low heat for 4 minutes in 3 tablespoons butter, without browning. Add 1 teaspoon curry powder and stir rapidly into butter; then add beans, and stir to coat well. Serve at once.

1½ pounds green beans
1 shallot
3 tablespoons butter
1 teaspoon curry powder

Minted Chocolate Rice Ring

Soften 2 envelopes gelatin in ½ cup water, then melt in top of double boiler, over hot water, with ½ cup light cream. Add half this mixture to 2 cups Basic Rice Dessert, below. Rinse a ring mold with cold water. Pour rice into it and chill for 40 minutes in freezer compartment of refrigerator, or 3 to 4 hours in refrigerator proper, until set. Invert and unmold on serving platter. While still very cold, with a pastry brush coat ring with following mixture: Remaining half of gelatin-cream mixture, 1 square semisweet chocolate (melted), and ¼ cup Garnier green *crème de menthe,* all blended together to a smooth consistency. Brush patiently, dipping repeatedly in glaze, until rice ring is well coated inside and out; it does not take long. Whip ½ cup heavy cream and, with a pastry tube, make a border of it around the ring. Chill again. Serve ice cold, with 1 cup hot Chocolate Sauce to which has been added ¼ cup *crème de menthe.*

2 envelopes gelatin
½ cup water
½ cup light cream
2 cups Basic Rice Dessert
1 square semisweet chocolate
½ cup Garnier green crème de menthe (in all)
½ cup heavy cream
1 cup hot Chocolate Sauce (see Index)

Basic Rice Dessert

In top of a double boiler, over high heat, bring 3 cups milk to boiling point. Add ½ cup Vanilla Sugar and ⅔ cup packaged precooked rice. Cook, covered, over boiling water for 1½ hours, stirring occasionally with a wooden spoon. Makes 2 cups.

3 cups milk
½ cup Vanilla Sugar (see Index)
⅔ cup packaged precooked rice

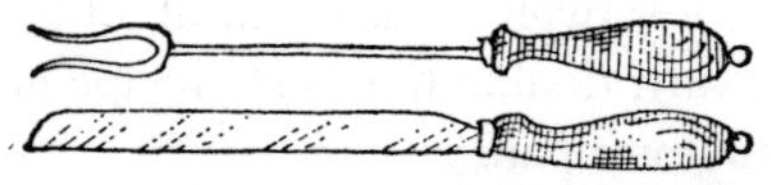

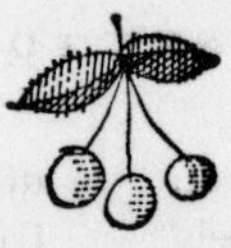

52

Informal Dinner for Four—I

Coquilles of Shrimp Mornay
Wild Rice Cheyenne
Tossed Green Salad with Curry Dressing
Fan Tan Rolls
Bremen Apple Torte
Coffee

WINES

Inexpensive: Gold Seal Keuka Rosé
Medium-priced: Chiaretto del Garda, or Tavel

Recipes, like jokes, have an odd way of going the rounds and cropping up simultaneously in two places, poles apart—which is exactly what happened with our Bremen Apple *Torte.* A New Yorker first showed us an old recipe handwritten in a "pinch of this" and "just enough of that" style. We happened to mention it as a great discovery a few days later at the home of a lady who hailed from San Francisco. She excused herself and came back two minutes later with *her* old handwritten recipe, no more than a pinch or two different from the first. The *Torte* she remembered well, she told us, as one of her mother's favorite party desserts.

We recommend this menu especially for entertaining without help, for four, as we have set it up, or for as many as twelve. Reserve about an hour and a half in the morning or early afternoon to get everything ready for the final touches. Fifteen or twenty minutes before dinner will give you time to reheat the completed Wild Rice Cheyenne (do this over low heat, and leave it in the pan to keep hot until servingtime), to toss the salad with the dressing, to pop the *coquilles* in a 350° oven for 12 minutes, and then to glaze them under the broiler. For twelve, glaze half at a time if you have only one broiler. And for that many, double the *Torte* recipe and bake it 10 minutes longer in a 9-inch springform pan.

Set a *coquille* at each place and then coax the assembled company to come to the table promptly. Serve the rice and the salad afterwards, passing plates down the table, family style.

We have served this dinner with great ease in quite another way. When the group numbers at least eight, we have the *coquilles* with cocktails in the living room. Since people linger over the shrimp while they are having their drink, we don't reheat the rice until we are ready for it. Then we have it, and the salad, rolls, and dinner plates all on a sideboard for selfservice as our guests come into the dining room.

Coquilles of Shrimp Mornay

Make 4 cups *Court-Bouillon* for Fish and in it poach 2 pounds shrimp in their shells for 5 to 6 minutes, or until they turn pink. Shell and devein them. Make 1½ cups *Sauce Mornay*, below. Trim the stems of ¼ pound mushrooms; wash, drain, and mince mushrooms, and sauté in a heavy skillet, over medium heat, with 2 tablespoons butter for 2 minutes. Sprinkle lightly with freshly ground pepper, a little salt, and 1 tablespoon chopped parsley. Combine shrimp, mushrooms, and *Sauce Mornay*, and spoon into 4 *coquilles* (scallop shells) or ramekins. Sprinkle each with 1 teaspoon grated Swiss cheese, then place under broiler until surface is just golden.

4 cups Court-Bouillon for Fish (see Index)
2 pounds shrimp
1½ cups Sauce Mornay
¼ pound mushrooms
2 tablespoons butter
Salt, pepper
1 tablespoon chopped parsley
4 teaspoons grated Swiss cheese

Sauce Mornay

Bring 1 recipe Béchamel Sauce, below, made with base of *Court-Bouillon* for Fish, just to boiling point. Remove from heat, stir in rapidly 1 lightly beaten egg yolk and 2 table-

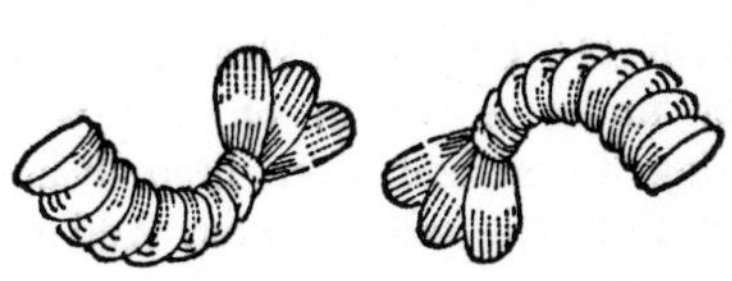

spoons grated Parmesan cheese, then incorporate 2 tablespoons butter. Makes 1½ cups.

This sauce is used over fish, vegetables, macaroni, poultry, or poached eggs in recipes which require glazing in the oven.

1 recipe Béchamel Sauce
1 egg yolk
2 tablespoons grated Parmesan
2 tablespoons butter

Béchamel Sauce

In a saucepan, over medium heat, melt 2 tablespoons butter and add 3 tablespoons flour. With a whisk or slotted spoon, mix rapidly, adding gradually 1½ cups hot milk as sauce thickens and bubbles. When all the milk has been added, boil sauce 8 minutes, stirring slowly until thick and reduced to about half its original quantity. Season with salt and pepper, stir in ½ cup heavy cream, then taste and correct seasoning. Keep warm until needed, but do not allow to boil again. Makes about 1¼ cups.

For fish, this sauce is made with *Court-Bouillon* for Fish instead of milk; for poultry, use chicken broth instead of milk.

2 tablespoons butter
2 tablespoons flour
1½ cups hot milk
or Court-Bouillon for Fish (see Index)
or chicken broth
Salt, pepper
½ cup heavy cream

Wild Rice Cheyenne

Wash 1½ cups wild rice in a colander under a stream of cold water. Bring to a boil over high heat 2 quarts lightly salted water. Add rice, bring water back to a boil, and keep at a rolling boil for 5 minutes. Drain and rinse, and repeat procedure, boiling rice this time for 20 minutes. Drain and rinse again under cold water. Place in the colander over boiling water, covered with a folded kitchen towel, to steam for 12 to 15 minutes, until fluffy.

Meanwhile, fry together over high heat for 4 minutes, with 1 tablespoon of butter: ¾ pound loose ground chuck, 2 medium onions, chopped, and 2 tablespoons chopped green pepper. Stir in cooked wild rice, and 2 teaspoons chili powder, ¼ teaspoon powdered thyme, and ⅛ teaspoon nutmeg. Turn out into a heated serving dish.

1½ cups wild rice
1 tablespoon butter
¾ pound ground chuck
2 medium onions
2 tablespoons chopped green pepper
2 teaspoons chili powder
¼ teaspoon powdered thyme
⅛ teaspoon nutmeg

Curry Dressing

To 6 tablespoons Basic French Dressing (see Index) add 1 teaspoon curry powder.

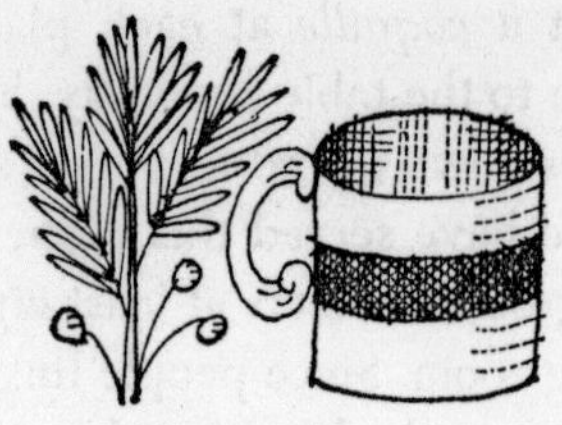

Bremen Apple Torte

Preheat oven to 325°. Peel, core, and slice 4 large apples. Cook, covered, over low heat, with 3 tablespoons Vanilla Sugar and 2 tablespoons butter until soft. When cool, add 3 well-beaten eggs, ½ pint sour cream, ½ cup sugar, ¼ teaspoon cinnamon, and juice and grated rind of ½ lemon. Return to heat and cook until thick, stirring constantly. Pour into 7-inch springform pan lined with Zwieback Crust, below, and sprinkle top with a little of the Zwieback mixture. Bake 30 to 40 minutes.

4 large apples
3 tablespoons Vanilla Sugar (see Index)
2 tablespoons butter
3 eggs
½ pint sour cream
½ cup sugar
¼ teaspoon cinnamon
Juice and grated rind of ½ lemon
Zwieback Crust

Zwieback Crust

With a rolling pin, on a piece of waxed paper, roll 10 Zwiebacks into fine crumbs. Pour into a bowl, and with the fingers, work 1½ tablespoons softened butter into crumbs. Press in even layer against bottom and sides of a 7-inch springform pan, reserving a spoonful for topping. Bake 7 minutes at 300°, and cool before filling.

10 Zwiebacks
1½ tablespoons butter

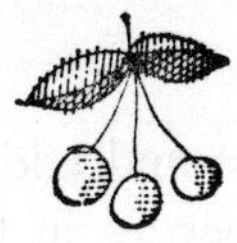

53

Informal Dinner for Four—II

CLAMS ON THE HALF SHELL
VEAL AND PEPPERS CASSEROLE
FETTUCCINE MILANESE
TOMATO SALAD *
TIVOLI PUDDING

WINES

Inexpensive: Cresta Blanca White Chianti, Livermore Valley
Medium-priced: Soave, Cantina Sociale

We have often wondered why certain dishes come to typify the cuisine of a country, while others equally good remain relatively unknown—so many of the unknowns are even better worth pointing out. This Italian dinner, as a case in point, is a happy departure from *scaloppine* and spaghetti.

Cook the Veal and Peppers early in the afternoon. Meanwhile, marinate the tomatoes and make the pudding. We ate this garnet-red delicacy at the home of an Italian lady who says she adapted it from a recipe sent to her by a cousin in the old country. We are still doubtful that the "old country" is Italy—this dessert is so much akin to Danish *rödgröd* or German *rote Grütze*—but she insists. We've adapted it one step further and sometimes use ¾ cup of Brandied Raspberries instead of the frozen berries and substitute ⅓ cup of the brandied fruit syrup for part of the water. Our plain English-speaking name for this is Brandied Raspberry Pudding—all part of the trans-Atlantic evolution of a recipe.

Every summer, we put up a few jars of Brandied Raspberries: Fill a quart jar with firm, ripe berries, sprinkling each layer with sugar and using 1½ cups of sugar in all. Hit the jar sharply on a counter top to settle the berries so you can get in as many as possible. Fill it with brandy and add 3 or 4 drops of red vegetable coloring (otherwise the berries get very pale in

* see Index

a short time). Taste for sweetness and add more sugar if desired. Put the cover on the jar and ripen the berries in the icebox for 6 months before using; they're worth waiting for.

Open the clams shortly before dinner. We used to plead with the fish market, with varying degrees of success, to deliver our opened clams as late in the day as possible so they wouldn't dry out. One day we spotted a special clam knife at the hardware store; granted, you have to learn to use it, but we plead no longer.

You can cook *pasta* an hour ahead and keep it hot in a colander over simmering water, but we prefer to make it at the last minute. Even with the oil in the cooking water to prevent its sticking together, *pasta* is at its best freshly cooked. While the noodles boil, reheat the veal over low heat. Toss the noodles with the buttered crumbs, and leave both veal and noodles in their hot pans while you eat the clams.

Veal and Peppers Casserole

Cut 2 pounds veal cutlet into 1-inch squares, and mince 2 medium onions. In a large deep skillet, over medium heat, heat ¼ cup olive oil, add onions and veal, and sauté together until the onion is pale gold. Add 2 tablespoons butter and 4 green peppers, seeded and cut into 1-inch strips. Sauté for 30 seconds, then pour in ¼ cup white Chianti, and season to taste with salt and pepper. Add ¼ teaspoon hot Italian pepper and 2 cups fresh or canned plum tomatoes, chopped coarsely. Cook over medium heat, uncovered, for 10 minutes, then cover and simmer slowly over low heat for 45 minutes.

2 pounds veal cutlet
2 medium onions
¼ cup olive oil
2 tablespoons butter
4 green peppers
¼ cup white Chianti
Salt, pepper
¼ teaspoon hot Italian pepper
2 cups fresh or canned plum tomatoes

Fettuccine Milanese

Drop 1 tablespoon olive oil and 1 pound narrow Italian egg noodles into 2 quarts rapidly boiling salted water, and boil over high heat for 12 minutes. Drain in colander. Meanwhile, in a heavy skillet, over medium heat, melt 4 tablespoons butter, add 1 cup coarse soft bread crumbs, and fry until golden. Toss *fettuccine* and crumbs together in skillet, and transfer to heated serving dish.

1 tablespoon olive oil
1 pound narrow Italian egg noodles
4 tablespoons butter
1 cup coarse soft bread crumbs

Tivoli Pudding

Defrost and drain ½ package frozen raspberries, reserving juice. Prepare 1 package Danish Dessert according to directions, substituting reserved juice for part of the water. Cool a little, fold in raspberries, then pour into a cut-glass serving bowl. Whip ½ cup heavy cream with 3 tablespoons Vanilla Sugar, and spread on top of pudding. Sprinkle with ¼ cup pistachio nuts or almonds, blanched and chopped. Chill for 3 hours.

½ package frozen raspberries
1 package Danish Dessert
½ cup heavy cream
3 tablespoons Vanilla Sugar (see Index)
¼ cup pistachio nuts or almonds

54

Hungarian Dinner for Six

HUNGARIAN GOULASH
CARAWAY BREAD
CUCUMBER SALAD
PALACSINTA PIE
Löwenbräu Beer, or
Dry Szamorodni Tokay, where available

Nowhere does the character of a people show up more clearly in its cuisine than in Hungary. The colorful, unrepressed quality of the Hungarian temperament manifests itself in a generous use of spices, a lavish abundance of butter and cream, a frequent contrast of sweet and sour. This is not a subtle, understated school of cooking. Flavors are distinctive. They may be wonderfully sweet in a tissue-pastried strudel or fruit-studded yeast cake, or fiercely hot in a soup flavored with a pea-sized scrap of fresh pepper. Bands of gypsies that roamed the countryside, cooking over open fires, left their imprint on the national cuisine in a wealth of stews such as goulash and paprikash; aromatic, hearty dishes as colorful as the gypsies themselves.

And the wine of Hungary, Tokay, is something apart; fiery and heady, with a unique bouquet, it is a fitting accompaniment to a virile cuisine. The vineyards, half the area of New York City, have a correspondingly small output that was originally reserved only for the royal family. While the supply of Tokay is still relatively small, it is generally available.

You might consider this menu as you do oysters, only during the "R" months, since it is not hot weather food. While the thermometer is at a reasonable level, and all during the winter, you are apt to use it time and again. It is a dinner for gourmet and steak-and-potatoes man alike. The seasoning of this goulash is exciting enough for the former, not too bizarre for the latter. The fresh taste of the Cucumber Salad and the moist texture of the Caraway Bread are perfect with it. Don't censure your guests if they use a crust to mop up the last bit of gravy; it's a compliment to both the food and to you. If you have a freezer, make a double batch of this bread; it is perfect to have on hand for cheese or sausage. The dessert is both handsome and delicious, and uses *palacsinta,* the Hungarian counterpart of the French *crêpe* or the Swedish thin *pannkaka,* in a new guise. Our menu is not elaborate; both main course and dessert are too filling to warrant extra folderol. When you have also chosen some hors-d'oeuvres to go with drinks, we know you will agree that the omission of a first course was wise.

This dinner takes several hours of concentrated work, either the same day or the day before, but everything is prepared in those few hours. The only thing left for the last minute is to light the oven.

Make the bread dough first. While it rises, start in on the main course, then back to the bread periodically when it needs attention. Goulash, like all stews, improves on standing, as the flavors permeate the meat thoroughly. Once it is cooked, put it in a covered casserole, and reheat it for serving for three quarters of an hour in a 350° oven, or on an asbestos mat over low heat on top of the stove. Neither will this salad suffer from standing. Years ago in Hungary, the provident housewife prepared crocks of marinated cucumbers and stored them in the ground to assure a winter's supply. The *Palacsinta* Pie can be oven-ready even the day before if you can store it in a freezer, but in that case allow five minutes additional baking time. If you don't have a freezer, do everything but the meringue early in the day, and whip up the meringue just before you serve dinner; it won't fall. In either case, you will only have to excuse yourself from the table to set it in the oven.

Crêpes are fine freezer candidates, too. Spend a free afternoon making a few batches. Package each batch in freezer foil and store. To defrost, loosen the foil, open the package a little and place in a 300° oven for 30 to 40 minutes, until the *crêpes* are thoroughly hot. If the top and bottom pancakes dry out, discard them. Pancakes take up little room in the freezer and are versatile for main courses with a fish or meat filling or served traditionally as Hungarian *Palacsinta.* For this, fill each hot *crêpe* with a heaping spoonful of strawberry or apricot preserve, roll up, dust with confectioners' sugar, and serve immediately.

Flexibility is the keynote for this evening, not only of preparation, but of the length of the guest list and the manner of service. Have as many people as you like. Oven space for the dessert is the only limiting factor. Otherwise, this menu is an excellent choice for a large group. The additional work is not too great when it is multiplied, particularly since the number of dishes to be prepared is small. As for service, take your choice. Anything goes, all the way from laps or small tables, since this is fork-but-no-knife food, to fairly formal seated service. Of course, you wouldn't pick this menu for a state occasion—it's not that sedate.

Hungarian Goulash

Preheat oven to 300°. In Dutch oven, over medium heat, sauté 3 medium onions, chopped, in 3 tablespoons chicken fat or shortening for 5 minutes. Cut 3 pounds beef chuck into 1-inch cubes. Add 3 tablespoons imported paprika, 3 teaspoons caraway seed, 2 cloves crushed garlic, the cubed beef, and 3½ teaspoons salt. Cook together for 5 minutes, then add ¾ cup tomato sauce and 3¾ cups water. Cover, and bake for 1½ hours. Peel 2 pounds potatoes and cut into 1-inch cubes. Remove goulash from oven, add potatoes, stirring in well, and return to oven for ½ hour more, or until meat and potatoes are tender. Skim fat from sauce. Serve goulash from a tureen or large deep serving dish.

3 medium onions
3 tablespoons chicken fat or shortening
3 pounds beef chuck
3 tablespoons imported paprika
3 teaspoons caraway seeds
2 cloves garlic
3½ teaspoons salt
¾ cup tomato sauce
3¾ cups water
2 pounds potatoes

Caraway Bread

Dissolve 1 package dry yeast in ¼ cup lukewarm water. To 1 cup scalded milk add 4 tablespoons honey, 1 teaspoon salt, the dissolved yeast, 2 well-beaten eggs, 1 teaspoon nutmeg, 4 teaspoons each crushed celery seeds and crushed caraway seeds, and about 4 cups sifted flour. Mix well and work dough until it is smooth. Then add 4 tablespoons melted butter and more flour if necessary to handle dough easily. Knead until smooth and elastic, then place in a buttered bowl, cover, and set in a warm place to rise until double in bulk, about 2 hours. Divide dough in half, shape into 2 loaves, and place in buttered loaf pans. Cover and let rise again until double in bulk, about 1 hour. Preheat oven to 425° and bake 15 minutes, then reduce heat to 375° and bake 20 minutes longer or until bread sounds hollow when tapped lightly.

1 package dry yeast
¼ cup lukewarm water
1 cup milk
4 tablespoons honey
1 teaspoon salt
2 eggs
1 teaspoon nutmeg
4 teaspoons celery seeds
4 teaspoons caraway seeds
4 cups sifted flour, more or less
4 tablespoons melted butter

Cucumber Salad

Peel 3 large cucumbers, slice paper thin, and sprinkle with ½ teaspoon salt. Chill for one hour, then press out all juice. Combine 3 tablespoons dill vinegar, 3 tablespoons water, 1 teaspoon sugar, and a pinch white pepper. Mix with cucumber slices, taste, and correct seasoning. Fold in ¾ cup sour cream, if desired, and sprinkle with 2 tablespoons of chopped fresh dill.

3 large cucumbers
½ teaspoon salt
3 tablespoons dill vinegar
3 tablespoons water
1 teaspoon sugar
Pinch white pepper
¾ cup sour cream (optional)
2 tablespoons chopped fresh dill

Palacsinta Pie

Preheat oven to 325°. Cut 8 *crêpes* in strips ¾ inch wide. Arrange in a large well-buttered pie plate or ovenproof dish. Sprinkle with ½ cup finely chopped walnuts, ¼ cup sugar, ¼ cup melted butter, and spread ½ cup apricot jam over all. Beat 6 egg whites until moist peaks are formed. Continue beating, gradually adding ¾ cup sugar, until stiff. Spread meringue over pie, bake for 15 minutes, and serve hot.

8 crêpes (see Index)
½ cup chopped walnuts
¼ cup sugar
¼ cup melted butter
½ cup apricot jam
6 egg whites
¾ cup sugar

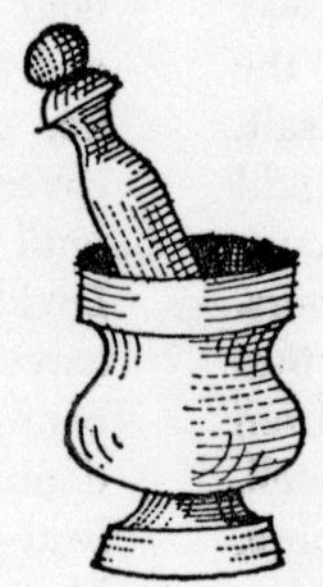

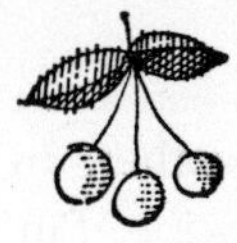

55

Informal Dinner for Six—I

Potage à la Parisienne
Pork Chops Charcutière
Tiny Peas à la Française
Potatoes in Their Jackets
Apple Tart Petit Châtelet
Coffee

WINES

Inexpensive: Beaulieu Vineyard Cabernet Sauvignon, Napa Valley
Medium-priced: B & G Médoc
Expensive: Château Haut-Brion, Graves, or Château Petit-Village, Pomerol

This is really a family dinner—definitely so in spirit, even if we haven't multiplied it to accommodate *all* the sisters and the cousins and the aunts. If you detect a French touch, that is no accident. France's home cooks specialize in unpretentious meals such as this, and the good ladies of French kitchens command respect no less than do their high-powered brothers, the chefs of *haute cuisine.*

Make the apple tart in the morning. Once it is in the oven, go on to the soup (but don't thicken it), and mix the sauce for the chops. For the three quarters of an hour before dinner you will be puttering in the kitchen, but encourage family and friends to wander in and out to keep you company or give you a hand. They may prefer to taste and advise, but if you're smart you'll press them into service. Someone can surely scrub potatoes, or wrap the pork chops in foil, or at least bring you a drink. While the meat is under the broiler, cook the potatoes and the peas, and thicken the soup. Serve the soup at the table from a tureen, and continue with family-style service throughout.

This meal is right for cool weather. In the fall, we often serve freshly pressed cider with it instead of wine. Put the pitcher of cold cider on the table, and also a crock of sweet butter and a whole-meal bread for those who prefer bread to potatoes for sopping up every last bit of sauce. In the winter, we like a bowl of polished apples for decoration, and, come spring, we deck the table with apple blossoms.

Speaking of apples brings us to apple tart and the some-like-it-hot, some-like-it-cold controversy. We are a dead-locked part of the controversy ourselves, one of us preferring the tart cold, the other warm. If you like it warm, don't make it till later in the day.

Potage à la Parisienne

Remove green tops and roots from 4 leeks. Split lengthwise and wash carefully under running water, then slice crosswise. Peel 4 medium potatoes, then rinse and slice thin. Place leeks and potatoes in a soup pot with 1½ quarts chicken broth or good meat stock. Add salt and pepper to taste, bring to a boil over high heat, then reduce heat and simmer 45 minutes. Blend 2 tablespoons butter and 2 tablespoons flour, drop into soup and cook 8 minutes, stirring almost constantly. Remove from heat, add ¼ cup heavy cream, taste, and correct seasoning. Serve from tureen, with a sprinkling of chives and parsley.

4 leeks
4 medium potatoes
1½ quarts chicken broth or meat stock
Salt, pepper
2 tablespoons butter
2 tablespoons flour
¼ cup heavy cream
Chives, parsley

Pork Chops Charcutière

Preheat broiler for 20 minutes. Make a barbecue sauce with ¾ cup bottled Escoffier Sauce Robert, ¾ cup corn oil, and ⅜ cup chopped gherkins. Place 6 thick loin pork chops on 6 pieces of double thickness aluminum foil, each large enough to wrap a chop. Season each chop with pepper, salt, paprika, and a portion of the barbecue sauce. Seal foil around chop and sauce. Place packages 4 inches from broiler heat and broil 20 minutes on one side, then turn packages and broil another 20 minutes. Unwrap and serve chops with juices on a large, heated platter. Accompany with potatoes and peas below.

¾ cup bottled Escoffier Sauce Robert
¾ cup corn oil
⅜ cup chopped pickled gherkins
6 thick loin pork chops
Pepper, salt, paprika

Tiny Peas à la Française

Drain the liquid from 2 No. 2 cans tiny June peas. In a pot, over low heat, melt 4 tablespoons butter, and add 2 tablespoons chopped shallots and 6 or 7 well-washed outer leaves Boston lettuce. Simmer lettuce and shallots, covered, about 6 minutes, until soft. Add peas, 1 tablespoon chopped parsley, ½ teaspoon sugar, and pepper and salt; taste, and correct seasoning. Heat well and pour into heated serving dish.

2 No. 2 cans June peas
4 tablespoons butter
2 tablespoons chopped shallots

6–7 leaves Boston lettuce
1 tablespoon chopped parsley
½ teaspoon sugar
Salt, pepper

Potatoes in Their Jackets

Wash and scrub 2 pounds new potatoes. Place in a 4-quart pot, cover with boiling water, add 1 tablespoon salt, and boil over high heat for 22 minutes, or until tender. Serve unpeeled, with sweet butter.

2 pounds new potatoes
1 tablespoon salt
Sweet butter

Apple Tart Petit Châtelet

Sandtorte Pastry *: Using fingers, blend together ¼ pound butter, 1½ cups unsifted flour, ¼ cup sugar, 1 teaspoon baking powder, and 2 egg yolks. Work mixture through fingers until it feels waxy, like modeling clay, and holds together in a ball. Preheat oven to 375°.

Pat pastry sparingly onto bottom of a 9-inch springform pan, and line sides evenly with a 1½-inch edge. Peel, core, quarter, and slice thinly 4 medium apples. Arrange apple slices, overlapping evenly, in concentric circles in tart shell. Bake for 40 to 45 minutes.

Heat ½ cup apricot jam with 2 tablespoons water, stir, and spread over apples while tart is hot. Serve cold. At the table, just before serving, ignite ¼ cup warm Calvados or domestic apple brandy, and pour it over the tart.

¼ pound butter
1½ cups flour
¼ cup sugar
1 teaspoon baking powder
2 egg yolks

4 medium apples
½ cup apricot jam
2 tablespoons water
¼ cup Calvados
or domestic apple brandy

* To make Salted *Sandtorte* Pastry for other uses, substitute ½ teaspoon salt for the ¼ cup sugar.

To make a baked pie shell, line pie plate as directed above, and bake in a preheated 450° oven for 15 minutes.

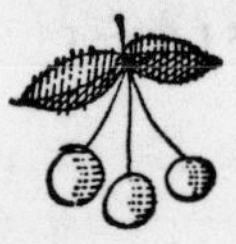

56

Informal Dinner for Six—II

South Seas Salad

Sautéed Calf's Liver

Potatoes Anna

Cucumbers and Peas

Celery Toast

Strawberry Bavarian Cream

Coffee

WINES

Inexpensive: Paul Masson Pinot Blanc, Santa Clara Valley

Medium-priced: Clos du Chapitre

Expensive: Bienvenue-Bâtard-Montrachet, Estate-bottled, Etienne Sauzet

We wade through many old cook books in search of ideas and forgotten recipes that should never have been forgotten. Often, we come upon directions to "stir the mixture for an hour" and we pause to admire the physical stamina of the women of past generations. And, we ask ourselves, how, without automatic washers, without vacuum cleaners, without electric mixers, did they ever find time to do all these things? With renewed gratitude, we count our blessings—or, at least, count all the appliances that make our life easier.

Compare our directions for Strawberry Bavarian Cream, made in a blender, with the directions in a cook book, *circa* 1905. Have you any idea how much time the blender saves? And, without sacrificing quality; if anything, the cream is more velvety. Use this same recipe for Raspberry or Boysenberry Bavarian Creams. Substitute frozen raspberries or boysenberries for the frozen strawberries, and garnish with the appropriate fresh berries. To make Peach Bavarian Cream, use frozen peaches, and fill the center of the ring with more frozen peaches or 4 fresh peaches, peeled and sliced shortly before serving.

Prepare the potatoes ahead and light the oven for them about an hour before dinner. After you put them in, put together the South Seas Salad, then peel and slice the cucumbers. The rest of the cooking goes very quickly, but you will have to do it just before dinner.

Since this is an informal meal, your friends will excuse you for the last twenty minutes while you cook the vegetables and the liver and reheat the Celery Toast. If you have frozen peas instead of fresh, cook them for only five minutes instead of eight. It's most important to have the pan hot to sauté the calf's liver. (This is true when you cook any liver.) Heat the pan first, then add the oil and butter, and let that heat half a minute or so before you put the liver and onion in. The liver is seared quickly, the juices are sealed in, and the meat doesn't get tough and dry as it does from slow cooking or overcooking. There's all the difference in the flavor and the texture! Heat the platter, too, so the liver and the vegetables will stay hot at one side of the stove while you eat your first course.

This is a case where we hope you know your friends well enough to say, "Come and get it," and let them know you mean it. The liver can wait for a *few* minutes, but not too long.

South Seas Salad

6 bananas
1 tablespoon lemon or lime juice
Salt
1 No. 2 can salmon
1 cup fresh or canned crushed pineapple
6 tablespoons Mayonnaise (see Index)
¼ cup finely chopped peanuts or madacamia nuts

Peel back a narrow strip of skin from 6 bananas. Fasten strips in rolls at ends of bananas with toothpicks. Carefully cut out bananas into a bowl, slice by slice. Sprinkle slices with 1 tablespoon lemon or lime juice and a little salt. Drain juice from 1 No. 2 can salmon over bananas. Flake salmon, mix with 1 cup fresh or canned crushed pineapple and 6 tablespoons Mayonnaise, then add to banana slices. Pile mixture into banana shells, and sprinkle with ¼ cup chopped macadamia nuts or peanuts.

Sautéed Calf's Liver

Rub 6 slices calf's liver with cut end of a lemon, squeezing lemon ever so slightly. Season with salt and pepper, then dip lightly in flour. Over high heat, sauté liver quickly with 1 tablespoon minced onion in 2 tablespoons each corn oil and butter. Remove liver from pan with as much onion as will stick to it, and place on a heated serving platter. Discard all fat in the pan. Replace pan over high heat, and in it melt 3 tablespoons butter. Add 1 tablespoon chopped parsley and ¼ cup dry white wine, swirl sauce around in the pan, and pour over liver.

6 slices liver
Lemon
Salt, pepper
Flour
2 tablespoons corn oil
5 tablespoons butter (in all)
1 tablespoon minced onion
1 tablespoon chopped parsley
¼ cup dry white wine

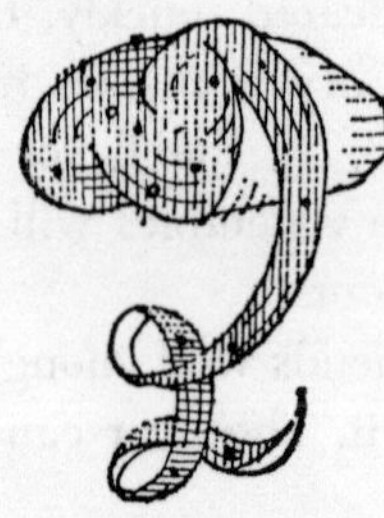

Potatoes Anna

Preheat oven to 450°. Peel and slice very thinly 6 medium potatoes. Wash slices and leave in ice water for ½ hour, then drain and dry on a towel. Butter a Pyrex bowl and place a layer of slices on bottom and sides of bowl. Pour a little melted salt butter over first layer. Repeat until potatoes are used up, using no more than 6 tablespoons melted butter in all. Bake 40 to 50 minutes, or until potatoes are soft. Turn out on a serving dish, and sprinkle with 1 tablespoon chopped parsley.

6 medium potatoes
6 tablespoons melted salt butter
1 tablespoon chopped parsley

Cucumbers and Peas

Peel 4 large cucumbers, cut in fourths lengthwise, and scrape out seeds; then cut into ½-inch lengths. Fill a medium-size pot with salted water ½ inch deep, bring to a boil, and add cucumbers. Simmer over low heat, covered, for 5 minutes, then add 2 cups peas and continue to simmer until both vegetables are just tender, or about 8 minutes longer. Drain thoroughly. Blend 5 tablespoons sour cream with 1½ teaspoons lemon juice and dash white pepper. Pour over vegetables and toss lightly. Taste, and correct seasonings.

4 large cucumbers
2 cups peas
5 tablespoons sour cream
1½ teaspoons lemon juice
Dash white pepper

Celery Toast

Remove heels from 2 loaves day-old unsliced salty-rye bread or French bread. Spread cut end of loaf thinly with butter, cut off very thin slice with serrated knife, butter cut end again, and continue until loaves are finished. Place slices on cooky sheets sprinkle with celery seed, and bake in 275° oven for 20 minutes. Edges will curl and toast will be golden and dry. Store in airtight container in refrigerator or cool place, and re heat before using.

2 day-old loaves salty-rye bread o
French bread
½ pound butter
Celery seed

Strawberry Bavarian Cream

Heat 1 package frozen strawberrie to boiling point, but do not boi Place in electric blender with 2 er velopes gelatin and ¼ cup hot ligh cream. Blend 40 seconds, then add 2 eggs and 1 tablespoon kirsch. Cover and blend 5 seconds. Add 1 heaping cup crushed ice, 1 cup heavy cream, cover, and blend another 20 seconds. Pour into 2-quart ring mold and refrigerate 12 to 24 hours.

One hour before servingtime, run tip of a sharp knife around inside of mold to loosen cream. Dip mold into a pan of hot water for a few seconds. Invert mold and turn out cream onto a serving platter. (When cream is free of mold, it will make a coughing noise). With paper towels, mop all moisture from platter.

Rinse 1 pint unhulled strawberries and pat dry. Lightly beat 1 egg white, dip berries (but not hulls) in it, then dip in Vanilla Sugar, and decorate outside of Bavarian-cream ring with the sugared berries. Place in refrigerator until servingtime.

1 package frozen strawberries
2 envelopes gelatin
¼ cup light cream
2 eggs
1 tablespoon kirsch
1 heaping cup crushed ice
1 cup heavy cream
1 pint strawberries
1 egg white
Vanilla Sugar (see Index)

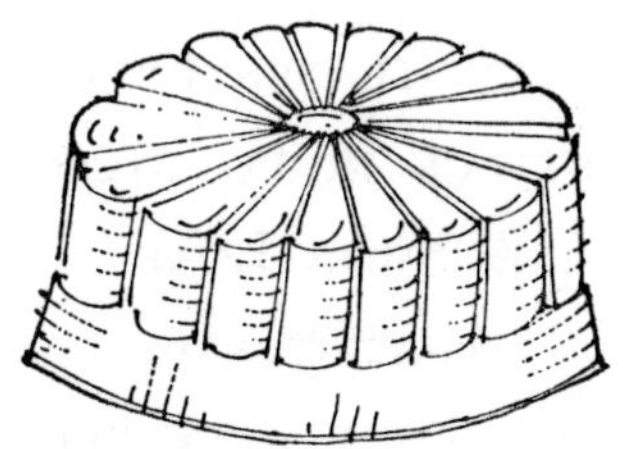

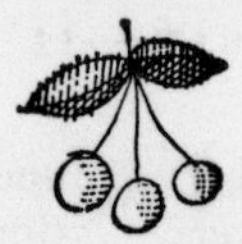

57

Swiss Dinner for Six

FONDUE BOURGUIGNONNE WITH SAUSAGE AND CHEESE
AND WITH BEEF AND VEAL
QUICK HOLLANDAISE SAUCE
SAUCE VALOIS
SWISS SAUCE PIQUANTE
PICKLED ONIONS
SPICY GLAZED FRUIT
ENDIVE AND LETTUCE BOWL, MUSTARD DRESSING
A SWISS LOAF
HEITISTURM
HAZELNUT LECKERLI

WINES

Inexpensive: Beer instead of wine, or
Medium-priced: Neuchâtel
Expensive: Château Chasse-Spleen, Vintage

This Swiss dinner with its do-it-yourself *Fondue Bourguignonne* works ou beautifully for informal entertaining for small groups. Six is about the maxi mum number of people that can do their cooking in one pot. If you hav two suitable pots, these can be placed at either end of a big table and yo can then handle twelve. Special *Fondue Bourguignonne* equipment is im ported from Switzerland but substitutes can easily be improvised: You' need a deep, heavy pot, six to eight inches in diameter, and a chafing-dis cooking stand fueled with either Sterno or alcohol. You need a high hea so a candle burner won't do here. You'll also want forks with long handle that do not conduct heat.

Today we consider *Fondue Bourguignonne* a typically Swiss dish, ye it is not rooted in the culinary tradition of Switzerland. Indeed, it was firs thought of as a Turkish dish and has been known there only since the war. It was introduced in private homes and captured the attention of restaurateurs who saw its possibilities as a novel entry on their menus. Sampled by American tourists, it has achieved quite a vogue in our country as an entertaining innovation. No one seems to know how it came by its present name, since it is not a *fondue* (though it uses similar cooking equipment), nor is it Burgundian.

When you set your table, the pot must be placed in the center within easy reach of your guests. Dinner plates are set in front of each person, as well as smaller plates holding individual portions of meats, cheese, or whatever. Originally this *fondue* was made only with fillet of beef, but to consider the budget and to vary the theme, it may now also be composed of cheese, sausage, or veal, or a combination of any of these.

The system we favor is to have the *fondue* in two installments. Put the equipment on a small table in the living room before dinner and bring out the sausage and cheese to cook and eat with cocktails. Later, take the pot to the dinner table and serve the beef and veal there. Bowls of sauces, relishes, and spiced fruits are placed on the table, and from these each guest helps himself to a spoonful of several kinds on his own plate. Both the Hollandaise and the Valois are rich sauces. Though we wouldn't normally suggest two butter sauces served together, the Swiss like it that way; after all, Switzerland is a dairy country. We give some recipes and suggestions for these accompaniments, though almost anything else you might want will do. If you make your own relish or conserve, do serve that. And there are many commercially prepared relishes, mustard pickles, and thick meat sauces that could well be substituted for our suggestions.

The cooking and eating work this way: Spear a piece of meat, or of cheese and sausage combined, on the long-handled fork and leave it in the bubbling oil in the pot until it is cooked to the desired doneness. Have an extra eating fork for each person. Transfer the meat to the eating fork, dip it in one or more of the sauces, or eat it with one of the pickles or relishes. In the meantime the next bit can be speared on the cooking fork and placed in the pot. A bite of fruit between pieces of meat serves to sweeten the palate.

If, as we suggest, you serve the cheese and sausage with cocktails, one small plate will do for each person. Near the *fondue* pot, set a bowl of cheese and one of sausage from which everyone can help himself. For accompaniment, perhaps just the pickled onions on toothpicks.

To go with the second installment, a simple salad and a good crusty bread, homemade if you have the time; if not, a fresh French or Italian loaf from the bakery. In either case, serve the bread hot. You'll notice that we give a recipe for a large batch of bread, but you'll want some with the cheese and sausage, then some for the meat, and then, there *is* something about homemade bread. For dessert, a simple but delicious peasant dish, traditionally made with blueberries—*Heiti* means blueberries. When they're not in season, though, strawberries, which are available almost all the year round, may be used. Again, if you don't want to bother with home baking, any good nut cookie that your pastry shop offers may be substituted for the *Leckerli.*

By nature this dinner calls for simple, rugged table accessories—earthenware, pewter or wood platters, a straw basket for bread, a crock for the butter, stainless-steel flatware. Have your color scheme bright—it's lusty, earthy food you're serving. This is definitely conversation-piece dining, an ice-breaker guaranteed to launch a gay evening.

Fondue Bourguignonne with Sausage and Cheese

Remove skin from ½ pound cervelat. Cut into ⅔-inch cubes. Cut rind from ½ pound imported Swiss cheese and cut cheese into equal number of cubes. Fill a deep heavy saucepan with cooking oil to a depth of 1½ to 2 inches, and add 2 tablespoons butter. Place on chafing dish stand, light fire, bring oil and butter to a boil, and add a piece of raw potato; this prevents fat from spattering.

Spear a piece of sausage and one of cheese on a fork. Hold in fat until cheese starts to melt and eat as directed above. If fat boils too hard, lower flame a little.

½ pound cervelat
½ pound imported Swiss cheese
Cooking oil
2 tablespoons butter
Piece of raw potato

Fondue Bourguignonne with Beef and Veal

Use 1 pound each fillet of beef and fillet of veal, trimmed weight. Or use all beef or all veal. Cut meat into bite-size cubes and proceed as in recipe for *Fondue Bourguignonne* with Sausage and Cheese, above.

1 pound fillet of beef, trimmed weight
1 pound fillet of veal, trimmed weight
Cooking oil
2 tablespoons butter
Piece of raw potato

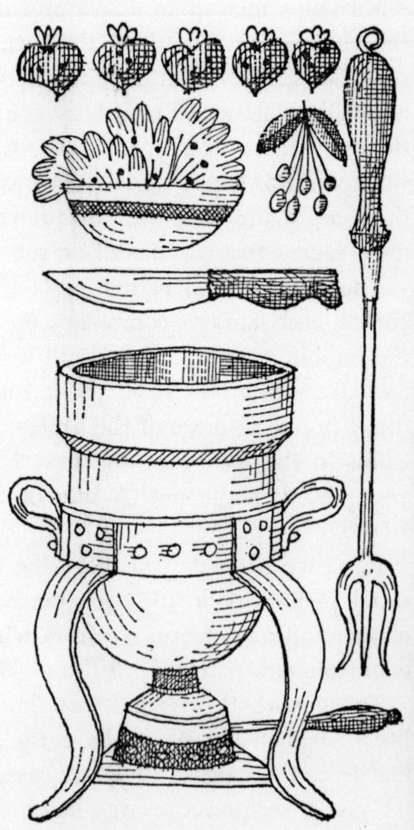

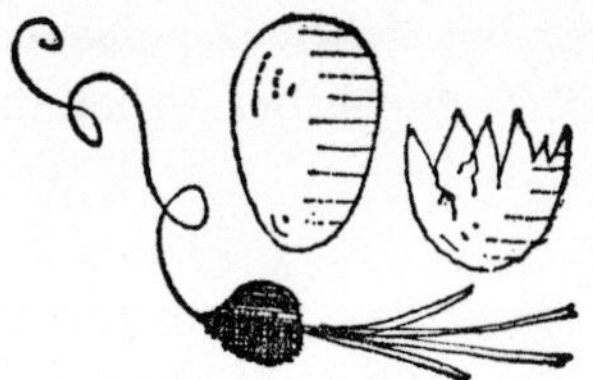

Quick Hollandaise Sauce

In a small saucepan combine 5 tablespoons butter, melted, 2 egg yolks, juice of ½ lemon, a pinch of salt, dash cayenne, and 2 teaspoons water. Set over medium flame and stir briskly with spoon or whisk until thick.

5 tablespoons butter
2 egg yolks
Juice of ½ lemon
Pinch salt
Dash cayenne
2 teaspoons water

Sauce Valois

In the top of a double boiler, over low heat, cook together 1 tablespoon tarragon vinegar, 2 tablespoons water, ⅛ teaspoon white pepper, ½ teaspoon dried chervil, and ½ tablespoon minced shallot, until liquid is reduced to 1 tablespoon. Drain off liquid. Add 3 egg yolks, one at a time, to the seasonings, blending well after each one. Have water in bottom of double boiler hot but not even at simmering point. Now set yolk mixture over hot water, and add ¼ pound butter, bit by bit, stirring constantly. Remove from heat and stir in ½ teaspoon beef extract.

1 tablespoon tarragon vinegar
2 tablespoons water
⅛ teaspoon white pepper
½ teaspoon dried chervil
½ tablespoon minced shallot
3 egg yolks
¼ pound butter
½ teaspoon beef extract

Swiss Sauce Piquante

Combine the following:

⅓ cup sour cream
⅓ cup thick commercial French dressing
3 tablespoons India relish

Pickled Onions

Toss together until onions are lightly coated:

Small jar medium-size cocktail onions, well-drained
1 tablespoon catsup

Spicy Glazed Fruit

Drain 1 medium-size can Elberta peaches (or pears, apricots, or pineapple). Cook juice over high flame until syrupy and reduced to about 3 tablespoons. Blend in 2 to 3 teaspoons dry mustard, depending on your taste, and coat drained fruit with spicy syrup.

Medium can Elberta peaches or pears, apricots or pineapple
2–3 teaspoons dry mustard

Endive and Lettuce Bowl, Mustard Dressing

Separate leaves of 3 heads endive. Chill. Remove dark green outer leaves of 2 heads Boston lettuce and discard. Wash remaining lettuce, drain well, and crisp in refrigerator.

In large wooden salad bowl, blend 2 tablespoons wine vinegar with ½ teaspoon salt, freshly ground pepper to taste, and 2 teaspoons dry mustard. Stirring with the flat of a fork, add gradually 6 tablespoons salad or olive oil until dressing is homogenized. Add 1 tablespoon chopped parsley. Tear

Boston lettuce into bite-size pieces and toss with dressing. Arrange endive over lettuce sun-burst fashion, with tops of leaves pointing outward.

3 heads endive
2 heads Boston lettuce
2 tablespoons wine vinegar
½ teaspoon salt
Freshly ground pepper
2 teaspoons dry mustard
6 tablespoons salad or olive oil
1 tablespoon chopped parsley

A Swiss Loaf

Sauté 1 small minced onion in 2 tablespoons butter until soft and yellow. Dissolve 1 package dry yeast in ¼ cup warm water. Scald 2 cups milk. Add 2 tablespoons sugar and 2 teaspoons salt to milk, and stir in dissolved yeast. When milk and onion are lukewarm, combine them in a large bowl, add 6 cups flour, and mix well. Put dough on lightly floured board and knead until smooth. Return to bowl, cover, and set in warm place to rise until double in bulk. Put risen dough on board, punch down, divide in four, and shape into 4 round loaves. Place on 2 greased cooky sheets, let rise again until double in bulk, and bake in a 400° oven for ½ hour.

1 small onion
2 tablespoons butter
1 package dry yeast
¼ cup warm water
2 cups milk
2 tablespoons sugar
2 teaspoons salt
6 cups flour

Heitisturm

Wash and drain well 1 quart fresh blueberries. Mix ½ teaspoon cinnamon with 2 tablespoons of sugar. Whip 1 cup heavy cream until stiff, adding cinnamon-sugar mixture. Put cream in a serving dish and chill. Dice 4 slices firm white bread, crusts removed, in ⅓-inch squares. Melt ¼ pound butter in large pan (one that will go to the table is preferable). Add bread and sauté until crisp and golden, stirring with a fork. Add ⅔ cup sugar, and continue stirring until croutons are coated.

All this may be done in advance. Just before serving, reheat croutons in butter-sugar mixture, add berries, and continue heating until berries are just warmed through; do not let them cook. Serve warm, with the chilled cream.

1 quart fresh blueberries
½ teaspoon cinnamon
2 tablespoons sugar
1 cup heavy cream
4 slices firm white bread
¼ pound butter
⅔ cup sugar

Hazelnut Leckerli

Beat 1 egg white until it stands in moist peaks. Gradually add ½ cup granulated sugar and a scant ½ teaspoon cinnamon, and continue beating until stiff. Add 2 teaspoons kirsch, and fold in ½ cup each hazelnuts and almonds, all ground. Sprinkle 2 tablespoons sugar on a board, and with

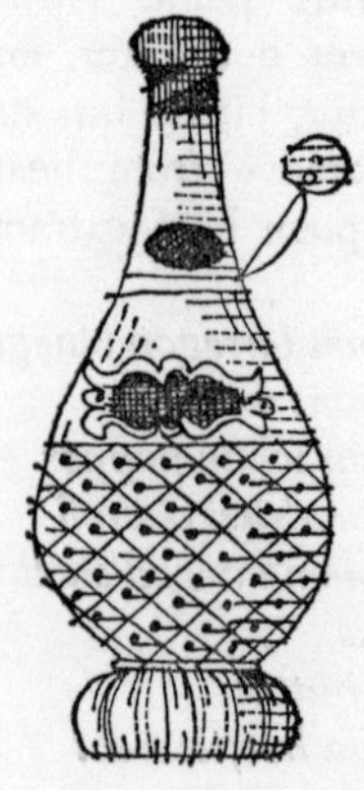

a sugared rolling pin roll out mixture lightly into a rectangle ¼ to ⅓ inch thick. Sprinkle with 1 tablespoon granulated sugar, cut into 24 squares, and place on a well-buttered cooky sheet. Let stand for 1½ hours, then bake in a preheated 400° oven for 7 minutes. *Leckerli* stay chewy inside.

1 egg white
½ cup granulated sugar
Scant ½ teaspoon cinnamon
2 teaspoons kirsch
½ cup ground hazelnuts
½ cup ground almonds
3 tablespoons granulated sugar, about
Butter

58

Low-Calorie Dinner for Eight

CELERY ROOT PARMA
CHICKEN PAPRIKA
PFARVEL AND SPINACH
BASIL BAKED TOMATOES
CARAWAY TOASTS
SWEDISH LEMON FROMAGE

WINES

Inexpensive: California Rhine Wine
Medium-priced: Chilean Riesling, Gran Vino or Reservado
Expensive: Dry Szamorodni Tokay

You've noticed, whether you want to or not, how often people talk about dieting? They are either just on the verge of starting, right in the middle, or nervously getting up the courage to face what they think must be a grimly Spartan regime. Have you ever labored long and lovingly over a beautiful dish, only to find that half your guests partake of it sparingly or not at all because, "I wish I could, but it has so many calories!" Medical statistics stress the hazard of overweight; health agencies plead, insurance companies threaten, and the beauty industry capitalizes on the whole business. It's not a plot to give you, as a hostess, an added problem, but it might as well be. Your guests accept with pleasure, but add, rather fiercely, that they pay strict attention to those medical statistics.

This is where you need low-calorie menus that don't have an aura of austerity. Such menus are not a matter of magic, but of mathematics. You will find calorie charts in some cook books, and you can buy inexpensive pocket-size calorie tables. They reveal many more exciting possibilities for the same number of calories than steak, lettuce, and grapefruit.

We chose low-calorie vegetables and chicken for this menu so that we could add some butter, cream, and sugar to produce a delectable meal to be enjoyed without a twinge of conscience. When you reckon with calories, the sum total is the important figure. Allot each calorie where it counts most—where you can taste it; butter to round out a sauce, cream where it is the perfect finishing touch. A little bit goes a long way.

In all probability, though, not everyone at your party is diet minded. Be generous to the fortunate few who either don't diet or don't have to, and plan extras for them. Have additional French dressing for the celery root; pour only part of the sauce over the chicken, reserving the rest in a sauceboat for more generous servings. You might provide a moist, light pumpernickel and sweet butter to go with the main course, and a cup of cream, whipped and sweetened, to be spooned over the *Fromage.* The traditional Swedish fruit *fromage* often has cream incorporated right into it; if you want the richer version on another occasion, follow this recipe but, before folding in the egg whites, fold in 1 cup of heavy cream whipped with 3 tablespoons of sugar.

Two hours, early in the day, will take care of the bulk of dinner preparation. Boil and marinate the celery. Cook the chicken and leave it in its pan juices; it will only gain in flavor. Reheat it and finish the sauce with the sour cream later. While the chicken is simmering, get the tomatoes and caraway toasts ready for the oven; whip up the *Fromage* and set it to chill; and wash and chop the spinach. You can stop right there and handle the *Pfarvel* and Spinach and the finishing touches described in the recipes in about twenty minutes before servingtime.

This dinner aims to please the figure conscious, but it is hardly a meal of deprivation. Decide on formal or informal service for it, according to the occasion. Like the basic black dress, it can be dressed up or dressed down. Dressing up might be the order of this day. Festivity boosts the weight watcher's morale, and the weight watcher might even be you.

Celery Root Parma

Blanch 8 slices celery root, cut 1 inch thick, for 2 minutes in boiling salted water. Add a dash monosodium glutamate to ½ cup Basic French Dressing. Pour over celery root and marinate for 3 hours or more. Drain thoroughly an hour or so before serving. On individual plates place 1 slice celery root (2 slices if canned), and top with 2 crisscrossed strips pimiento. Put a rolled anchovy in center, and sprinkle a little sieved hard-cooked egg over all.

8 slices celery root,
16 slices if canned
½ cup Basic French Dressing (see Index)
Dash monosodium glutamate
16 thin strips pimiento
8 rolled anchovies
1 hard-cooked egg

Chicken Paprika

In a covered Dutch oven, over very low heat, cook 4 large onions, diced, in 2 tablespoons chicken fat until soft and transparent but not brown (¾ of an hour). Stir in 2 tablespoons imported paprika. Add 2 large broilers, cut in pieces, and ½ seeded green pepper. Pour in ½ cup stock or water, and season with 1 teaspoon salt and ⅛ teaspoon pepper. Cover, bring to a boil over high heat, then reduce heat and simmer until chicken is tender, about 35 to 45 minutes. Discard green pepper and remove chicken to hot serving platter. Stir 2 teaspoons flour into ⅓ cup sour cream and dilute with a few spoonfuls of pan juices. Add this to pan juices and simmer, stirring constantly, until sauce is thickened. Taste, correct seasonings, and pour over chicken.

4 large onions
2 tablespoons chicken fat
2 tablespoons imported paprika
2 large broilers
½ green pepper
½ cup stock or water
1 teaspoon salt
⅛ teaspoon pepper
2 teaspoons flour
⅓ cup sour cream

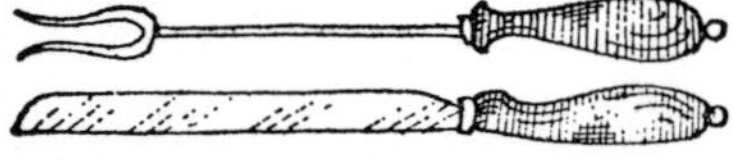

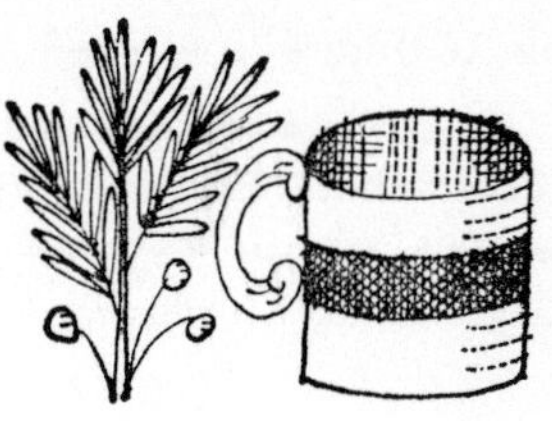

Pfarvel and Spinach

Drop ¾ cup *pfarvel* * in 1 quart boiling salted water and cook 15 to 18 minutes, until just tender. Rinse under hot water and drain thoroughly in a colander. Pick tough stems from 4 pounds fresh spinach, wash spinach, and chop coarsely (or use 3 packages frozen chopped spinach). Place in pot with only the water that clings to leaves. Steam, covered, for 3 to 5 minutes. Drain in a colander and press out excess moisture with a fork. Combine spinach and cooked *pfarvel,* add 1 tablespoon butter, and season to taste with salt and pepper. Pack in a bowl and invert at once onto a heated serving platter.

¾ cup pfarvel *
4 pounds spinach
or 3 packages frozen chopped spinach
1 tablespoon butter
Salt, pepper

Basil Baked Tomatoes

Cut slice from stem end of 8 tomatoes and discard. Mix together 4 tablespoons dried bread crumbs, 1 tablespoon melted butter, ½ teaspoon salt, and 1 teaspoon dried basil, and sprinkle mixture on tomatoes. Bake in 350° oven for 25 minutes.

8 medium tomatoes
4 tablespoons dried bread crumbs
1 tablespoon melted butter
½ teaspoon salt
1 teaspoon dried basil

* This is an egg barley which may be bought in most groceries.

Caraway Toasts

Spread 2 tablespoons soft butter on 16 pieces rye Melba toast. Sprinkle 4 teaspoons of caraway seed over all. Place in 350° oven for 8 to 10 minutes.

16 pieces rye Melba toast
2 tablespoons soft butter
4 teaspoons caraway seed

Swedish Lemon Fromage

Soak 1 tablespoon gelatin in ¼ cup cold water. Grate rind of 2 lemons, squeeze out juice, and reserve. Beat together 6 egg yolks and ¾ cup sugar until thick and light. Beat in lemon juice and half the grated rind. Dissolve gelatin over heat and beat into yolk mixture. Then beat 6 egg whites stiff and fold into yolk mixture. Spoon into individual serving dishes or one large bowl, and sprinkle with remaining lemon rind.

1 tablespoon gelatin
¼ cup water
2 lemons
6 eggs, separated
¾ cup sugar

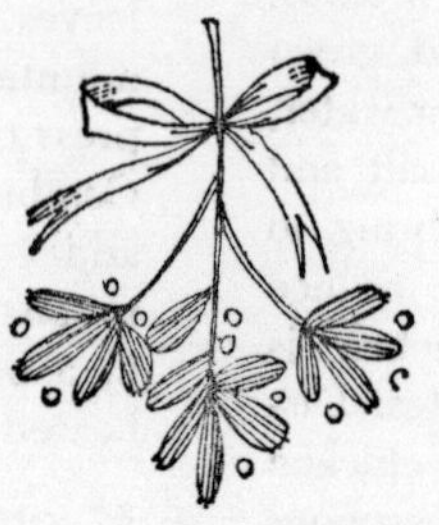

59

Fish Dinner for Eight

Artichokes, Sauce Chiffonnade
Halibut à la Flamande
Parslied Potatoes
Cheese Sticks
Open Orange Tart

WINES

Inexpensive: American Riesling
Medium-priced: Alsatian Riesling
Expensive: Bernkasteler Doktor

We have often listened to women bemoaning in quiet, or not so quiet, desperation the unhappy chance that they must give a dinner without serving meat. This complaint has cropped up so many times that we hastened to work out this particular menu when we first started our book.

Whoever decided on fish for fast days simply did not understand fish—and, when you stop to think of the magnificent dishes created with it, seriously underestimated the imagination of the world's good cooks besides. New England chowders, Scandinavian fish puddings, Chinese sweet-and-pungent fish bear testimony to that! Furthermore, we can all use a change, even from good red meat.

In setting up this menu we have borrowed an idea from the West Coast—our first course serves as both vegetable and salad. This is not to telescope two courses into one, but to avoid a conglomeration that would be anything but a symphony of flavors; the vinegar dressing on the artichokes would rudely overpower the delicately flavored fish were they to be served together. That such combinations will not do comes as no news to most of us, but a special charm of obeying this basic rule of menu planning is less obvious. This is simply that a delectable sauce, a delectable recipe, particularly for vegetables, does not have to go by the board because it will not "go with" the main course. Far better to include it and savor it by itself, as has been done for many years in Europe where vegetables often follow the main course in solitary splendor, as indeed the artichokes might do in this case.

Our dessert has a dividend we'd like to mention. The recipe for the crust can be used for superb cookies we call Yvette's Crescents: Pinch off marble-size balls of the dough and roll them between the palms of your hands, making baguettes about 2 inches long with tapered ends. Bend these into crescent shapes, place them on lightly buttered cooky sheets, and bake them at 375° for about 12 minutes. Remove them from the tins and, while they are still hot, dust them generously with sieved confectioners' sugar. If you're not in the mood for a tart, you could have the chilled orange sections simply anointed with the liqueur and pass these cookies separately.

Last-minute preparation and service shouldn't present any special problems. The artichokes and their sauce are done ahead. Crust for the tart may be made even several days before and kept in the refrigerator; the same with the Cheese Sticks (we always keep a supply of these in the freezer, all baked, needing only to be reheated for a few minutes in a 375° oven). The fish can be ready to bake and needs no attention during cooking. Just mind your watch and cook the potatoes while the fish is in the oven.

For table decoration for seafood and fish dinners, we like to use shells. We started collecting them some years ago on Florida's Gulf Coast where *everybody* seems to go shelling. Came home with quite a boxful and have added some since, purchased at stores that supply shell collectors who don't get to Florida. We never seem to arrange them twice the same way. We decide on our color scheme, put the shells in a bowl or on a flat platter, and play around with them until we've got what we want. Their shapes, their delicacy and translucency give enchanting results. And try them in combination with flowers!

Artichokes, Sauce Chiffonnade

Wash 8 large artichokes under running water, steep for 10 minutes in salted water, and drain. With kitchen shears cut ¼ inch off each leaf, and with a sharp knife cut off stem and bottom leaves. Boil, uncovered, in a pot of boiling salted water for 30 minutes. Drain and cool.

To serve, press forefinger into center of artichoke and enlarge hole by gently spreading leaves to the side. With a grapefruit knife remove heart and choke from artichoke bottom, scraping it clean. Artichoke now has shape of a bowl. Fill with *Sauce Chiffonnade,* below, and place on large individual plates.

8 large artichokes
Sauce Chiffonnade

Sauce Chiffonnade

In a saucepan, over medium heat, melt 2 tablespoons butter. Blend in 2 tablespoons flour, and add gradually 1½ cups chicken broth, stirring very rapidly with a whisk or wooden spoon as sauce thickens and bubbles. When broth has all been added, boil sauce rapidly for 8 minutes, stirring almost constantly. Season to taste with salt and pepper, and remove from heat. When sauce has completely stopped boiling, stir in 1 egg yolk. When quite cold add 2 tablespoons tarragon vinegar. Fold in 1 stiffly beaten egg white just before serving.

2 tablespoons butter
2 tablespoons flour
1½ cups chicken broth
Pepper, salt
1 egg yolk
2 tablespoons tarragon vinegar
1 egg white

Halibut à la Flamande

Arrange 8 individual halibut steaks in a thickly buttered shallow ovenproof dish. Peel and slice 2 lemons and 2 onions, and arrange slices over fish. Season generously with freshly ground pepper, salt, and ⅛ teaspoon allspice, and moisten with ½ cup dry white wine. Mix together 2 tablespoons bread crumbs, 3 tablespoons grated Swiss cheese, and 1 tablespoon chopped parsley. Sprinkle this over all and dot with butter. Bake, uncovered, in preheated 350° oven for 25 minutes. The juice by this time should be reduced by two thirds. Serve sprinkled with 1 tablespoon chopped parsley.

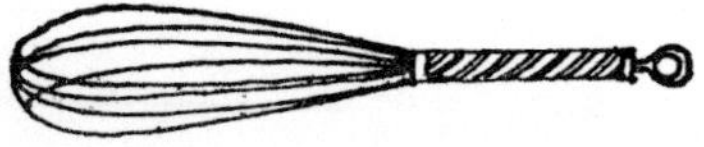

¼ pound butter, in all
8 individual halibut steaks
2 lemons
2 onions
Pepper, salt
⅛ teaspoon allspice
½ cup dry white wine
2 tablespoons bread crumbs
3 tablespoons grated Swiss cheese
2 tablespoons chopped parsley

Parslied Potatoes

Peel 6 large Idaho potatoes and cut them in 1-inch cubes. Cook, uncovered, in plentiful boiling salted water, over high heat, for 10 minutes. Drain quickly while still steaming. Replace in pot over high heat. Shake pot constantly for 20 seconds to allow all liquid to evaporate, so that the potatoes look floury, fluffy, and even fall apart a little. Place in a heated serving dish with 2 tablespoons butter in the middle, and sprinkle with 2 tablespoons chopped parsley.

6 large Idaho potatoes
2 tablespoons butter
2 tablespoons chopped parsley

Cheese Sticks

In a bowl work together to a smooth paste 2⅓ cups flour, 1¼ cups grated Cheddar cheese, ½ pound soft butter, and salt and pepper to taste. Chill dough for 20 minutes. With a floured rolling pin roll out ¼ inch thick on a floured board. Cut into strips ½ inch wide and 8 inches long; use a pastry wheel if you have one. With a pastry brush paint sticks with 1 egg first beaten with 1 tablespoon water. Sprinkle with ½ cup celery seed. Bake on an unbuttered baking sheet in 350° oven for 12 minutes. Makes 5 dozen cheese sticks. Reheat before serving.

2⅓ cups flour
1¼ cups grated Cheddar cheese
½ pound butter
Salt, pepper
1 beaten egg
1 tablespoon water
½ cup celery seed

Open Orange Tart

Place following ingredients for crust in a bowl and work together with hands until dough feels like modeling clay:

¼ pound plus 2 tablespoons butter
⅔ cup granulated sugar
1 cup sifted flour
1½ cups grated almonds
1 teaspoon grated lemon rind
⅛ teaspoon cinnamon
2 egg yolks
1 hard-cooked egg yolk, sieved

With fingers pat three-quarters of dough evenly on bottom of 9-inch springform pan. Pat remaining quarter of dough into an edge ½ inch high around inside of pan.

Drain 3 No. 2 cans orange sections. Arrange sections, slightly overlapping, in concentric circles until bottom of tart is covered. Bake at 315° (325° is just a little too hot!) for about 50 minutes. Do not brown. Dilute 4 tablespoons orange marmalade with 1 tablespoon Grand Marnier, heat, and pour evenly over fruit. Serve cool.

3 No. 2 cans orange sections
4 tablespoons orange marmalade
1 tablespoon Grand Marnier

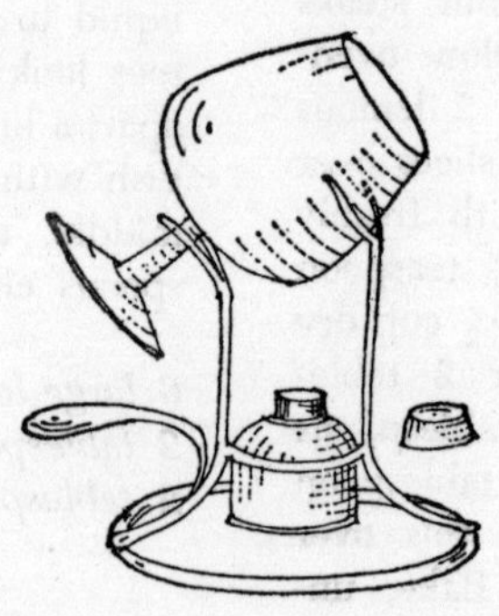

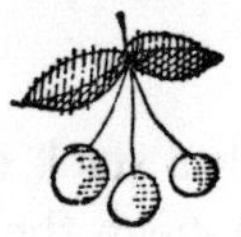

60

Steak Dinner for Twelve

Shrimp in the Pink
Baked Steak with Mushrooms
Potato Rösti
Onion-Filled Onions
Tomato Slices
Dunking Bread
Upside-Down Chocolate Cake

WINES

Inexpensive: California Burgundy or Zinfandel
Medium-Priced: Moulin-à-Vent, Domaine Burdelines
Expensive: California Martin Ray Cabernet Sauvignon, Vintage

And then there are always those who eat everything—as long as it's steak and a chocolate dessert. Actually, dreaming up dinners for the steak-and-potatoes, chicken-and-apple-pie set is quite a challenge. If you can figure out something different and interesting, and really good besides, then you've done it! So use the steak-and-potatoes theme, but depart from the hackneyed in concept and preparation; it can be done. This type of menu you will want, too, for guests whose tastes you don't know well. Play it safe for visiting firemen, at least the first time.

The most exciting feature of this dinner is the method of cooking the steak. By oven-roasting it you achieve the broiled look and taste, with a bonus of as good a sauce as you've ever dunked a piece of French bread in. Furthermore, you can cook a quantity of steak (for as many as two dozen people) that you just can't manage in one broiler. Here, by using the oven, you can broil as many steaks as can fit on both shelves.

The Shrimp in the Pink can be served either on individual plates as a first course at the table, or with cocktails before dinner. In the latter case, have them in one large bowl with a stack of small plates and forks handy. If your guests are calorie minded, heap the shrimp alone in one bowl with the sauce in another. A plea—don't overcook the shrimp; they end up dry and tough. Take a lesson from the Chinese. Juicy, tender shrimp are the result of cooking just until they change color and lose their transparency. Another plea—get good, solid, meaty tomatoes, sweet and flavorful. If there are only the watery, acid ones around, substitute another salad.

Since this is not a dinner that takes care of itself for the last half hour or so, you will have to count on slipping out to the kitchen twice during that time; first, to put the steak in and start the potatoes browning. Back to your guests, renew yourself with a cocktail if you wish, and then into the kitchen for fifteen minutes to get everything ready. (So the eleventh-hour rush will not floor you, as it otherwise might, cook and fill the onions earlier in the day. Reheat them in a covered pan, on an asbestos mat over low heat, for this last quarter hour before dinner.)

This is a substantial dinner, a he-man meal that tolerates no chi-chi. In setting your table, follow through with simple china and linen (a red-checked cloth is fine), stainless steel, wine bottles right on the table, cruets of vinegar and oil for the tomatoes, the pepper mill, bread kept hot in napkin-lined baskets. (An imported beer, incidentally, would be as appropriate as wine with this dinner.) Family-style service is just right—host carving at one end of the table, sending the plates down to your end for potatoes and onions. Have the tomatoes on several small platters on the table for guests to help themselves.

If your table doesn't seat twelve, or if you've enlarged this party, use several smaller tables but keep to the same scheme. The only differences are that you will have to serve from a buffet table where your host will carve, and, since service will be longer, you may need candle warmers.

Shrimp in the Pink

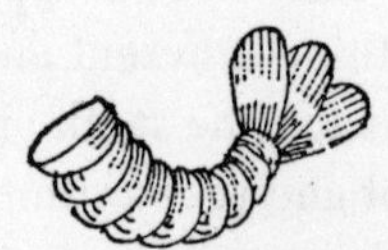

Make a *Court-Bouillon* for Fish: Bring to a boil in a large pot 2 quarts water with 1 tablespoon salt, 10 crushed peppercorns, 2 tablespoons lemon juice, 1 bay leaf, 1 celery stalk, and 1 carrot. Reduce heat, then simmer 20 minutes. Add 4 pounds raw shrimp and bring to a boil again. Skim thoroughly, reduce heat, and simmer until shrimp turn pink. Remove from heat and cool shrimp in broth. Shell, devein, and drain thoroughly on absorbent paper.

Drain 1 No. 2 can of julienne beets, reserving ¼ cup of liquid from can. Combine 1½ cups sour cream, ½ cup mayonnaise, ¼ teaspoon salt, and 1 tablespoon grated horseradish. Mince ½ cup beets, fold into sour cream mixture, and add reserved beet liquid to make the Pink Dressing.

Toss shrimp with dressing. Arrange in individual shrimp-cocktail glasses or on small plates. Garnish with some of remaining beet strips. Chill before serving.

2 quarts water
1 tablespoon salt
10 crushed peppercorns
2 tablespoons lemon juice
1 bay leaf
1 celery stalk
1 carrot
4 pounds shrimp

1 No. 2 can julienne beets
1½ cups sour cream
½ cup Mayonnaise (see Index)
¼ teaspoon salt
1 tablespoon grated horseradish

Baked Steak with Mushrooms

Have ready the following garnish and basting mixtures:

Garnish: Trim stems of ½ pound button mushrooms to within ½ inch of caps. Wash and drain mushrooms and slice ¼ inch thick. Over high heat melt 2 tablespoons butter; when it sizzles, reduce heat to medium. Add mushrooms and sauté until they are golden and soft. Stir ½ teaspoon meat extract or beef concentrate into pan juices. Taste, season with salt and pepper, and sprinkle with 1 tablespoon chopped chives.

Basting: Crush 1 clove garlic and 2 tablespoons minced onion in a garlic press. Blend together garlic, onion, ¼ cup Worcestershire sauce, 1½ tablespoons salt, ¼ teaspoon freshly ground pepper, and 6 tablespoons very soft butter.

Steaks: Preheat oven to 550° for ½ hour. Trim fat and tail from 2 or 3 porterhouse steaks weighing 10 pounds altogether. Place steaks in shallow baking pan, and brush with ½ of basting mixture. Bake 12 minutes, then turn steaks and insert meat thermometer into one of them. Brush second sides with rest of basting mixture.

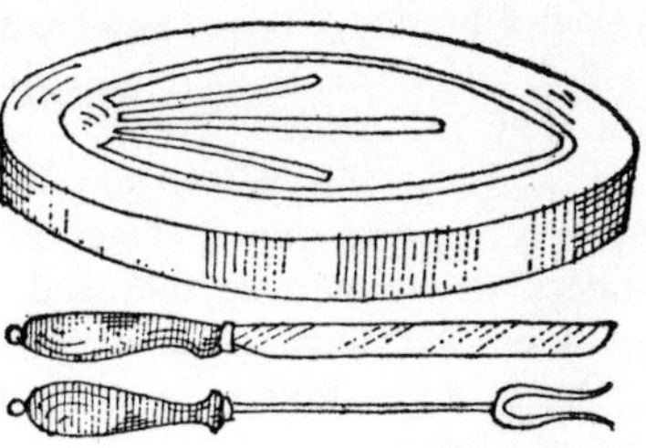

Bake to temperature recommended for rare (130° to 140°) or medium rare (160°). Remove steaks to heated serving platter. With perforated spoon, heap mushrooms on steaks, reserving their juice. Place baking pan over high heat on top of stove. Deglaze drippings with ¼ cup cold water, and add mushroom juice and 1 tablespoon butter. Taste, correct seasoning, and pour sauce over steaks.

½ pound button mushrooms
2 tablespoons butter
½ teaspoon meat extract or beef concentrate
Salt, pepper
1 tablespoon chopped chives

1 clove garlic
2 tablespoons minced onion
¼ cup Worcestershire
1½ tablespoons salt
¼ teaspoon freshly ground pepper
6 tablespoons butter

2 or 3 porterhouse steaks (10 pounds)
¼ cup water
1 tablespoon butter

Potato Rösti

Boil 4 pounds medium potatoes in their skins until just tender. Peel and slice thin. Add 1 tablespoon salt and 1 medium minced onion. In a large heavy skillet, over high heat, melt

¼ pound butter. When it sizzles, add potatoes and sauté, shaking pan often, until they are golden. You may put them aside at this point, and finish just before servingtime. Then press potatoes down with spatula and fry over low heat until crust is formed on the bottom. Invert on a heated serving platter.

4 pounds medium potatoes
1 tablespoon salt
1 medium onion
¼ pound butter

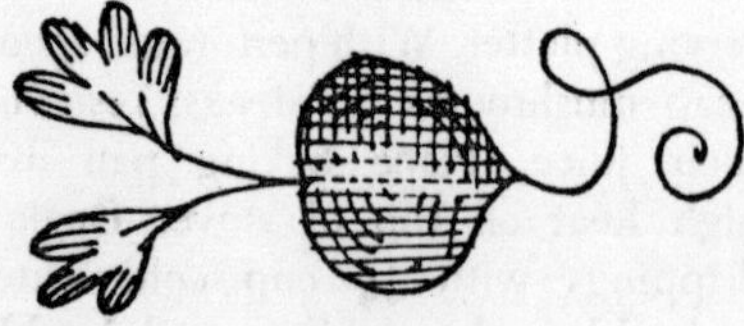

Onion-Filled Onions

Peel 12 large onions. In a large heavy pan, melt 2 tablespoons butter, and add 2 tablespoons sugar and the onions. Brown over high heat, shaking pan to brown onions on all sides. Add ⅓ cup water, cover pan, and turn heat low. Cook until tender, adding more water if necessary.

Peel 1 pound very tiny white onions, or use 1 No. 2 can of same. Brown in 2 tablespoons butter and 2 tablespoons sugar in same manner as large onions. Add ⅓ cup water, or more as needed, and cook until tender. (Canned onions only need browning in the butter and sugar.)

To serve, cut a thin slice from top of each large onion. Scoop out enough pulp to make room for the small onions, and arrange small onions in the large onion shells.

12 large onions
2 tablespoons butter
2 tablespoons sugar
⅓ cup water
1 pound tiny white onions or 1 No. 2 can same
2 tablespoons butter
2 tablespoons sugar
⅓ cup water

Tomato Slices

Use 5 pounds solid, ripe tomatoes, beefsteak if available. Dip one at a time in boiling water, then quickly in cold water (or hold over gas flame until skin blisters slightly), and peel. Slice and chill. Arrange slices on platters and serve with oil and vinegar in cruets at the table.

5 pounds beefsteak tomatoes
Oil
Vinegar

Dunking Bread

Quarter 2 loaves French bread by cutting in half lengthwise, once horizontally, then again down center of each half. Cut crosswise twice to separate sticks into thirds. Brush cut surfaces lightly with about ⅜ pound butter, melted. Place on baking sheets, cut edges up, and heat in 300° oven for 3 to 5 minutes. Place in napkin-lined baskets to keep warm.

2 loaves French bread
⅜ pound butter

Upside-Down Chocolate Cake

Preheat oven to 350°. Cream together 4 tablespoons butter and ¼ cup dark brown sugar. Mix in ¾ cup light corn syrup and 1 cup chopped pecans or walnuts. Grease a 9-by-12-inch pan and spread mixture on bottom of pan.

Cream together 6 tablespoons butter and 1¼ cups Vanilla Sugar until light. Meanwhile, melt 4 ounces bitter chocolate over hot water. Beat 2 egg yolks into butter-sugar mixture, and add melted chocolate. Mix 2 cups flour with 2 teaspoons baking powder. Add dry ingredients to chocolate mixture alternately with 1½ cups milk. Beat 2 egg whites until stiff and fold into batter. Pour into cake pan and bake 55 minutes. Invert on board or platter, cool, and serve cut in squares.

4 tablespoons butter
¼ cup dark brown sugar
¾ cup light corn syrup
1 cup chopped pecans or walnuts
6 tablespoons butter
1¼ cups Vanilla Sugar (see Index)
4 ounces bitter chocolate
2 eggs, separated
2 cups flour
2 teaspoons baking powder
1½ cups milk

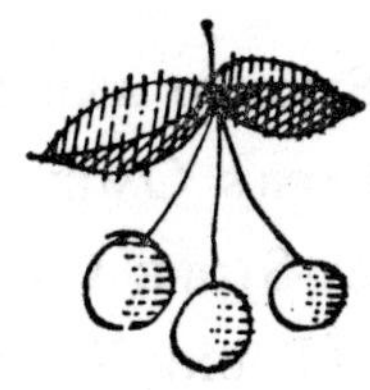

61

Buffet Supper—Smörgåsbord for Sixteen

PLATTER OF SMOKED AND PICKLED FISH
FARMER'S OMELETTE
COUNTRY-STORE CASSEROLE
DRÖTTNINGHOLM (PRUNE-FILLED VEAL ROLLS)
ASSORTED COLD MEATS AND SAUSAGES
BROWN BEANS
CASTLE SALAD FOR A PARTY
SCANDINAVIAN RYE BREAD AND CRISP BREADS
SWEDISH AND DANISH CHEESES
WORLD'S BEST APPLE DESSERT
FINGER COOKIES
Aquavit and Beer

Smörgåsbord derives from the Swedish, *smör,* butter, *gås,* goose, and *bord,* table. A groaning *bord* it is, but it takes its name from the hollowed-out wooden scoop, goose-like in shape, that was used to skim the freshly-churned butter. The scoopful of butter was then brought to the table. The *smörgåsbord* probably originated in the inns of the Scandinavian country-side, where innkeepers needed a wide assortment of dishes always ready for stagecoach travelers. The names of many of these dishes, translated literally, have an ingenuous charm; we have not changed them.

Preparing a *smörgåsbord* is an ambitious project, but gratifying. Though the menu need not list as many as 134 dishes (the minimum selection at a famous restaurant in Lund, Sweden), there should be both hot and cold dishes and a variety of meats, fish, eggs and cheeses. You will have to pre-

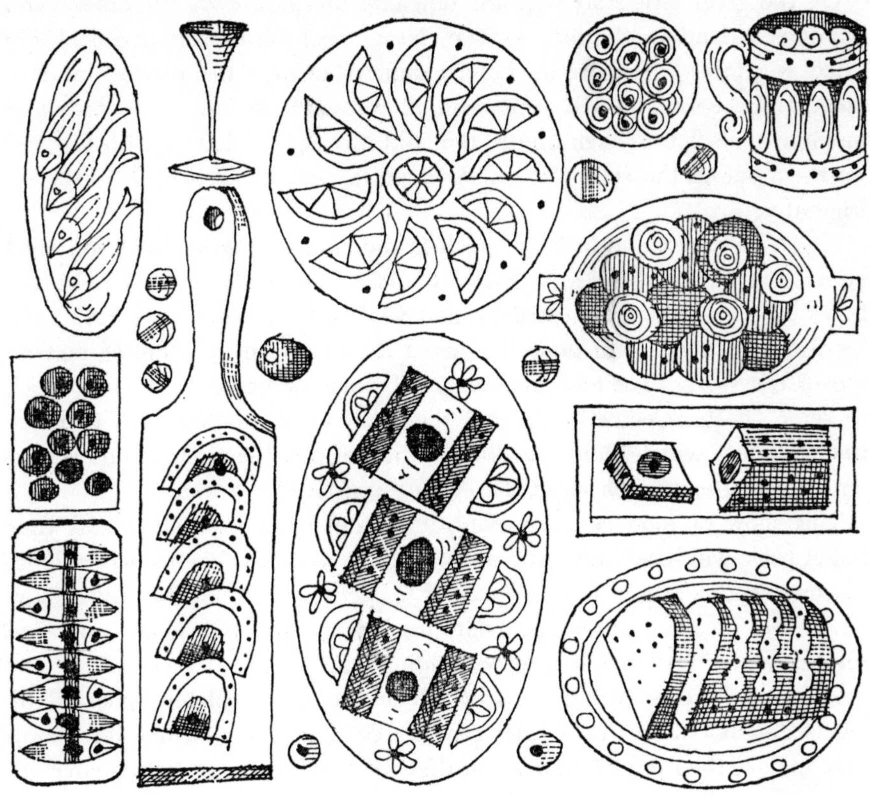

pare a number of the dishes yourself, but a fair share of this splendid array —the smoked and pickled fish, the cheeses, breads, and cold meats—you will buy at a good delicatessen or Scandinavian food shop. Fortunately, the *smörgåsbord* allows for much advance preparation, but give yourself free time for a day or even two before, and time just before serving to take care of last-minute cooking and arranging of platters on the buffet.

This would be a Gargantuan job of cooking to leave for the day of the party. You might get it done, but it would just about do you in, too. So market at least the day before (you will have quite an imposing list!), and prepare the casserole, the veal rolls, and the beans. Setting a buffet and tables to seat sixteen people could present problems. Solve these the day before too; tomorrow you'll want to concentrate on getting things done, not on meeting unforeseen emergencies. You must, for instance, have several hot plates, chafing dishes, or candle warmers; beg or borrow enough so that you can keep hot on the buffet the omelette, the casserole, the veal rolls, and the beans. And with that, you do have quite a slice of work behind you.

On the great day, start with the omelette makings; cook the onions and potatoes and mince the fish or meat. Next, bake the dessert and cook the salad vegetables. Two hours before dinner, arrange the platters of fish, meat, and cheese. You will want them all at room temperature, for they lose much of their flavor when they're too cold. Cover the platters with foil and set them out on the *smörgåsbord.* Arrange the salad, but keep it in the refrigerator.

If you have no stand-in for yourself in the kitchen, that's where you must be on and off for the last forty-five minutes before dinner, to handle the following: To reheat the casserole and veal rolls, covered, in a 350° oven for three-quarters of an hour; to reheat the beans on an asbestos mat on top of the stove, over low heat; to put baskets of breads, a chilled crock of *smör* (butter, remember?), and the salad on the buffet; and to make the omelettes, which should be done at the last possible moment and served on a hot platter or on a large, flat chafing dish over hot water.

This show of food certainly constitutes the major decoration and your buffet table will have little extra space. Still, it would be gay to have a long, narrow wooden tray in the background massed with either blue and yellow flowers for Sweden, or red and white for Denmark, or red, white, and blue for Norway. Your last job is to persuade your guests that this feast is best eaten in the proper installments of fish first, on small plates, followed by meats and hot dishes on dinner plates. We don't know when you found time to bake the Finger Cookies, but they keep well for ages, tightly covered, and with the World's Best Apple Dessert, aren't they worth it?

Platter of Smoked and Pickled Fish

Select a variety of fish, some pickled, some smoked: smoked salmon and eel, herring (called *böckling*), Swedish anchovies (less salty than the Portuguese and packed in brine rather than oil), mussels, sardines, and pickled herring. The canned products are acceptable if no others are to be found.

Farmer's Omelette

Over low heat, sauté 1/4 cup minced onion in 1 tablespoon butter until soft and yellow. Meanwhile, dice 4 peeled boiled potatoes, and dice enough left-over fish or meat to make 1 1/2 cups. Combine sautéed onion,

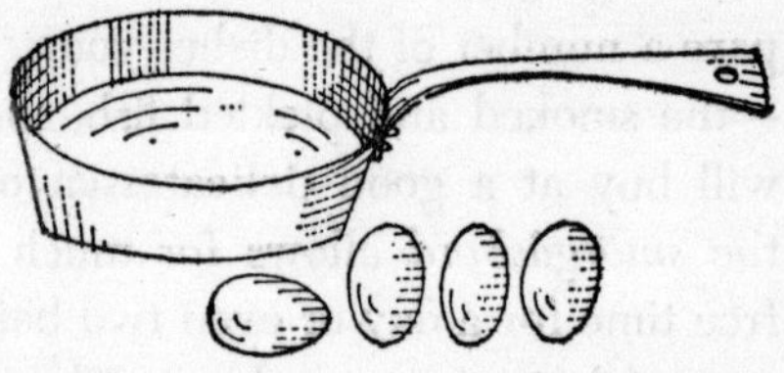

potatoes, and meat or fish, and heat all together. Just before servingtime, beat 8 eggs with 1 teaspoon salt and a little pepper until just blended. In a heated 12-inch skillet or omelette pan, over low heat, melt 2 tablespoons butter; when it stops sizzling, pour in eggs. Cook over low heat, pulling in edges with a fork to let uncooked egg run to bottom. Do not brown bottom of omelette. When set but still moist on top, spread filling mixture over eggs. Roll omelette with aid of a fork or a rubber spatula, and turn out on a serving platter.

8 eggs
1 teaspoon salt
Pepper
3 tablespoons butter, in all
¼ cup minced onion
4 boiled potatoes
1½ cups diced left-over fish or meat

Country-Store Casserole

Slice thinly 3 veal kidneys and sauté over high heat in 2 tablespoons butter for 2 or 3 minutes; remove from pan and reserve. Slice 1 pound fillet of pork ⅓ inch thick, and sauté in same pan in another 2 tablespoons butter; remove from pan and reserve. Peel and slice thin 4 pounds potatoes and 4 large yellow onions. In a large casserole arrange alternating layers of potatoes, meat, and onions, starting and ending with potatoes; sprinkle each layer with salt and pepper. Pour 2 bottles Lager beer over all, cover, and bake in a 350° oven for 1 hour. Uncover and bake ½ hour longer.

3 veal kidneys
1 pound fillet of pork
4 tablespoons butter
4 pounds potatoes
4 large yellow onions
1 tablespoon salt
¼ teaspoon pepper
2 bottles Lager beer

Dröttningholm or Prune-Filled Veal Rolls

Remove crusts from 2 slices white bread and soak in ¾ cup water. In a large bowl, mix together 1½ pounds ground veal, ½ pound ground pork, 3 lightly beaten eggs, the bread soaked in water, 1 tablespoon salt, and ¼ teaspoon each pepper and nutmeg. Work thoroughly with hands. Divide into 16 portions, and form each portion into a ball around 1 large cooked and pitted prune. In a large heavy pan, over high heat, melt 4 tablespoons butter. Add meat rolls and sear on all sides. Reduce heat, and add 1 cup chicken stock (or 1 chicken bouillon cube dissolved in 1 cup boiling water). Cover and simmer over low heat for 30 minutes or until done.

1½ pounds ground veal
½ pound ground pork
2 slices white bread
¾ cup water
3 eggs
1 tablespoon salt
¼ teaspoon pepper
¼ teaspoon nutmeg
16 large prunes
4 tablespoons butter
1 cup chicken stock
or 1 chicken bouillon cube dissolved in 1 cup water

Assorted Cold Meats and Sausages

Arrange a platter of assorted cold meats and sausages, allowing about 2 pounds in all: thinly sliced ham, roast beef, cold roast pork, smoked pork loin, *medwurst, cervelat,* cold chicken or turkey—as many varieties as your fancy dictates.

Brown Beans

Wash 2 cups brown beans * and soak overnight in water to cover, about 2 quarts. Bring to a boil in same water. Turn heat low, cover, and simmer 1 hour. Then add 2 teaspoons salt, ⅓ cup light molasses, and ⅓ cup vinegar, and continue to cook for ½ hour, or until tender. (Add more salt, molasses, and vinegar if a more pro-

* Brown beans are a Scandinavian species found in certain specialty stores only. Substitute red kidney beans if necessary.

nounced flavor is desired.) Mixture should be as thick as oatmeal; if not, uncover and cook rapidly, stirring constantly, until of desired consistency.

2 cups brown beans
2 quarts water
2 teaspoons salt
1/3 cup light molasses
1/3 cup vinegar

Castle Salad for a Party

Cook, according to directions on package, 1 package each frozen green beans, peas, and lima beans. Drain and chill. Drain 1 No. 2 can diced beets. Toss together lightly the cooked vegetables, the beets, and 1 minced medium onion, 1/4 cup minced black olives, and 2 tablespoons capers. Blend together 2 teaspoons prepared mustard, 1/4 cup salad oil, and 3/4 cup dry white wine. Toss vegetables with dressing and mound on a serving platter. Garnish around base with 2 sliced hard-cooked eggs.

1 package frozen green beans
1 package frozen peas
1 package frozen lima beans
1 No. 2 can diced beets
1 medium onion
1/4 cup minced black olives
2 tablespoons capers
2 teaspoons prepared mustard
1/4 cup salad oil
3/4 cup dry white wine
2 hard-cooked eggs

Scandinavian Rye Bread and Crisp Breads

Limpa is the name of the most readily available Scandinavian rye bread in this country. It is delicately sweet. But any assortment of good rye breads and light or dark pumpernickels will go well with *smörgåsbord.* In addition, there should be one or more varieties of crisp breads, from the paper-thin *flatbröd* to the fairly thick *knäckebröd.* Failing these, use Rye Krisp or similar products.

Swedish and Danish Cheeses

Choose one or more among the following:
Gräddost—firm-textured cheese made of cream
Kryddost—firm cheese with a liberal sprinkling of caraway seeds
Crème Chantilly—soft, delicately flavored, very rich cheese, made of cream
Gjetost—goat cheese with unusual, sweet flavor; must be shaved thin to serve
Primula—soft, delicately flavored, medium-rich cheese

World's Best Apple Dessert

Preheat oven to 350°. Peel, core, and slice 12 firm cooking apples. In a large pot, over low heat, dissolve 1/3 cup sugar in 2/3 cup water. Add apples and cook until just tender. Drain off juice and place apples in one large or two medium-size ovenproof dishes. Cream together 1 1/3 cups sugar and 1/2 pound less 2 tablespoons softened butter until light and fluffy. Beat into creamed mixture 4 egg yolks, 1/2 teaspoon almond extract, and juice of 1 lemon, and fold in 4 ounces blanched ground almonds. Beat 6 egg whites until stiff but not dry. Fold carefully into batter, and spoon over apples. Bake 40 minutes, or until golden. Serve at room temperature.

12 firm cooking apples
1/3 cup sugar
2/3 cup water
1/2 pound less 2 tablespoons butter
1 1/3 cups sugar

4 egg yolks
½ teaspoon almond extract
Juice of 1 lemon
4 ounces blanched ground almonds
6 egg whites

Finger Cookies

Preheat oven to 300°. To make about 3 dozen finger cookies, blend together with hands to make a smooth dough ½ pound less 2 tablespoons butter, 7 tablespoons sugar, 2 cups plus 2 tablespoons flour, ½ teaspoon baking powder, ½ beaten egg, and ½ teaspoon almond extract. With palms of hands shape pieces of dough into rolls ½ inch in diameter. Cut diagonally into slices 1 inch long. Flatten each slice slightly with one finger, brush with remaining ½ beaten egg, and sprinkle with 24 chopped almonds. Bake on ungreased cooky sheet for 25 to 30 minutes, until light gold.

½ pound less 2 tablespoons butter
7 tablespoons sugar
2 cups plus 2 tablespoons flour
½ teaspoon baking powder
½ teaspoon almond extract
1 egg
24 almonds

FORMAL DINNERS

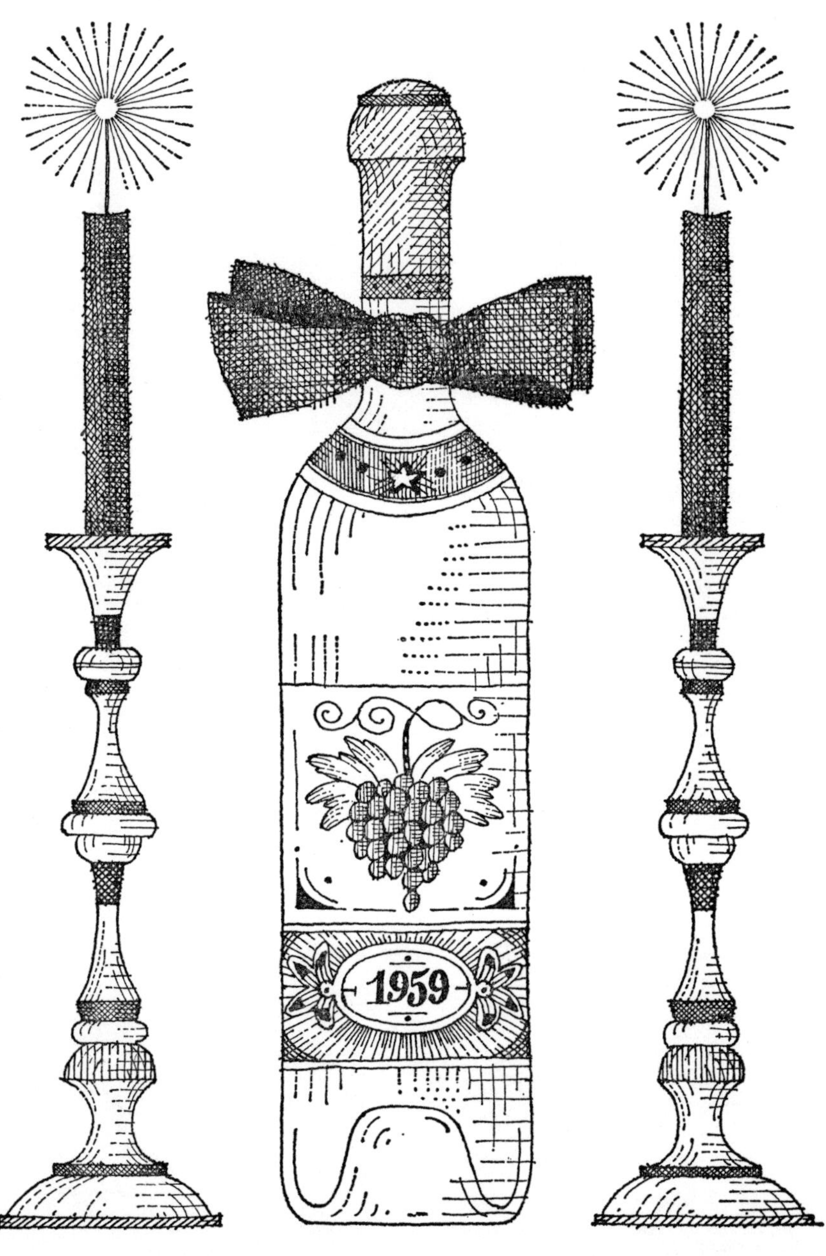

62

Summer Formal Dinner for Four

PALACE COURT SALAD
LOUIS DRESSING
MUSHROOMS NEAPOLITAN
FUSILLI
FLAN À LA CÉVENOLE
DEMITASSE

WINES

Inexpensive: Cresta Blanca Chianti
Medium-priced: Bertani Chianti
Expensive: Ruffino Chianti, Reserva Ducale

The palace of Palace Court-Salad fame has nothing in common with Buckingham or Versailles. A famous San Francisco landmark, the Palace Hotel caters to commoners and kings alike. The court the recipe refers to is an enormous, high-ceilinged dining room decorated in the opulent style of the late 1800's. In a city that makes a fetish of fine food, the Palace maintains its reputation for excellent cuisine. First-time visitors are invariably advised to order the *spécialité de la maison,* the renowned salad made with chicken, or lobster, or tiny shrimp, as well as with crabmeat; rarely is anyone disappointed, whether eating it for the first time or the hundred and first.

Since the salad is a substantial first course, it makes sense to follow it by a fairly light main course, which, in turn, permits a rich dessert. In the morning, get the *Flan* in the oven first. (Substitute 1½ cups of canned, unsweetened puréed chestnuts for the whole ones if you don't have a blender; it's hard work to purée them finely enough. If you use the canned purée, add the liquid slowly to get a smooth mixture.) While the chestnut custard is baking, boil the artichokes, make the salad dressing, and prepare the Mushrooms Neapolitan but don't add the parsley and vermouth to these yet. Remove any bones that may be lurking in the crabmeat, and that's all for the moment. Visit the kitchen at some point in the afternoon, when the *Flan* is cold, to whip the cream and spread it on top.

We list this as a formal dinner, though formal service isn't necessary, particularly for so few people. After you've had a cocktail, go out to the kitchen if you're on your own, to boil the *Fusilli*. While the noodles are boiling, make coffee, arrange the individual salads, and reheat the Mushrooms Neapolitan over low heat and add the parsley and wine. (Or, reheat them in a chafing dish set on a small table next to you in the dining room or outdoors.) Drain the noodles, leave them in the pot (they'll keep warm until you come for them in a few minutes), and bring the salads to the table.

To use this menu for six people, augment the recipes accordingly, but leave the *Flan* recipe as it is; it makes half a dozen servings. For twelve people, double the *Flan* recipe, and triple everything else; in this case plan buffet service with one person to help, or two waitresses for seated service. Make a note too, to serve Palace Court Salad for lunch some day. When San Francisco ladies are on a binge, they order a rich chocolate dessert to follow it, for which the hotel is famous. We don't have that recipe, but serve Viennese Chocolate Roll (see Index), instead.

Palace Court Salad

4 large artichokes
2 large tomatoes
1 cup shredded Simpson lettuce
1 pound fresh crabmeat
1½ cups Louis Dressing
1 hard-cooked egg

Cut off 1 inch from tops of 4 large artichokes and remove outside leaves. Boil artichokes in plenty of salted water until a leaf can be plucked with ease. Place upside down on a rack to cool. Then spread outer leaves apart a little, remove conelike center leaves, and scoop out choke without damaging bottom. Place each artichoke on a ½-inch-thick center slice of beefsteak tomato, or other large tomato, first covered with ¼ cup finely shredded Simpson lettuce. Fill center of artichokes to top with approximately ½ cup fresh crabmeat. Over this pour 3 tablespoons Louis Dressing, below, then sprinkle with sieved hard-cooked egg. Serve additional dressing in a sauceboat.

Louis Dressing

To make 1½ cups dressing, mix 1 cup Mayonnaise with ½ cup chili sauce and 2 teaspoons each finely minced chives and pimientos.

1 cup Mayonnaise *(see Index)*
½ cup chili sauce
2 teaspoons minced chives
2 teaspoons minced pimientos

Mushrooms Neapolitan

Dip 3 ripe tomatoes in boiling water, then quickly in cold water, peel and seed them, then chop finely. Over low heat, cook tomatoes in 2 tablespoons butter until they form a purée. In a large skillet, over medium heat, sauté 1 pound sliced fresh mushrooms in 3 tablespoons butter until lightly browned. Season with salt, freshly ground pepper, and $\frac{1}{2}$ teaspoon Italian seasoning. Add 1 pound ground raw veal, and cook, uncovered, for 12 minutes. Add the tomato purée, 1 tablespoon chopped parsley, and 1 tablespoon Italian dry vermouth. Serve at once, with a sprinkling of grated Parmesan on each serving.

3 tomatoes
5 tablespoons butter, in all
1 pound mushrooms
Salt, pepper
$\frac{1}{2}$ teaspoon Italian seasoning
1 pound ground veal
1 tablespoon chopped parsley
1 tablespoon Italian dry vermouth
$\frac{1}{2}$ cup grated Parmesan

Fusilli

In a large pan, over high heat, bring 3 quarts salted water to a rapid boil, and add 1 tablespoon olive oil and 1 pound *fusilli* (corkscrew noodles). Continue boiling rapidly for 18 minutes, drain, add 3 tablespoons sweet butter, and serve with Mushrooms Neapolitan.

3 quarts water
Salt
1 tablespoon olive oil
1 pound fusilli
3 tablespoons sweet butter

Flan à la Cévenole

Preheat oven to 275°. Scald 2 cups milk with $\frac{1}{4}$ cup Vanilla Sugar and $\frac{3}{4}$ cup plain granulated sugar. Beat together 2 eggs and 4 yolks, and stir hot milk and sugar into eggs. In an electric blender or a food mill, purée 25 cooked or unsweetened canned chestnuts with just enough milk to obtain a smooth purée. Stir into custard mixture. Pour into a Pyrex baking dish and place in a pan containing hot water to within 1 inch of top of baking dish. Bake for 45 minutes, cool, then chill. Whip $\frac{1}{2}$ cup heavy cream with 1 tablespoon kirsch and 2 tablespoons Vanilla Sugar. Spread on top of custard and serve very cold.

2 cups milk
$\frac{3}{8}$ cup Vanilla Sugar, in all (see Index)
$\frac{3}{4}$ cup granulated sugar
2 eggs
4 egg yolks
25 cooked or unsweetened canned chestnuts
$\frac{1}{2}$ cup heavy cream
1 tablespoon kirsch

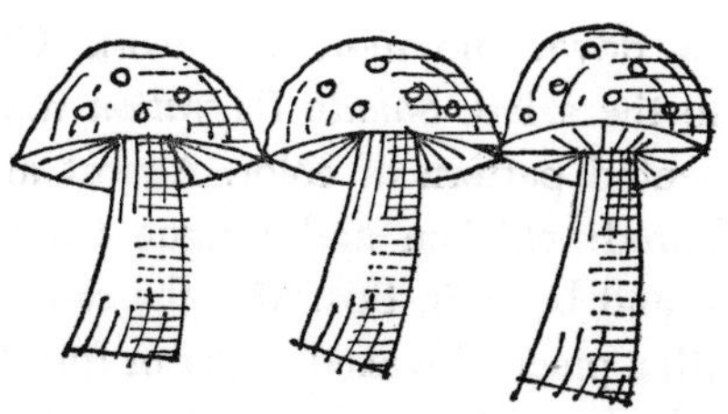

63

Summer Formal Dinner for Six—I

ICED CREAM OF CARROTS
SALADE BAGRATION
PÊCHES MELBA
LANGUES DE CHAT *
DEMITASSE

WINES

Inexpensive: Louis Martini Dry Semillon
Medium-priced: Pouilly-Fuissé
Expensive: Montrachet Les Ruchottes

A heat-wave special with double-barreled temperature control; cool, light, refreshing food for the guests, a minimum of slaving over a hot stove for the hostess, and a menu that's equally suitable for noon or night.

It's not that we want to rout you out of bed at an unearthly hour, but our best advice is to get into the kitchen in the dawn's early light, before the sun is a ball of fire. You should be finished in an hour or so, with dinner practically ready. Boil the macaroni and eggs for the salad, cook the vegetables in broth for the soup and purée them, and poach the peaches. Leave *Langues de Chat* (see Index) on the menu only if you have them already on hand. If not, buy something equally light and fragile at the pastry shop; no lighting of ovens today. Keep the electric fan whirring instead.

Now, you can slow down—no more hot work. Chill the peaches and the soup, and turn to the salad. *Salade Bagration* makes a handsome picture, the top a segmented pattern of color. Almost all the ingredients are bought already prepared: chicken and tongue from a delicatessen, artichoke hearts, truffles, and beets in tins. Mix the salad, put it in its serving bowl, and cover it with a piece of waxed paper or foil. Mince the ingredients for the top, wrap each separately in foil, and set everything in the refrigerator. Finish the decorating an hour or less before you eat, so the top of

* see Index

the salad won't have a chance to dry out. Also in the morning, spoon the ice cream into its serving dish, put it in the freezer, and whip the cream. (For a professional finish, put the whipped cream into a pastry tube and keep it in the refrigerator until you're ready to garnish the peaches.)

At this point, head in the coolest possible direction and stay put, or at least out of the kitchen, for the rest of the day. Dinner involves little more than helping yourself from the icebox: Finish the salad, and add cream to the soup and ladle it into individual cups. Dessert will only take three or four minutes to assemble, and since you can buy the Melba Sauce that Escoffier invented, it's no trick to duplicate this famous recipe. Dame Nellie must have captivated *le Grand Maître;* he paid her inspired homage in the language he knew best.

Iced Cream of Carrots

Slice 8 medium carrots, and mince 2 celery stalks and ½ onion. Cook all together with ½ bay leaf and 2 cloves in 3 cups chicken broth until tender. Remove cloves and bay leaf. Place soup, a little at a time, in an electric blender (or force through a food mill) until a very smooth purée is obtained. To last batch done in blender, add 1½ tablespoons Worcestershire and 5 sprigs parsley. If food mill is used, chop parsley finely and add to purée with Worcestershire. Taste; soup should be highly seasoned. Cool, then chill. Before serving, stir in ½ cup heavy cream. Serve in chilled individual cups.

8 medium carrots
2 celery stalks
½ onion
½ bay leaf
2 cloves
3 cups chicken broth
1½ tablespoons Worcestershire
5 sprigs parsley
½ cup heavy cream

Salade Bagration

Combine 3 cups cooked elbow macaroni, 2 cups minced cooked chicken,

½ cup chopped raw celery, ½ cup small artichoke hearts, halved, and 1½ cups Mayonnaise; place in a glass serving bowl. Mince, all separately, the yolks and whites of 3 hard-cooked eggs, ¾ cup julienne beets, 1 large truffle, enough boiled tongue to make ½ cup, and enough parsley to make ½ cup. With chopped ingredients make design like a pie cut in five sections on top of salad, filling in one triangle each of beets, egg white, parsley, tongue, and egg yolk, in that order. In center place a little mound of chopped truffle. Chill, and toss at table just before serving.

3 cups cooked elbow macaroni
2 cups minced cooked chicken
½ cup chopped raw celery
½ cup small artichoke hearts
1½ cups Mayonnaise (see Index)
3 hard-cooked eggs
¾ cup julienne beets
1 large truffle
½ cup minced boiled tongue
½ cup minced parsley

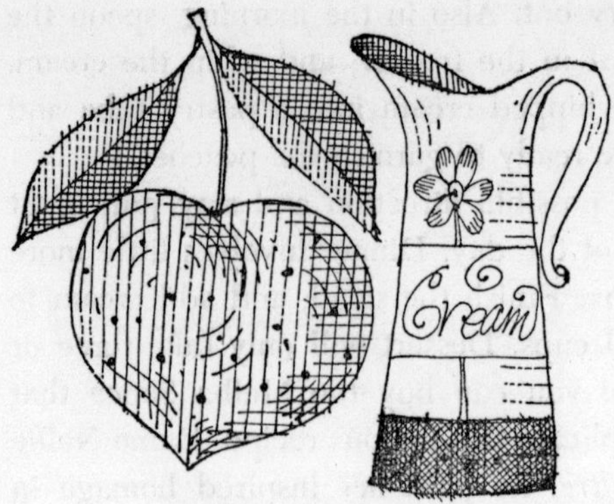

Pêches Melba

Make a syrup by boiling together 1 cup Vanilla Sugar and 1 cup water. Peel 6 ripe freestone peaches, leave them whole, and poach them until tender in the syrup. Cool and chill. Reserve syrup for other uses; it keeps well in refrigerator. Spread 1½ pints vanilla ice cream evenly on bottom of a fairly deep silver or glass bowl. Over this, pour about three quarters of a bottle of Escoffier Sauce Melba. On this, arrange chilled poached peaches in a circle; give top of each peach a blush by brushing it with some of remaining sauce. Whip 1 cup chilled heavy cream with ¼ cup Vanilla Sugar. Garnish bowl with whipped cream between peaches and in center. Serve very cold, with *Langues de Chat* (see Index).

1¼ cups Vanilla Sugar, in all (*see Index*)
1 cup water
6 freestone peaches
1½ pints vanilla ice cream
1 bottle Escoffier Sauce Melba
1 cup heavy cream

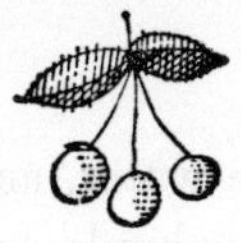

64

Summer Formal Dinner for Six—II

AVOCADOS WITH GREEN TURTLE SOUP
TROUT BRAISED IN PORT
POTATOES À L'ANGLAISE WITH CHERVIL
BOWL OF LIMESTONE LETTUCE WITH FRENCH DRESSING
CHERRY STRUDEL

WINES

Inexpensive: Beaulieu Vineyards Château Beaulieu
Medium-priced: Barsac, Cru Bouscla
Expensive: Château Filhot

The best skiers, so the story usually goes, were practically born on skis, and the most proficient equestrians learned to ride before they could walk. Could it be that all the great-aunts who make tissue-thin strudel leaves played with pastry dough instead of dolls when they were young? We must remember to ask. For us, who played with dolls, the ready-made frozen strudel dough we buy is a great comfort. Strudel is a delicacy we'd hate to do without, but our attempts to stretch the dough still result in something that looks like a large sheet of Swiss cheese.

With the prepared dough, it's reassuringly easy to make Strudel, and that's what you'll do first for this dinner. (There are many other fillings you can use, almost as many as for pie. A favorite variation of ours is Coconut Strudel: Beat together 3 egg yolks and ⅓ cup of sugar until thick and light. Add 1 cup of flaked coconut, the juice and grated rind of ½ a lemon, and fold in 3 stiffly beaten egg whites. Spoon the mixture on the strudel leaves and roll up as for the Cherry Strudel, but bake about 20 minutes in a 400° oven.) While the Strudel is in the oven, set the soup in the icebox to jell, wash and drain the lettuce, put it in the icebox too, and make the French Dressing (see Index).

Toward the latter part of the afternoon, prepare the fish for baking, peel the potatoes and put them in ice water, and split and stone the avocados. Since this is a formal dinner, you should have someone to serve and finish the cooking, though the bulk of the work is done.

Instruct the waitress to allow a half hour to bake the fish and finish the sauce. After it goes into the oven, she should cook the potatoes, and cube the jellied soup and heap it in the avocados. She can arrange the salad bowl after she has served the first course. Strudel is even better eaten warm than cold. Tell the waitress to reheat it in a 350° oven for 10 minutes, after she takes the fish out, and to dust it very generously with confectioners' sugar just before she passes it at the table.

Avocados with Green Turtle Soup

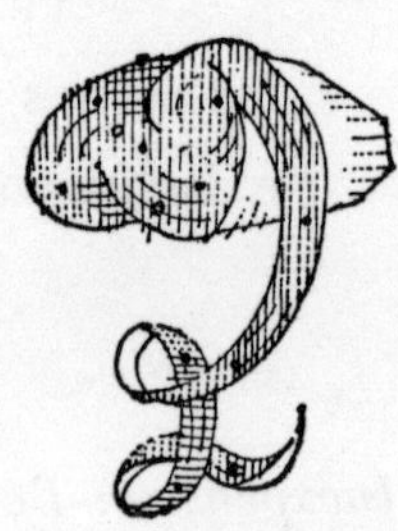

To contents of 2 cans green turtle soup add ½ cup Madeira, and chill and jell in a square or loaf pan. Halve and seed 3 ripe avocados, and season very lightly with lemon juice, freshly ground white pepper, and salt. Unmold jellied turtle soup, cut into cubes, and with it fill hollows of avocados. Garnish with rosette of sour cream forced through fluted nozzle of a pastry tube.

2 cans green turtle soup
½ cup Madeira
3 avocados
Lemon juice
White pepper, salt
6 tablespoons sour cream

Trout Braised in Port

Have fishmonger split a 4- to 5-pound salmon trout and remove backbone. In a skillet, over medium heat, sauté together for 2 minutes in 3 tablespoons butter ½ cup fine julienne strips of carrots, ½ cup chopped mushroom stems, 1 tablespoon minced truffle, and ¼ cup finely minced celery. Add ½ cup chicken stock, and simmer over low heat for 5 minutes. Add 3 tablespoons heavy cream, and season with freshly ground pepper and salt. Remove from fire and thicken with 1 egg yolk. Cool a little, then spread mixture over one trout fillet, then place second fillet on top to reconstitute fish, and wrap securely in cheesecloth.

Make ½ cup *Court-Bouillon* for Fish and to it add 1 cup white port. Place trout on a rack in a long narrow fish kettle, or in a small roasting pan, and cover with the *Court-Bouillon* and port mixture. Add 12 large mushroom caps and braise, covered, for 20 minutes in a preheated 350° oven. Remove fish from pan, unwrap carefully, and place on a heated serving platter.

Strain pan juices, add ¼ cup heavy cream and ¼ cup white port, and measure. For each cup of liquid add 1 tablespoon butter kneaded with 1 tablespoon arrowroot or cornstarch. Season with a pinch of cayenne pepper, then pour over fish. Garnish with the mushroom caps and Potatoes *à l'Anglaise,* below, and serve at once.

1 salmon trout, 4 to 5 pounds
3 tablespoons butter
½ cup julienne strips carrots
½ cup chopped mushroom stems
1 tablespoon minced truffle
¼ cup minced celery
½ cup chicken stock
3 tablespoons heavy cream
Salt, pepper
1 egg yolk

½ cup Court-Bouillon for Fish (see Index)
1¼ cups white port (in all)
12 large mushroom caps
¼ cup heavy cream
Butter
Arrowroot or cornstarch
Cayenne

Potatoes à l'Anglaise with Chervil

Peel evenly 12 small Idaho potatoes, then pare them down to even shapes. Boil in hot salted water until tender, over high heat. Pour off water and replace potatoes over heat to allow moisture to evaporate. Add 2 tablespoons melted butter, roll potatoes in it, and sprinkle with 1 tablespoon chopped fresh chervil. Serve at once.

12 small Idaho potatoes
2 tablespoons butter
1 tablespoon chopped chervil

Easy Cherry Strudel

Preheat oven to 375°. Drain well 2 cans No. 2 pitted black cherries. Defrost 1 package frozen strudel leaves for 3 hours at room temperature. Have ready 1 cup melted butter, ½ cup toasted bread crumbs, ½ cup Vanilla Sugar, and 1 tablespoon grated lemon rind. Spread slightly damp kitchen towel on table, and have all ingredients close at hand. Open strudel package, quickly divide the 4 leaves of dough, place on towel, and brush each leaf with melted butter (use about ½ cup in all). Sprinkle with crumbs, and stack leaves on top of one another. Cover one end of last layer with cherries, sprinkle with Vanilla Sugar and lemon rind, then gently lift the towel from that end and let the strudel roll itself up. Place on a buttered baking sheet and brush with half of remaining melted butter. Bake 35 minutes, or until golden brown, basting occasionally with remaining butter. Serve warm or cool, dusted with confectioners' sugar, and cut in thick slices.

2 No. 2 cans black cherries
1 package frozen strudel leaves
1 cup melted butter
½ cup toasted bread crumbs
½ cup Vanilla Sugar (see Index)
1 tablespoon grated lemon rind
Confectioners' sugar

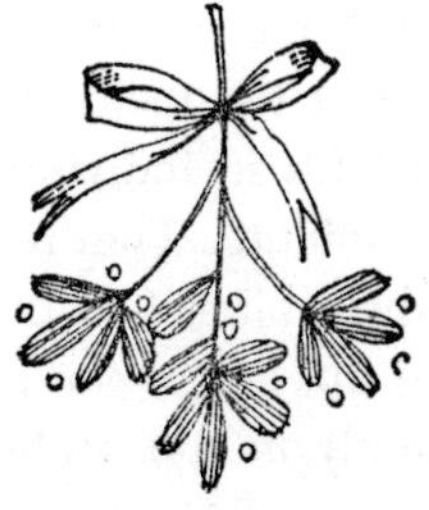

65

Summer Formal Dinner for Eight

ICED HONEYDEW

POULET NORMAND

WATER CRESS AND LETTUCE BOWL WITH FRENCH DRESSING

PETITS POTS DE CRÈME

DEMITASSE

WINES

Inexpensive: Wente Sauvignon Blanc, Livermore Valley

Medium-priced: Vouvray

Expensive: Graves, Château Bouscaut (white)

Escoffier, alone, lists well over a hundred and fifty ways to cook chicken. Cook book authors have devoted whole volumes to that one subject. It's indeed a puzzlement to decide whether to broil or roast, poach or braise, etcetera, etcetera, etcetera. When it comes to chicken recipes, there is an *embarras de richesses.*

But we rate Chicken Normand a particular treasure. Delicately flavored and divinely rich, it's a beautiful company dish. Nor is it difficult to make, though there is one hitch; it should be prepared just before dinner, so skip this menu if you don't have help. Unless, of course, you feel free to disappear for three quarters of an hour, which is up to you to figure out.

The rest of the dinner is as easy as pie, or should we say easy as *Pots de Crème,* since these little custards are much simpler to make than a pie. While they're in the oven, wash and drain the salad greens and make the French dressing. That leaves just the melon to be cut into wedges or, for an exotic touch, serve melon balls in individual fruit cups, sprinkled with a few rose petals at the last minute. They're delicately sweet, and quite edible, if you find the idea disturbing. Cut the flowers early in the morning, just as the dew is drying up, and while the essence of the blossom is still strongest. Wash them gently in cool water, shake off excess moisture, and keep the flowers in water in the refrigerator until you're ready to use them.

Stick to your theme by using the palest pink or green cloth and, for the centerpiece, a low bowl massed with the same roses. Or, switch the theme to Nasturtium Coupe: Substitute cantaloupe or Persian melon balls for the honeydew, with a single nasturtium centering each portion; the flavor of nasturtiums is reminiscent of honey. For the table, use a pale yellow or orange cloth and a bowl of nasturtiums.

We think Ferdinand the Bull knew what he was about when he sat under his tree all day munching flowers, but we do recommend following his example with a certain restraint and with guests who take pleasure in trying the unusual.

Poulet Normand

Preheat broiler to highest heat. Split four 2-pound broilers, rub them inside and out with a damp towel, and season with freshly ground pepper and salt. Place them in broiler pan, skin side down, and place 1 tablespoon butter in each cavity. Broil 4 to 6 inches from heat for 12 to 15 minutes, or until chicken is well-browned. Turn, brush skin with melted butter, broil again for 10 minutes, then turn off broiler and put in the heated oven 10 minutes longer to bake. Remove chicken to hot platter.

Meanwhile, peel, quarter, core, and slice 6 crisp apples, and sauté in 3 tablespoons butter until transparent. Season with pepper and salt, and transfer to one side of heated platter. Mix 2 cups sour cream with 2 tablespoons flour. After placing chicken on platter, place broiler pan over high heat, pour in 1/4 cup cold water, and deglaze pan juices. Warm 1/2 cup Calvados or apple brandy, ignite, and when flames subside, pour into pan juices, add sour cream, and stir until well blended. Pour over chicken and sprinkle with slivered blanched almonds. Serve with Steamed Rice (see Index), if desired.

4 2-pound broilers
Salt, pepper
1/2 pound butter in all, more or less
6 apples
2 cups sour cream
2 tablespoons flour
1/4 cup cold water
1/2 cup Calvados
or apple brandy
Slivered blanched almonds

Petits Pots de Crème

Preheat oven to 325°. Scald 2 1/2 cups cream with 1/2 cup Vanilla Sugar and cool. Beat together 3 eggs and 5 yolks. Then pour cooled cream into eggs, stirring rapidly. Pour into *pots de crème* or custard cups and set in a pan of hot water. Cover and bake for about 15 minutes, or until a knife inserted in center comes out clean. Serve chilled.

2 1/2 cups cream
1/2 cup Vanilla Sugar (see Index)
3 eggs
5 yolks

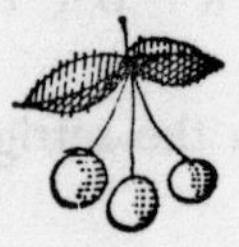

66

Summer Buffet for Twelve

HALIBUT À LA RUSSE
POULET DIABLE
SPINACH NOODLES
ARTICHOKE BOTTOMS CROWNED WITH SPINACH
CHINESE CABBAGE BOWL WITH WATER CRESS
MERINGUE À L'ANCIENNE
DEMITASSE

WINES

Inexpensive: Widmer's Riesling
Medium-priced: Dienhard Bernkasteler, Hans Christof, en carafe

An outstanding professional cook once remarked that she plans a meal first with her eyes and then with her palate, picturing each finished platter before she decides on it. You can find no more appropriate occasion than a rather grand summer buffet to apply the theory. As you read the recipes that follow, conjure up an image of the effect they will make spread out on a buffet table, complete with your best china and silver. We hope both you and your guests will be tempted beyond endurance.

The crowning glory of this buffet is an elaborate halibut platter. It takes time and patience to make—and is handsome enough to warrant the effort. Get to work the day before, or get up *early* in the morning to poach the fish, make the aspic and the *Sauce Russe,* cook the vegetables, and boil the eggs. Finish the platter anywhere from two to four hours before you need it, and store it in the icebox. Arrange the salad and keep that in the icebox too. Then prepare the artichoke bottoms and put them in the saucepan, ready to reheat. And make the *Sabayon* Sauce for the meringue now, too.

Since meringues keep for days in a tightly covered tin, and indefinitely in a freezer, make the meringue shell well ahead. (If you can't get beautiful raspberries for this dessert, use strawberries instead). Allow about three quarters of an hour for the chickens. When you turn them, put the water on for the noodles and drop them in when it boils.

Because of these last minute jobs, it's wiser to handle this party with help. Last minute help will do, though this depends on how well you know your guests and whether you want to treat this as an informal evening or a formal party.

And now for a bonus of practical instruction—the old teaser about what to do with left-over egg yolks or egg whites. Before the days of freezers, there was no help for it but to get back to the kitchen as soon as possible and cook something. In the case of this menu, for instance, after beating up 12 whites for the meringue, and using 1 yolk in the *Sauce Russe* and 4 in the *Sabayon,* you'll still have 7 yolks to deal with. The next day, you could make Mayonnaise or a *Crème Brûlée* (see Index); or, you could be in no mood for cooking after the previous day's labor, in which case freeze them as follows: Beat them lightly with ⅓ teaspoon salt *or* 1½ teaspoons sugar per 6 or 7 yolks, pour into a container, and freeze. (Don't forget, when you defrost them, to adjust the salt or sugar in the recipe in which you use them; you'll never remember which is which, so label them.)

The yolk-white ratio can as easily tip the other way, leaving you with more whites than you know what to do with. To freeze whites: Drop each into a separate small muffin tin or plastic cup as you separate the eggs, and place in the freezer. When they are solid, run hot water over the bottom of the tins or cups for 2 or 3 seconds. Pop these into a plastic bag, and replace in the freezer. To use frozen egg whites, put them in a large bowl in a warm place. They should defrost in about a half hour, but to hasten the process, cut them up with a knife after they have been in the bowl for five minutes.

Just to remind you of what you already know, you can't win at this yolk-white game. If you made the meringue for this party ahead, as suggested, you were saddled with a *dozen* yolks that day. The freezer is the best answer we know to that.

Halibut à la Russe

Soften 1 envelope unflavored gelatin in 2 tablespoons water, and dissolve in 1¼ cups of hot rich beef consommé. Pour liquid into large shallow platter or baking tin, and place in freezing compartment of refrigerator for 30 minutes (or in the refrigerator proper for 3 hours) to set thoroughly.

Prepare a *Court-Bouillon* for Fish (see Index). In it poach together 12 unshelled jumbo shrimp and a 7-pound piece of halibut (the tail end or a chunkier piece cut from the middle of the fish) for 12 to 20 minutes; time depends on thickness of fish. Cool fish in *Court-Bouillon,* then skin and remove oily film which lies under skin. Slice skinned fish in half horizontally, remove bones and chill halves thoroughly in refrigerator.

Prepare a *Sauce Russe* in an electric blender: Blend together for 2 seconds 1 whole egg, 1 egg yolk, 1 teaspoon prepared mustard, ¼ teaspoon

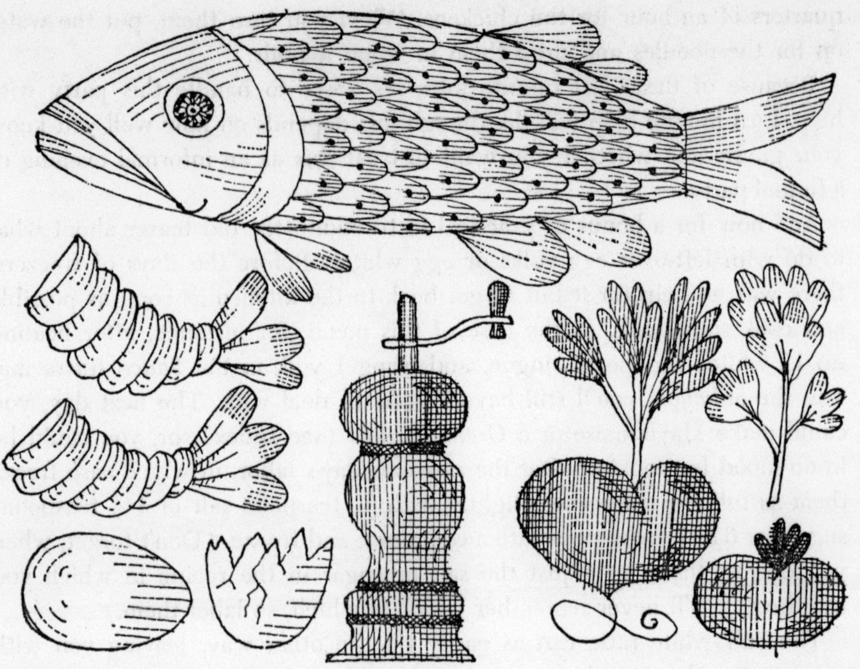

white pepper, and ½ cup unflavored white wine vinegar. Then immediately begin pouring in gradually 1½ cups salad oil in a steady stream, and blend until it is completely absorbed. Turn off blender at once. Add 4 tablespoons red caviar and ¼ teaspoon cayenne pepper. Turn on blender and blend sauce for no more than 20 seconds. (Makes 2 cups.)

Prepare a *Salade Russe:* Combine in a mixing bowl 3 sliced boiled potatoes and 3 cups cooked, cooled, and well-drained French-cut string beans. Add 1 cup *Sauce Russe,* toss lightly to blend, and chill thoroughly in refrigerator.

To complete the Halibut *à la Russe* have ready: 3 hard-cooked eggs, the whites and yolks chopped separately; ⅓ cup chopped cooked beets; ⅓ cup finely chopped parsley; 4 ounces black caviar; and 2 truffles, peeled and sliced, and the peelings finely chopped. Now combine ¼ cup *Sauce Russe* with chopped truffle peelings and spread on inner sides of two halves of halibut. Reassemble halves and place fish at one end of a long silver or glass serving platter. Cover fish evenly and neatly with remaining ¾ cup *Sauce Russe.*

Decorate with the slices of truffle and a few pieces of the jellied consommé cut into small shapes with a cooky cutter. Place cooked shrimp, still in their shells, in a semicircle around the base of the fish to form a scalloped edge. At the other end of the platter, heap the *Salade Russe* and mold it into a dome. (If you are using a tail of halibut, mold the salad to complete the shape of a fish.) On the salad mark out with the tip of a knife four equal-size isosceles triangles, the long points meeting at the top of the dome. Cover each of the triangles with one of the following, in the order named; chopped beets, chopped egg white, chopped parsley, and chopped egg yolk. Outline triangles with black caviar. Around base of the salad dome arrange a semicircle of more jellied consommé shapes. Chill the completed Halibut *à la Russe* in the refrigerator until servingtime. If weather is very hot, place serving platter on the buffet over another platter filled with cracked ice.

Court-Bouillon for Fish (see Index)
7-pound piece of halibut
12 jumbo shrimp

SAUCE RUSSE:
1 whole egg
1 egg yolk
1 teaspoon prepared mustard
¼ teaspoon white pepper
½ cup white wine vinegar
1½ cups salad oil
4 tablespoons red caviar
¼ teaspoon cayenne pepper

SALADE RUSSE:
3 potatoes
3 cups French-cut string beans
1 cup Sauce Russe, above

GARNISHING:
1 envelope gelatin
1¼ cups beef consommé
1 cup Sauce Russe, above
3 hard-cooked eggs
⅓ cup chopped cooked beets
⅓ cup chopped parsley
4 ounces black caviar
2 truffles

Poulet Diable

Preheat broiler. Split 6 squab chickens in halves, wipe inside and out with damp towel, and place skin side down in broiler pan. Place 1 tablespoon butter in each cavity, and season with salt and pepper. Broil 6 inches from heat until nicely browned. Meanwhile, combine into a sauce 1 cup Dienhard Bernkasteler Hans Christof (if you substitute, use a good dry white wine) with ½ cup melted butter and 1 cup bottled Escoffier Sauce Diable. Turn chicken skin side up. With a pastry brush, coat skin of chicken with sauce. Reduce broiler heat or place chicken 4 inches further away from heat. Broil until nicely browned, then turn off broiler, but leave chicken to bake 7 minutes longer. Transfer to heated serving platter, add remaining sauce to juices in the pan, and pour over chicken. Garnish with little bunches of parsley.

6 squab chickens
6 tablespoons butter
Salt, pepper
1 cup Dienhard Bernkasteler Hans Christof
or other good dry white wine
½ cup melted butter
1 cup bottled Escoffier Sauce Diable
Parsley

Artichoke Bottoms Crowned with Spinach

Wash and remove stems from 3 pounds very fresh spinach. Place leaves in boiling salted water over high heat and boil at a rolling boil for 5 minutes. Drain well. Purée in an electric blender, a small portion at a time, with just enough stock or chicken broth to purée with ease; blend each portion 30 seconds. (Or, purée through food mill.) Add 2 tablespoons butter and ¼ teaspoon grated nutmeg. Spoon purée into and mound on 12 canned artichoke bottoms. Just before serving, place garnished artichokes in a large skillet with stock ¼ inch deep, cover, and reheat over low heat without boiling. Arrange around mound of spinach noodles, below.

3 pounds spinach
2 tablespoons butter
Stock or chicken broth
¼ teaspoon nutmeg
2 No. 2 cans artichoke bottoms

Spinach Noodles

Drop 1½ pounds spinach noodles into 6 quarts rapidly boiling salted water. Add 3 tablespoons olive oil, and boil at a rolling boil for 12 minutes, then drain in colander. Replace in pot and stir in 6 tablespoons butter. Mound on a heated serving platter and garnish with Artichoke Bottoms, above.

1½ pounds spinach noodles
3 tablespoons olive oil
6 tablespoons butter

Water Cress and Chinese Cabbage Bowl

Pick stems from 2 bunches water cress. Slice 2 heads Chinese cabbage into rounds ¼ inch thick without loosening leaves. Separate 3 hearts of chicory. Wash, drain, and dry greens carefully. Slice 1 large onion into rings; use only 12 of the largest rings. Arrange greens in a decorative pattern in a wooden bowl and top with onion rings. Just before serving, toss with ⅔ cup Basic French Dressing.

2 bunches water cress
2 heads Chinese cabbage
1 large onion
3 hearts of chicory
⅔ cup Basic French Dressing (see Index)

Meringue à l'Ancienne

Preheat oven to 250°. In large bowl of electric mixer, beat 12 egg whites until they stand in soft peaks. Continue beating, adding 1½ cups confectioners' sugar 2 tablespoons at a time. Beat in 1 teaspoon vinegar and 1 tablespoon almond extract. Cover 4 baking sheets with waxed paper, and mark outline of a 10-inch dinner plate twice on each sheet. On three of the circles, with a pastry bag and wide fluted tube, press out meringue 2 inches wide; complete circle quickly and smoothly. For the fourth circle, press out a series of rosettes, each touching the next. Bake meringues 40 minutes. Then turn off the oven but keep door open a crack by inserting a pencil in it, and let meringues dry until oven is cold, approximately 40 minutes. Remove circles from waxed paper, and pile them on top of one another, rosette circle last, sticking them lightly together with a little Hard Sauce. Just before serving, fill with 2 quarts fresh raspberries and pour 1 cup *Sabayon* Sauce, below, over berries. Serve second cup of *Sabayon* from a sauceboat.

12 egg whites
1½ cups confectioners' sugar
1 teaspoon vinegar
1 tablespoon almond extract
Hard Sauce (see Index)
2 quarts raspberries
2 cups Sabayon Sauce

Sabayon Sauce

Beat together 4 egg yolks and ⅔ cup sugar until foamy and light. Cook in top of double boiler over boiling water, stirring constantly, until mixture is thick and creamy. Cool over cracked ice, beating constantly. Fold in ⅔ cup heavy cream, whipped, and chill. Pour over raspberries just before serving.

4 egg yolks
⅔ cup sugar
⅔ cup heavy cream

67

New Orleans Dinner for Six

Oysters Rockefeller

Jambalaya

Beet Salad Creole

Southern Biscuits

Crème Brûlée

Café Brûlot

WINES

Inexpensive: Pinot Chardonnay, Santa Clara Valley

Medium-priced: Chablis Butteaux

Expensive: Chablis Vaillon, Estate-bottled, Marcel Servin

Though New Orleans belongs to the deep South, it maintains a culinary identity all its own. The influences of a French, Spanish, and Negro population blend in a unique cuisine—possibly the only *haute cuisine* America can claim as its own. Private homes, as well as the restaurants that flourish as gourmet meccas, perpetuate it still.

A yen for the Southern tradition of leisurely elegance lurks in the heart of every hostess. This menu will suit that mood when it overcomes you. To achieve it, time is of the essence, plenty of time; but the advance preparation involved makes the dinner surprisingly practical in the end. This holds true even for the Oysters Rockefeller which will want last minute attention only for the final baking. Our version of this recipe comes from an old Louisiana family which, like many another, tried to duplicate this specialty of New Orleans' famed restaurant, Antoine's. Nobody has succeeded in weaning the secret formula from the chef. As a result, there exist innumerable variations, some claiming to be *the* original; no one will ever know. An amusing aside as to the origin of the name has it that the chef at Antoine's, inspired by the classic French treatment of snails with an herb butter, sought a similar unctuous complement to the succulent oyster. He evolved this outrageously rich sauce at the time when the Rockefeller name first symbolized riches—what more fitting association!

The name jambalaya, too, has its story. The early Creoles pronounced rice *ya. Jambon au riz* (ham with rice) became jambalaya in their colorful language. You may cook it ahead and place the uncovered casserole over a pot of simmering water for about an hour to reheat thoroughly; or reheat it on an asbestos mat over very low heat. If your broiler is small, you will have to broil the oysters in relays. When the last batch is done, bake them all together, using both shelves of the oven. Make your biscuit dough early in the day. Roll it out, cut the biscuits, and put them on cooky sheets. They will wait in the refrigerator for baking when the oysters are done, just in time for the second course. The salad and *Crème Brûlée* recipes both require that you finish them ahead of time. When you serve the *Crème*, do not be dismayed by the apparently impenetrable, brittle surface. This is as it should be. It needs only the first light tap of a serving spoon to shatter it. *Café Brûlot* warrants formal service in the living room, with all the attendant ceremony of lighting and pouring the brandied coffee. Best do it on a tray.

We suggest this menu for a formal dinner for an intimate group, though it presents no problem of preparation or service for double the number of people. If you are looking for an occasion to pull out all your fanciest table trappings, your best crystal, as much silver as you want, this is the time to do it. Add a damask cloth, candlelight, a lavish flower arrangement—and dress yourself up to the nines, too, while you're about it.

It may seem contradictory, but you can convert the same menu, minus the Oysters Rockefeller, to an informal meal, a splendid Sunday-night supper with an absolute minimum of last-minute work. The jambalaya is also a fine choice for the hot dish on a buffet table, while Oysters Rockefeller, French bread and a simple salad, plus a light fruit dessert such as Blueberries Aragonaise (see Index), constitute an excellent luncheon. In that case, allow six oysters for each serving.

Despite its elegance, this is not a fussy, frilly dinner. There is an abundance of substantial food to delight the men of the party who may or may not think it important that you are also recreating a bit of gracious living from old New Orleans.

Oysters Rockefeller

Drain liquor from 2 dozen fresh oysters, reserve it, and add enough water to make 2 cups liquid. Place oysters on their half shells in a shallow pan of milk; they will greedily drink up the milk and get very plump. Meanwhile, in an electric blender, purée together coarsely 3 shallots, ⅛ teaspoon thyme, 1 cup spinach leaves, packed, and 1 stalk green celery. Do this a small portion at a time, adding a little oyster water each time. Or grind all vegetables in a food chopper. Mix vegetables with remaining oyster water, place over high heat, and boil for 5 minutes. Remove from heat, add 2 lightly beaten egg yolks. Then stir in bit by bit ½ pound butter, cut in pieces. Stir until butter is all melted, and add 2 tablespoons Herbsaint, or Pernod, or ¼ teaspoon of ground green anise seed, and 1 tablespoon Worcestershire sauce. Keep sauce warm over hot but not simmering water.

Fill 6 small Pyrex, aluminum, or stainless-steel ovenproof pie plates with a ½-inch layer of rock salt, and preheat under the broiler. Place 4 oysters on each plate and broil under medium heat until edges begin to curl. Spoon sauce over the oysters, using enough to fill the shells, and sprinkle ½ cup dry toasted bread crumbs over all. Return to hot oven (450°) for 5 minutes and serve immediately on the salt-covered plates.

2 dozen oysters
Oyster liquor and water to make 2 cups
3 shallots
⅛ teaspoon thyme
1 cup spinach leaves, packed
1 stalk green celery
2 egg yolks
½ pound butter
2 tablespoons Herbsaint or Pernod or ¼ teaspoon ground green anise seed
1 tablespoon Worcestershire sauce

Jambalaya

Make a *Court-Bouillon* for Fish: Bring to a boil 1 quart water and 1 quart dry white wine with 1 carrot, 2 sliced onions, ¼ teaspoon thyme, ½ bay leaf, 1 sprig parsley, 6 crushed peppercorns, and 1 tablespoon salt. Reduce heat, then simmer 45 minutes. Then add 1½ pounds raw shrimp and bring to a boil again. Skim thoroughly, reduce heat, and simmer until shrimp turn pink. Remove from heat and cool shrimp in broth. Shell, devein, and reserve.

Dip 2 tomatoes, one at a time, in boiling water, then in cold water, and peel. Mince and reserve. In a large skillet or flameproof casserole, over high heat, sauté together until golden brown ½ cup diced salt pork and 2 minced onions. Add 2 cups brown rice and salt and pepper to taste. Sauté mixture, stirring, 1 minute longer. Then add minced tomatoes, ½ bay leaf, ½ pound fresh lean pork, cubed, ½ pound smoked ham, also cubed, and ½ pound sliced mushrooms. Cover with 5 cups cold *Court-Bouillon,* ½ cup Madeira, and ¼ cup California Burgundy. Bring to a vigorous boil over high heat. Reduce heat to low and cook, covered, 35 to 40 minutes. All the liquid should be absorbed. Add reserved shrimp about 10 minutes before rice is done.

1 quart water
1 quart dry white wine
1 carrot
2 onions
¼ teaspoon thyme
½ bay leaf
1 sprig parsley
6 crushed peppercorns
1 tablespoon salt
1½ pounds shrimp

2 tomatoes
½ cup diced salt pork
2 onions
2 cups brown rice
Salt, pepper
½ bay leaf
½ pound fresh lean pork
½ pound smoked ham
½ pound mushrooms
½ cup Madeira
¼ cup California Burgundy

Beet Salad Creole

Marinate 1 No. 2 can shoestring beets, drained, and ¼ cup minced green pepper for 1 hour in ½ cup basic French dressing to which has been added 1 tablespoon concentrated frozen orange juice and 1 tablespoon grated orange rind. Serve on individual glass salad plates.

1 No. 2 can shoestring beets
½ cup minced green pepper
½ cup Basic French Dressing (see Index)
1 tablespoon concentrated frozen orange juice
1 tablespoon grated orange rind

Southern Biscuits

Sift together twice 2 cups flour, 5 teaspoons baking powder, and ½ teaspoon salt. Work in 2 tablespoons butter with tips of fingers. Add gradually ¾ cup milk, more or less, cutting in with a knife to make a soft dough. Flour rolling pin and board, roll out dough, then fold it over on itself in four layers. Roll out again, to a thickness of ¼ inch, and cut with a biscuit cutter. Bake about 12 minutes in a 450° oven.

2 cups flour
5 teaspoons baking powder
½ teaspoon salt
2 tablespoons butter
¾ cup milk, more or less

Crème Brûlée

Heat 1 pint heavy cream in top of a double boiler, covered, until hot but *not* scalding. Have water in bottom of double boiler hot but not boiling; test cream by dropping a bit on your finger to be sure it is actually hot. It will reach right temperature in 5 to 7 minutes. Remove from heat, add 1 tablespoon Vanilla Sugar, and stir until dissolved. Beat yolks of 4 eggs, then beat yolks into hot cream.

Pour custard into 7½-inch Pyrex pie plate. Set plate in a pan of hot water, and bake in 300° oven, on the middle shelf, until set (50–60 minutes). The only sure way to tell whether custard is properly set is to insert a round-ended knife into the middle; it must come out clean. Chill thoroughly. (It's best to make custard the day before and refrigerate overnight; it should be *icy* when the broiling process takes place.)

Now the tricky part—the *brûlée* topping. Have ready ¾ cup sieved light-brown sugar. (After sieving, let it fall lightly into the cup; do not press it down.) Sprinkle sieved sugar ¼ inch thick over entire surface of custard. Do this lightly and do not press down on it. Preheat broiler to 350° and adjust broiler rack 6 inches from heat. Put in the *crème*, watch it, and turn it around occasionally to be sure browning is even. A fine, just-darker-than-golden crust takes about 3 to 4 minutes. Remove from broiler, cool a few minutes, and refrigerate again for at least 2 hours.

1 pint heavy cream
1 tablespoon Vanilla Sugar (see Index)
4 egg yolks
¾ cup sieved light-brown sugar

Café Brûlot

In top pan of a chafing dish, over direct heat, place 1 strip lemon rind, 1 strip orange rind, 4 teaspoons Vanilla Sugar, 2 cloves, and one 2-inch piece stick cinnamon. Add 1 cup brandy and blaze as soon as it is warm. Gently pour in 2 cups hot *espresso* coffee. When brandy has burned itself out, ladle carefully into demitasse cups.

1 strip lemon rind
1 strip orange rind
4 teaspoons Vanilla Sugar (see Index)
2 cloves
2 inches stick cinnamon
1 cup brandy
2 cups hot espresso coffee

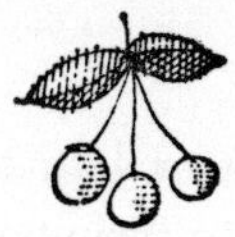

68

Viennese Dinner for Eight

Potato Pancakes Franz Josef
Filet Wellington
Braised Cucumbers and Peas
Fresh Mushroom Salad
Biscuit Glacé
Demitasse

WINES

Inexpensive: White—High Tor Rockland White
Red—High Tor Rockland Red
Medium-priced: White—Liebfraumilch Gebruder Lob
Red—Château Brane-Cantenac
Expensive: White—Brauneberger Juffer Spätlese, Estate-bottled, Ferdinand Haag
Red—Château Smith-Haut-Lafitte

This menu in the elegant-little-dinner tradition really requires formal service. Though you will prepare almost everything in advance, the half hour or so just before dinner is very busy. Have someone in to help, so you can enjoy all this good food and wine with your guests, and relish talking about it as well. With this menu especially, select only one or two cocktail accompaniments to go before; more than that gilds the lily.

Don't let the length of the *Filet* recipe frighten you. The procedures are not difficult; the applause you will get makes the whole effort worthwhile. While you roast the beef, make the stuffing, and while the beef cools, make the dessert. This recipe for *Biscuit Glacé* comes from a Canadian gentleman and businessman with a passionate interest in cooking. Where other men carry notebooks or newspaper clippings of bridge problems or stock-market quotations, his pockets are filled with scraps of paper and backs of menus covered with recipes. Business takes him to Europe several times a year. He travels by boat and manages to insinuate himself into the kitchen for a time each day. In Paris, he visits one of his favorite restaurants every morning to spend a few hours in the kitchen, peeling potatoes or some such, while he watches the chef at work. The success of a trip is gauged as much by the number of new recipes as by the volume of new business. His *Biscuit Glacé*, by the way, can be unmolded and decorated about one or two hours before servingtime and replaced in the freezer, or your waitress can do this while you're having the main course.

The pastry-covered *Filet* goes into the oven when the guests arrive. This allows forty-five minutes for cocktails and the first course. If you want to be more leisurely, have the waitress wait for the signal from you to put the beef in. She will prepare the cucumbers and peas just before dinner, and while they are cooking, she can arrange the salad. There's time for her to put the *Filet* on a platter and garnish it with water cress after the pancakes are served.

This is the occasion to use your grandest table appointments; such a feast warrants them: a multiple-branch candelabra at either end of the table, small bunches of delicate white flowers tied to the arms, tall white tapers—elegant. Though six single, low glass candle holders from the 5-and-10, with flowers massed around the base of each candle, will do just as well. This scheme is designed for a white cloth. If you prefer color, follow through with cloth, flowers, and candles all in shades of the same color.

Potato Pancakes Franz Josef

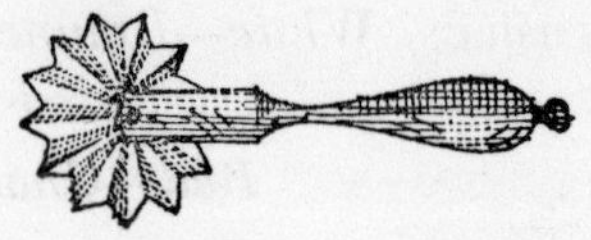

Peel and grate 1 pound potatoes and and ½ onion. Beat 1 egg lightly and combine with 2 tablespoons sour cream and 2 tablespoons flour, then combine with grated potatoes and onion. Over high heat, in a heavy pan or griddle, melt 1 tablespoon fat or shortening. Reduce heat, drop half of potato mixture by spoonfuls into pan, and spread to make 4 thin pancakes. Fry until golden on one side, then turn and fry other side. Transfer to heated platter. Place another tablespoon of fat in pan and repeat for 4 more cakes.

Cut 8 ounces smoked Nova Scotia salmon into julienne strips. Mix ½ pint sour cream with 1 tablespoon flour, add salmon and 4 tablespoons capers, and heat together in a saucepan. When hot, divide mixture among the 8 pancakes and serve at once, with a good dry white wine.

1 pound potatoes
½ onion
1 egg
2 tablespoons sour cream
2 tablespoons flour
2 tablespoons fat
8 ounces smoked Nova Scotia salmon
½ pint sour cream
1 tablespoon flour
4 tablespoons capers

Filet Wellington

For the pastry enclosing *Filet* Wellington, make a Cream-Cheese Pastry dough by combining with hands 1 cup flour, 1/4 pound butter, and 1/4 pound cream cheese. Chill.

Meanwhile, season with salt and pepper a 3 1/2-pound fillet of beef. Sear it on all sides in a heavy pan in its own fat. Add 1 carrot and 1 onion, both sliced, 2 tomatoes, diced, and 1/4 cup water. Roast, uncovered, at 350°, inserting meat thermometer in center of meat; roast to 130° to 140° for rare, or 160° for medium rare, as desired. Take out thermometer, remove meat from pan, and cool.

While beef is roasting, make a stuffing: Soak 2 slices bread in milk, then squeeze dry and reserve. Sauté 1 minced onion in 2 tablespoons butter, over low heat, for 5 minutes. Add 2 tablespoons chopped parsley, the reserved bread, 1 beaten egg, and 2 tablespoons cream. Cook all together, stirring constantly, for 2 minutes. Remove from heat, and add 1 pound ground raw veal, and salt and pepper to taste. Work mixture thoroughly with fingers until well blended.

Now take chilled pastry and, on a floured board, roll it out in a sheet large enough to enclose fillet. Spread 1/4 of stuffing down center of pastry to fit under fillet, and place fillet on it. Spread remaining stuffing over top and sides of fillet. Enclose loosely with pastry on all sides. Place, seam side down, on a greased cooky sheet. Brush top with 1 egg yolk mixed with a little water. Cut 6 evenly spaced air vents in herringbone pattern down length of pastry. Refrigerate until 45 minutes before servingtime. Bake at 350° for 30 minutes, then turn heat to 400° and bake 10 minutes longer. Fillet, protected by crust and stuffing, will not cook any more.

1 cup flour
1/4 pound butter
1/4 pound cream cheese
1 egg yolk

3 1/2-pound fillet of beef
1 carrot
1 onion
2 tomatoes
1/4 cup water

2 slices of bread
Milk to soak bread
1 onion
2 tablespoons butter
2 tablespoons chopped parsley
1 egg
2 tablespoons cream
1 pound ground raw veal
Salt, pepper

Braised Cucumbers and Peas

Peel 8 cucumbers and cut them in chunks 1 1/2 inches long. In a heavy skillet, over high heat, melt 3 tablespoons butter. Add cucumbers, season with pepper and salt, and sauté for 5 minutes. Reduce heat to medium, then add 3 cups shelled peas and 1/2 cup stock, and continue cooking another 5 minutes for frozen peas, or 8 minutes for fresh. When cucumbers have a glassy look, remove from heat, sprinkle with 1 tablespoon chopped parsley and 1 teaspoon chopped chives, and transfer to a heated serving dish.

8 cucumbers
3 tablespoons butter
Salt, pepper
3 cups peas
½ cup stock
1 tablespoon chopped parsley
1 teaspoon chopped chives

Fresh Mushroom Salad

Scrub and rinse 2 pounds very fresh, even-sized mushrooms; remove stems and slice each mushroom *very* thin without completely separating it on one side, so that it can be spread like a fan or a handful of cards. Marinate for 2 hours in a dressing made of 6 tablespoons finest olive oil, juice of 1 lemon, pepper, salt, 1 teaspoon monosodium glutamate, and 1 teaspoon chopped parsley. Turn mushrooms once while they marinate. To serve, lift out of marinade and decorate with sprigs of water cress.

2 pounds mushrooms
6 tablespoons olive oil
1 lemon
Salt, pepper
1 teaspoon monosodium glutamate
1 teaspoon chopped parsley
Water cress

Biscuit Glacé

Split 1½ packages lady fingers and line bottom and sides of a 3-inch-deep, 1½-quart mold with them. Beat 8 egg yolks with ½ cup sugar in electric mixer until very thick and light. Beat 1 cup heavy cream stiff with ¼ cup sugar. Add ¼ cup Grand Marnier, 2 tablespoons cognac, and ¼ cup coarsely grated semisweet chocolate to yolks, and fold into whipped cream. Pour into lined mold, and place in freezer until firm, at least 3 hours.

Beat ½ cup heavy cream stiff. Unmold *Biscuit Glacé* onto a serving platter. With a pastry tube, decorate with whipped cream in center, around edges, and on sides, as desired.

1½ packages lady fingers
8 egg yolks
½ cup sugar
1 cup heavy cream
¼ cup sugar
¼ cup Grand Marnier
2 tablespoons cognac
¼ cup grated semisweet chocolate
½ cup heavy cream

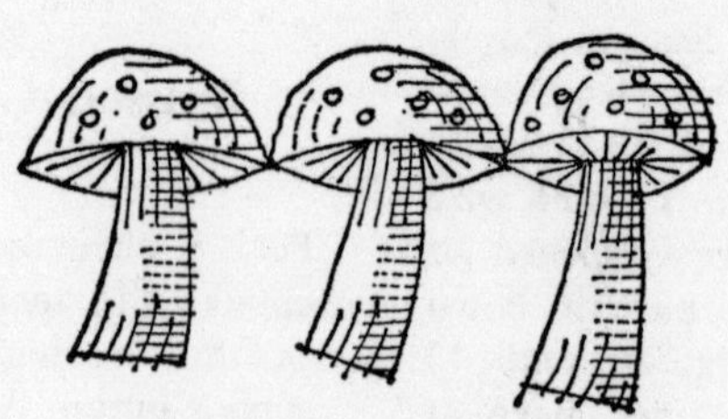

69

Winter Formal Dinner for Eight—I

LOBSTER BISQUE
RACK OF VENISON, SAUCE PIQUANTE
CRAB APPLES EN BELLE VUE
PURÉE OF CHESTNUTS
FRENCH STRAWBERRY TART
DEMITASSE

WINES

Inexpensive: Sherry—Widmer's New York State Dry
Red—Beaulieu's Beaumont Pinot Noir, Napa Valley
Medium-priced: Sherry—Duff Gordon Nina
Red—Hermitage Des Moines
Expensive: Sherry—Harvey's Bristol Dry
Red—Romanée-Conti

People are either venison lovers or they would happily settle for a good hamburger, so poll your guests before you decide on this menu. We're reminded of a friend of ours, married to a European. On their wedding trip to Europe, the groom's family and friends went all out to entertain the newlyweds with a series of the most elegant dinner parties. You know the outcome—venison every night for a week. Our friend developed an unprecedented yearning for hamburger.

But, venison, or wild duck, is a rare treat to many others. Once you've collected your game-loving friends, here's how you go about getting ready for them: Marinate the venison a day ahead. If you have bought it, you won't have to lard the meat yourself; the butcher at a fancy food market is equipped with a larding needle and the know-how to do such a perfect job that the meat arrives looking like a picture in a food ad. But if a sporting friend is the source of your supply, you'll have to struggle along yourself; venison is a dry meat and needs fat to keep it juicy. With a small, sharp knife make rows of incisions one inch deep and about two inches apart over the surface of the roast; cut the fat into julienne strips and tuck a piece into each incision.

This menu is a good deal more imposing than the work involved. If you plan to tackle any of our formal dinners unaided, this one is as easy as any, for you really can take care of it by stages: In the morning, bake the *Sandtorte* Pastry and prepare the custard and the strawberries; purée the chestnuts, prepare the crab apples, and make the *Espagnole* for the *Sauce Piquante.* Calculate the time necessary to roast the meat, and, when you put it into the oven late in the day, complete the Strawberry Tart. That leaves you with the simple but last-minute jobs of assembling the Quick Lobster Bisque, chestnut purée, and *Sauce Piquante.* Without help, you'll have to go into the kitchen from time to time and dinner will be slower, but you have nothing so complicated to attend to that you can't afford to have your attention divided between cooking and guests.

Use the same menu for non-game-eaters by substituting not hamburger, but a saddle of lamb for the venison. Marinate the lamb for only 5 hours, but roast it just as you do venison, in a hot oven for about 45 minutes to 1 hour, or until a meat thermometer registers 165°, and serve it with *Sauce Piquante.*

Quick Lobster Bisque

In top of a 2-quart double boiler heat to boiling point 3 cans lobster bisque; add a dash of cayenne pepper. Add 1 small chopped truffle to ½ cup Cognac, warm, and ignite. When flames subside, pour Cognac into bisque and reserve truffle. Whip lightly ½ cup chilled heavy cream with ¼ teaspoon salt. Pour bisque into heated cups, and top each cup with 1 tablespoon whipped cream and a dash of chopped truffle. Serve with dry sherry.

3 cans lobster bisque
Cayenne pepper
½ cup Cognac
1 small truffle
½ cup heavy cream
¼ teaspoon salt

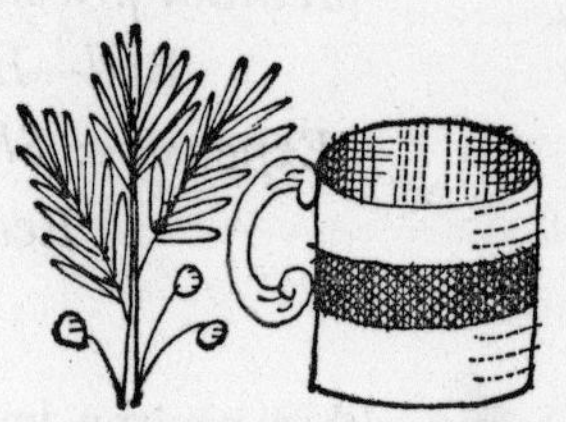

Roast Rack of Venison

Cover rack of venison with marinade made of ½ pound sliced carrots, ½ pound sliced onions, ¼ pound chopped celery tops, 6 crushed juniper berries, 3 sprigs parsley, 6 crushed peppercorns, 2 bottles Napa Valley Pinot Noir, and ½ cup olive oil. Place meat in refrigerator for 24 hours, then lift from marinade and dry thoroughly. Lard meat with small strips of fatback and cover with 3 large slices of same. Season with salt, place in roasting pan, and roast in preheated 450° oven about 45 minutes for first 6 pounds, and 5 minutes longer per pound in excess of that. Venison should be served rare. Remove fatback, and place meat on heated serving platter.

To make *Sauce Piquante,* pour off all fat from pan and, over high heat, deglaze with 1 cup marinade. Add ¼ cup wine vinegar and 1 tablespoon finely minced shallots. Boil together, uncovered, until reduced to half the original volume. Stir in 1½ cups Household Sauce Espagnole, below, reduce heat, and simmer 3 minutes. Then add 2 teaspoons chopped gherkins, 1 teaspoon chopped parsley, and a pinch of dried powdered tarragon. Carve venison, pour a little sauce over it, and serve the rest in a sauceboat.

½ pound carrots
½ pound onions
¼ pound celery tops
6 crushed juniper berries
3 sprigs parsley
6 crushed peppercorns
2 bottles Napa Valley Pinot Noir
½ cup olive oil
½ pound fatback, about
Salt

1 cup venison marinade
¼ cup wine vinegar
1 tablespoon minced shallots
1½ cups Household Sauce Espagnole
2 teaspoons chopped gherkins
1 teaspoon chopped parsley
Dried powdered tarragon

Household Sauce Espagnole

Wipe a small skillet with paper towels to make absolutely sure it is greaseless. Place 4 tablespoons flour in skillet and, over high heat, stir gently with a fork and let burn evenly to a peanut color. Remove from heat at once and stir until pan has cooled. In a saucepan, over high heat, melt 3 tablespoons butter. Add browned flour, stir with a whisk, and moisten with a few drops of canned consommé Madrilène. As sauce bubbles and thickens, add gradually ¼ cup more Madrilène and 2 cups beef consommé, stirring constantly. Then boil over high heat at a rolling boil until reduced to 1½ cups, or for about 8 minutes. Makes 1½ cups.

4 tablespoons flour
3 tablespoons butter
¼ cup consommé Madrilène
2 cups beef consommé

Crab Apples en Belle Vue

Drain crab apples from 2 large jars and reserve juice. Place apples stem side up in a shallow silver or crystal bowl. Soften 1 envelope gelatin in ¼ cup water. Measure 2¾ cups apple juice and heat to boiling point. Add ¼ cup raspberry liqueur and gelatin, and stir until completely dissolved. Pour over apples, cool, and let set in refrigerator. Serve from same bowl.

2 large jars crab apples
¼ cup raspberry liqueur
1 envelope gelatin
¼ cup water

Purée of Chestnuts

Drain 1 can unsweetened chestnuts, reserving liquid. Place chestnuts, a few at a time, in electric blender and purée until very smooth, adding just enough liquid to give consistency of mashed potatoes. (Or, force through food mill and moisten with a few drops of liquid; in this case, beat purée with electric mixer after adding remaining ingredients.) Heat over medium heat, adding ½ cup chicken broth, 2 tablespoons heavy cream, freshly ground pepper, salt, and a dash of nutmeg. Serve hot, with venison.

1 can chestnuts
½ cup chicken broth
2 tablespoons heavy cream
Salt, pepper
Nutmeg

French Strawberry Tart

Make 2 cups Vanilla Custard, below, and spread on bottom of a well-cooled baked *Sandtorte* pie shell. Hull 1½ quarts strawberries, rinse and drain them, then dip each one in strained currant jelly. Arrange in concentric circles and stemside down on custard filling. If desired, whip ½ cup chilled heavy cream with ¼ cup Vanilla Sugar, and garnish edge of tart lavishly with large rosettes of cream forced through fluted nozzle of a pastry tube.

2 cups Vanilla Custard
1 Sandtorte pie shell (*see Index*)
1½ quarts strawberries
1 cup strained currant jelly
½ cup heavy cream (*optional*)
¼ cup Vanilla Sugar (*see Index*)

Vanilla Custard

In top of a double boiler, over low heat, warm 2 cups milk with ¼ cup Vanilla Sugar, then place over boiling water. Pour ½ cup of sweetened milk into a bowl and beat 4 egg yolks into it. Add 2 tablespoons cornstarch, ¼ teaspoon salt, and 2 tablespoons butter. Return to top of double boiler and cook, stirring occasionally, until custard is thick. Cool and pour into pie shell. Makes 2 cups.

2 cups milk
¼ cup Vanilla Sugar (*see Index*)
4 egg yolks
2 tablespoons cornstarch
¼ teaspoon salt
2 tablespoons butter

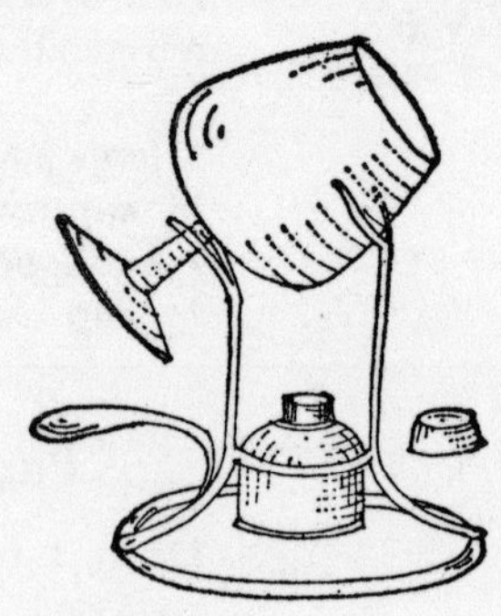

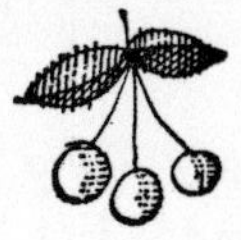

70

Winter Formal Dinner for Eight—II

Mushrooms à la Crème

Crown Roast of Pork Bigarade with Orange Stuffing

Onions à la Grecque

Walnut Soufflé

Demitasse

WINES

Inexpensive: Cresta Blanca Sauvignon Blanc, Livermore Valley

Medium-priced: Pouilly-Fuissé

Expensive: Hermitage Chante-Alouette

A proper name tacked onto a recipe is often that of the chef or gourmet who created the dish, or of a famous person for whom it was named. Though from the sound of the word you might expect to find in French history a *bon vivant* called the Duc de Bigarade, it turns out that *bigarade* refers instead to an ancient variety of orange grown centuries ago near the Mediterranean. Smaller than the bitter Seville orange, it was used by a fourteenth-century chef, Taillevent, in creating the original *bigarade* recipe that we term familiarly *à l'orange.*

Devote the morning to this dinner, and the real work is largely finished. To be specific: Sauté the mushrooms and the onions; prepare the *Béchamel* for the mushrooms, orange stuffing for the roast, and sauce for the onions; and complete the soufflé to the point where you beat the egg whites.

Aside from spooning the stuffing into the crown roast and putting it in the oven 3 hours before you eat, then putting the onions in the oven with the pork 2 hours later, the rest is a question of assembling what is already prepared.

Since you'll probably have a waitress in for this dinner, tell her to handle the remaining details this way: Immediately before dinner, heat the mushrooms and *Béchamel* together and toast the bread for them; and whip the egg whites and fold them into the soufflé. (This would seem to require three hands if it's to be done quickly; it's not as bad as all that, though it helps if the waitress knows what she's about.) The pork comes out of the oven, and the soufflé goes in. After the waitress serves the mushrooms, she'll finish the sauce for the roast and arrange the meat platter. You may have to wait a few minutes for dessert, but there's no telling how quickly everyone will eat, or how many good stories will slow down the pace and pep up the party. It's of no matter anyway; we're all familiar with the advice that it's better for guests to wait for the soufflé than the other way around.

Mushrooms à la Crème

Rinse and scrub well 1½ pounds very fresh mushrooms. Slice them, and sauté, over medium heat, in 3 tablespoons butter with 1 teaspoon finely minced shallot. Reduce heat and simmer with ½ cup heavy cream. Season with salt and freshly ground pepper. When tender, add 2 tablespoons white wine and 1 cup Béchamel Sauce. Serve hot, on toast.

1½ pounds mushrooms
3 tablespoons butter
1 teaspoon minced shallot
½ cup heavy cream
Salt, pepper
2 tablespoons white wine
1 cup Béchamel Sauce (*see Index*)

Crown Roast of Pork Bigarade

To make stuffing: Peel, seed, and remove all fibers from 2 large oranges. Chop coarsely and, in a large saucepan, mix with 3 tablespoons sugar, ¼ pound melted butter, 2 cups toasted bread crumbs, ½ pound ground pork, 1 tablespoon grated orange peel, 1 teaspoon each salt, freshly ground pepper, and mace, 2 tablespoons finely minced onion, and 1 pressed clove of garlic. Cook over medium heat for about 10 minutes, stirring often, then cool completely.

Preheat oven to 325°. Stuff a 14-rib crown roast of pork with mixture, and place roast in a large roasting pan. Season with salt and freshly ground pepper. Warm and ignite ½ cup cognac; when burned out, pour over meat. Add a veal shank (bone only), 4 carrots, 1 bay leaf, 1 sprig parsley, and ½ cup stock or beef broth to pan. Roast for 3 hours.

Meanwhile, wash 4 unpeeled oranges and cut into quarters; poach for 15 minutes in a syrup made of 1 cup Vanilla Sugar and 1 cup water. Remove meat from pan when done and keep hot on a serving platter. Pour all fat from the pan, then deglaze bottom and sides with 2 cups orange juice. Add 3 tablespoons butter kneaded with 3 tablespoons cornstarch, and bring sauce to a rolling boil over high heat, stirring constantly. Arrange Onions *à la Grecque,* below, and the orange quarters alternately around roast. Moisten stuffing with 3 tablespoons sauce, and serve rest of sauce from a sauceboat.

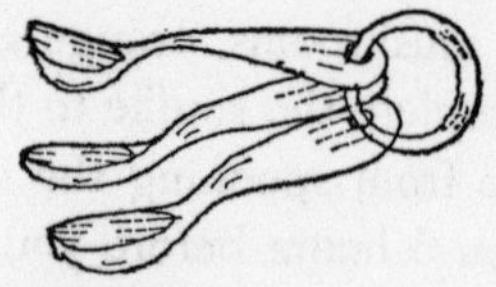

2 large oranges
3 tablespoons sugar
¼ pound butter
2 cups bread crumbs
½ pound ground pork

1 tablespoon grated orange peel
1 teaspoon each salt, pepper, mace
2 tablespoons minced onion
1 clove garlic

14-rib crown roast of pork
½ cup cognac
1 veal shank (bone only)
4 carrots
1 bay leaf
Sprig parsley
½ cup stock or beef broth

4 oranges
1 cup Vanilla Sugar (see Index)
1 cup water
2 cups orange juice
3 tablespoons butter
3 tablespoons cornstarch
Onions à la Grecque

Onions à la Grecque

Preheat oven to 325°. Over medium heat, sauté 3 pounds small white onions in 3 tablespoons butter. Combine 2 cups consommé, ½ cup wine vinegar, 1 cup seedless raisins, 1 tablespoon tomato paste, 2 tablespoons salad oil, ¾ teaspoon salt, ¼ teaspoon crushed red pepper, ¼ teaspoon thyme, and 1 bay leaf. Simmer sauce 3 or 4 minutes and add freshly ground pepper. Arrange onions in shallow baking dish, cover with sauce, and bake for 1 hour or until tender.

3 pounds small white onions
3 tablespoons butter
2 cups consommé
½ cup wine vinegar
1 cup seedless raisins
1 tablespoon tomato paste
2 tablespoons salad oil
¾ teaspoon salt
¼ teaspoon crushed red pepper
¼ teaspoon thyme
1 bay leaf
Pepper

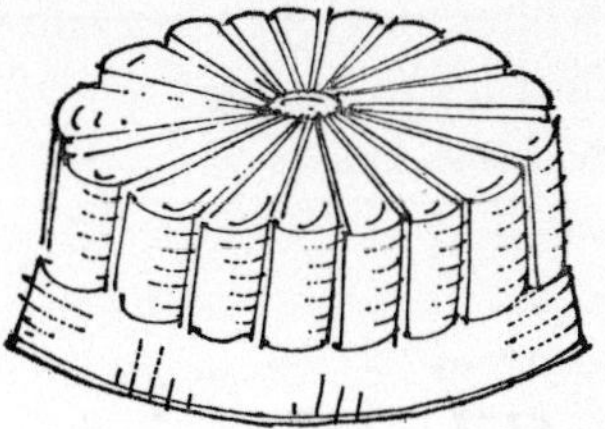

Walnut Soufflé

Preheat oven to 350°. In a saucepan, over high heat, melt 6 tablespoons butter; add 6 tablespoons flour and with a whisk or slotted spoon stir rapidly, adding slowly 2 cups light cream. Continue stirring while sauce thickens and bubbles for about 5 minutes. Remove from heat and cool. Add 3 tablespoons cognac and ⅛ teaspoon almond extract, and mix well. Beat 6 egg yolks until light in color, and add ½ cup Vanilla Sugar, 1 teaspoon grated lemon rind, dash of salt, and ½ cup chopped walnuts. Mix well and combine with cream mixture, beating all the while. Butter a 2-quart soufflé dish and dust with 3 tablespoons finely ground walnuts. Beat 7 egg whites until stiff but not dry. Fold carefully into yolk mixture, and pour into soufflé dish. Place dish in a pan of hot water and bake 35 to 40 minutes. Serve at once.

6 tablespoons butter
6 tablespoons flour
2 cups light cream
3 tablespoons cognac
⅛ teaspoon almond extract
6 egg yolks
½ cup Vanilla Sugar (see Index)
1 teaspoon grated lemon rind
Salt
½ cup chopped walnuts
Butter
3 tablespoons ground walnuts
7 egg whites

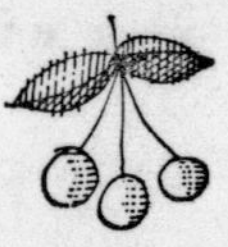

71

Thanksgiving Dinner for Twelve

PORTO FLIP

CHEESE COOKIES *

LOBSTER PUFFS WITH HOLLANDAISE SAUCE

ROAST TURKEY MONTMORENCY

WILD RICE WITH PISTACHIO NUTS

GREEN-BEAN SALAD

PUMPKIN TARTS

DEMITASSE

WINES

Inexpensive: Gold Seal Delaware

Medium-priced: White Hermitage

Expensive: Montrachet

DESSERT WINES

Inexpensive: Wente Sweet Semillon, Livermore Valley

Medium-priced: Château Climens

Expensive: Château d'Yquem

You know us well enough by now to expect the unexpected, even on a Thanksgiving menu. We wouldn't dream of severing relations with turkey and pumpkin pie, but we are not about to limit ourselves to strictly traditional fare. As a result you can use this menu for any fall or winter formal dinner; it's definitely not labelled "Thanksgiving only."

As for service, that depends: For a family dinner, where you're chief cook and everyone's a bottle washer, you can serve from a buffet or family style; on the other hand, you can plan it for an elegant dinner party on Thanksgiving Day or any time from December to March, with formal seated

* see Index

service and two waitresses. For a holiday table setting, arrange a bacchanalian centerpiece of grapes piled high on a bed of gold-sprayed grape leaves, with, here and there, a few leaves tucked between the bunches.

There's much you can do a day ahead: Bake the Cheese Cookies (see Index) and make the Hollandaise (store the sauce in a heatproof bowl in the icebox, and reheat it over hot water); blanch the pistachio nuts; cook and marinate the beans (it won't hurt them to marinate more than the three hours specified); mix the tart pastry, press it into pie plates or springform tart rings, and set them in the refrigerator overnight.

Fill and bake the tarts in the morning. Start the turkey 4 hours before you expect to eat; once it's in the oven, cook the lobster tails and shell them. Then, boil the wild rice, steam it, and leave it in the colander covered with a towel, ready to be reheated over boiling water 25 minutes before dinner. A few minutes before you reheat the rice, start heating the fat for the lobster and mix the beer batter. From now on, things will be buzzing; if this is a family affair, ask for a volunteer to finish the salad while you fry the Lobster Puffs. (Or, make them about an hour earlier, leave them on a brown paper-covered baking sheet, and reheat them in a 400° oven for 8 to 10 minutes.) The volunteer salad tosser can also help by reheating the Hollandaise. Your husband should have enlisted in the family act some time before this by getting busy with the Porto Flips.

Eat the lobster fresh and hot, then declare an intermission while your host carves the turkey, you make the sauce, and your efficient volunteer takes charge of the rice and puts salad on individual plates. In the meantime, since no one wants to be left out of an act, we assume that the table is being cleared and hot dinner plates brought out. After the grand finale of Pumpkin Tarts, coffee in the living room and a long, long pause before anyone makes a move to clean up.

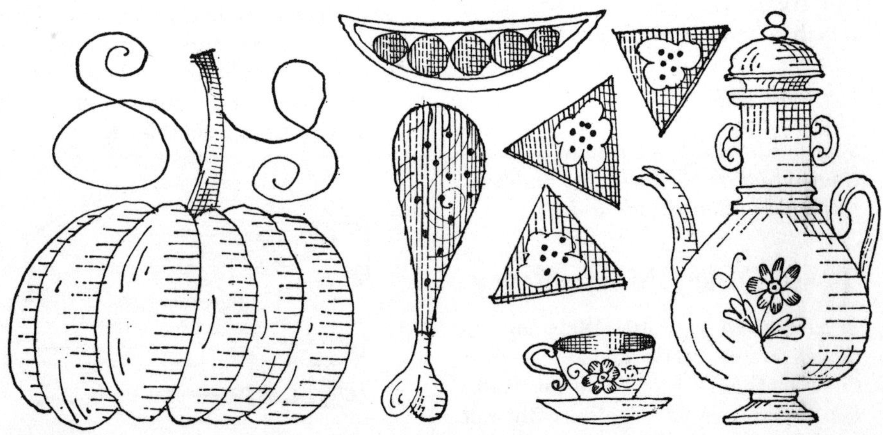

Formal service involves much the same schedule, but with two people coming to help, leave more of the cooking to them. And, if the mythical volunteer we've invented doesn't exist, engage at least one person to help even for a family group. We don't want you so exhausted at the end of this that you confine your thanks to a mere "thank-goodness-that's-over" when the last guest has departed.

Porto Flip

In an electric blender or quart-size cocktail shaker, place 2 egg yolks, ½ cup heavy cream, 2 cups chilled ruby port, and 1 ice cube. Add 1 teaspoon grated nutmeg. Blend or shake until smooth and frothy, and pour into stemmed wine glasses. For 12 you will have to make this recipe 3 times, with:

6 egg yolks
1½ cups heavy cream
6 cups ruby port
3 ice cubes
1 tablespoon grated nutmeg

Lobster Puffs

To make a Beer Batter for fritters, mix 1½ cups flour with 1½ cups light beer and blend until smooth. Poach 6 medium rock-lobster tails in *Court-Bouillon* for Fish for 12 minutes. Meat will be slightly underdone. Cool, then extract meat from shell. Halve lobster tails, coat lightly with beer batter, and fry in deep fat at 400°. Serve very hot, with Hollandaise Sauce.

1½ cups flour
1½ cups light beer
6 medium rock-lobster tails
Court-Bouillon for Fish (see Index)
Hollandaise Sauce (see Index)

Roast Turkey Montmorency

Preheat oven to 450°. Wipe an 18-pound turkey inside and out with a damp cloth, and remove all pin feathers. Season cavity lightly with salt and freshly ground pepper, and rub skin with salt and pepper and 1 teaspoon celery salt. Place turkey in deep roasting pan, breast side up, and add ⅓ cup water to pan to prevent scorching of drippings. Cover turkey breast and thighs with cheesecloth into which ⅛ pound butter has been rubbed. Roast for 3 hours without opening oven door, then reduce temperature to 400°. Remove cheesecloth, baste turkey with pan juices, and roast ½ hour longer, or until joints move easily when prodded. Remove to a heated serving platter.

Pour off all fat from roasting pan, leaving only brown glaze, then deglaze pan with cold juice from 4 No. 2 cans pitted sour cherries; add 1 cup port. Blend 6 tablespoons arrowroot or cornstarch with 6 tablespoons butter until smooth. Place roasting pan on high heat, bring liquid to a rapid boil, add butter paste, and stir until sauce is slightly thickened. Warm ⅓ cup Cherry Heering or cognac, ignite, and add to sauce when flames subside. Then add cherries and heat through. Carve turkey, pour part of sauce and fruit around turkey meat, so as not to impair crispness of skin, and serve rest from a sauceboat.

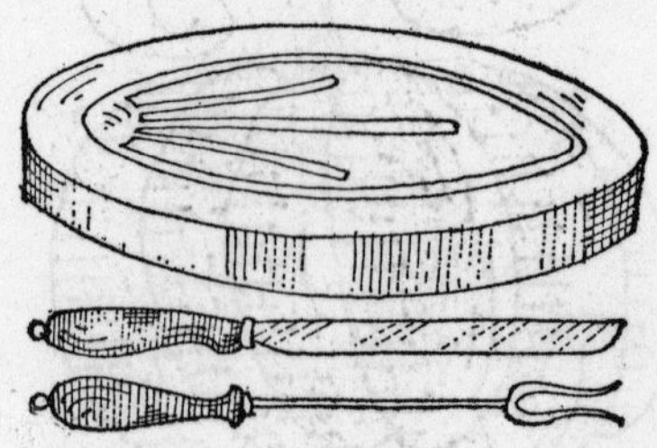

18-pound turkey
Salt, pepper
1 teaspoon celery salt
⅓ cup water
⅛ pound butter

4 No. 2 cans sour cherries
1 cup port
6 tablespoons arrowroot or cornstarch
6 tablespoons butter
⅓ cup Cherry Heering or cognac

Wild Rice with Pistachio Nuts

Pour 4½ cups washed wild rice into 3 quarts rapidly boiling salted water, and continue boiling for 5 minutes. Pour off water; replace it with fresh boiling water, and boil 20 minutes. Drain rice in colander or sieve, rinse with cold water and place, still in colander, over boiling water. Cover colander with folded kitchen towel, and steam rice over low heat for 20 minutes. Blanch 1 cup pistachio nuts in boiling water, and slip off skins by pressing them between thumb and index finger. Stir 1 teaspoon freshly ground pepper, ⅛ pound butter, and pistachio nuts into rice, and serve with Turkey Montmorency.

4½ cups wild rice
3 quarts boiling salted water
1 cup pistachio nuts
1 teaspoon pepper
⅛ pound butter

Green-Bean Salad

Boil 4½ pounds green beans in salted water until tender. Drain, cool, and chill. Make 1½ cups Basic French Dressing and add to it ¼ cup finely minced shallots and 1 tablespoon chopped parsley. Marinate beans in dressing for at least three hours, then lift from dressing and place in a bowl. If you wish, slice 4 large truffles thinly over beans. Toss just before serving.

4½ pounds green beans
1½ cups Basic French Dressing (see Index)
¼ cup minced shallots
1 tablespoon parsley
4 large truffles (optional)

Pumpkin Tarts

Preheat oven to 375°. To make 2 pumpkin tarts, serving 8 each, prepare 2 unbaked *Sandtorte* Pastry shells. Brush bottoms with thin coating of currant jelly and sprinkle with ¼ cup blanched slivered almonds. Set in refrigerator while preparing filling.

Beat together 2 eggs, 4 egg yolks, 1 cup sugar, and 3 cups light cream. Into this beat 3 cups mashed cooked pumpkin, 1 teaspoon each salt, ground ginger, and cinnamon, and ¼ teaspoon mace. Blend thoroughly and pour into shells. Bake for 10 minutes, then reduce heat to 325° and bake 30 to 35 more minutes, or until a knife inserted in center of custard comes out clean. Dust with confectioners' sugar just before serving; serve very cold, with a sweet dessert wine.

2 unbaked Sandtorte Pastry shells (see Index) 203
¼ cup currant jelly
¼ cup blanched slivered almonds
2 eggs
4 egg yolks
1 cup sugar
3 cups light cream
3 cups cooked pumpkin
1 teaspoon salt
1 teaspoon ginger
1 teaspoon cinnamon
¼ teaspoon mace
Confectioners' sugar

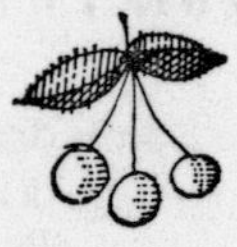

72

Christmas Dinner for Six

PINEAPPLE SURPRISE

PHEASANT EDOUARD HERRIOT

WATER CRESS BOWL

BÛCHE DE NOËL

DEMITASSE

CHAMPAGNES

Inexpensive: Korbel, Brut, California

Medium-priced: Moët et Chandon, White Seal, Brut

Expensive: Krug Extra Sec, English Market, Vintage

"And we wish you a Merry Christmas" in the best way we know. We would like to share our Christmas dinner with you—a menu we consider a rare gastronomic treat and a handsome spectacle besides. We had a soul-searching time making up our minds whether or not to include the pheasant recipe, since we have long guarded it with a special few in the top-secret file. The holiday spirit finally won out. It bears the name of the late Edouard Herriot, who was almost as well known a gourmet as a statesman. A one-time mayor of Lyons, the heart of *the* gastronomic district of France, he was quite as active in affairs of the palate as in affairs of state.

This is not a dinner we would choose for mass production. Enjoy it with a few intimate friends who respect beautiful food. If it is impossible to pare down your list, you could plan for as many as twelve, but not more. You can easily handle all the cooking yourself, but we do suggest someone to help serve.

Most of us would simply never get through the festivities of Christmas without at least half a dozen lists of things-to-remember. To remember for this dinner: The pineapple must marinate at least six hours (overnight may be more convenient); find a quiet hour to decorate the tops and to make the holly wreaths; make the *Bûche* ahead, in the morning if you wish, and keep it in the refrigerator; truss the pheasants; and wash, dry, and chill the water cress. (We don't use a dressing for the cress, but, if you insist, use Wine Dressing; see Index.)

That done, you can tear up the list. You've only the cooking of the pheasant left to do. For these, if you couldn't find walnut oil in a delicacy shop, use peanut oil instead. The flavor is not as delicate, but it will do. Cook the birds for their first hour. When you are about to have drinks, add the shellfish and vegetables, let the pheasant finish cooking, and thicken the sauce just before you announce dinner.

The pineapple is particularly appropriate as a Christmas decorative theme, since for centuries past it has symbolized hospitality. With paint in an aerosol can, it's no job at all to spray the leaves. Buy the tiny red baubles in two sizes to trim both the pineapples and their wreaths. Make six extra holly wreaths about five inches in diameter, and put them on very low holders for tall red candles. The platter of pineapples will be in the center of the table, and the candles lit, when you come into dinner. This applies, of course, to an evening dinner on Christmas Eve or Christmas itself. For a midday meal, set the pineapples at each place and, instead of candles, have a miniature Christmas tree, made of five holly wreaths in sizes graduating from three to ten inches. Wire red baubles to them, and pile them one on top of the other, with one large red ball on the very top. A prickly job, all of this, but fun. *Joyeux Noël!*

Pineapple Surprise

6 small pineapples
1 can Mandarin orange sections
18 glacéed cherries
½ cup Myers dark rum

Can green aerosol paint
Holly
Wire and red baubles

Cut off tops of 6 small pineapples one third of the way down. Remove meat from tops without crushing fronds. Remove meat inside pineapples, and discard cores. Cube all the meat and replace in shells with 5 canned Mandarin orange sections and 3 glacéed cherries for each shell. Warm and ignite ½ cup Myers dark rum, and pour a little into each pineapple. Cover with foil and marinate in refrigerator for 6 hours or more. With aerosol can, spray fronds bright green, and then wire with small red baubles. Make 6 little holly wreaths, wire with more red baubles, put on serving plates, and put the plates on a platter or tray. Just before serving, remove foil from chilled pineapples, replace decorated tops, and set each pineapple in its holly wreath.

Roast Pheasant Edouard Herriot

Wipe 2 pheasants inside and out with a damp cloth, and truss carefully. In a Dutch oven, over medium heat, sauté birds, one at a time, in 3 tablespoons walnut oil and 2 tablespoons butter until light brown on all sides. Discard oil and butter. Add to birds 4 sprigs of parsley, ¼ teaspoon thyme, ¼ bay leaf, 4 tablespoons butter, pepper, salt, and ½ cup white port. When butter sizzles, lower heat, cover, and simmer for 1 hour. Then add 2 large truffles, chopped, 12 large mushroom caps, 1 package frozen artichoke hearts, 6 whole peeled shallots, 4 raw unshelled fresh-water crayfish tails * (or 8 jumbo shrimp), another ½ cup white port, and 2 tablespoons heavy cream. Simmer 25 minutes longer.

Carve pheasants in kitchen and place on deep heated serving platter. Arrange vegetables and shellfish as garnish on top of and alongside meat. Measure juices in the pan. For each cup of liquid blend together to a paste 1 tablespoon butter and 1 tablespoon arrowroot. Add to juices, stir until slightly thickened (the process is almost instantaneous), and pour over pheasant and garnishes.

2 pheasants
3 tablespoons walnut oil
2 tablespoons butter
4 sprigs parsley
¼ teaspoon thyme
¼ bay leaf
4 tablespoons butter
Salt, pepper
1 cup white port, in all
2 large truffles
12 large mushroom caps
1 package frozen artichoke hearts
6 shallots
*4 fresh-water crayfish tails **
or 8 jumbo shrimp
2 tablespoons heavy cream
Butter
Arrowroot

Bûche de Noël

Sift together twice ¼ cup sifted flour, ½ teaspoon salt, and 4 tablespoons cocoa. Beat 5 egg yolks until pale yellow and frothy, adding gradually 1 cup confectioners' sugar. Add 1 teaspoon vanilla and fold sifted ingredients into egg yolk-sugar mixture. Beat 5 egg whites stiff, and fold into batter. Spread in a well-greased jelly-roll pan, and bake at 375°, about 6 inches away from bottom of the oven, for 15 to 20 minutes. With a sharp knife cut edges off cake, loosen under side with spatula, and turn out onto a damp cloth. Roll up cloth and cake like a jelly roll, and store in refrigerator until needed. Meanwhile, make 1 recipe Mocha Butter Cream, and whip 1 cup heavy cream.

Unroll the cake, spread it very lightly with 5 tablespoons Mocha Butter Cream and thickly with whipped cream, and roll up again. Spread roll

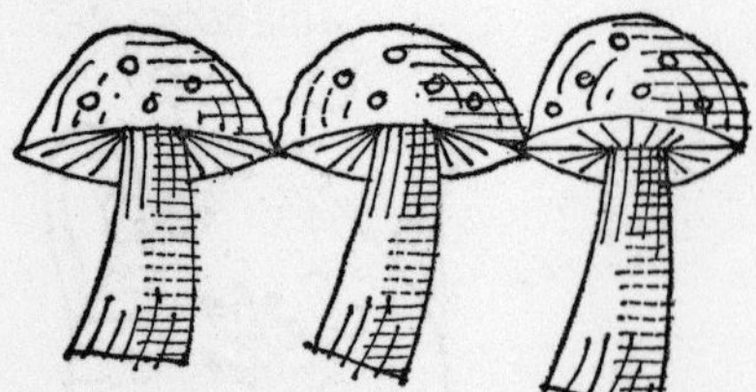

* Crayfish tails are not always in season; they may be purchased cooked in jars from some delicacy shops. These should be added at the last, since they must not be cooked again.

with ¾ cup Mocha Butter Cream, and score with a fork to make a rough, barklike surface. Decorate with swirls of remaining Mocha Cream forced through pastry tube, and sprinkle ends of log with chopped blanched pistachio nuts.

¼ cup sifted flour
½ teaspoon salt
4 tablespoons cocoa
5 egg yolks
1 cup confectioners' sugar
1 teaspoon vanilla
5 egg whites
1 recipe Mocha Butter Cream (see Index)
1 cup heavy cream
½ cup chopped blanched pistachio nuts

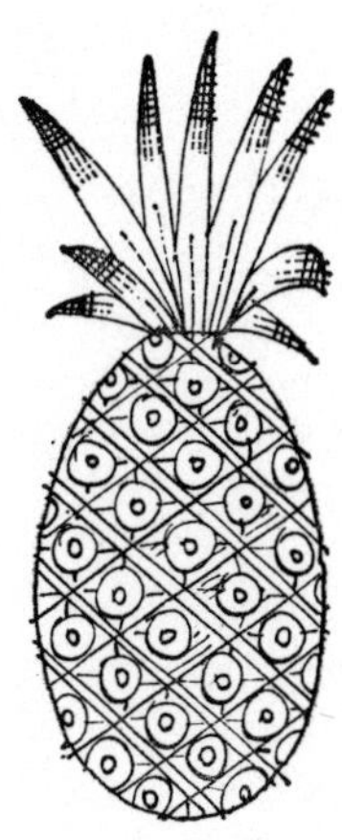

Menu Planner

The recipe index which follows is designed to serve as a menu planner as well as to locate recipes by name. The entries, therefore, include the following categories:

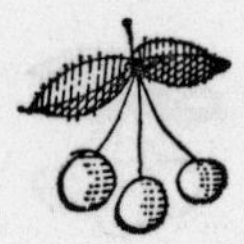

Recipe Index